America Celebrates!

America Celebrates!

A Patchwork of Weird & Wonderful Holiday Lore

Hennig Cohen
&
Tristram Potter Coffin

DETROIT   CHICAGO   WASHINGTON, D.C.   LONDON

America Celebrates!

A Patchwork of Weird and Wonderful
Holiday Lore

Published by Visible Ink Press,
a division of Gale Research Inc.
835 Penobscot Building
Detroit, MI 48226-4094

Visible Ink Press is a trademark of Gale Research Inc.

ISBN 0-8103-9407-3

Editor: Diane L. Dupuis
Art Director: Arthur Chartow
Interior Design: Kathleen Palmer
Illustrations: Terry Colon, Kyle Raetz
Cover Design: Cynthia Baldwin
Cover Illustration: Jim Dryden

10 9 8 7 6 5 4 3 2 1

CONTENTS

Preface xv

Introduction xvii

America Celebrates!

AMERICA CELEBRATES

CONTENTS

AMERICA CELEBRATES

CONTENTS

AMERICA CELEBRATES

CONTENTS

AMERICA CELEBRATES

CONTENTS

AMERICA CELEBRATES

CONTENTS

PREFACE

*A*merica Celebrates! A Patchwork of Weird and Wonderful Holiday Lore presents the folklore associated with calendar customs and festivals that have become an integral part of the social habits of North Americans in general, as well as regional, occupational, or ethnic groups in particular. While some holidays have arisen from ancient practices, others are fresh attempts to celebrate neglected festivals or, in some cases, the results of political or ethnic groups wishing to strengthen their sense of identity. Still other holidays have been created by the passage of laws. The traditional lore surrounding a given holiday, regardless of its origin, comprises the heart of this book.

Celebrating Diversity

America Celebrates! contains over 200 items of folklore associated with more than 60 North American holidays and festivals. Holidays included in *America Celebrates!* range from well-known religious and secular holidays, such as Christmas and Independence Day, to more obscure celebrations like Tater Day. The equally diverse items of folklore accompanying each holiday vividly illustrate the rich body of history behind these special celebrations.

America Celebrates! reflects the ever-evolving culture of America from colonial times to the present. Oral traditions brought from already-established cultures in the Old World to North America evolved as immigrants intermingled their

traditions and developed new ones. With the changes in immigration patterns, North American culture—and thus its folklore—changed as well. Therefore, alongside the Irish St. Patrick's Day Parade, readers will find Vietnamese Tet. Some holidays and types of folklore may be more extensively treated than others simply due to the limitations of available published material. But *America Celebrates!* aims to capture the spirit and richness of North American festivals and represent the vast range of associated lore: legends, beliefs, proverbs, superstitions, charms, sayings, songs, recipes, processions, parades, pageants, fairs, food, games, gifts, dances, contests, poems, riddles, music, plays.

The Search for Authentic Lore

The items of folklore in this book were selected by the authors from a wide range of published sources and unpublished collections, including scholarly journals in the areas of folklore and local history, doctoral dissertations, public and private archives, private collections, and newspapers, magazines, souvenir programs, and publicity materials. Without the numerous scholars, collectors, and reporters who located, investigated, and documented the North American holidays and their lore included in these sources, compiling this book would not have been possible.

Arranging Celebrations

Chronologically arranged according to the Gregorian calendar, *America Celebrates!* begins with New Year's Day,

AMERICA CELEBRATES

PREFACE

January 1, and concludes with Kwanza, a period that returns to the Gregorian New Year. Each holiday's name is accompanied by its date or inclusive time frame. Since some festivals are moveable both in relation to the Gregorian calendar and to their own calendars (Chinese, Jewish, lunar, or other), these idiosyncracies are noted. A description of the holiday's origins, historical background, and general characteristics is provided, and associated items of folklore follow in subgroupings.

Acknowledgments

Material for *America Celebrates!* was selected and edited by Diane L. Dupuis from the second edition of the authors' mammoth reference classic, *The Folklore of American Holidays*, with assistance from Marie J. MacNee.

The authors are indebted to the collectors, reporters, and others mentioned in the "Source" sections who have located and described the material included in *America Celebrates!*. In particular, we would like to thank the following people for their invaluable assistance: Leland Agan, Peter Bartis, Nancy Cheng, Leonard P. Deleanis, Patricia C. Fry, Morton H. Fry, Henry Glassie, Kenneth S. Goldstein, Theodore Holmberg, Ruth Kelly, Michael Licht, Adolph Matz, Teresa Pyott, James W. Renny, Reverend H. Seki, Reg Slater, Patty Stout, William Strachan, Joanne Takagi, Betty Takagi, Priscilla C. Whitford, and Don Yoder. We are also grateful to the staffs of the Brown University Library, University of Pennsylvania Library, and University of Rhode Island Library for making their resources available to us. But most of all we owe a debt to our research assistant, Steve Stuemfle, who worked long, hard, and careful hours for us.

INTRODUCTION

Few women dancing about a maypole on an American college campus are aware that they are paying tribute to the reproductive powers of the phallus; few workers having a drink at a Christmas party in the factory believe that they are to be transformed by the power of the liquor just as the barren landscape is to be transformed by returning spring; few revelers think the horns and bells and shouting on New Year's Eve are for the purpose of frightening whatever evil spirits are abroad. Yet year after year North Americans and Western Europeans perform such rituals by rote. That's part of what this collection of holiday lore is all about. To understand how we as a culture went from fearing evil spirits to crooning "Auld Lang Syne," a look at time-keeping history is helpful.

Agricultural Communities and the Seasonal Cycle

Once a community gives up hunting and food gathering and settles down more permanently to plant crops and to live in villages, the changing seasons assume deeper magic and religious significance. Winter, spring, summer, fall— want, promise, fulfillment, harvest—the cycle recurs year after year, generation after generation. With a limited understanding of the ways of nature, agricultural peoples may see the weakening of the sun in winter, the death of vegetation, and the barren landscape as phenomena that threaten to last forever. Only

with the help of prayer, sacrifice, and sympathetic magic, they believe, will spring return with its green fertility and will survival be possible. By the same token, the flowering of the crops, the reproduction of the women and animals, and the eventual harvest seem almost too wonderful to be true. Each part of the cycle of the year is deemed delicate, crucial, and sacred. It is only natural that the religions of farming peoples center about these changing seasons and those rites that insure the successful completion of each cycle.

For these cultures, the phenomenon of the seasons is often embodied in a god-force that is born each year, grows strong, weakens, and dies, only to be replaced by a new god-force. The sun, with its daily rising and setting, its seasonal strengthening and decline, is usually the symbol or the embodiment of this power. The sun "fertilizes" the earth, and together their mutual role in producing food is seen as parallel to the roles of the male animal and the male human in consort with their female counterparts. Plants that retain their green in the barren months of winter (holly, ivy, mistletoe) suggest that this reproductive god-force is not dead, but simply absent, able to return (if it will) in spring. Liquors and hallucinogens, made from plants and fruits harvested from the summer just past, assure that the force of one year is transferred to the next. A desire to cleanse whatever has been evil in the old seasons is present. The new year, especially as it is born,

AMERICA CELEBRATES

INTRODUCTION

must be freed from the curses of the past; for this reason, purges, noise to scare evil spirits, or frivolities to mask the seriousness of the situation are felt to help.

A typical calendar of an agricultural people, then, would begin with a celebration not unlike the one practiced in the mid-nineteenth century by some Missouri and Pennsylvania German groups that featured feasting, drinking, rioting, and noisemaking (especially music and the shooting of guns). In the spring they would hold another festival, heralding the first appearance of the crops and the birth of animals and children. At this time they would bless the livestock, worship phallic symbols such as the maypole, and hunt for and decorate eggs. Midsummer rites, such as those connected with voodoo ritual in New Orleans, glorified the full growth of the fruit of the crops and often included bonfires, a symbol of the full-burning sun. Here, as in other celebrations, dancing, sexual license, feasting, and drinking were common. Finally, the agricultural year closed with harvest celebrations at the time when they would gather the crops and recall the animals from the fields. These were feasts of thanksgiving during which they would consume surplus food and slaughter animals that could not be kept for the winter. At this time, people would offer thanks for the richness of the year past and prepare themselves for the long, hard winter ahead.

The Development of Formal Calendars

Because the cycles of the seasons were so important to early peoples and because they studied them so closely, it was not long before they devised a means to calculate and record the cycles' passage. Thus, formal calendars were developed by most peoples as they began to advance technologically. From the basic unit of the day (measured from dawn to dawn, from midnight to midnight, from sunset to sunset), formal calendars evolved. Days were grouped so as to correspond with the cycles of the moon (months). Later, shorter groupings of four, six, seven, or ten days were used to establish periods between market days. Our seven-day week was originally Hebraic and was adapted by the Roman world during the first century B.C., and was subsequently observed by the Christian world.

The grouping of days by the cycles of the moon appealed because it approximated closely the menstrual cycle of women, but it was not fully suitable for determining the seasons of the year, whether they were divided into two (wet and dry), into three (flood, seeding, harvest), or into four. Seasons of the year depend on the sun. As the sun's varying positions result in a year of approximately 365 days and as the lunar month is 29 1/2 days, the two systems are never fully compatible. Even early civilizations recognized this, and the history of the calendar is a search for means of harmonizing the lunar and solar calculations, the seasons, and the established holidays.

We do not know when the first calendar came into use, but we can say that all known communities have had at least the rudiments of a calendar. People have always noticed the changing seasons; the movements of the sun, moon, and stars; and the migration patterns of animals, if only because they are crucial to survival. Where these matters have been recorded, a certain level of social organization with an accompanying system of number, measurement, and script or proto-script must be present. Moreover, the calendar implies the sort of human awareness of an environment that is associated with deities, rituals, and social organization. The resemblance of calendars across the world also suggests a similarity in the development of cultural patterns, the general similarity of instincts and mental processes creating equivalent modes of behavior and institutions. For while some calendars have been carried from one society to another along trade and migration routes, it is difficult to account in this fashion for the agreement between pre-Columbian Native American calendars like the Mayan and ancient Mediterranean calendars like the Egyptian.

The Chinese Lunar Calendar

In *America Celebrates!* the lunar calendar is well illustrated by the old Chinese calendar, discarded by the Chinese Republic in 1912 in favor of the solar Gregorian calendar borrowed from the West. Chinese native festivals, however, are still celebrated according to the old calendar, even in New World cities like New York and San Francisco. In the Chinese lunar calendar, the first day of the year comes with the first new moon after the sun has entered Aquarius, a date that falls between January 21 and February 19. The calendar includes twelve months or moons, designated simply as First, Second, and so forth. Each month, which lasts 29 1/2 days, begins with the new moon. As needed, an intercalary month is added to make the lunar and the solar years correspond. This additional month is inserted at varying intervals, often at the beginning of the year, but it does not affect the month in which a given festival is normally held, because festivals continue to be celebrated in their regular lunar months.

The calendar fits nicely with the four seasons, allowing three months for each, with the Ninth Day of the Ninth Month, the autumn equinox, and the Fifth Day of the Fifth Month, the summer solstice, assuming particular importance as agricultural dates. There are also two complex methods of identifying the years: one based upon the reigns of emperors; the other involving combinations of characters. The years are given twelve popular names. Nineteen ninety-two is, for example, the Year of the Monkey. The monkey is followed in sequence by the cock, dog, boar, rat, ox, tiger, hare, dragon, serpent, horse, and sheep, until the monkey is reached again and the pattern recurs.

AMERICA CELEBRATES

INTRODUCTION

The Jewish Lunar Calendar

The Jewish calendar is primarily lunar, numbering the years from what their historians believed to be the "birth of the world" on October 7, 3760 B.C. Nineteen ninety-two, for instance, is the equivalent of 5762. To adjust the lunar month of 29 1/2 days, the Jewish calendar alternates twelve months of 29 and 30 days. The calendar also introduces leap years and an extra month seven times in every nineteen years in order to regulate it. The Jewish calendar begins in late September or in October, and each day in the calendar begins the night before in keeping with the Biblical concept that the night precedes the day.

The Solar Gregorian Calendar

The solar Gregorian calendar is now universally used by all historically Christian nations, as well as many others, and probably will soon be the only calendar by which the business of the world is conducted. It was introduced by the Roman Catholic Pope Gregory in a papal bull dated March 1, 1582, to replace the Julian calendar, devised under the auspices of Julius Caesar, which had been in use since 46 B.C. In the Julian calendar, which was also solar, the year was too long, and every 128 years the error added up to a full day. By the sixteenth century the Julian calendar was no longer in harmony with the agricultural practices of the time, and the farmers who were planting and reaping in accordance with the holy and feast days of the church found nature and the church out of step. By 1582 the calendar was ten days off, an error that Gregory corrected by changing the date of October 5 to October 15. The change, which was required in all Roman Catholic countries, was ignored in Protestant Britain and subsequently in the British colonies.

It was not until 1752 that the English-speaking countries adopted the Gregorian calendar. By then, the discrepancy between the two systems was eleven days. Moreover, the Eastern church did not accept the Gregorian calendar as official until 1923, by which time a thirteen-day discrepancy had accumulated. The result has been that many festivals celebrated by the common folk, who are often ignorant of or indifferent to official calendars, appear idiosyncratic in their dating.

It is also important to know that while the Western church establishes Easter from the Gregorian calendar, the Eastern church, even after adopting the Western system, continues to establish Easter by means of the Julian calendar. The result is serious differences in the dates of Easter and many moveable feasts among the Western Christians and the Albanians, Greeks, Bulgarians, Russians, Syrians, and others within the Eastern church. Nor is there any consistency among the various Eastern churches. For instance, the Greeks use the Julian calendar only for Easter and associated dates, while the Russians use the Julian calendar for all festival dates.

Pagan Foundations of Christian Holidays

The variety of calendars ranges greatly, from the Armenian, Hindu, and Persian calendars of today to the Babylonian, Egyptian, Aztec, and Incan calendars of the past. The dates of folk festivals are not always adjusted to meet the changes of place, religion, and computation that go with calendar adaptations and revisions. As a result, one finds what appear to be inconsistencies and confusions in the dates of folk holidays. Furthermore, a large amount of overlapping has occurred in the various festivals as people have migrated, acculturated, and changed religions. Each society had its own day or period during which it conducted its particular rites, often employing remarkably similar mimes, processions, feasts, orgies, sacrifices, and such. For each, the time chosen was dependent on many factors: geography, climate, local traditions, chance. Moreover, as Roman Catholicism spread, it became the policy of the church not only to establish new holidays, but to appropriate pagan holidays into Christian ones, since local celebrations could not be suppressed.

This practice accounts for a number of saints' days included in *America Celebrates!*, for, in fact, their chance of survival is enhanced by the pagan element they retain. Thus, Midsummer's Day and St. John's Day are made to coincide; the Easter season has become both a celebration of Christ's death and a fertility rite; and Christmas has assumed many of the characteristics of the Teutonic and Roman New Year's festivals.

Climate, of course, was a major influence in determining the character of holidays. The weather in England on St. John's Day is much warmer than the weather in Sweden on the same date. It is no accident, therefore, that the Anglo-American St. John's Day features the midsummer solstice rites, while the Swedish celebration on the same date is centered on spring and the first flow of the sap. Whitsunday, forty days after Easter, is for England a rough equivalent to St. John's Day in Sweden.

Perhaps nowhere is the juxtaposition of pagan celebrations with church holidays better shown than in the fusion of the Roman custom of gift-giving at the midwinter Kalends with Santa Claus and Kris Kringle. Santa, who is actually St. Nicholas (Sanct Herr 'Claus), was a legendary saint who supposedly saved three impoverished virgins from prostitution by throwing money down the smoke-hole of their cottage and into their stockings drying by the fire. St. Nicholas mingled with pagan gift-givers and judges of behavior such as Befana and Knecht Ruprecht and developed into an elf with a fur-trimmed cardinal robe or suit who gives presents to the good and whips the bad. This confusion was further complicated by his association with the tradition that the Magi and shepherds took gifts to the newborn Christ, so that the Christ-Child (Christ Kindl or Kris Kringle) actually became the gift-giver and a fig-

AMERICA CELEBRATES

INTRODUCTION

ure identical to Nicholas. Furthermore, when one realizes that sometimes, as in North Carolina, St. Nicholas and Old Nick (the devil) became confused, one gets an idea of how difficult a festival's history may become.

Ethnic Roots of North American Festivals

North American culture is anything but static. Even the flow of immigrants into the land is forever changing. In a feature article in the *Providence* (Rhode Island) *Journal* of March 24, 1980, Richard Polenberg made the following remarks:

... On the eve of World War II, more than one in four Americans was a first- or second-generation immigrant. Ethnic culture, European in linguistic origin, Roman Catholic and Jewish in religion, flourished in such cities as New York and Boston. In the last 15 years, the sources of immigration have shifted from Europe to Asia and Latin America.

Today, the United States receives fewer immigrants from Italy and Greece combined than from India alone, fewer from West Germany than Thailand, fewer from Ireland than from Egypt. Spanish is the most commonly used foreign language, and there are more homes in which Chinese, Japanese, Korean and Filipino is spoken than homes in which people ordinarily use Italian.

America Celebrates!, like the sources from which it was drawn, reflects these changes. Thus, alongside the Irish St.

Patrick's Day Parade we have the Vietnamese Tet. The book also reflects the firmly established, confident ethnicism of some of the groups that have been on this continent now for 100 years or more. Not only have the Rhode Island Portuguese picked an utterly American date, Labor Day, for their festa, but an African group has selected Christmas as a time for preserving black customs in a new land. And Italians, finding that Columbus Day has been made a national holiday, have chosen to celebrate it as an ethnic holiday as well, while the Norwegians have responded by creating a Leif Ericson Day.

Festivals, whether genuine, revived, or artificial, do take on characteristics that reflect their ethnic roots, the time of year in which they occur, and the saints' days associated with them. Thanksgiving is predictably characterized by food and drink; Mardi Gras by miming, costumes, and music; May Day by maidens, flowers, and planting customs; and the Fourth of July by outdoor events, noise, and parades. Sometimes, one holiday will even encourage one of its major characteristics in another. American Jews, influenced by the lavish gift-giving of Christmas, have increased the amount of gift-giving at Hanukkah. Nor is it unusual for two or more holidays to share beliefs or customs. The idea that if it rains on St. Swithin's Day it will rain for forty days and nights is also common to St. Medard's Day, Ascension Day, and Whitsuntide. The variety of lore associated with American festivals is vast indeed.

The Durability of Folk Festivals

Folk festivals, because they are so durable, commonly preserve much lore that would otherwise vanish. Often we find what was once a religious festival surviving as a secular drama, dance, or game. Greek dramas, the great plays of Aeschylus, Sophocles, and Euripides, evolved from old Dionysian rites and were still performed in Athens in the fifth century B.C. as a part of a quasi-religious service. Robin Hood plays and St. George plays, performed into the twentieth century, retained elements common to the May Day vegetation ceremonies of medieval England. The Mexican dances in which Moors oppose Christians are survivals of ancient European fertility rites enacted as sexual confrontations and once mimed as part of the New Year rituals. Even North American square dancing can be traced directly to similar rites. Bullfights are modern elaborations of the ritual killings of the male fertility symbol, the bull, perhaps as part of the festival involving the death of the king of the old year. Soccer (English football) and American football are disciplined forms of ancient rivalries between villages once involving a struggle for the possession of a skull or inflated animal bladder. In fact, some scholars (surely with too much enthusiasm) have seen all narrative art, from myths to short stories and comic strips, as having evolved from ritual and the miming that results from it.

This is not to say that there are no folk festivals emerging in North America today. A commercially or politically sponsored occasion may in time become fully traditional. The Kentucky Derby with its juleps, parties, and post parade, as well as the Darlington "500" Stock Car Race with its growing superstitions and tales, and the Boston Marathon, the Army-Navy football game, the many state fairs, and the various jazz and music festivals all are close to being events that might be called "folk festivals." They are certainly modern variations of the races, games, dances, fairs, and musical performances that have come and gone throughout the traditions of various cultures, and much lore has grown up about them.

Selection of Festivals

So, when all is said and done, the key word is "tradition." Whether the festival has arisen from ancient practices, is a fresh attempt to celebrate an older festival that has been disregarded for a time, or has been artificially created by the passage of a law, a Chamber of Commerce decision, or a political or ethnic group that wishes to strengthen its sense of identity, the authors have included it in this book only if we have been able to see it as an integral part of the social habits of North Americans at large or of a regional, occupational, or ethnic group within the nation. The questions asked were: "Would this calendar custom or festival continue to be celebrated if there were no legal or commercial reason to celebrate it?" and "Is the event creating or

AMERICA CELEBRATES

INTRODUCTION

did it at some time in the past create its own set of traditions, with associated legends, anecdotes, superstitions, food and the like?" If the answer is "yes" to either or both, the festival and the associated materials were included.

Dating Holidays, Beginning the New Year, Beginning This Book

For the early farming cultures, any point in the lunar or solar year could be used as the starting point for the annual round of agricultural and sacred rites. The Gregorian calendar begins just after the winter solstice, the Chinese about three to seven weeks later; the Julian calendar begins on March 1, the Jewish calendar close to the autumn equinox; the solstices and the equinoxes are natural beginning points. Because many points in the lunar or solar year have been used to begin the annual round of agricultural and sacred rites, the authors had to ask themselves: "Precisely when does the New Year begin? Where should this volume start?" Is it when the death of winter is succeeded by the birth of spring? Or is it after the harvest, when the growing season is over and the fields lie fallow and asleep?

In either case, ancient farming peoples patterned their calendars after the changes on the face of the land. Their wise men also watched the sky and observed that the seasons of the earth were matched by the seasons of the heavens. The priest-astronomers of the Babylonians and Druids and Aztecs learned how to measure out the year by the course of the stars. Yet here, too, was a question of where to begin. Did the new year commence with the longest day, at midsummer, when the sun showed its might in the firmament, or the shortest, when it was at the depth of its decline but at the point that it would start once more its upward arc? Or with the vernal equinox?

There was still another way of ordering time and of indicating the place of its annual beginning. This was the chronicle of the experience of humankind itself, its history. Time began with the creation of the world, and the new year marked its anniversary; or the new year commemorated the birthday of a messiah, king, or culture hero or the revelation of a prophet. Whether the new year is determined by the cycle of the agricultural season, the circular path of heavenly bodies, or the turning wheel of history; whether it is the new year of aboriginal North Americans or recent immigrants from Southeast Asia, any collection of festival folklore makes two things clear: humankind has had many new years, and these various and almost arbitrary points on the calendar encompass both end and beginning.

As our starting point we have simply chosen the New Year's Day of the Gregorian calendar, January 1, and let the natural flow of holiday lore structure the contents, concluding with Kwanza, which returns to the Gregorian New Year's Eve. The result is a cycle, never-ending, and it is as such a circle the book should be viewed. We have also used the Gregorian calendar as a basic means of dating holidays, even though these days may be set according to the Chinese, Jewish, or other calendars.

Moreover, many of the festivals are moveable, moveable both in their relationship to the Gregorian calendar and to their own calendars. (We designate as "moveable" only the latter.) Easter, for instance, moves according to a fixed pattern within the Gregorian calendar, as do all the days dependent on it. Labor Day (the first Monday in September) and Thanksgiving (the last Thursday in November) also move, but are predictable. On the other hand, a rattlesnake round-up or a graveyard decoration outing may be as casually dated as "late winter or early spring" or "a week-day in July or August." The Seneca Green Corn Festival is merely "called" when the tribal leader decides the crop has reached the proper stage of ripeness. Other dates, like Passover or the Chinese New Year, are fixed within the Jewish or Chinese calendars, but move within the Gregorian. This is also true of the Iroquois White Dog Feast, which comes after the first new moon in what we call January.

Other days, like Thanksgiving (once the last, now the fourth Thursday in November), have been changed over the years by legal decree. Recent federal regulations have also rescheduled old holidays like Columbus Day (once October 12) to the second Monday in October and Washington's Birthday (once February 22) to the third Monday in February. Thus, holidays and festivals that were formerly fixed have become moveable. There are even examples such as the one in Honolulu in 1978 where city officials urged parents to keep their children home on Halloween because of the heavy rains, saying a "make-up Halloween" would be declared when the weather cleared.

Flexible Celebration

A conclusion with a wider application may be drawn from this rainy Halloween in Honolulu: festivals are remarkably flexible and this flexibility makes for their remarkable ability to survive. Pagans and popes and public officials, even the power of nature herself, may alter and shape them. They may erode, revive, merge, flourish, decline, sink almost into oblivion; and, if the rain is heavy, it may even be necessary to issue a local rain check. But the danger of a festival's being washed completely away by the floods of time is not as great as one might expect. Besides, if old ways and holidays are swept off, new ones are forever appearing on the scene.

America Celebrates! suggests in its range and diversity the durability of holiday lore, especially its power of survival through adaptation to new environments and its capacity for being put to new uses.

Hennig Cohen
Tristram Potter Coffin

America Celebrates!

January

1

NEW YEAR'S DAY

New Year's festivals once included rites which were supposed to ward off the barrenness of winter and insure the return of spring with its fertility. In pre-Christian times among certain peoples, these midwinter rites included the actual or symbolic killing of the king of the old year and the welcoming of a new king. Sometimes a sacred animal was sacrificed, to be replaced by a new one; sometimes a scapegoat, upon whom the sins of the tribe were visited, was driven out to wander or die. New

Mummers strut their stuff

Year's in America, which occurs at the midpoint of the Twelve Days of Christmas and aside from Christmas itself is the most festive celebration of this joyous season, brings to the Christ-Mass many pagan vestiges: the veneration of evergreens, the burning of the yule log and the kindling of new fires, indulgence in sexual license and intoxicating drink, processions of mummers and maskers, ritualistic combat between opposing parties, and the pledging of good resolves in order to redeem the bad behavior of the past.

New Year's Eve at Times Square

Jennifer Lin filed the following account of New Year's Eve revelry at New York City's Times Square:

New Year's Eve is a precise ritual for Tama Starr. At 5:30 P.M., she will climb on to the roof of One Times Square at the south end of the famous intersection of Broadway and Seventh Avenue [New York].

She will be wearing three wristwatches: two digital and one Mickey Mouse. At 7, 9 and 11 P.M., Starr will tune in a shortwave radio for the correct time from WWV, the broadcast station for the National Bureau of Standards, in Fort Collins, Colorado.

Then, at *precisely* 11:59 P.M., and unbeknown to hundreds of thousands of revelers, Starr will let the fun begin.

On her signal, a crew of workers will use a pulley to lower a glowing six-foot apple 70 feet in a New Year's Eve's tradition with which her family's business, the Artkraft Strauss Sign Corp., has been entrusted for the last 80 years.

"For me, New Year's Eve is a cross between a very moving, religious ritual and being present at the fall of Saigon. You're really in the eye of a hurricane with excruciating boredom and mind-numbing tension," Starr said.

Adding to the tension this year is a special attraction: When the ball hits bottom after 60 seconds, it will shimmer with a strobe light and spinning mirrors to mark the "leap second," an extra second added to 1987 to correct for the slightly slowing rotation of the earth.

Tama Starr has her grandfather to thank for her role on New Year's Eve. The late Jacob Starr, a Russian immigrant who took a job as a metalworker and signmaker after arriving in New York, built the first ball for New Year's Eve in 1907, after the city outlawed fireworks for the celebration.

He later earned the title "The Lamplighter of Broadway" by making theater marquees and neon signs.

Source

Philadelphia Inquirer, December 31, 1987.

Philadelphia Mummers Parade
Parade Traditions

Charles E. Welch, Jr., penned this description of the Philadelphia Mummers Parade traditions:

[It is 1966.] The sound comes before the sight—*Oh, Dem Golden Slippers*, barely heard, then swelling as thousands of banjos and glockenspiels feed out of the narrow lively streets into Broad Street. They come out of the heart of Philadelphia, these unique "Shooters" in their stunning and incongruous magnificence, and the rest of Philadelphia—at least a million and a quarter people—stand to watch them: a Viking carrying a hundred square feet of costume, a Fancy Captain with a train a block long, uncountable clowns in indescribable array, a myriad of musicians—the work of a year expended on one day of glory.

[By the 1960s the Philadelphia Mummers were represented by three groups of marchers: the Comic Clubs, the Fancy Clubs, and the String Bands.]

The earliest of all the Mummer clubs anyone can remember is the Chain Gang, which was believed to have been organized about 1840. A Comic Club as we know it today, this group organized and took a name with the expressed purpose of parading over New Year's Eve and the next day. Nothing else is known of this, our first organized club.

Shortly after the organization of the Chain Gang, some members of the Shiffler Hose Company, also known as Santa

Anna's Cavalry, made the rounds in South Philadelphia on New Year's Eve and New Year's day in costumes. They wore simple costumes, and uncomplicated makeup.

In the years immediately preceding the Civil War, the residents of Southeast Philadelphia paraded on a fairly regular basis over the New Years' endings. This era has become known as the lampblack period, because the marchers used a combination of lard and lampblack to disguise themselves. Wearing this disguise, and generally, jackets turned inside out or women's clothes, etc., they would roam the area of Smoky Hollow, Stone-house Lane, Prospect Bank, Martin's Village and other sections east of League Island, in the southeastern portion of Philadelphia. The paraders quite often carried stockings filled with flour with which they would sock unwary pedestrians.

These neighborhood excursions were discontinued for five years during the Civil War. At the war's end, many clubs were organized. Among them were: the Bright Star, Morning Star, Golden Crown, and Silver Crown. Some of these clubs were short-lived, by 1882-83 the Morning Star had already disbanded. These clubs were all Fancy, though they were not yet so classified....

One of the first Comic Clubs organized was the Cold Water, which first went out in 1884. This club had a notable reputation for many years, and won many prizes. In 1900 it changed its name to Forty Sevens, and continued to make the folks on the sidelines laugh. This club soon after the turn of the century disbanded, and its members joined other clubs. Many of these old Comic Clubs had picturesque names, there were: the Hardly Ables, the Dill Pickles, the Red Onions, the Dark Lanterns, Mixed Pickles, Energetic Hoboes, and the Blue Ribbons. Later, as we shall see, the clubs were named after prominent Philadelphians.

It is difficult to separate Comic from Fancy Clubs in these early days; some clubs started as Comic and ended Fancy....

When the winds blow cold up Broad Street, the longest straightest street in the world, and the coldest when the breezes blow, the Mummers suffer intensely. The great street forms a kind of wind tunnel which throws the capes of the Fancies around as if they were sailboats on a pond. Stately and serene in fair weather, the capes become menacing burdens in foul.

This was not always so, for the early Parades were relatively small affairs. The Shooters kept close to home, and usually wore simple costumes, the kind that could be whipped up in a hurry. Clowns, Indians and Devils were much in evidence. A favorite costume was a greatcoat turned inside out. This continued until after the Civil War when the Shooters east of Broad Street, in 1875, organized the Golden Crown Club. Then on the west side of Broad Street a rival sprung up, the Silver Crown Club. Founded in 1875 the Silver Crown lasted longer than any of the other fancy clubs, marching into the thirties. It

NEW YEAR'S DAY

Philadelphia Mummers Parade

was these two clubs which brought in the Fancy Dress idea.

Following the fashion set by the "Crown" clubs, in the early eighties the following Fancy Clubs were organized: William Banner, George A. Baird, Independents, Thomas Clements, Sr., and Thomas Clements, Jr. These clubs were loosely organized, and many soon dropped out, but not without making contributions to the tradition of the Parade. For example let's take the Independents and their founder Samuel Coett. When the Independents took to the street, the costumes of the paraders were quite simple, there were none of the flaring headpieces, the widespread collars, and the flowing capes. The idea for these was conceived by Mr. Coett, assisted by his wife, daughter, and son-in-law Billy Walton. Billy Bushmeier took out the cape designed by Mr. Coett in 1880, and this was the first cape requiring page boys.

This was a period of great rivalry, and the beginning of prizes for the best paraders. This money was given by local merchants; cakes and other food items were also presented to the marchers. The Thomas Clements, Sr. Club won the first cash prize in Mummer history in 1888; this prize was presented at the McGowan Political Club. As the prizes grew in number, the rivalry grew. A custom grew up of the winners serenading the losers with a funeral march, or some similar piece. This solicitude on the part of the winners for the losers often resulted in fierce fights. During this period the Baseler Club and the Cle-

ments, Sr. Club staged a fight that resulted in a riot call.

The String Bands were not on hand to welcome in the twentieth century, but they missed it by only one year. The late Bart McHugh and the late Abe Einstein suggested to John F. Towers that he lead his band in the Parade.

Source

"The Philadelphia Mummers Parade: A Study in History, Folklore, and Popular Tradition," Ph.D. Dissertation, University of Pennsylvania, 1968, 12-13, 61-62, 75-76, 87-88.

The Parade's Golden Sunrise New Year's Association

Edgar Williams compiled this report on preparing for the Mummers Parade:

It was chilly inside the former slaughterhouse, but John Lucas was mopping his brow.

"Nerves," he said. "I get morning sickness, afternoon sickness, all kinds of uptight sickness. But once we move out for the parade, I'm fine."

Lucas, 47, is captain of the Golden Sunrise New Year's Association. Tomorrow [January 1, 1981], barring weather that is less than clement, he will lead about 300 club members up Broad Street in the Fancy Division of the 1981 Mummers Parade.

But yesterday was Lucas's last full day to inspect personnel and equipment because this morning, at 7:45, there begins the 24-hour countdown for the parade.

In the former slaughterhouse in South Philadelphia, the Golden Sunrise's clubhouse since 1974, Lucas was busier than a behind-schedule beaver. He moved from costume to costume, checking them out with the people who will wear them. Then he turned to the "captain's suit" that will be his attire.

Calling Lucas's costume a suit is like calling a deep-sea diver's outfit a bikini. The outfit, titled "Oriental Fantasy," is 15 feet high. Dominated by a pagoda-like structure on top, it is 35 feet long, including a huge plastic dragon that stretches like a pre-inflation dollar and weighs about 800 pounds.

The part with the pagoda rolls on wheels, with two muscular aides, stationed inside, providing the foot power. Two other men are at the front and back of the dragon for propulsion purposes.

The suit's colors are predominantly red, orange and gold. "I feel," Lucas said, "as though I'm surrounded by flames."

What is rocking Lucas's dreamboat is the long-range forecast for New Year's Day issued at 5 P.M. yesterday by Gordon Tait, the forecaster for the National Weather Service.

"We are looking for increasing cloudiness Wednesday, with snow likely Wednesday night," Tait said. "On New Year's Day, we look for a possible snowfall of one to three inches."

"If snow falls on the plastic dragon, or on a lot of other items that are far from weatherproof, we're in big trouble," Lucas said....

The Golden Sunrise Club, which finished third in the Fancy Division in last January's parade (it last won in 1978), will put close to $100,000 worth of costumes on the street.

Keeping busy throughout the day was Palma Lucas, the captain's wife, who did just about everything from stapling costumes to making sandwiches. She maintained her cool all the way.

"And why not?" she said. "The day after the parade, the sun is going to rise, no matter what."

Source

Philadelphia Inquirer, December 31, 1980.

The Parade and Television

Philadelphia Mummers Parade

From an article headlined "Broad St. strut grows glitzier each year" by Beth Gillin comes this assessment of the modern-day Mummers Parade:

Tomorrow [January 1, 1987], weather permitting, about 20,000 Philadelphia Mummers arrayed in sequins and spangles or clothed in outrageous outfits that satirize the issues of the day will strut up Broad Street in the 88th consecutive Mummers Parade.

Ordinary Philadelphians by the thousands have been doing this every year since 1901, cheerfully enduring a 2½-mile march from South Philadelphia to City Hall, often in bone-chilling weather.

AMERICA CELEBRATES

NEW YEAR'S DAY

It's a raucous and noisy ritual whose original purpose was to frighten away any evil spirits who might be lurking around, planning to stir up trouble in the new year.

Over time, though, the Mummers Parade has gotten bigger, longer, louder and glitzier. In recent years, performances have incorporated high-kicking chorus girls and complicated mechanical devices, and the parade has acquired a sheen suggestive of a Broadway musical or a Las Vegas revue.

For as primitive as its roots are—and some trace the origins of the Mummers Parade all the way back to the worship of Momus, the ancient Greek god of mimicry—the modern-day festival, with its increasingly brilliant costumes and polished choreography, is also very much a child of television.

"The era of television, and especially color television, has drawn a lot more viewers. In order to attract attention to themselves, the groups, especially the string bands and fancy divisions, have had to come up with more and more elaborate presentations," said parade coordinator George V. Karalius.

Attracting attention to themselves is, after all, the major consideration for parade participants, who compete for prizes in four divisions: comic clubs, fancy clubs, string bands and brigades.

"They all want to win first prize, which is the name of the game," said Norma Gwynn, executive director of the Mummers Museum, the official repository of Mummer lore at Two Street and Washington Avenue. "They all want to be number one."

Even before television, the Mummers were extremely competitive, said Karalius, a deputy recreation commissioner for the city. "There are records of brawls between clubs in the 1920s and 1930s."

But television stations, by contracting for the right to broadcast the annual event, added to the competition. By pouring more money into club coffers, television has made it possible for clubs to purchase increasing quantities of feathers, sequins and spangles with which to bedeck their members, and to hire more and more professional help....

While millions are expected to view the parade in the comfort of their living rooms, up to a million Philadelphians and visitors have lined the streets in years past to observe the festival up close.

Gwynn noted that when the Mummer tradition began, "it was a homey-type celebration, where people visited from house to house. Then it evolved into a neighborhood ritual, and then a citywide celebration, and with each evolution it became a bit more elaborate."

Source

Philadelphia Inquirer, December 31, 1987.

Springtime Mummers Parade

A composite of two articles by Michael Bamberger and Mark Fazlollah shows a new twist to the Mummers Parade tradition:

They marched on the wrong day—the 98th day of the year, not the first. And they marched the wrong way—south on Broad Street [Philadelphia], not City Hall-bound.

But the thousands of screaming, cheering and clapping spectators who packed stoops, windowsills and sidewalks along 18 blocks of Broad Street yesterday [April 8, 1989] didn't seem to mind. The Mummers were back, and they weren't in buses.

"January first was the worst," said Sylvia Romano of the 1600 block of South Broad Street, remembering the drenching rains of New Year's Day, the traditional day for the Mummers Parade. The rain that day drove many of the string band performers—and their elaborate costumes of feather and satin—to the safety of buses.

But there was no need for artificial shelter in yesterday's brisk, refreshing breeze and squinting sunshine.

"C'mon, drill for us," Romano screamed at the penguin who led the Quaker City String Band. The band strutted its considerable stuff, to Romano's shrieking delight. "This more than makes up for" the aborted New Year's Day parade, she said.

The shindig yesterday was a stripped-down version of the usual affair: just 23 string bands in a 3 ½-hour parade. There were no fancy brigades, comics, judges or prizes. And fewer people than usual. . . .

A spectator could enjoy all the wonderful sounds of a Mummers Parade. Whistles and glockenspiels and cornets and banjos. Children shrieking. Pretzel vendors hawking. The soft hum of a Cadillac convertible idling. The muted roar of a subway running underneath Broad Street. . . .

Donna Muraresku, a member of the Duffy String Band, said she was pleased to have a second chance after the New Year's Day debacle. "You could hear the people screaming," she recalled yesterday, " 'Get off the bus and march! Be a string band!' They were throwing tomatoes and bottles. What a mess. Today, people were happy that we were out."

But Muraresku found it strange to be marching down Broad Street in spring, not winter, and going southbound, not northbound. "It was awkward, 'cause you kept looking for City Hall and not seeing it. You kept wondering how many more blocks you had to go."

She was talking at the finishing point of the parade, at Marconi Plaza at Broad Street and Oregon Avenue, several blocks north of Veterans' Stadium.

Several hours earlier, at the parade's starting line, Frank Foidl, music director of the Polish-American String Band, said he

Philadelphia Mummers Parade

felt he was making history. He's been a Mummer for 35 years, and he's never marched on Broad Street on a day other than January 1.

"Lots of other streets on lots of other days, but the Mummers Parade *is* Broad Street and it *is* New Year's Day. This is nice," Foidl said of the spring air and the festive surroundings. "Nice for the marchers and nice for the people, but it's not the same thing."...

[Nonetheless,] some radicals even suggested that Mummers Parades should regularly be held in the spring rather than January 1.

"They ought to always have it in April," said Andrea Wasser, a Fairmount resident whose daughter Molly, 1, was just a little frightened at seeing her first Mummers Parade yesterday.

"It's beautiful. The sun is shining on the sequins and feathers and everything," said South Philadelphia resident Yolanda Ciarrocchi. "Today was the right day."

Donna Howard, 33, of Holmes, bragged that her family had been "the best crowd and the loudest crowd" at Broad and Mifflin Streets since she was 2 years old.

But was an April Mummers Parade really the same?

"We had the same spirit [as on New Year's Day]. We had a good time," she said. "It was beautiful today, it was exceptional, it was really nice. . . . We had good weather, nobody got wet."

Howard and others who had attended the Jan. 1 parade said they were willing to forgive the city for the New Year's Day fiasco, when the snow and rain ruined costumes and forced many parade participants to ride buses—past vocally disappointed onlookers—up Broad Street to Walnut Street, where they resumed marching.

Source

Philadelphia Inquirer, April 9, 1989.

La Guiannée

An Associated Press feature by J. L. Schmidt, filed from Prairie du Rocher, Illinois, describes New Year's festivities on the Mississippi River.

The walls of once-powerful Fort de Chartres have crumbled and the mighty Mississippi River has changed its course, but the centuries-old French New Year's tradition of *La Guiannée* lives on in this southern Illinois town.

Liberally translated as "mistletoe of the New Year," the singing and drinking fest today will continue as one of the oldest folk traditions still observed in this country.

The tradition reminds the 650 inhabitants of this 260-year-old community, nestled under the cliffs overlooking the Mississippi, of an era when nearby Fort de Chartres was the strongest French colonial strong-hold in North America.

The fest starts as soon as the 6:30 A.M. Mass ends at St. Joseph's Catholic Church. Revelers don costumes, many made from cornhusks, and begin a door-to-door trek to sing traditional French songs.

Townspeople who want to be serenaded telephone ahead to schedule the singers, who now travel by bus. In years past, everyone walked.

Fort de Chartres will be the second stop this year, and that stop will be "the only real chance the public will have to see the singers," said Steve Anderson, a site interpreter.

The fort will be illuminated with torches and candles and the singers will see a roaring fire in the hearth and a long oak table laden with cold meats, cookies and mulled cider, Anderson said.

At private homes, they will be tempted with whiskey, wine or homemade cherry brandy, a return to the custom in which mummers performed for alms or refreshments.

Source

Philadelphia Inquirer, January 1, 1982.

And that's not all:
see "Cajun Country Mardi Gras."

First Night Revels in Boston

Diego Ribadeneira and Alexander Reid describe New Year's celebrations in "Bean Town":

With organizers promising the celebration would be bigger and better than ever, an estimated 600,000 revelers jammed Boston's chilly streets yesterday to bid

farewell to 1987 and usher in 1988 at the city's 12th annual First Night extravaganza.

Turning Boston into a stage, more than 1,000 artists and performers entertained children and adults at 58 indoor and outdoor sites. More than 200 events were featured, including opera, dance, storytelling, juggling, ice sculptures, face-painting and laser shows.

The lively sounds of jazz and the pungent smells of spicy sausages and salty pretzels filled the 34-degree air.

As night came, dozens of vendors swarmed onto Boylston Street hawking gaudy masks, colorful balloons, party hats, favors and horns. "So far so good," reported vendor Mary Salvadore. "Little by little, they are selling."

Although the day's events officially began in the early afternoon, most people agreed that First Night didn't really get into gear until the sun went down and the parade began. And it didn't end until midnight, with the three-minute fireworks display over Boston Harbor.

As the parade kickoff drew near, hordes of party-goers squeezed onto the streets and sidewalks near the Prudential Center, many admiring the colorful lights of the giant Christmas tree in front of the building.

For the 60 minutes the parade lasted, Boylston Street resembled Times Square on New Year's Eve as people stood shoulder-to-shoulder, sporting garish costumes,

NEW YEAR'S DAY

many singing and yelling. The blaring sounds of party horns competed with the shouts of vendors trying to attract customers.

First Night organizers had encouraged people to wear costumes, have their faces painted and don masks to break down the barrier between performer and audience.

Forming on Boylston Street in front of the Prudential Center shortly after 5:30 P.M., the nearly quarter-mile procession with its several thousand marchers captured the eclectic essence of First Night.

A convoy of police cruisers led the way, slowly inching through a gauntlet of party-goers squeezing in from both sides of the street. Following Mayor Flynn and his family was a Father Time figure dressed in white and carrying three doves in a wooden cage.

The colorful column cut a swath through Boston from the Back Bay to the Boston Common. Among other things, it featured a giant inflated spider, skeletons atop stilts, Chinese dancers, unicyclists and the Geometric Progressions marching band.

Many of the marchers wore oversized heads, arms and hands, adding a touch of Mardis Gras to the scene.

An 8-foot-tall ice sculpture with the dates 1987 and 1988 carved in it sat atop a trailer. As the parade streamed down Boylston Street, a sculptor slowly picked away at 1987 and by the time the procession

reached the Common, the old year had disappeared. . . .

The start of a New Year has traditionally been a time for people to make resolutions. In response, First Night organizers crafted a 25-foot "Resolution Tree" out of pine. With holes drilled into the tree, passersby could jot down resolutions on green and white silken leaves and stick them in the slots.

Source

Boston Globe, January 1, 1988.

Kissing Day

Holiday customs on the Minnesota frontier during the nineteenth century are described by Bertha L. Heilbron. She quotes the manuscript Boutwell Diary, January 1, 1834, and correspondence in the Minnesota Historical Society collections.

When missionaries began to work among the Minnesota Indians, particularly among the Chippewa of the North, they found that the natives made much of New Year's Day. They celebrated the holiday, which they called "Kissing day," after the manner of the French-Canadian traders and voyagers. The puritanical religious leaders often were obliged, much against their wishes, to observe the day in the native manner. William T. Boutwell, who went to Leech Lake in 1833, found that the Indians there were in the habit of visiting the resident trader on January 1 to receive presents, "when all, male and female, old and young, must give and receive a kiss, a cake, or something else."

At Red Lake twelve years later a band of missionaries planned a New Year's celebration which seemed to please the natives, who "honored" them "with a salute of two guns." The missionaries at this place recognized the Indian custom and took part in the celebration. According to Lucy M. Lewis, the wife of one of the missionaries, all the mission workers gathered at early dawn at the house of their leader, "the most convenient place to meet the Indians who assemble to give the greeting and receive a cake or two & a draught of sweetened water. It is the custom through the country to make calls & receive cakes." But instead of offering kisses, these Indians sang a "New Year's hymn learned in school for the occasion." The Red Lake missionaries marked New Year's Eve by assembling the pupils of the mission school and giving them presents. In 1845 the gifts consisted of flannel shirts for the boys and "short gowns" for the girls.

Source

Minnesota History, XVI (1935), 375-76.

New Year's on a Louisiana Plantation

From an essay on "Customs and Superstitions in Louisiana" by Alcée Fortier, historian and folklorist, at Tulane University, New Orleans, comes this portrait of New Year's Day in that region:

At daylight, on the 1st of January, the rejoicing began on the plantation; everything was in an uproar, and all the negroes, old and young, were running about, shaking hands and exchanging wishes for the new year. The servants employed at the house came to awaken the master and mistress and the children. The nurses came to our beds to present their *souhaits* [wishes]. To the boys it was always, "*Mo souhaité ké vou bon garçon, fe plein l'argent é ké vou bienhéreux*" ["My wish is that you are a good boy, that you lot of money and that you have good luck"]; to the girls, "*Mo souhaité ké vou bon fie, ké vou gagnin ein mari riche é plein piti*" ["My wish is that you are a good girl, that you marry a husband rich and kind"].

Even the very old and infirm, who had not left the hospital for months, came to the house with the rest of *l'atelier* [hands] for their gifts. These they were sure to get, each person receiving a piece of an ox killed expressly for them, several pounds of flour, and a new tin pan and spoon. The men received, besides, a new jean or cottonade suit of clothes, and the women a dress and a most gaudy headkerchief or *tignon*, the redder the better. Each woman that had had a child during the year received two dresses instead of one. After the *souhaits* were presented to the masters, and the gifts were made, the dancing and singing began. The scene was indeed striking, interesting, and weird. Two or three hundred men and women were there in front of the house, wild with joy and most boisterous, although always respectful.

Their musical instruments were, first, a barrel with one end covered with an ox-hide—this was the drum; then two sticks and the jawbone of a mule, with the teeth

AMERICA CELEBRATES

NEW YEAR'S DAY

still on it—this was the violin. The principal musician bestrode the barrel and began to beat on the hide, singing as loud as he could. He beat with his hands, with his feet, and sometimes, when quite carried away by his enthusiasm, with his head also. The second musician took the sticks and beat on the wood of the barrel, while the third made a dreadful music by rattling the teeth of the jawbone with a stick. Five or six men stood around the musicians and sang without stopping. All this produced a most strange and savage music, but, withal, not disagreeable, as the negroes have a very good ear for music, and keep a pleasant rhythm in their songs. These dancing-songs generally consisted of one phrase, repeated for hours on the same air.

In the dance called *carabiné* [vigorous, spicy], and which was quite graceful, the man took his *danseuse* by the hand, and made her turn around very rapidly for more than an hour, the woman waving a red handkerchief over her head, and every one singing—

> "*Madame Gobar, en sortant di bal,*
> *Madame Gobar, tiyon li tombé.*"

> ["Madame Gobar, leaving the dance, Madame Gobar, the little one, she fell."]

The ball, for such it was, lasted for several hours, and was a great amusement to us children.

Source

Journal of American Folklore, I (1888), 136-37.

New Year's Calling

Alonzo Gibbs describes, in general terms, the New Year's custom of "calling" in New York. The time is not specified but is presumably the latter part of the nineteenth century.

New Year's calling was a pleasant custom of the late nineteenth and early twentieth centuries. On New Year's Day all doors were open to the young men of the city [New York]. There were no fixed invitations. The callers wandered from home to home—tenement or brownstone front—whether they had ever before visited in this place or that. The one requirement for entry was a calling card. On this point the girls of the household were insistent. A desire for cards prompted all preparations. No matter how divergently one might talk about the custom, say in terms of girls meeting eligible boys or parents renewing old friendships, the cards none-the-less underlay the whole business. In quality and quantity, they, to the female mind, meant social success or failure.

For this reason each young man sought a type face compatible with his personality and a quality cardboard distinguished to the touch. All during December local printers were kept busy duplicating the samples in their show windows, conservative and bearing austere block letters on a white background, cards printed in crimson capitals filigreed with gold, novelty cards to which a small mug bearing the caller's nicknames was attached by a red or green ribbon, cards that stood up by themselves or that glittered open under the springy thrust of an accordion fold.

On New Year's Day, the caller appeared at the door, probably in the old Scotch tradition of "first-foot," and was welcomed by the head of the house—usually Father in his smoking jacket. Then surrounded by girls, the young man was led to a cut glass bowl at a table in the hallway. Here he drew from his vest pocket a leather or silver case pranked with delicate designs, opened it, and tossed a card into the twinkling bowl.

With such importance placed on these tokens, no wonder consternation and fretting prevailed if the first arrivals, as so often happened, were delayed. Horsecars and buggies moved slowly when snow was copious and backs of animals steam under fallen flakes. But eventually, through the wintry day in sleighs of jingling bells or on foot, ankledeep in drifts, with scarves blowing back over shoulders, hats awry, the callers came. Sometimes they came in groups, a little tipsy and singing as they came....

On the sideboard in the parlor the callers found decanters surrounded by plates of sugared *pfefferneusse*, spicy and hard as stones. Across the room, sarsaparilla, creamy and effervescent, splashed into stoneware mugs, and on the table glimmered many-tiered cakes, covered with glazed fruits or lush with different colored icings....

Under mistletoe and jaded boughs of Christmas, the first day of the new year was celebrated to its end. The hostesses insisted that "tomorrow will be Ladies' Day," but few really intended to go calling next morning. Ladies' Day was more of a threat than a custom.

Source

New York Folklore Quarterly, XVI (1960), 295-97.

And that's not all:
The popular *Hill's Manual of Social and Business Forms* (... edition [of] 1880) has an extensive section on the etiquette of the New Year's "call":

Of late years it had become fashionable, for ladies in many cities and villages, to announce in the newspapers the fact of their intention to receive calls upon New Year's Day, which practice is excellent, as it enables gentlemen to know positively who will be prepared to receive them on that occasion; ...

Upon calling, the gentlemen are invited to remove overcoat and hat, which invitation is accepted unless it is the design to make the call very brief.... Gloves are sometimes retained upon the hand during the call, but this is optional. Cards are sent up, and the gentlemen are ushered into the reception room. The call should not exceed ten or fifteen minutes, unless the callers are few and it should be mutually agreeable to prolong the stay....

The two or three days succeeding the New Year's are ladies days for calling, upon which occasion they pass the compliments of the season,

NEW YEAR'S DAY

comment upon the incidents connected with the festivities of the holiday, the number of calls made, and the new faces that made their appearance among the visitors. It is customary upon this occasion of ladies meeting, to offer refreshments and to enjoy the intimacy of a friendly visit. This fashion of observing New Year's Day is often the means of commencing pleasant friendships which may continue through life.

New Year's Calling in Early Wisconsin

In "Social Life in Wisconsin," Lillian Kruegar describes this New Year's custom as she treats the territorial period through the mid-1860s; footnotes credit Milwaukee and Madison newspapers of the 1850s as a major source:

In frontier Wisconsin the New Year was made welcome with the ever popular ball. Barely had the participants recovered from their Christmas revelry when they made ready for the New Year day visitors. Making a round of calls on that day was a recognized social practice, noticeably participated in by the men of the community. Convention required the serving of refreshments by the 'at home' hostesses. In Milwaukee 'the first day of New Year [1851] ... was enjoyed, apparently, by all concerned. The Ladies were "at home" to receive visitors and had no lack of calls thro' day and evening. The pleasant weather and capital sleighing did much to make the day pass off agreeably.' January 1, 1857, 'the streets were alive with people

enjoying the holiday, there were numbers of sleighs filled with gentlemen paying the annual visit of congratulation.' There was less calling in 1859 though New Year's eve was one of general hilarity: 'There was considerable jollity about our city, Friday night, and a very general seeing of "the Old Year out and the New Year in." There were four, or five Balls, during the evening.... The "calling" was not general, though quite a number of gentlemen went the rounds....'

A Madison journalist in 1857 says of this holiday: 'The day passed off very pleasantly. The social custom of calling was quite generally observed. The day was an admirable one for the purpose, the sleighing capital, and the streets in good condition for pedestrians.' He informs the public of an accident to mar the day's pleasures. A large sleigh containing people from Lake Side watercure overturned on the corner of Washington avenue, near the Episcopal church, but no one was severely injured.

Source

Wisconsin Magazine of History, XXII (June 1939).

And that's not all:
See "New Year's Calling."

Japanese New Year

Japanese Customs in America

In Japan Shōgatsu, or New Year's, is probably the gayest and most significant celebration of a national culture unusually rich in festivals. Preparations begin during the last week of December and the festive season continues until the middle of January. (Japan now uses the solar calendar.) It is an occasion for settling accounts, giving presents, having reunions of family and friends, and eating holiday dishes. Some of them require elaborate preparations and are designed to appeal to the eye as well as the mouth. Although Japanese-Americans note the passing of traditional practices, within the family circles many of them, especially food traditions, survive. "Miss N.I.," a researcher for Paul Radin, collected and reported material on the customs and beliefs of the oriental minorities in the San Francisco Bay area for a 1934 study directed by Radin.

In contrast to the elaborate manner in which New Year is welcomed in Japan, the same holiday as celebrated by Japanese in America [c. 1934] is quite simple. In chatting with members of the older generation, there was disclosed the interesting fact that, graphically illustrated, there has been a distinct curve in the degree of observance of Japanese New Year. Though exact dates and figures cannot be given without more extensive research, the following observations, though they indicate only roughly the trends that have taken place, are nevertheless revelatory.

For about ten years after the 1890s—which may be considered the beginning of extensive Japanese settlement in Alameda County [California]—the Japanese holidays, not even excepting the all-important New Year, were scarcely observed. Not only the scarcity of Japanese people at that time, but also the lack of appropriate paraphernalia for celebrating the holidays and the fact that these pioneers were too busily occupied in the task of colonization, account for this seeming absence of feeling for the festivals of their mother country. However, from about 1900 and for some twenty years after, a renewed interest in

their national holidays developed, literally flared up.

A rather large Japanese community, added to greater leisure after the first years of hard work and the opening of stores handling merchandise from Japan, encouraged the Japanese people to satisfy their instinctive wish to celebrate the festivals of their home country. According to one of the older members of the Japanese community in Oakland [California], until about the year 1906 approximately one-tenth of the Japanese kept strict observance of the New Year spirit in the Japanese style by arranging the triple-tree decoration ... just outside their doors. He added that though this custom was not preserved in private homes after 1906, proprietors of large Japanese concerns, particularly in San Francisco, elaborately bedecked their store-fronts with pine, bamboo, and plum tree branches until as late as 1920.

Another new feature of the New Year celebration was the setting out of the American and Japanese flags, a practice retained by three-fourths of the Japanese people in America until about the year 1917. Since that date, flags have not been prominently displayed outside the houses, except in front of large stores or, less conspicuously, inside the homes. The year 1917 also seems to mark the decline of the observance of the custom of making New Year calls, a proceeding which up to that time the Japanese had followed almost one hundred percent. Furthermore, only until about 1917 or 1918 did the Japanese girls

AMERICA   CELEBRATES

NEW YEAR'S DAY

spend part of New Year's day playing battledore and shuttlecock, whereas *karuta*—a Japanese card game—and *sugoroku* (backgammon) parties were popular even as late as 1928 and 1929. The custom of exchanging New Year gifts has been steadily fading out among the Japanese in America, giving way to the more universal Christmas presents.

The one feature of the New Year celebration which has been preserved even to this day, at least within the family, is the provision and consumption of some of the special New Year foods and the drinking of wine. Many members of the older generation chuckled when asked whether they were forced to give up their custom of imbibing *sake* during the period of prohibition. A very great minority of them, even to this day, spend some days before New Year's Day pounding out rice into *mochi* [characteristic New Year's food, rice dumpling, steamed and pounded] . . . . The bright red lobster—supposed to be a symbol of old age on account of its crooked back—which is a feature of the outdoor decoration in Japan, has been given a less conspicuous place. Nevertheless, it still adorns the interior of many homes. . . .

Yet it is to be doubted whether here in America, even at the time of the fullest and most elaborate New Year celebrations, the holidays lasted more than a day, for economic exigencies demanded resumption of business as soon as possible. The one clear cut manifestation of the holiday spirit even today is the three-day period of non-publication observed by all the Japanese newspapers, a luxury indulged in on no other occasion. As a whole, therefore, New Year's as celebrated by the Japanese in America has lost that air of relaxation and carefree rejoicing so easily submitted to and so contagious during the New Year holidays in Japan.

A questioning of the members of the younger generation of Japanese in America brought to light also the fact that they are slowly but surely discarding Japanese traditions of the New Year celebration. The custom of giving the house a thorough cleaning, for instance, as well as that of remaining at home on December 31st to welcome the New Year, are both disappearing. Boisterous hilarity with confetti, bells, horns, and so forth, and going to New Year's Eve dancing parties and midnight-shows seem to be more to the taste of the younger Japanese. Today, there still exists an unresolved conflict between the parents' desire to have the entire family home on New Year's Eve, and the children's desire to celebrate it in the American style. This circumstance accounts, in part, for the relatively poor attendance at dances given on that evening.

With the passing of the years, however, there is an indication that the younger folk will do as they please, and that their elders will have to resign themselves, as best they can, to the influence of American modes and manners on their children. Whether or not they go out on New Year's Eve, it is true that today the younger generation no longer spend New Year's Eve playing Japanese cards and backgammon, nor do they indulge in the simple pastimes of spinning tops, flying kites, and playing battledore and shuttlecock.

As to the matter of food, it is to be expected that in families in which the parents are of the first generation, the special preparation and partaking of Japanese foods will continue.

Source

Southwestern Journal of Anthropology, II (1946), 166–68.

Japanese Food for New Year's

This recollection of traditional New Year's customs and foodways, and the accompanying recipes, were obtained in 1978 by Joanne Takagi, of Albertson, New York, a student at the University of Pennsylvania, from her mother, Betty Y. Takagi, born in Seattle, Washington, in 1923.

Prior to World War II, I can remember the call for community Japanese males, both *issei* (first generation) and *nisei* (second generation) in Seattle, Washington, to participate in the making of *mochi* [rice cakes, made from cooked rice pounded into a sticky paste in wooden mortars]. The rice-pounding was usually done on the weekend before New Year's. It was a communal social event where there was much merry-making as each took turn pounding the rice. Each family had already ordered the quantity of *mochi* they desired, so they had a general idea of how much was necessary. For several days, my sisters and I helped mother prepare special foods. The central item would be broiled red snapper or sea bream, called *tai....* It would be broiled whole, and it was important to skewer it carefully so that it appeared to be in motion. Sometimes they would improvise by tying the head and tail to shape it.

A great variety of *sushi* [rice cooked in wine vinegar and spices topped with various kinds of seafood, sometimes uncooked, or combinations of specially cooked vegetables] are prepared. Analogous to the foods associated with our Easter celebration, many foods such as eggs, fingerlings of the sardine family, cod roe, bamboo shoots and beans—indicating new life and new beginnings—were prepared and arranged in the *jubako* [a lacquered box with four tiers, beautifully arranged, the first tier with sweet foods, the second broiled foods, the third boiled, and the fourth raw fish and vegetables].

Early on the New Year's morning the soup, *ozoni* [rice cake soup] was made. It consists of stock made variously in the different provinces in Japan, a few pieces of green vegetables about one and a half inches in size, slices of carrots which have been decoratively cut, dried mushrooms and *mochi* which has been toasted on a wire rack over an open flame. Other dishes such as *kombu* [kelp] and *umani*, a dish consisting of meat and vegetables with a soy sauce-sugar flavoring, were also served. The entrance would be decorated with a branch of pine and plums to assure longevity, and on the hall table two rice cakes of different sizes would be placed on top of each other, with a tangerine above.

Japanese New Year

AMERICA CELEBRATES

NEW YEAR'S DAY

My father would leave the house around 6:30 A.M. on New Year's Day to make calls on friends, relatives and business associates. He chose this early hour because it was traditional to visit and eat and drink at each home, but to avoid overeating and drinking, he would leave his calling card on the doorsteps of as many as possible before the families had arisen. He would be gone all day, and I remember that he would sometimes be drunk by the time he came home in the evening.

The rest of us arose a few hours later. We would post ourselves in the living room to invite the callers in for food and *toso-sake* [sweet sake spiced with medicinal herbs to encourage longevity]. The traditional greeting, "*Shinen omedeto gozaimasu,*" was exchanged, which is equivalent to "Happy Year." The visits were usually brief, 15-30 minutes, as they also had other calls to make.

In the evening we would play *karuta*, a Japanese card game. The caller would say the beginning of a poem on the subject of love and the object would be to find the matching half of the poem as quickly as possible. Shuttlecock was also played. My father is tone deaf, and he would make us laugh uproariously by exaggeratedly singing songs off key.

This type of New Year's celebration has greatly diminished since World War II. Many first generation Japanese are now deceased, and the second generation are involving themselves less and less with feast making, probably due to the great effort required and the dearth of some of the foods. I note the use of more and more instant foods and canned goods among the recent Japanese immigrants, and I am told they now use electric *mochi* makers. My sister who still resides in Seattle said that many of the *niseis* visit on New Year's Day but are now served a combination of traditional Japanese New Year's foods with a greater concentration of American foods served buffet style. As for the third generation, I do not know any who follow the Japanese New Year's traditions although I must confess that our contacts with those of Japanese heritage are minimal.

My husband, who is also a *nisei* but was born and reared on the East Coast, specifically, New York and New Jersey, also remembers the special New Year's foods and the social calls from a few Japanese friends. He is a gourmet and a gourmand and has made it a point to make certain that we have these special foods on New Year's. In lieu of preparing them, we have gone to those Japanese restaurants in New York City that serve these items and dined out about three days successively. At one time, there were quite a few restaurants, namely *Miyako, Nippon, Suehiro, Aki,* etc., that offered these dishes, but they are dwindled to a very few. This is probably due to the labor involved, and many Japanese prefer to cook at home for the holidays. The consumption of *ozoni* and *mochi* persists today. The *mochi* can be bought at the Japanese food stores in New York City either fresh or frozen.

The practice of closing businesses at this time of year still exists in New York. All Japanese business firms are closed for about three to five days. Many of the Japanese restaurants are closed on New Year's Day here, and some a few days additionally.

Ozoni

2   chicken breasts, skinned and boned (Pork slices may be substituted.)
3   dried Japanese mushrooms
¼-   pound leaf spinach
12   pieces of *mochi* (rice cakes)
6   cups *dashi*
     salt
     pepper
     soy sauce
6   pieces lemon rind

Soak dried mushrooms in boiling hot water about twenty minutes, drain, cut off stem, and cut into about six pieces.

Boil six cups of water and add three packets of instant *dashi-no-moto* to make soup base. Salt, pepper, and soy sauce may be added to taste. Add mushrooms and chicken breasts and boil six minutes, longer if pork is substituted. Pork must be fully cooked.

Meanwhile, peel carrots, slice crosswise, and cut into flower petal shapes. Add to soup and cook until tender.

Wash spinach leaves and boil in small amount of water, cooking until barely tender, but still green.

Toast cubed *mochi* on wire rack over open burner flame, turning frequently until lightly browned and puffy.

Slice lemon rind into thin slivers, to represent pine needles, an evergreen symbolizing long life.

Serve soup in bowls and place chicken or pork pieces, mushrooms, carrots, spinach leaf, lemon slice, and two pieces of *mochi* into each bowl, arranging it so that it is appealing to the eye.

Tai

Gut and scale a whole red snapper, leaving intact the tail, head, and fins. Skewer fish with long, thin bamboo sticks or use a string or thread and tie it around the tail, pulling string taut and tying it around the head. This is to shape the fish so that it appears to be swimming.

Sprinkle with coarse salt and broil until done.

Arrange cooked fish on platter with green pine branch and lemon slices.

Serve with dip of soy sauce mixed with lemon juice.

Turnip and Carrot Salad

3   turnips
1   carrot
6   teaspoons cider vinegar or rice wine vinegar
1   teaspoon *mirin* or light white wine
     salt
1   teaspoon sugar

AMERICA CELEBRATES

NEW YEAR'S DAY

Wash turnips and slice crosswise into one-quarter inch slices. Then slice again lengthwise into thin slices.

Peel carrot and slice similarly.

Place vegetables into dish and sprinkle with salt. Squeeze slices to remove moisture, and let stand for about thirty minutes.

Add vinegar, sugar, and *mirin*, mix well, and let stand for another thirty minutes.

Source

University of Pennsylvania Folklore Archives, unclassified, 1980.

And that's not all:
see "New Year's Calling."

What to Eat on New Year's Day

Georgia

Ronald Steiner collected this from an anonymous informant at Grovetown, Columbia County, Georgia.

To have good luck all the year, eat a piece of boil [sic] meat on the first day of January.

Source

Journal of American Folklore, XII (1899), 265.

Tennessee

This advice comes from a selection of "superstitions at home" contributed by Mrs. Marion T. Faye of St. Bethlehem, Tennessee, who grew up on a farm.

We always ate hog jowl and blackeyed peas on New Year's Day for good luck. Many people say you should put a dime in the peas, but we never did that.... My oldest brother had a cook who truly believed that it was bad luck for a woman to come to your house first on New Year's Day. So she always had the hired man go to the house and go into every room before she would cook breakfast. That meant late breakfast on New Year's Day.

Source

Tennessee Folklore Society Bulletin, XX (September 1954), 54.

North Carolina

Joseph D. Clark interviewed first-year students in English at North Carolina State College, Raleigh, in 1955-56 and 1960-61.

On New Year's Day cook something that swells for a prosperous year. Eat turnip greens, hog jowls, blackeyed peas, and peaches on New Year's day to bring health and wealth during the year.

Hog jaws, cabbage, and blackeyed peas for New Year's dinner will bring luck.

Eat collard greens at New Year's to have paper money all the year. Cook blackeyed peas and hog head on New Year's Day and have plenty to eat all year.

Rice and peas on New Year's Day bring good luck.

Money cooked in blackeyed peas on New Year's means you will have money all year.

Source

Southern Folklore Quarterly, XXVI (1962), 210-11.

Pennsylvania Dutch

From an article on sauerkraut by Don Yoder, the first saying is from Mrs. Lilly Hyle of Rexmont, Pennsylvania; and the second from J. S. Greiner of Elizabethtown, Pennsylvania.

Eat sauerkraut on New Year's Day to keep well the rest of the year.

If people eat sauerkraut on New Year's Day they become rich.

A common explanation as to why Pennsylvanians today eat turkey on Christmas and pork (with sauerkraut) on New Year's Day is that pork symbolizes the "forward look" of the turn of the year. A fowl scratches backward—a pig roots forward. . . .

There are a few references to sauerkraut at New Year's from the 19th Century. They would appear to be associated with the Christmas-New Year's custom of feasting on sauerkraut. One of the earliest of these references comes from Norristown, where sauerkraut was featured on New Year's Day, 1861: "Saur Kraut lunches were the order of the day at the different lager beer saloons" (Norristown *National Defender*, January 1, 1861).

In the 20th century, it is a widespread custom. In Central Pennsylvania the custom is so common that pork and sauerkraut advertisements appear in the commercial columns of the newspapers throughout the dying days of December. One such ad, from the *Altoona Mirror* of December 27, 1960, emanating from Pielmelet's Market, Corner 1st Ave. and 15th St., urges readers to "Follow the Tradition for New Year's Day," by serving "Sauerkraut and Pork," and adds the bid for confidence "We make our own Kraut." On December 29, 1960, The "Endress Market" advertised "Sauerkraut: Our Own Make! It's Truly Delicious! Serve it for Your New Year's Dinner." In the same issue of the *Mirror*, the "Sanitary Market" informs the readers that "Blocher's Fresh Dressed Pork will guarantee the success of your New Year's dinner," while "Honsaker Bros." advertises "Pork for New Year—Spare ribs, loin and ham cuts, shoulder cuts, tenderloin, sausage." It was obvious that Altoona was preparing for New Year's in the (more or less) traditional Dutch fashion.

Source

Pennsylvania Dutchman, XII (Summer 1961), 62.

New York German

This advice was collected by Alice P. Whitaker from Mrs. Matilda Popp, age fifty, and Lilian Wind, "about fifty," both of whom learned them from their German parents.

[It was believed c. 1940] in the old German section of Buffalo [New York] that if you kept cabbage or herring in the house on New Year's Eve, you will have money all year . . . if you *eat* a piece of herring at the stroke of midnight, you will be *lucky* all year.

Source

New York Folklore Quarterly, XI (1955), 258.

AMERICA CELEBRATES

NEW YEAR'S DAY

New Year's Beliefs

Tennessee

The first two beliefs are from a collection by Ruth W. O'Dell of Newport, Tennessee; the third is collected in "Middle Tennessee" by Neal Frazier.

If you wash your clothes on New Year's Day, you will wash someone out of your family.

If a woman comes to see you on New Year's Day, the chickens will all be pullets; if a man comes, they will all be roosters.

On New Year's night, place a gold band in a glass of water, go into a dark cellar, and see your husband's picture in the bottom of the glass.

Source

Tennessee Folklore Society Bulletin, X (December 1944), 4 and II (October 1936), 12.

The Alleghanies

J. Hampden Porter interviewed "mountain whites . . . in remoter parts of the Alleghanies between southwestern Georgia and the Pennsylvania line."

If a girl wishes to know whether her future husband will be a stranger or from the vicinity, she can find out by going alone and after night on New Year's Eve, standing silently by a peach-tree and shaking its stem. Should a dog bark, her suitor comes from a distance, but if a cock crows his home is near.

Source

Journal of American Folklore, VII (1894), 108.

The Ozarks

From a collection of mountain white superstitions recorded by Vance Randolph.

Always make sure the salt-shaker is full on New Year's Day, and you will prosper throughout the year.

Source

Journal of American Folklore, XLVI (1933), 17.

Creole Louisiana

These beliefs were collected by Hilda Roberts in Iberia Parish, southwestern Louisiana.

If you sew on New Year's Day, you will sew a shroud before the year is out.

Always wear something new on New Year's Day for good luck during the year.

Source

Journal of American Folklore, XL (1927), 190.

Illinois

Lelah Allison collected these beliefs from southeastern Illinois.

If you cry on New Year's Day, you will be sorry throughout the year.

What you do the first hour of the New Year will be what you do most of the year.

Animals kneel at midnight on New Year's Eve.

Source

Journal of American Folklore, LXIII (1950), 314-15.

North Carolina

A collection of superstitions made by Joseph D. Clark in 1955-56 includes these beliefs provided by students of North Carolina State College, Raleigh.

Whatever you do on New Year's Day, you'll do the rest of the year.

Don't do anything on New Year's that you don't wish to do all year.

Source

Southern Folklore Quarterly, XXVI (1962), 211.

Hawaii

Gwladys F. Hughes collected these beliefs at Waialua sugar plantation, thirty-four miles from Honolulu, in 1946-47. Informants were children of Japanese ancestry, many of whom "speak broken English." Yet most of these items are well known on the mainland, especially to those of Anglo-Saxon origin.

Don't sweep the house during the day.

Don't sweep the house during the evening.

Girls must not go out early in the morning of New Year's Day.

Men do most of the work on New Year's Eve.

Bad luck comes if a girl is your first visitor: good luck, if a man comes first.

Luck will go away if you open the front door.

Source

Journal of American Folklore, LXII (1949), 296, 298.

January

1

EMANCIPATION DAY

There have been a number of Emancipation or "freedom" celebrations. The first was held on January 1, 1808, to commemorate the legal termination of the importation of slaves into the United States. Regional celebrations have also taken place honoring various military proclamations such as that of General David Hunter, Commander of the Department of the South, who on May 9, 1862, freed the slaves in South Carolina, Georgia, and Florida, and General Gordon Granger who issued an order freeing the Texas slaves on June 19, 1985. And there were smaller celebrations of a more obscure origin that are less easily explained but apparently recall

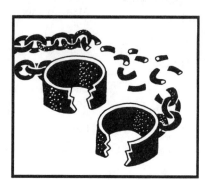

that date on which slaves in a particular locality learned that they were free at last.

President Lincoln issued a formal Emancipation Proclamation on January 1, 1863, after a preliminary announcement on the previous September 22. The latter date was celebrated also, but it is on the anniversary of Lincoln's official proclamation that the most important observances take place, in part because January 1 is both a traditional and legal holiday. One of their notable features is the reading of his proclamation, often in a rhythmic, dramatic style that elevates the language of a government document to the level of folk poetry.

Emancipation Day, Sacred and Profane

William H. Wiggins, Jr., a folklorist and historian, discusses the origin of Emancipation Day and its ritualistic celebration.

There has never been a day in Afro-American history equal to January 1, 1863.... Free blacks and white abolitionists gathered in churches across the Northeast, anxiously awaiting the dawn ... and its statement of freedom. In northern cities like Boston and New York, racially mixed

congregations spent the last night of 1862 singing and praying for freedom in special Emancipation-watch night services.... Soon after midnight their prayers were answered when a copy of President Lincoln's Emancipation Proclamation was read to them just moments after it arrived over the telegraph wire. After the reading of this document, there was much applause and speechmaking in praise of President Lincoln for having the courage to issue such a statement and of the eternal God for giving him the wisdom to see that it must be done....

[I]ndicative of the sacredness of the celebrations is the serious attitude that most celebrants bring to it. Mingo Scott used the term "intellectual" to describe the ambiance of January 1 celebrations:

> It's more on the basis of an intellectual celebration. There you come with the reading of the Emancipation Proclamation, speeches are made, appropriate music and then some of the most outstanding speakers among black people come and they are very prepared.

But there were some lighter, secular aspects of the celebration. Perhaps the most spectacular is the parade. In 1973, for example, parades were held in Charleston, South Carolina, and Phenix City, Alabama. Both affairs were modest .... The Charleston, South Carolina, parade had less than a hundred marchers. In its ranks were a uniformed scout troop, about five motorcycles, two cars decorated with crepe-paper streamers and placards on the doors. The

procession was led by a motorcycle policeman and the American flag was carried by the scout troop.

Mrs. J.C. Cook, the wife of a local Baptist preacher, described the Phenix City, Alabama, parade in the following conversation:

> Now yesterday they formed their parade in the yard of the Mount Zion Baptist Church and marched from North Phenix City to Phillips Temple. There were quite a few men in the march. I know most all of the men, but I can't recall right now. One is the president of the Association, the Betterment Association of Russell County. They had cars that were decorated and the Mount Olive School band led the parade. They gave music right out of Fort Mitchell School. That parade began some few years back. I can't recall now, just how far back that's been.

This parade was routed through the black community and appears to be similar in size to the 1890 January 1 parade witnessed by Clara Neale, a ninety-year-old, retired schoolteacher, in rural South Carolina. She recalled past celebrations as days where there was "music and different people spoke ... and the band.... And the speaking, different people spoke. And some who had horses and mules and things dressed them up and paraded around."

Many of the celebrations in such smaller communities as Fitzgerald, Georgia; Phenix City, Alabama; and Hopkins, South Carolina, included meals after the noon

AMERICA   CELEBRATES

EMANCIPATION DAY

program. Leila Blakey tells how it was done in Monticello, Georgia: "Well . . . it was . . . I guess you couldn't say it was spread on the ground. This was January 1 and you know winter time. And in Monticello we had winter. So they had this long table all set up where you could go around and just pick up what you wanted, that type of thing."

In Hopkins, South Carolina, a meal was also served after the Emancipation Program, but unlike this free meal at Monticello, Georgia, the celebrants had to pay for the food. Wilemenia Crelow, a retired South Carolina schoolteacher, remembers:

> They'd kill a big hog and sell barbecue. You could get a 25 cents sandwich and a 50 cents plate. [With] lemonade and cokes [to] drink. [But] this wouldn't necessarily be at the church. Barbecues wouldn't be at the church. That would be at another meeting place, at the school house or something, or someplace like that. See, we would have this service at the church. Then we leave there and go on to the school house or some other community house and have barbecues.

The Nashville, Tennessee, celebration also has had after-program dinners, but not on an annual basis. (Mingo Scott notes that the January celebration in this city is sometimes "concluded or climaxed with a banquet.")

The most important part of the celebration is the program that comes after the parade and before the eating. This program has evolved over the years into a highly ritualized religious service. Original chance actions, such as the reading of the Emancipation Proclamation, have become essential segments of the service, as has the singing of James Weldon Johnson's song "Lift Every Voice and Sing." And always at the center has been the spoken word—the major address or sermon to be given on that day. These three parts of the program form the tripod foundation on which all else done in that one-and-a-half-to two-hour service is based. The opening paragraph of a 1941 Atlanta *Daily World* editorial underscores this fact:

> And they came here: it was January first, the official celebration day of the Emancipation. From the little country schoolhouse to the large city metropolitan churches they gathered and sang "Lift Every Voice and Sing," listened to the reading of the Emancipation Proclamation and the fine phrased eulogy from the great spokesman.

And the following statement by the Reverend Kelly Miller Smith, pastor of the First Baptist church in Nashville, Tennessee, and a former speaker at past January 1 celebrations, further confirms this cultural fact: "Well, in Nashville here, prior to last year it was an observance which was on or about January 1, which included a major address, always the singing of 'Lift Every Voice and Sing,' always the reading of the Emancipation Proclamation. Those were the must items, the must ingredients in the observance."

Tradition has fashioned a ritualistic order in which the Emancipation Proclamation is always read before the major address is given. However, such a fixed place has not yet been accorded the song "Lift Every Voice and Sing." For example, in 1973 it served to open the celebration in Columbus, Georgia, but closed the celebrations in Atlanta, Georgia, and Indianapolis, Indiana. In both programs it was sung just prior to the benediction, and on the Indianapolis program it was called the "Closing Hymn of Challenge." In all cases, the address climaxes the celebration and comes very late in the program. As the Reverend William Holmes Borders, the pastor of the historic Wheat Street Baptist church in Atlanta, Georgia, and a past speaker at numerous May 5, August 1, and January 1 Emancipation celebrations, has commented: "the addresses which I have made have always been last, the climax of the whole thing, the program."

The majority of these celebrations has some sort of printed program. In 1973, as a case in point, the programs of Atlanta, Georgia, and Indianapolis, Indiana, were mimeographed, while the programs of Phenix City, Alabama, and Columbus, Georgia, were printed. This latter program was printed in black ink on pages of folded 8 ½- by 11-inch gold paper.

There is an important cultural aesthetic beneath this formal program. In the 110-year history of the Emancipation celebration, Afro-Americans have come to attach different values and standards to the three foundation pillars of this celebration. For example, the reading of the Emancipation Proclamation has evolved over the years from a straightforward news report to a highly developed genre of oral narration within Afro-American culture. Tradition has also dictated that the reader of this precious document must be young, preferably in his or her late teens or early twenties and preferably female, though young men have been selected with some success. . . .

Source

Prospects: An Annual of American Cultural Studies, IV (1979), 331-32, 335-41.

And that's not all:
see "Juneteenth."

January
4-8

OLD CHRISTMAS, EPIPHANY, TWELFTH NIGHT

January 6, the twelfth night after Christmas, is the present date of the Feast of the Epiphany. According to the New Testament's Gospels, on this date the Magi or Three Kings venerated the Infant Jesus. Literally, the word "Epiphany" means "manifestation," and in addition to this first manifestation of Christ, two others are commemorated—the baptism in the Jordan River, and the transformation of

Midwinter merrymaking

water into wine at the marriage feast in Cana, Christ's first miracle. The Eastern Church emphasizes the journey of the Three Kings to Bethlehem, eventually reserving the eighth day of the Epiphany season to honor the baptism. In England and America, the change from the Julian to the Gregorian calendar in 1752 eliminated eleven days from the year; this and the fact that the Nativity was a moveable feast in the Western Church until the designation of December 25 as Christmas, has created much confusion. "Old Christmas" on January 6, prior to the acceptance of the calendar reform, is not altogether forgotten, though it has been generally superseded by "New Christmas" on December 25. Furthermore, in some places various dates from January 4 through January 8 are observed as "Old Christmas." Twelfth Night, the eve of the Feast of Epiphany, is an occasion for merrymaking. It marks the end of Christmastide and the beginning of the carnival season, which reaches its climax with Mardi Gras. According to the reckoning of the Julian Calendar, it falls on the same day as "Old Christmas." This coincidence compounds the confusion.

The Cherry-Tree Carol

*The British ballad "The Cherry-Tree Carol" is well
known on both sides of the Atlantic. The variant
presented here was collected near Hindman, Knott
County, Kentucky. The text derives from an
apocryphal story in the Pseudo-Matthew Gospel. The
earliest English versions appear in fifteenth-century
mystery plays, where, as here and other English
versions, the cherry tree figures. In some Continental
versions the date tree, which has the authority of the
Apocrypha, is preserved. Others substitute an apple
tree. Josephine McGill collected this version of the
carol from Will Wooten; he learned it from his
grandmother, who was from North Carolina. She
"died about thirty years ago at a very advanced
age." The reference in stanza 9 to "the sixth day of
January" evidences the continued celebration of Old
Christmas.*

Among ... additions to the list of
American versions of British ballads is "The
Cherry-Tree".... This [variant of the]
quaint and beautiful carol was found ... in
the mountain region of Kentucky....

When Jo-seph was an old man, An old man was he. He mar-ried Vir-gin Ma-ry, The Queen of Gal-i-lee, He mar-ried Vir-gin Ma-ry, The Queen of Gal-i-lee.

2. As Joseph and Mary
   Were walking one day:
   "Here are apples, here are
   cherries
      Enough to behold."

3. Then Mary spoke to Joseph
   So meek and so mild:
   "Joseph, gather me some cherries,
   For I am with child."

4. Then Joseph flew in anger,
   In anger flew he:
   "Let the father of the baby
   Gather cherries for thee."

5. Then Jesus spoke a few words,
   A few words spoke he:
   "Let my mother have some
   cherries;
      Bow low down, cherry-tree."

6. The cherry-tree bowed low
   down,
      Bowed low down to the
   ground,
   And Mary gathered cherries
      While Joseph stood around.

7. Then Joseph took Mary
   All on his right knee:
   "O, what have I done?
      Lord have mercy on me!"

8. Then Joseph took Mary all,
   All on his left knee:
   "O, tell me, little baby,
      When thy birthday will be."

9. "On the sixth day of January
   My birthday will be,
   When the stars in the elements
      Shall tremble with glee."

Source

Journal of American Folklore, XXIX (1916), 293-45, 417.

OLD CHRISTMAS, EPIPHANY, TWELFTH NIGHT

Kings' Day at Santo Domingo Pueblo

Charles H.Lange, at the time an anthropologist at the University of Texas, describes ceremonies at Santo Domingo, a Keresan pueblo on the Rio Grande in northwestern New Mexico, which he observed on January 6, 1940.

Upon arrival at the Pueblo of Santo Domingo [New Mexico], about 2 P.M., [January 6, 1940] we found the celebration of Kings' Day, or Reyes Day, already in progress. A crowd of several hundred celebrants was gathered in front of a house which proved to be that of the newly appointed governor of the pueblo. A chorus of singers was in the house, and the crowd was waiting their reappearance. Later, it was learned that the chorus had entered this home and that of the newly appointed lieutenant governor. Homes of other new officers and those of people having the name of Rey or Reyes, whose day was being celebrated were visited but not entered.

After a few minutes the chorus emerged; they were dressed as French chefs. (In 1939, the chorus had been dressed as Chinese.) There were twenty-seven in the group, mostly younger men. The face of each was painted with pink clay and adorned with some form of false mustache. White aprons and chef's caps were made from flour sacks. The chorus formed an arc facing the doorway as they sang. Three men stood in front of the others, also facing the door. In front of all stood the leader who wore a very heavy,

dark beard and mustache, a black sheepskin wig or hat, and an olive-drab smock. One chorus member carried a small, two-headed drum.

After several songs by the chorus, the house occupants threw presents from the roof to the crowd. Then the chorus, followed by the crowd, moved to another house where more songs were sung and presents were again thrown from the roof. The crowd was composed almost entirely of Santo Domingo residents as neighboring pueblos were holding their own celebrations that day. Some Spanish-Americans and a few Anglos were present. We were told that there were about sixty-five houses at which celebrations occurred, of which we watched the proceedings at about thirty-five. The ceremonies had begun shortly before noon and continued until about five o'clock that evening. At that time the people returned home to eat and rest for the dancing which began soon after six o'clock and continued until well after midnight.

Presents distributed from the housetops included the following items: cigarettes, Bull Durham and papers, candy bars, stick candy, candy suckers, packages of hard candy, gum, tin trays, pails, wash tubs, biscuit tins, dippers, pans, flour sifters, egg beaters, oranges, apples, grapefruit, glass bowls, 50 lb. sacks of flour, loaves of bread (mostly of native baking), cans of sardines, canned fruits and vegetables, 10'-12' halter ropes, rolls of linoleum, cooking utensils, cookies, wafers, crackers, crackerjack, yards of cloth, handkerchiefs, and head scarves.

Ready-made cigarettes and the tin ware seemed most popular. Everything was received enthusiastically, however, and the people throwing the presents were constantly urged by members of the crowd to throw an object in their direction. The crowd remained jovial throughout the day. Non-Indians were treated hospitably, and no objection was raised to their scrambling for presents. Occasionally, struggles for presents became quite spirited, but the losers usually shifted their attention quickly to the next offerings with a minimum of animosity.

Many presents were thrown toward the chorus; a few were purposely directed toward friends or relatives, especially women and small children. For the most part, however, presents were thrown at random.

Singing by the chorus included native songs and also adaptations of such pieces as "La Varsuviana," and other Spanish songs. While singing, the chorus members usually remained motionless although there were some of the hand and arm gestures commonly seen in Pueblo Indian dance choruses.

The atmosphere of the entire afternoon was one of gaiety and good-naturedness which are not always present at Santo Domingo ceremonies, at least when non-Indian visitors are concerned. The same gaiety and hospitality characterized the events of the evening.

After eating supper in one of the homes, the woman guided us to a neighboring house where dancing was to occur. After a futile wait, a small boy was directed to escort us to another home where a group of dancers was known to be. During the evening, seven groups were observed, several of them in a number of different homes. . . .

For each of the seven groups of dancers there was an older man, only one of whom appeared to have donned any special dress for the occasion. This one person had put on his best clothing, dressing very much like the chorus members for a Feast Day dance; the others appeared in their daily work clothes. In each group, this leader was clearly in charge, entering the house first, leading the dancers from the house at the end, and making the decision as to whether encores were deserved and, if so, how many.

On the average, there were a half dozen in each chorus, including one drummer. Three groups performed without a chorus or drum: these were primarily clown groups. In one or two choruses, the members wore red velvet shirts, false mustaches, and sunglasses, in imitation of the Navajo. In several houses, these chorus members also danced. The seven dance groups were as follows:

First Group: Nine dancers. There were three men on each side of a woman (actually a male impersonator) in a line with two leaders in front of them. The woman wore a yellow Navajo skirt. The six

OLD CHRISTMAS, EPIPHANY, TWELFTH NIGHT

men in the line had their thighs painted white, bells at their knees, and knee-length black stockings and high, dark brown moccasins. The two men in front wore regular long pants of white cotton. All had on dark colored, velvet shirts, and wore many strings of turquoise, coral, and other beads. They wore a silver bow-guard on the left wrist, concho belts, and kilts of various sorts, saddle blankets. Saltillo serapes, but not one of the usual Hopi dance kilts. In their right hands, the men in the line carried black gourd rattles and in their left, fan-like objects of sticks and ribbons. A pendant foxskin hung from the belt in back. At the neck of this foxskin there was a glass or metal disk from which long ribbons hung. One of the leaders carried a rattle and sprigs of Douglas fir; the other carried a rattle and a foxskin. The men's hair was not flowing but confined under a large headdress of feathers (most of these were turkey but one or two men had eagle feather headdresses) and ribbons. This headdress was arranged as a fan, three or four feet wide, the outer edge of which had four ribbons, two in front and two in back, which hung down on either side to the dancer's waist. A few men had a scarf around their head. Face painting consisted of a black and red smudge across the cheeks and nasal bridge, and the lower jaw was painted white. In the back of the headdress, concealing the ties, there was a cluster of turkey breast feathers.

Second Group: Nine dancers. This group was almost identical with the first.

Third Group: Nine dancers. This group also had a line of seven dancers with two leaders in front. However, there were three female impersonators, arranged alternately with the four men of the line. Except for small tassels of down on each feather tip of the headdresses, these were essentially the same in costume and behavior as the first two groups.

Fourth Group: Six dancers. However, the chorus with this group included seven singers, five of whom also drummed. This was perhaps the most spectacular group, the increased size of the chorus and greater volume of the singing and drumming supplementing the more active type of dancing which was a modification of the so-called "Comanche War Dance."

The bodies of three dancers had been completely blackened. Beaded moccasins, white breechcloths, bow-guards on the left wrists, straps of several sleigh bells from the waist down the outside of each leg to the ankle, headdress, short spears in the right hand, and a small round shield in their left hands completed the costumes. The headdress appeared based on a sort of winter cap, or helmet, with flaps coming over the ears and fastening under the chin. This was dark brown, and there was a roach attached to it from front to back. Two large eagle tail feathers were attached to the roach, and at the nape of the neck were two smaller eagle feathers.

The other three dancers had large eagle feather headdresses, based on a similar arrangement although composed of many eagle feathers in a line from front to back along the roach. Two had the left side of their bodies painted green, with the other side unpainted. All of the face was green. The third dancer wore trunks and a vest of bright yellow. All three had the straps of sleigh bells as noted for the first three. The second three also wore bustles of eagle feathers fastened just above the buttocks and consisting of a semi-circle of feathers which flapped loosely with the dancers' movements. In the center of this bustle was a glass or piece of tinsel with many bright ribbons attached. On each side of this bustle, a single eagle wing feather, tipped with a purple plume, reached straight up to the dancers' shoulders.

Fifth Group: Five dancers. This group consisted of five men dressed as Negresses and was accompanied by neither chorus nor drum. All wore sunglasses. The performance of this group lacked the routine of the already described groups, each performance being largely improvised as it proceeded. However, the songs, mostly parodies, and comic dialogue were apparently well done as the group's efforts were received enthusiastically by all.

Sixth Group: Four dancers. This was another group of clowns, all wearing blackened sheepskin wigs. Again there was no chorus nor drum. Other items of costuming included ordinary European clothing, one or two straw or felt hats, false beards and mustaches, and blackened faces. The acts consisted primarily of song parodies and comic dialogues, partly Keresan, partly

Spanish, and some in English. Again, their antics were received with great bursts of laughter from the entire crowd.

Seventh Group: Seven dancers. The costumes of this group were very similar to the other clown groups. They included sheepskin wigs, false beards and mustaches, blackened upper faces, and ordinary street clothing, except for moccasins. The middle man of the line wore a sun helmet instead of the sheepskin wig. Each wig had a bare portion over the forehead on which there was painted a yellow, or red, cross. One dancer had a New York World's Fair pennant stitched across the front of his sweatshirt; another had the words, "Ouch, Papa, Push More," stitched across his. Again, there was no chorus nor drum; their slow, jovial actions, songs, and jokes were an obvious adaptation of the minstrel show.

As noted, the chorus in the afternoon had frequently rendered *"La Varsuviana,"* and other familiar Spanish songs. In the evening, these and many others were used by all three clown groups to the great delight of everyone. Some of the songs used, most often as parodies, included: "Reuben, Reuben," "She'll be Comin' 'Round the Mountain," "The Old Grey Mare," "Joy to the World," "I Wish I Were Single Again," *"Frère Jacque,"* and "This is the Way We—." This last selection included "iron our clothes," "wash our hands," "comb our hair," "march to school," and other activities associated with Indian Boarding School routine. The songs were

OLD CHRISTMAS, EPIPHANY, TWELFTH NIGHT

all well received, and several Indians were openly interested in our understanding and appreciating the satire.

At almost every home the host asked for more numbers and sometimes received as many as half a dozen encores. As the group finally departed, the woman of the house gave a present of food to one of the attendants accompanying each group. This was native bread, pieces of uncooked meat, or a dish of stew. These were taken to some central place where they were kept for the group's feast after the night's festivities had ended. Presents were given at every house.

Source

El Palacio, LVIII (1951), 398-400, 402-05.

Epiphany Celebration of the Sponge Fishermen

Edwin Clarence Buxbaum described and discussed this celebration in the Greek-American community of Tarpon Springs, Florida.

The Epiphany celebration involves the entire town for about three days. The town is decorated with banners and signs that are sold by the Epiphany committee and the receipts are used for the expenses of the Epiphany day celebration. Thousands upon thousands of tourists, both Greek and American, come from all parts of the United States to witness the celebration and events connected with it. There is a gala atmosphere in the city. After an elaborate church service which includes the "blessing of the waters" by a very high ranking church official, usually the Arch-

bishop of North and South America, there is a parade from the church to the Spring Bayou where the "recovery of the cross from the waters" takes place. The parade lasts perhaps an hour or more, and during this time, all of the shops in the city close. There are costumed paraders from the Greek groups in the neighboring towns of Clearwater, Tampa and St. Petersburg, and several bands, including high school bands, are in the procession. Crowds line the streets and the edge of the water around famous Spring Bayou. The governor of the state usually attends the ceremonies as do many other state officials, senators, and civil representatives from many Florida cities. The high officials of the Greek AHEPA [fraternal club] are always there.

It is only in the last few years [c. 1965] that Tarpon Springs had been named the "focal point" of the Epiphany celebration by the Archdiocese of North and South America. It has always been the mecca of the older Greeks from all parts of the United States when they wanted a place to retire.

The climax of the morning's ceremony comes when the golden cross is thrown into the water and then is retrieved by one of many young men who have signed up for the privilege of diving for the cross. The lucky one who recovers the cross from the water, receives a blessing from the archbishop and is supposed to have good luck for a year. This good luck also extends to his family. In the afternoon, many hundreds go to the sponge exchange where a

Greek dinner is served, and there is Greek *bouzouki* music and Greek dancing. This is called a *glendi* and it is an annual affair looked forward to by young and old. The large enclosure of the sponge exchange seems to be appropriate for this very Greek celebration. In the evening and on the following day, dances are given by various Greek groups.

Although many thousands come to the celebration, most do not stay longer than one day. Although the merchants claim that the visitors to Tarpon Springs do not buy very much, the restaurants, camera shops, motels and the hotel do excellent business. This is the one day of the year when the Greek group is completely in charge of all attractions in the city. Americans accept this and seem to take some pride in the fame which the city has acquired because of this ceremony. When the only notice about Tarpon Springs in guide books is about the Epiphany day celebration, these same people are not so pleased. There seems to be an unexpressed pleasure among the Greeks that for at least one day in the year, the Greek group is dominant again as it was during the affluent years of the sponge fishing industry.

Source

"The Greek-American Group of Tarpon Springs, Florida," Ph.D. dissertation, University of Pennsylvania, 1967, 342-44.

January

FIRST QUARTER MOON
IROQUOIS WHITE DOG FEAST

The Iroquois League, a collection of numerous Native North American groups of the eastern United States and eastern Canada, were considered to have had the most advanced material culture of the East Woodlands area tribal groups. Approximately 29,000 Iroquois now reside in the United States and Canada, and many continue to practice the customs of their forefathers. The sacrifice of the white dog or dogs at the New Year ceremonies of the Iroquois tribes was dedicated to Teharonhiawagon, the Master of Life. He was believed to have revealed through his dreams that a sacrificial victim and an offering of tobacco were necessary to

insure the return of spring and the rebirth of all life on earth, and thus to thwart the Gods of Winter and Famine. Joshua Clark, who described the ritual in 1849, compared the white dogs to the biblical scapegoat "laden with the sins of the nation." At that time, the ceremony was performed in a longhouse or assembly hall, a bark- covered rectangular structure that became the symbol of the Five Nations. The sacrificed animals were usually eaten, and fires, dances, games, and other New Year ceremonies accompanied the sacrifice. Still celebrated, the festival lasts for a number of days, constituting the culture's major mid-winter rite.

White Dog Feast at the Onondaga Reservation

Harriet Maxwell Converse, an adoptive member of the Seneca tribe, published this article in the Elmira (New York) Telegram, *January 29, 1888.*

This religious festival is usually "called" during the first quarter of the moon in the month of January [1888]. It may be held on various days during that period, its special beginning being named by the sachems of each nation, and continues for six successive days, including in

its various ceremonies nearly all the features of the Iroquois religion. In accordance with olden customs such feast was "called" last week by the Onondagas on their reservation near Syracuse [New York]. . . .

On the first day of the "new year jubilee" a white dog is selected and strangled. It must be, by the law, "spotless and free from all blemish"; they are careful not to shed its blood nor break its bones. It is decorated with ribbons and red paint, and ornamented with feathers, and the very pious, who are taught that with each gift to the sacrifice a blessing is bestowed, hang upon its body trinkets and beads of wampum. Thus decorated, it is fixed to a cross-pole and suspended by the neck about eight feet from the ground. There it hangs until the fifth day, when it is taken down and carried by "faith keepers" to the council-house, and laid out upon a bench, while the fire of the altar is kindling, while a priest, making speeches over it, relates the antiquity of this institution of their fathers, and its importance and solemnity, finally enjoining the people to direct their thoughts to the Great Spirit, concluding with a prayer of thanks that the lives of so many have been spared through another year. On this occasion, at "noon by the sun," twelve young warriors who were stationed at the northern corner of the council-house, firing their rifles, announced the procession as formed. Headed by four "faith keepers," who bore the sacrifice, and who were followed by the priests and matrons, and the old and young people, the procession slowly moved toward the main council-house, under which the remains of the celebrated prophet Ga-ne-o-di-yo (Handsome Lake) are buried. Passing through the building from the western to the eastern door outward, and around the council-house, reentering it at the eastern door, they laid the sacrifice on the altar; and, as the flames surrounded it, a basket containing tobacco was thrown on the fire, its smoke rising as incense, as the priest, in a loud voice invoking the Great Spirit, chanted as follows: "Hail, hail, hail! Thou who has created all things, who ruleth all things, and who givest laws to thy creatures, listen to our words. We now obey thy commands. That which thou hast made is returning unto thee. It is rising to thee and carrying to thee our words, which are faithful and true."

This was followed by the "great thanking address" (given by the priest and people). . . . This concluded the religious rite, after which the people dispersed in various directions, to reassemble in the afternoon, attending the exciting and peculiarly Indian "snow snake" game. The fifth being a day devoted to religion, there were no dances. The "great f[e]ather dance," a religious one, was given the next afternoon, followed by the "trotting," "berry," "fish," and "raccoon" dances. Previous to the sacrifice the "cousin clans" were divided: the Wolf, Turtle, Snipe, and Bear sat in the new council-house; the Deer, Beaver, Eel, and Hawk were in the old council-house, from whence the procession formed. Sachem Ha-yu-wan-es (Daniel Lafort, Wolf), Oh-yah-do-ja-neh (Thomas Webster,

AMERICA CELEBRATES

IROQUOIS WHITE DOG FEAST

Snipe), hereditary keeper of the wampum belts, were masters of the religious ceremonies in which about two hundred Indians participated.

Source

Journal of American Folklore, I (1888), 83-85.

And that's not all:
In the "snow snake game" a stick carved in the shape of a snake was thrown on the ice in a contest for distance. W. M. Beauchamp reports on the decline of the White Dog sacrifice: ". . . no dog has been burned at Onondaga for two years past. I asked Chief Lafort why this happened, and he said the sacred breed of dogs had run out. Other Indians, however, think this is but an excuse for discontinuing the sacrifice, which had lost its solemnity. Forty years ago the Onondagas burned two white dogs on an altar pile; then but one; then it was dropped into a stove, and now the white dog seems to have finally disappeared." See *Journal of American Folklore*, I (1888), 195.

Games at the White Dog Feast

W. M. Beauchamp read this account at the annual reading of the American Association for the Advancement of Science in 1896.

Some Iroquois games have a high antiquity, having survived the test of time. Two forms of the game of white and black still exist, and there are frequent allusions to one of these in the Jesuit Relations, where it is termed that of the plate or dish. It excited the highest interest; for though it was of the simplest nature, nation played against nation, and village against village. From the floor to the ridgepole of the cabin the eager spectators looked at the two players, showing their sympathy by their cries.

Two forms of this simple game of chance remain, and perhaps there were never more than these. Father Bruyas alluded to one of them in his Mohawk lexicon of radical words, speaking of it as the game in which the women scatter fruit stones with the hand. This distinction of throwing remains, although disks of bone or horn are now used instead of the stones of fruit. L. H. Morgan described this as the game of deer buttons, called *Gus-ga-e-sâ-ta* by the Senecas. They used eight circular buttons of deer horn, about an inch in diameter, and blackened on one side. These are about an eighth of an inch in thickness, and bevelled to the edge. He said: "This was strictly a fireside game, although it was sometimes introduced as an amusement at the season of religious councils, the people dividing into tribes as usual, and betting upon the result." In public two played it at a time, with a succession of players. In private two or more played it on a blanket, on which they sat and threw. His counting differs at first sight from that which I received, but amounts to the same thing. Beans were used for the pool, and Morgan said that six white or black drew two, seven drew four, and all white or black drew twenty. Less than six drew nothing, and the other player had his throw until he lost in turn.

Among the Onondagas now eight bones or stones are used, black on one side and white on the other. They term the game *Ta-you-nyun-wât-hah*, or Finger Shaker, and from one hundred to three hundred beans from the pool, as may be agreed. With them it is also a household game.

In playing this the pieces are raised in the hand and scattered, the desired result being indifferently white or black. Essentially, the counting does not differ from that given by Morgan. Two white or two black will have six of one color, and these count two beans, called *O-yú-ah*, or the Bird. The player proceeds until he loses, when his opponent takes his turn. Seven white or black gain four beans, called *O-néo-sah*, or Pumpkin. All white or all black gain twenty, called *O-hén-tah*, or a Field. These are all that draw anything, and we may indifferently say with the Onondagas, two white or black for the first, or six with the Senecas. The game is played singly or by partners, and there is no limit to the number. Usually there are three or four players.

In counting the gains there is a kind of ascending reduction; for as two birds make one pumpkin, only one bird can appear in the result. First come the twenties, then the fours, then the twos, which can occur but once. Thus we may say for twenty, *Jo-han-tó-tah*, you have one field, or more as the case may be. In the fours we can only say, *Ki-yae-ne-you-sáh-ka*, you have four pumpkins, for five would make a field. For two beans there is the simple announcement of *O-yú-ah*, Bird. There is often great excitement over this game.

The game of peach stones, much more commonly used and important, has a more public character, although I have played it in an Indian parlor. In early days the stones of the wild plum were used, but now six peach stones are ground down to an elliptic flattened form, the opposite sides being black or white. This is the great game known as that of the dish nearly three centuries ago. The wooden bowl which I used was eleven inches across the top and three inches deep, handsomely carved out of a hard knot. A beautiful small bowl which I saw elsewhere may have been used by children.

The six stones are placed in *Kah-óon-wah*, the bowl, and thence the Onondagas term the game *Ta-yune-oo-wâh-es*, throwing the bowl to each other as they take it in turn. In public playing two players are on their knees at a time, holding the bowl between them. When I played, simply to learn the game, we sat in chairs, the bowl being on another chair between us. Beans are commonly used for counters, but we had plum stones. Many rules are settled according to agreement, but the pumpkin is left out, and the stones usually count five for a bird and six for a field. All white or all black is the highest throw, and five or six are the only winning points. In early days it would seem that all white or all black alone counted. The bowl is simply struck on the floor; and although the game is said to be sometimes intensely exciting, the scientific spirit restrained my enthusiasm. I was not playing for beans, but for information.

This ancient game is used at the New Year's or White Dog Feast among the Onondagas yet. Clan plays against clan, the Long House against the Short House, and, to foretell the harvest, the women play

AMERICA   CELEBRATES

IROQUOIS WHITE DOG FEAST

against the men. If the men win, the ears of corn will be long, like them; but if the women gain the game, they will be short, basing the results on the common proportion of the sexes.

Source

Journal of American Folklore, IX (1896), 269-70. From a paper on "Iroquois Games."

And that's not all:
For a "game of peach stones," see "Seneca Green Corn Dance." Universally, games played on certain holidays often serve the double purpose of adding to the jollity of the occasion while implying the importance of the force of fortune. The Jewish festival, Hanukkah, celebrating the rededication of the temple at Jerusalem after the victory of the Maccabees over King Antiochus of Syria, features the spinning of a *dreydl* or top with four sides, each of which is marked to indicate whether the player wins or loses from a store of nuts and candy. The Japanese traditionally play card games and dice games on New Year's Day. During New Year's White Dog Feast, a gambling game is an exciting but at the same time serious part of the festivities. Clan plays against clan, and the women, who live in the "Long House" and in the matrilineal Iroquois society have a powerful role, play the unmarried men. The results of the game predict the quality of the corn crop.

January   February

21 <small>to</small> 19

CHINESE NEW YEAR

New Year's is the principal holiday of the Chinese calendar and one which has attracted public attention in the United States for the pageantry of its Golden Dragon Parade. The date is determined by a lunar calendar, with solar adjustments so that holidays recur in a pattern of seasonal regularity. The holiday begins with the first new moon after the sun enters the sign of Aquarius. The years are named for a sequence of twelve symbolic animals—rat, ox, tiger, hare, dragon, serpent, horse, ram, monkey, rooster, dog, and boar. Festivities extend over several days, the first day being essentially a family celebration. Homage is paid to ancestors at household shrines, and visits are exchanged among relatives and intimates. To avoid bad luck, impeccable behavior is insisted upon. The climax of the holiday period is the Dragon Parade, a gala event in the Chinatowns of many American cities. The Dragon is thought to dispel evil spirits, a process aided by firecrackers, drums, and gongs.

New Year parade in Chinatown

Observing Chinese New Year

William Hoy participated in California Chinese native festivals in San Francisco's Chinatown for more than a decade. He also observed celebrations of the Chinese New Year in more than a dozen California cities and mainland China in 1944-46. He provides this description of the Chinese New Year. Chinese New Year's Day occurs between January 20 and February 19, and begins properly at midnight on New Year's Eve. Certain ancient customs are still observed, such as the mothers' admonishing their children to avoid the use of all vulgar words, or words which may be interpreted as bad. Persons who are financially in debt try their best to repay their debtors before the old year dies, but if they are unable to do so they are no longer morally obligated to do away with their lives, as ancient custom once dictated.

All the meeting halls and headquarters of [San Francisco] Chinatown's fraternal, district, clan, trade guild, and other associations are brilliantly lighted at the time the New Year dawns. This is one custom observed in all Chinatowns. In recent years the practice of hoisting the national flag of China was added, as a

AMERICA   CELEBRATES

CHINESE NEW YEAR

gesture of nation-consciousness, a spirit which was lacking among most California Chinese up to fifteen years ago [c. 1932].

At least twenty-four hours before the advent of the New Year, the floors of all mercantile houses, association buildings, and private homes are swept, cleaned, and washed thoroughly, and they must not be swept again until the New Year's celebration is over. This follows the ancient practice of symbolically avoiding misfortune, since the sweeping of floors in this period means the sweeping away of all good luck for the new year.

The shooting of firecrackers—to call the attention of the gods and scare away malignant devils at the same time—is, of course, a *sine qua non* of any Chinese New Year's celebration, past or present. The firecrackers start exploding promptly at midnight, if permission from the local police authorities has been obtained.

But the most important custom which heralds the beginning of the new year is a gastronomic one. It is the eating of *lohan chai*, a vegetarian dish adapted for common use from a recipe of Chinese adherents of Buddhism. *Chai* denotes a vegetarian meal, whereas *lohan* is the Buddhist term for 'saints' as it pertains to Chinese Buddhism.

Another meatless dish eaten in the first twenty-four hours of the New Year is *yu sang*, which means "raw fish." That is, the basic ingredient of this repast is raw fish which has been skinned, boned, and

neatly sliced into thin strips. It is then made palatable and delicious by mixing it, salad-fashion, with chopped green onions, peanut oil, ground roasted peanuts, lemon juice, sesame seeds, chopped raw ginger, Chinese parsley, soy sauce, sliced turnips, and crisp fried-rice noodles. This Cantonese epicure's delight is eaten along with bowls of steaming rice gruel called *congee*.

Sweets eaten at the New Year's celebrations include homemade steamed and fried pastries; "thousand-layer" sweet cake—a symbol of longevity—and deep-fried sweetmeats flaked with sesame seeds, and other pastries made from rice flour. The recipes for all these are traditional, handed down orally from one generation to another.

Fruits for this festive season are the orange and tangerine—because their skins are red, the color of good luck; preserved lichee nuts (actually a fruit and not a nut); and sugar cane. Candies include candied melon, sugared plums, lotus seeds, melon seeds, preserved sugared ginger, lotus roots, and a variety of sweets made from Chinese fruits.

Flowers which are highly prized for this holiday are the plum blossom, pussy willow, azalea, peony, and the traditional water lily or narcissus.

For those who still adhere to the ancient religious rites at least one visit must be made to a public temple in the week of the New Year, to make sacrificial offerings and to propitiate the gods. This is usually attended to by the womenfolk and the smaller children. In San Francisco's Chinatown, at this writing, there are still three public temples where New Year sacrifices may be made: the T'ien Hou temple on Waverly Place, the Kong Chow temple on Pine Street, and the Lit Sing Kung temple on Spofford Alley. The deities which the California Chinese favor are Kwan Ti (God of War), Kwan Yin (Goddess of Mercy), and Hou Wang (Duke Hou). It is interesting to note that of these three gods two were actual historical personages: Kwan Ti was the famous General Kwan Yu of the Three Kingdoms period in the second century of this era, and Duke Hou, a Cantonese, was a benevolent magistrate in Canton's Chungshan (formerly Heungshan) district some centuries ago. After his death and during a plague Hou appeared in a dream to a farmer and gave him a remedy to alleviate a scourge. The remedy worked, and in time the folk imagination deified him as a god. Only the Goddess of Mercy has no real earthly beginning, since her origin stemmed directly from the Buddhist religion. Chinese popular religion has attributed her origin to a sainted Chinese woman, but this is a myth, conjured up to make Kwan Yin more acceptable to the masses.

Since there is no congregational worship in popular Chinese religion, the faithful may go to the temple at any time of the day they please and perform the ceremonies of burning incense and paper money, offering wine and meat to their favorite gods, and reciting the proper incantations. Those who still maintain ancestral shrines in their own homes light incense sticks and red candles in front of the spirit tablets. The proper amount of food and wine is also placed there.

The colorful lion dance, of course, is also an integral part of the New Year's festivities. The lion, Buddhist symbol of courage, majesty, and constancy, is also a harbinger of good luck, and so he is enticed to dance and prance before every door. In San Francisco's Chinatown in the early days, the temples—and there were over half a dozen then—used to sponsor the lion dance through the streets and alleys of the quarter, and the plentiful silver collected went into the coffers of the temple keepers. Sometimes the august Chinese Six Companies took the privilege and hired local operatic actors and acrobats to perform the intricate but conventionalized dancing of the ceremonial lion. Today, by community consent, the community-sponsored Chinese Hospital holds the lion dances during the New Year. The money, wrapped in lettuce leaves, is collected from persons before whose doorways or shops the lion prances and roars, to the accompaniment of beating drums, clashing cymbals, and exploding firecrackers, and goes into the general fund of the hospital for charity cases. Thus an old Chinese New Year's ritual is well adjusted to modern needs.

On the social side a "must" on every family's calendar between the first and third day of the New Year is the paying of social calls to the homes of relatives and friends. On these visits tea (sweetened by

AMERICA CELEBRATES

CHINESE NEW YEAR

Chinese red dates), red melon seeds, and sweetmeats are ceremoniously offered to each guest. The sweets repose usually on a traditional octagonal black-and-red lacquered tray, which takes its shape from the eight-sided *pa kua* used in Chinese divination. Taking several pieces of sweets from the tray, the visitor, if an adult, places a folded red-paper package containing silver on the center compartment of the tray. This package, called *lay shee* (good-luck piece), is also given by adults, especially the married ones, to all unmarried children and babies. The giving of *lay shee* at New Year's is one of the oldest, most universal, and unchanged customs of the Chinese people, and symbolizes the giving and receiving of good luck. Notice how the color of red permeates this portion of the New Year custom—the red date in the tea, red melon seeds, the red tray, and red *lay shee* packages.

Since, except for the catering trade, everyone stops working during the New Year's celebration, there must necessarily be social festivities and recreation for the celebrants to while away the three to five days of this period. Home and restaurant banquets are continually given at noon, evening, and midnight. Where women and children are not present, these banquets are occasions for drinking bouts accompanied by the game of finger guessing. All night mah-jongg sessions are held in homes, bachelor quarters, and family tong headquarters. The less energetic usually attend the Mandarin theater to view special Cantonese operas, or go to the Grandview and Great China theaters on Jackson Street to see Cantonese-language moving pictures, either locally made or imported from Hongkong. And each afternoon everybody can follow the lion-dance troupe as it dances up and down every Chinatown street, or shoot firecrackers during the hours allowed by the police.

On the third day of the New Year, if a family has decided that a three-day celebration is sufficient, the ceremony of "opening the year" (*hoi nien*) is performed. This, however, is more or less a duplication of the rituals attending the first day. A visit may be paid to a temple, where more incense sticks, candles, and paper money are offered to the gods. There is a final big dinner, either at home or in a restaurant, and the shooting of the last rounds of firecrackers. And if the New Year's social calls have not yet been completed the last must be paid on this day.

In this manner the three days of this festival pass quickly enough, and another Chinese year begins.

Source

Western Folklore, VII (1948), 243-46.

Year of the Horse

The association of each new year, in many oriental cultures, with a symbolic animal is at least two thousand years old. But more recent and American elements such as the drum and bugle corps and "Miss Future Chinatown" are emerging traditions. Somewhere between is the association of the new "Year of the Horse" with good luck at the race track and the old "Year of the Snake or Serpent" with a layoff from a job. Names have always exerted their magic. Julia Cass filed this news item on Philadelphia's celebration:

The ferocious gold, green and pink Komada Dragon may have been an unnecessary precaution at yesterday's [February 13, 1978] Chinese New Year's Parade.

Though the huge creature was belligerently swinging its tail, snapping its jaws and flashing its red eyes to scare off evil spirits for the coming year, the parade's organizers were expressing nothing but optimism for the year 4676, the Year of the Horse, which officially began last Tuesday.

"It will be a very good year," promised John Ton, the young, stylishly dressed coordinator of the parade sponsored by the Chinese Benevolent Association and the Philadelphia Chinatown Development Corp.

"The horse means power, strength, love, success and women," Tom said. "The way I interpret it, it means a lot of luck at the race track."

Last year—the Year of the Snake—not even a dragon could help. "The snake is such a bad year, we didn't even have a parade," sighed Cecilia Moy Yep, the other coordinator of the parade, who said she was laid off from her job last year.

Despite the year's hopeful portents, the traditional Chinese warders-off of evil—the clanging symbols, exploding firecrackers, the dragon and several lions—made their way along Race Street yesterday in Philadelphia's Chinatown.

They were joined by a not-so-traditional Chinatown drum and bugle corps, the police and firemen's band, a float carrying Miss Chinatown (Helen Louie) and various other misses, and city dignitaries riding electric golf carts.

Leading this group was Fire Commissioner Joseph Rizzo, whose department forgets its firecracker regulations for the parade.

"Firecrackers? What firecrackers?" he asked over the crackle of dozens of explosions, when asked about the rules.

"The bands, the beauty queens, they are Americanization," said Richard Den, Secretary of the Benevolent Association, who remembers the New Year's parades of his native province of Hunan, on the Chinese mainland. There, he said, business leaders marched with representatives of each district and each surname—the Lees, Lings and Wongs and so on.

Bringing up the rear at yesterday's parade was Miss Future Chinatown, eight-year-old Susie Wong, who rode on a cart with her father.

Asked what year it was, the Americanized Miss Future Chinatown answered, "1978."

Source

Philadelphia Inquirer, February 13, 1978.

Year of the Monkey

Jill Smolowe describes the festivities in New York city's Chinatown:

Greetings of *"kung hay fat choy,"* the Cantonese expression of good fortune competed with a volley of firecrackers yesterday [February 16, 1980] as thousands of people jammed the narrow streets of [New York's] Chinatown to usher in the Chinese lunar year 4678, the year of the monkey.

Eight teams of youths accompanied lion dancers through the streets, striking gongs and drums to chase away evil spirits from local shops. At the culmination of each dance, the lion would snatch a red envelope and a chunk of lettuce strung on a pink cord in front of each shop.

"We bring the stores luck," explained Stanley Leung, a member of the team that danced along Bowery Street. After a 15-minute dance, the lion would grip the envelope between its teeth and dash off with a small sum of "lucky money," the team's reward for saving the proprietor from demons.

Dragons also dizzily wended their way along Mott Street, with young people holding the colorful bodies high above their heads on gold posts. Red, yellow and silver flags accompanied the processions that moved along Pell and Bayard Streets.

The monkey, one of 12 animals that cyclically rule the lunar calendar for a year, represents craft, charm and intelligence. The humorous creature is supposed to

portend 12 months of improved communication between the peoples of the world.

The Chinese also draw upon the Western depiction of the monkey as representing the absence of evil, since it hears none, sees none and speaks none. Yesterday, those who defied the rain and snow to celebrate the new year behaved like the traditional triumvirate of monkeys, covering ears, eyes and mouths to shut out the deafening pops, bright white flashes and smoke of the firecrackers.

"This isn't the time to worry about catching a cold," said Raymond To, who had brought his five children from South Orange, N.J., to see the processions. "I want my children to know what the Chinese costumes and traditions are about—the American New Year is never as exciting as this."

People nestled in doorways and sought refuge from wet weather beneath awnings and umbrellas, but few complaints were heard. Paul Ling, a 31-year-old who came to the United States from Hong Kong 19 years ago, spoke for many when he said: "I wouldn't miss the Chinese New Year for anything. It really makes me feel like I'm back home."

Friday night, the eve of the new year, many Chinese families gathered for the traditional reunion dinner, at which seemingly endless platters of pork, chicken, beef and vegetables were served. The dishes also included *"yu"* (fish). Most of the new year's dishes have names that contain a special greeting, and the word for fish closely resembles *"yao yu,"* the word for abundance.

Source

New York Times, February 17, 1980.

And that's not all:
see "Chinese New Year" for firecrackers, food, and dragons.

Sweets for the Year of the Dragon

Marilyn Marter reported on a traditional Chinese sweet:

"Usually the Chinese would celebrate the New Year for five days. During that time, there would be no work. They would concentrate on eating, playing games and gambling. At least that's the way it used to be at the turn of the century," said Fu Shen Chang, a chef born and trained in Beijing....

"During the New Year period, it is winter in northern China, and people there gather together in the evening, play games and eat sweets or snacks. And this is one of them," said Chang as he started to shape bean-paste centers for sweet rice dumplings....

The task of making these holiday snacks, in the old days, would have fallen to the Chinese wife or grandmother. She would have made the bean paste from scratch, soaking the beans, removing the skins, grinding the paste, blending in the sugar. Now, however, at Asian markets the sweet red-bean paste comes canned and ready to use.

"Or some people will use peanut butter," said the younger Chang. He runs the restaurant Ming Dynasty ... at which the senior Chang is executive chef. The *Tong Yuen* or New Year's Dumplings will be included in the eight-course New Year's banquets that the restaurant has scheduled on Monday evenings into March.

The round shape of the dumplings offers a symbolic hope for a well-rounded New Year. They typically are served, too, at the Lantern Festival, which marks the end of the official New Year's celebration. This occurs on the 15th day of the first lunar month.

With either filling ingredient, the dumplings are a change for the American palate. The glutinous rice-flour coating is a bit gummy after the traditional boiling. To get around this, chef Chang offers the option of deep-frying, which gives a firmer texture and more familiar feel to the sweet.

Just as the recipes are being Westernized, so, too, is the holiday itself.

Traditionally, everything must be cleaned and put in order before the New Year. And for the first month, it is the habit to wear new clothing. When you meet someone on the street, it is customary to clasp hands and wish each other luck in the New Year.

"And they don't do it these days anymore," says Chang, "but traditionally

CHINESE NEW YEAR

on the fifth night of the New Year celebration, the younger generation is supposed to thank the older generation, within the family, by bowing to the ground as in prayer."

Though officially 15 days long, the public or business celebration has been steadily shortened. Even in Taiwan, the work holiday has been cut to just the first three days of the New Year, says Chang. But for a few days afterward, banquets and parties are given by business owners for their employees.

"During those banquets," says Chang, "you usually have a chicken dish, and it is tradition that whoever the chicken head points to is being laid off work and won't be around that next year."

And what if the full staff is going to stay? Then the chicken head is directed at the owner.

Particularly among farm families and in northern China, where the New Year period and icy cold winters coincide, it is traditional to gather together in the evening to play games and eat sweets or snacks. Tong Yuen is one of those sweets. Although originally associated with the New Year's celebration, the sweet is eaten now throughout the year, says Chang.

Hung Tong Tong Yuen (Red-Bean New Year's Dumplings)

1½ teaspoons black sesame seeds
1   can (18 ounces) sweet red bean paste
1   tablespoon sesame or other oil
2   cups rice flour, approximately

Water

Heat dry wok or skillet over medium flame. Add black sesame seeds, and cook, stirring, for about one minute or until aroma is released. Remove. Let cool. Using straight roller or mortar and pestle, grind dry seeds to a powder. Combine sesame with bean paste, blending thoroughly.

Moisten palm with oil and roll small amounts of bean paste into balls one-half inch to three-quarters inch in diameter. Place on plate or waxed paper that has been lightly oiled. Pour flour into large mixing bowl. Drop the balls, six at a time, into flour.

Remove and place coated balls in strainer. Ideally, the strainer should be the flat ladle type to allow for separation of dumplings. Dip dumplings into water in second mixing bowl, holding them under water for just a few seconds to wet the rice flour. Remove and drain. Drop wet dumplings back into flour. Shake or stir to coat again. Repeat wetting and coating procedure five times. After final coating with rice flour, set dumplings aside, or refrigerate for at least two hours to allow moisture in the coating to even out. When set, the coating will have a matte finish and be very smooth.

To cook dumplings, bring water to low boil in wok or large saucepan. Cook dumplings, a few at a time so as not to crowd, a few minutes until coating is translucent. Serve in bowl with some of the cooking liquid. The water may be sweetened as desired with sugar or honey. Makes about 36 dumplings, enough for 12 to 18 servings.

Note: As an alternative cooking method, the dumplings may be deep-fried in oil heated to 325 degrees. The oil is purposely kept at a lower temperature than for normal frying because hot oil will make the dumplings puff up and pop open, releasing bits of the filling into the oil. Fry gently until dumplings are golden.

Some Chinese cooks substitute peanut butter sweetened with brown sugar and flavored with ground sesame for the traditional sweet red-bean paste in the recipe above.

In Fujian, an eastern province of China, the cooked dumplings are frequently sprinkled with or rolled in sesame seeds, ground peanuts and sugar.

Source

Philadelphia Inquirer, February 17, 1988.

Fortune Cookies for the Year of the Rooster

Ruth Glick published this recipe during the during the Chinese New Year period:

If you would like to usher in the Chinese New Year with fortune cookies this year [1981, the Year of the Rooster], you can improve on both the cookies and the fortunes by making your own. Unlike their store-bought counterparts, homemade fortune cookies have a buttery taste and melt-in-your-mouth texture. And they can be filled with bits of your own cleverness or personal wishes rather than factory wit. . . .

3 egg whites
⅔ cup sugar
⅛ teaspoon salt
¼ teaspoon vanilla
½ cup melted butter
2 tablespoons strong tea
1 cup flour

Prepare fortunes, fold and set aside.

In a medium bowl, combine egg whites, sugar, salt and vanilla. Stir in melted butter and tea. Mix well. Stir in flour until batter is smooth. Chill batter at least 30 minutes.

For each cookie, place a rounded teaspoonful of batter on a greased baking sheet. With the back of a spoon, spread out batter to form a thin circle about 3 inches in diameter. Bake no more than 2 or 3 cookies at one time, because they must be folded before they begin to cool and harden.

Bake in a preheated 350-degree oven for 3 to 5 minutes or until edges of cookies are brown. Remove baking sheet from oven and carefully remove one cookie with a spatula. Lay cookie flat on a clean plate and place a fortune on top. Working quickly, fold the cookie in half to form a semicircle and enclose the fortune. Lay the semicircle across the rim of a glass and press the folded edge against the glass, half inside and half outside. The curved edge should be left to flare out, to give the cookie its

AMERICA CELEBRATES

CHINESE NEW YEAR

characteristic "nurse'scap" shape. Set completed cookiein the well of a muffin tin to hold the shape while it cools. Repeat procedure with subsequent cookies.

Note: As cookies must be shaped when hot, handle with care. Makes 45.

Source

Washington Post, February 5, 1981.

January   February
21 ^{to} 19

TET

Tet, a seven-day festival, is an abbreviation for *"Tet Nguyen-Dan,"* a Vietnamese phrase meaning "first day." It celebrates both the beginning of a new year and of spring, and is considered to be Vietnam's most important festival. In keeping with the Chinese belief (and, for that matter, certain American folk beliefs as well), it is important that only good things occur during Tet, for the year will proceed as it begins. It is a time for family reunions and feasting. Old debts are cleared, houses repainted, and new clothes bought. Seven days before Tet, a household spirit—the kitchen god Ông Táo—is said to travel to the abode of the Jade Emperor to report on the affairs of the family. For this reason a preliminary ceremony is held to send him off in a good mood. While he is gone, the *Cây Nêu* —a tree made of bamboo and red paper symbolic of Buddha—is erected

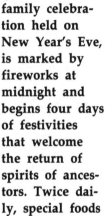

in front of the house in order to ward off evil spirits. As an extra precaution, a bow and arrow are sometimes drawn in lime in front of the threshold, and sacrifices are made to deceased members of the family. *Giao Thùà*, a family celebration held on New Year's Eve, is marked by fireworks at midnight and begins four days of festivities that welcome the return of spirits of ancestors. Twice daily, special foods are put on the family altar, and gifts and money are exchanged among family members. Tet is also a time for visiting, and, according to superstition, a prosperous first guest will assure an auspicious beginning to the new year. Such visits are far from random: the first day is devoted to the father's relatives, the second day to the mother's relatives, the third to friends and teachers, and on the fourth day, the spirits are believed to return to heaven.

AMERICA   CELEBRATES

TET

Vietnamese Tet Comes to America

This 1977 celebration of Tet, the Vietnamese New Year, is not simply an instance of recent immigrants observing a traditional holiday in their adopted homeland. Because of the circumstances of their emigration, it conveys their psychological, political, and social needs with unusual immediacy. As these are satisfied, Tet celebrations may well become, like those for the Chinese New Year in San Francisco and New York, a time of feasting, relaxation, an expression of pride in cultural origin, and a part of the diversity of the American scene. The report was filed by Judith Cummings.

Several hundred Vietnamese refugees and their friends gathered in Queens [New York] yesterday [February 19, 1977] to hold a celebration for Tet, which, while it offered a showcase for the gay dances and fireworks that normally adorn the New Year holiday, also represented a deliberate effort to help buttress a flagging sense of community and pride.

There was merriment enough as befits a proper welcoming of the Year of the Serpent, but organizers spoke of a more sober purpose that was reflected in some of the dances and songs.

The festivities were held at the Catholic Preparatory Seminary, at 56-25 92d Street in the Elmhurst section.

As a half-dozen young girls in the background performed a dance to "Song of the West," alluding to their new life, Le Thanh Hoang Dan, a leading organizer of refugees here, said cooperation had been sought from various local Vietnamese organizations to join in a single celebration, in what for most of them was their second new year in this country. The primary goal, he said, was to raise money to be distributed by the Red Cross to help other Vietnamese refugees now scattered in Thailand, Malaysia, Hong Kong, and other parts of Southeast Asia.

The $500 that was expected to be raised, according to Mr. Dan, a City University doctoral student, would be more symbolic than anything else—a gesture intended to demonstrate that these earlier refugees, most of them intellectuals and professionals who fled in 1975—had not forgotten countrymen who remained when Vietnam went under Communist control. . . .

"We are trying to feel proud of our community. It's not that we haven't wanted to help before, but we are poor," Mr. Dan said. A former lecturer on the philosophy of education at the University of Saigon, he works at a bakery, in this country he said. His wife, My Chau, is a bank teller.

Huong Marra, a self-described housewife who lives with her husband, an engineer, in Huntington, L.I., looked away from the folk dancing to say that Tet in this country was treated "as a Memorial Day, to think about our country."

Source

New York Times, February 20, 1977.

January-February

15th Day of Shevat
TU B'SHEVAT

Tu B'Shevat, the New Year of the Trees, is the fifteenth day of the Jewish month Shevat. The day is also called Hamishas Asar, the New Year of the Trees. It is reserved as a day for respecting and appreciating plants and trees.

Originally, it had no religious significance, with no celebration or liturgical observation, though the day was used to reckon tithes on fruit. In medieval times the custom of eating

fruits associated with the Holy Land arose as a means of recalling the Jewish homeland. Then, in the 17th century a special ceremonial, inspired by the verse "For man is like the tree of the field," was developed mostly by the kabbalists. Today, in the State of Israel, Tu B'Shevat has become an arbor day for tree-planting by children. Because of this, the day is being popularized across the world. Its observance shares common elements with Arbor Day and Earth Day, both celebrated in April. On these occasions, too, children often participate in tree-planting activities, spurred in recent years by concern for the global environment.

The New Year of the Trees
Origins of the Holiday

Marilyn S. Lieberstein reported on the holiday for the Jewish Exponent:

On Tuesday night, as the 15th day of the Hebrew month of Shevat unfolds, Jews will take note of Tu B'Shevat—an ancient minor holiday that may one day become a major Jewish festival celebrating the natural world.

Also known as Rosh Hashanah L'eilanot, the New Year of the Trees, Tu B'Shevat has its roots in the ancient custom of reckoning the age of a tree in order to tithe its fruits.

The observance is mentioned in the Talmud, but not in the Torah.

Observing that most of Israel's rainfall occurs before the 15th day of Shevat, Rabbi Hillel ruled that the age of a tree

AMERICA   CELEBRATES

TU B'SHEVAT

would be counted from that day. Thus, whatever fruits the tree yielded after that day would be tithed as fruits of the new year.

Knowing the age of a tree is also important in order to fulfill the halachic [Religious law] injunction against eating the fruit of a tree less than four years old.

The *Encyclopaedia Judaica* notes that it was traditional among the Ashkenazic communities in Europe to observe Tu B'Shevat by eating 15 different kinds of fruit, with special preference given to fruits grown in Eretz Yisrael.

The New Year of the Trees

To Sephardic Jews, the encyclopedia reports, the New Year of the Trees took on a greater significance. During the 16th century, the kaballists of Safed expanded the Sephardic liturgy and customs for the festival and devised a special order of service for the day—a Tu B'Shevat seder [Ritual Meal].

To Dr. Arthur Green, president of the Reconstructionist Rabbinical College in Wyncote [Pennsylvania], the kaballists' centuries-old order of service can serve as a model for modern times. In his view, Tu B'Shevat is an ancient holiday with a modern message: Care about, preserve and protect the natural environment....

It is also a new age in human history, Green said—an age in which the very existence of the earth is threatened by nuclear weapons and assaults on the environment.

"I think this means something for us as Jews," he said. "We who have been victims of destruction have to bear an extra sensitivity."

Tu B'Shevat, if observed as a major Jewish holiday, can foster such sensitivity, he said. A Tu B'Shevat seder, he said, is "a time of education, of reflection, of celebrating the divine within creation and realizing that creation remains fragile and we have to protect it."

Source

Jewish Exponent, January 29, 1988.

Children Plant New Year Trees

Robert Leiter provided further coverage:

"Does anyone know what bark is?" the young woman asked.

Several small hands darted up, fingers stretching urgently.

"It's the tree's skin," a little girl answered in a near whisper, though with evident pride.

She was one of 15 children—kindergarteners, first-, second- and third-graders from Congregation Or Ami—who participated Sunday in the annual Tu B'Shevat celebration at the Morris Arboretum of the University of Pennsylvania.

The Tu B'Shevat program, held in the arboretum's Widener Education Center, was begun eight years ago at the suggestion of volunteer guides Gerry Schneeberg and Beverly Miller, who wished to broaden the facility's outreach to children during a season when most people would rather stay indoors.

The celebration, which, in the words of Education Intern Catherine Maxwell, strives to introduce the children to "all the ways we use trees and all the ways trees help us," has three parts.

First the children watched a film, donated by the Central Agency for Jewish Education, which depicts the founding, 10 years ago, of Israel's Jewish Children's Forest.

The worldwide project was a cooperative effort by the Jewish National Fund, Israel's president, prime minister and the Ministry of Education. The goal was to create a bond between Israeli children and Jewish children in the Diaspora every Tu B'Shevat.

Each Israeli child would plant two trees, one for himself and one for his pen pal in the Diaspora. A third tree would be planted in honor of a child who perished in the Holocaust.

In a pre-screening introduction, Phyllis McGusty of the arboretum spoke of Tu B'Shevat—the New Year of the Trees— and its importance to Israel's ecological system.

"Israel knows that it has to plant trees to replenish all the forests and groves that have been destroyed over the years," McGusty said. "Without trees, there's a lot of erosion. The soil dries out, the winds blow the soil away and there's lots of decay. So we plant trees to renew the landscape."

Source

Jewish Exponent, February 5, 1988.

February
2

CANDLEMAS OR GROUNDHOG DAY

In the Eastern Church, Candlemas celebrates the Presentation of Christ in the Temple; in the Western, the Purification of Mary. The blessing of the candles, for which this day is named, did not enter the ceremony until the eleventh century. In Europe, Candlemas was combined with pagan candlelight processions to purify and invigorate the fields before the planting season, for light was associated with the sun's power and with fertility and darkness with sterility. In Mexico, Candlemas coincides with the Aztec New Year.

Punxsutawney Phil and friends

On Candlemas, the woodchuck is said to emerge from his hibernation in order to look for his shadow. If he sees it, he will return to his burrow for six more weeks. If he doesn't, he knows spring will arrive soon. The belief is related to the association of Candlemas with the sowing of the crops, sunny weather foreboding harsh days and so poor planting. In Germany, the badger, and in England and France the bear, had analogous roles as weather prognosticators.

An Early Groundhog

This Groundhog Day reference is reprinted by Alfred L. Shoemaker from the files of the Pennsylvania Dutch Folklore Center at Franklin and Marshall College.

Of course everybody knows that February 2 is groundhog day. If the *dox* (the dialect word for groundhog) sees its shadow on this day, the belief is that six weeks of bad weather will follow; if the day is cloudy, however, the weather will be mild and moderate from then to spring.

The earliest reference we have to groundhog day at the Folklore Center is an entry in James L. Morris' diary under the date of Feb. 4, 1841. A storekeeper at Morgantown, Berks County [Pennsylvania], Morris wrote: "Last Tuesday, the 2nd inst., was Candlemas day, the day on which, according to the Germans, the Groundhog

peeps out of his winter quarters and if he sees his shadow he pops back for another six weeks nap, but if the day be cloudy he remains out, as the weather is to be moderate."

Source

Pennsylvania Dutchman, V (February 1, 1954), 11.

More Recent Groundhogs

Like the return of the migrating swallows to San Juan Capistrano in California a natural occurrence first accumulates a body of folk traditions and then attracts public attention through the mass media, providing an opportunity for various promotional enterprises—in the name of folklore, good clean fun, and local boosters. This article on Punxsutawney Phil, unsigned, was distributed to member newspapers of the Associated Press:

Punxsutawney Phil

Once again tomorrow [February 2] in a small town in north-central Pennsylvania [Punxsutawney], a four-legged oracle will predict when spring will come.

The famous forecaster is Punxsutawney Phil, the legendary groundhog said by believers to be nearly a century old and an infallible prognosticator of winter's end.

On Groundhog Day, according to the German folklore of this region, groundhogs, also known as woodchucks, emerge from their underground hibernation. If they see their shadows, the legend says, they scamper back into their burrows and winter continues for six weeks. If they do not, spring is just around the corner.

It is not clear just how Phil acquired his special status as spokesman for his species, but Punxsutawnians insist that their groundhog is the "seer of seers."

Perhaps accuracy has something to do with it.

"In 92 years of Punxsutawney Phil's emergence, he has never, never, never been wrong," says Charles M. Erhard Jr., president of the Punxsutawney Groundhog Club.

There was a miscue once, Erhard admits, but it wasn't Phil's fault.

"One year the weather was so terrible on Groundhog Day that Phil sent a message out that any durn fool would know enough not to go outside," he recalled.

"So since there wouldn't have been any shadow, we predicted an early spring. The worst part of winter followed, which just goes to show that when humans get involved, they can't get it right, but Phil never misses."

This town has a heavy stake in Phil's reputation, and the annual prediction is made amid great pomp and circumstance, ending with the trek up Gobbler's Knob to Phil's heated bunker to get The Word.

Erhard, clad in tails and striped pants, will lead the pilgrimage, rap with a special acacia wood cane at the stone facade of the burrow, speak intimately with Phil in "groundhog language" and translate for the assembled multitude.

AMERICA   CELEBRATES

CANDLEMAS OR GROUNDHOG DAY

Phil actually lives most of the year with his mate in a nearby park and must be installed at Gobbler's Knob in advance of the big event.

Animal authorities say woodchucks generally hibernate until March, and Phil is not always happy to have his sleep disturbed.

"A few years back, one of the inner circle had his finger bitten, and it gave us a scare," Erhard recalled. "But so far I've been on friendly terms with him."

Source

Philadelphia Inquirer, February 1, 1978.

More Recent Groundhogs

Pothole Pete

Donald Singleton reported on New York City's groundhog:

New York City's official groundhog-designate is hereby christened Pothole Pete.

The name for the still-hibernating critter was suggested by seven of the well over 50 entrants in *The News* groundhog-naming contest. The first two suggesters of Pothole Pete, whose entries arrived on the same day, were declared winners.

The reason for the contest—and the groundhog—was the fact that New York City found itself in the embarrassing position of being without a resident groundhog for Groundhog Day early this month. So *The News*, in the finest tradition of civic responsibility, bought one for the city.

At the moment, Pothole Pete is still hibernating in his box at the Space Wild Animal Farm in Beemerville, N.J. As soon as he comes to and finishes his spring cleaning—about May 1—Fred Space will make delivery. [*The News* will] turn Pete over to the city's Parks Department so he can be installed in a new cage at Flushing Meadow-Corona Park Zoo in Queens.

Source

New York *Daily News*, February 13, 1978.

Chipper and Sunshine

Boston Globe *readers were informed of Chicago's groundhog situation:*

Officials of the Brookfield (Ill.) Zoo are resorting to the inducements of food and sex, so determined are they to give Groundhog Day visitors a glimpse of Chipper, a groundhog with a bad attitude who spent the past three Groundhog Days inside of his hollow log. Today, Chipper is to be reunited with Sunshine, a 2-year-old female groundhog separated from him since November. Sunshine will be taken to the mouth of the log to see if she can entice Chipper to come out. In case that fails, there will also be a "Welcome to Spring" cake on hand for Chipper, concocted of his favorite foods—carrots, honey and oats.

Source

Boston Globe, February 2, 1981.

From Bear to Groundhog

Provençal Roots

H. Newell Wardle discusses "The Groundhog Myth and its Origins":

To the folk-lorist there are few pleasures which excel that of the discovery of a familiar superstition parading in ancient garb. Such was the writer's fortune, upon reading a discussion which took place before the *Société Préhistorique Française* in January of 1917. There M. Catelan records—

"On running through the numerous calendars that were given me for the *Capo d' Anno*, we noted that our *Studio* calendar bore for the 1st of February the fête of the Holy Bear (*Saint Ours*).

"Now, there is an alpine Provençal proverb which says, '*Si, pour le Chandeleur, l'Ours sorte de sa tanniére et voit son ombre, il rentre et de quarante jours ne sorte plus.*' ['If, on Candlemas, the Bear comes out of his den and sees his shadow, he returns for forty days more.']

"We have thought to interest our colleagues by calling attention to this date of the 1st of February and that of the 2d of February (*le Chandeleur*), both of which treat of the bear, and at the same time are brought into relation with the sun. In any case, we have brought a stone, perhaps useful, to the temple which is being rebuilt."

When and how this Provençal bear migrated to the New World may never be known; but there would seem to be no possible doubt of its identity with the American groundhog, which, on the 2d of February, annually casts its shadow across the pages of our daily press.

Source

Journal of American Folklore, XXXII (1919), 521.

Bear Dance

The Bear Dance is a ritual of regeneration, depicting the awakening of the bear from its winter sleep. It is associated with the coming of spring. Among the Utes it is mainly a social event. The Blackfeet, Crow and Kutenai traditionally perform the dance when the bear emerges from hibernation. J. Alden Mason collected this item "during the summer of 1909 from the Uintah Utes at White Rocks, Utah. The informant, Snake John, was an old White River Ute, reputed to have been the leader of the Meeker Massacre, 1879. His mother was a Shoshone."

In the fall the snow comes, and the bear has a wickiup in a hole. He stays there all winter, perhaps six moons. In the spring the snow goes, and he comes out. The bear dances up to a big tree on his hind feet. He dances up and back, back and forth, and sings, "Um, um, um, um!" He makes a path up to the tree, embraces it, and goes back again, singing "Um, um, um!" He dances very much, all the time.

Now Indians do it, and call it the "Bear Dance." It happens in the spring, and they do not dance in the winter. The bear understands the Bear Dance.

Source

Journal of American Folklore, XXIII (1910), 363.

February

3

POWAMÛ FESTIVAL

The Hopi, a group of Native Americans considered part of the Pueblo culture, populate villages in what is now northeastern Arizona. The villages are governed by a chief, who is also the spiritual leader. Pueblo villages are made up of members of various clans, who undertake both political and religious duties. The Hopi creation myth is central to many ceremonies. From the earth, which had always existed, the Hopi Indian Sky Father, represented by a hawk or eagle,

and the Earth Mother, represented by a spider, generated the human race and a number of marvelous animals.

Man emerged from beneath this earth through an opening, and upon his death is supposed to return to the underworld. The Sky Father, who is also known as the Sun God and by other names as well, symbolizes the male generative force. His arrival, in a personified form, and his departure, are occasions for two major Hopi festivals, which take place at the Walpi Pueblo, Arizona.

The Arrival of the Hopi Sky-god

J. Walter Fewkes compiled this report:

Hopi Indians personate in their worship the spirit ancients of their clans, by masked men wearing totemic designs characteristic of those clans. They also represent them by graven images and figures with like symbolism. The spirits of the ancients, their personations by men, the festivals in which these personators appear, and their representation by images and figures, are called Katcinas. The power which is personated objectively, or that which we call the spirit, is the magic potentiality conceived of as an anima or invisible aerial or breath body. . . .

In certain elaborate festivals these Indians also personate other beings besides clan-ancients, prominent among which may be mentioned the Sky-god. It is the author's purpose, in this article, to consider

at length the objective symbolism and acts of this personator in certain festivals. The distinction between the terms, Sky-god and Sun-god, is verbal, not real, for the sun is the shield or mask, a visible symbol of the magic power of the Sky-god conceived of as an anthropomorphic being. Both these names are used interchangeably in the following pages. . . .

In order to obtain a clear idea of the nature of Sky-god personations among the Hopi let us first describe those of the so-called Katcina clan, to be followed by a consideration of the modifications which appear among other clans.

The two most important festivals of this clan at Walpi [northeast Arizona] celebrate the advent and exit of personations of its clan-ancients. In one, the arrival, and in the other, their departure, are represented by men who personate these beings. They are supposed to enter the pueblo in February, an event dramatized in the festival called Powamû; to leave the pueblo, or go home, in July, and the representation of that event is called the Niman. In the intervening months the clan ancients are supposed to remain in the village or its neighborhood, publicly appearing from time to time in the pueblo in masked dances lasting a single day.

While these dramatizations of advent and departure are festivals of one clan, the actors are not restricted to this clan. Several others combine with it and personate their ancients, so that it has come about that while in the main these two great festivals

are controlled by one clan, whose chief is chief of the festivals, fragments of dramatizations by other clans survive in them, and personations of many clan ancients unconnected with the leading clan likewise appear. With all these additions, however, the main events are distinctly those of one clan or group of clans.

When the advent and departure of the ancients are dramatized a being is personated who leads them into the pueblo, and another who conducts them from it to their home, the underworld. The former leader represents the Sky-god as a Sun-god; the latter the same god, ruler of the realm of the dead, and god of germs.

The Sun-god of the Katcina clans, the advent of whom is celebrated at the Powamû festival, is generally called Ahüla, the returning one, although sometimes called the "Old-Man-Sun."

The author witnessed the public dramatization of the return of this god on the morning of February 3d, the opening day of the festival, at Walpi, in 1900. As this dramatization is a type of other presentations a somewhat detailed description of his dress and symbolism, with an account of the acts performed, is appended. Like most dramatizations the ceremony has two parts, a secret and a public exhibition. . . .

The man wears a mask which has a circular or disk form, with periphery bounded by a plaited corn-husk in which are inserted eagle-wing feathers, and a fringe of red horsehair representing sun's

POWAMÛ FESTIVAL

rays. The upper part of the face is divided into two quadrants, one of which is yellow; the other green, both decorated with black crosses. The middle is occupied by a triangular figure, and the chin, here hidden by a foxskin, tied about the neck, is black in color. A curved beak projects from one angle of the triangular symbol in the middle of the face.

The clothing consists of two white cotton ceremonial kilts, one tied over the shoulder, and the other around the loins. The leggings are made of an open mesh cloth with a fringe of shell tinklers tied down the side. In his right hand this figure carries a staff, to one end of which two feathers are tied, while midway in its length are attached a small crook, feathers, and an ear of corn. Among many objects carried in the left hand may be mentioned sprouts of beans, a slat of wood, a bag of sacred meal, and stringed feathers; the uses of these will be referred to in an account of the acts of this personage. The most characteristic symbolism, as is always the case, is shown on the face-shield or mask, which resembles somewhat that of the conventional Hopi Sun-disk.

A man who personated the Sun-god donned this characteristic mask and dressed near the sun shrine at Walla, northeast of the pueblos, and after certain preliminaries at this shrine, led by the Katcina chief, proceeded up the trail to the pueblos, first Hano, from which he proceeded to Sichomovi and Walpi, visiting the kivas and houses of all the principal chiefs

in these three villages. The acts at each house are substantially identical, so that one description may serve for all....

As the personator of the Sun-god walked through the pueblos he imitated the gait and general manner of an old man, using a staff for support as he proceeded from one room to another, and performed the following rites at each kiva. Having approached the hatchway of one of these rooms he leaned down, and drew a vertical mark with sacred-meal on the inside of the entrance, opposite the ladder. Turning to the east he made solemn inclinations of his body, bending backward and bowing forward, uttering at the same time a low, falsetto growl. He then turned to the kiva entrance and made similar obeisances, calling in the same voice; two or three of the principal men responded by coming up the kiva ladder, each bearing a handful of prayer-meal, and a feather-string which he placed in the hand of the Sun-god, at the same time saying a low, inaudible prayer.

At the houses of the chiefs the personator performed similar acts having the same import. Advancing to the doorway, he rubbed a handful of meal on the house wall, at the left of the doorway, making a vertical mark about the height of his chest. He then turned to face the rising sun, and made six silent inclinations of his body, uttering the falsetto calls, holding his staff before him at arm's length. Turning again to the doorway he bowed his body four times, and made the same calls.

The chief man or woman emerged from the house and placed in the hand of the personator a handful of prayer-meal and stringed-feather, saying at the same time a low prayer. In return for which the Sun-god handed him a few bean sprouts.

All the prayer offerings which the Sun-god had received in this circuit of the towns were later deposited in a sun-shrine, and the personator returned to the kiva, where he disrobed; the mask was carried to the house of the Katcina chief in whose custody it is kept, and to whom it is said to belong.

The above actions admit of the following explanations: The personator of the Sun-god enters the pueblos from the east at or near sunrise, receiving at each house the prayers of the inmates symbolized by the meal which each chief places in his hand, receiving in return sprouted beans symbolically representing the gifts for which they pray. The inclinations and obeisances with the accompanying calls may be theoretically interpreted as signs to his beneficent followers, the clan-ancients, and the bows to the doorways, gestures indicating the houses that he wishes them to enter, bringing blessing. The whole performance is a "prayer by signatures," or a pantomimic representation in which the desires of the Hopi are expressed by symbols and symbolic actions. The priests ask the Sky-god to aid them, and he answers in a symbolic way for himself and his followers, the ancients of clans.

The representation of the departure of the clan-ancients is not less dramatic than that of their advent; in it they are conducted or led away by a personage with symbols which are characteristic of another god.

Source

Journal of American Folklore, XV (1902), 14-19.

February

9

THE GASPARILLA PIRATE FESTIVAL

During the period of Mardi Gras celebrations in other cities along the Gulf Coast, Tampa, Florida, civic leaders, probably inspired by the "krewes" or men's clubs, began in 1904 to sponsor a parade of ships and a mock pirate invasion. Named in honor of José Gaspar, Tampa's legendary "patron pirate," the festival takes place in the downtown waterfront area. The invasion calls for a group of more than five hundred costumed pirates (usually some of the city's most prominent business and social leaders) to sail into Tampa harbor on a three-masted schooner (complete with cannons and a flying Jolly Roger flag), capture

the city, and kidnap the mayor. They then parade along Bayshore Boulevard accompanied by lavish floral floats and marching bands. Other activities held during Gasparilla week include distance-runs, a children's parade, and a bicycle race. The festival ends with Fiesta Day in Ybor City, a day-long party of dancing in the streets, Spanish bean soup, sidewalk artists, and a torchlight parade during which the pirates make their final appearance of the year. This invasion from the sea and other festivities now attract almost a million participants annually and have given rise to a few genuine folktales as well.

The Pirate Who Became a Civic Legend

The Real Gaspar

This information comes from a Greater Tampa chamber of Commerce brochure.

A curious quirk of his, this, that the bloodthirsty [José] Gaspar—who was accustomed to refer to himself as "Gasparilla"—should now be installed as a sort of civic patron rogue of the Florida West Coast. In Tampa his carnival time each February sets the populace to dancing in the streets and shouting his name.

Time has pretty well bleached out the memories of his sins. Tampans like to think of Gaspar as a hearty old swashbuckler, with courtly manners and possibly—just possibly—prankish habits; but never as a man to scuttle a ship or slit your throat.

In good truth, little enough is known of the worthy fellow, save that while a lieutenant in the Royal Spanish Navy he led a mutiny in 1783 aboard the Spanish sloop-of-war, the *Florida Blanca*, seized command of the vessel, and set sail for the Florida straits. Preying on the shipping of all nations, his freebooting exploits quickly established his status as one of the dreaded "Brethren of the Coast."

Research in the archives of the Spanish Navy at Madrid some years ago resulted in the discovery of Gasparilla's own diary of his first twelve years as a pirate. This remarkable fragment had fallen into Madrid's hands in 1795. In it Gasparilla boasted thirty-six ships captured and burned, their crews given the option of joining his ranks or walking the plank. Captive ladies were disposed of according to the fancy of the moment. How many other ships fell prey to Gaspar in later years is unknown. His buried treasure is still being sought by treasure hunters along the Florida coast.

The sea-rover's luck ran out in 1814 when he and his buccaneer band, emerging from their safe rendezvous in the shelter of an island in Charlotte Harbor south of Tampa—now the site of Boca Grande, near Punta Gorda—made their fatal mistake. About to pounce on a lone brig, apparently

a merchantman, Gasparilla saw to his consternation the Stars and Stripes break out at the masthead, and discovered that his proposed victim was a Navy warship, the U.S.S. *Enterprise*, Lieutenant Kearney commanding. The battle was joined, and in a few minutes Gasparilla's flagship, the *Gasparilla II*, was a burning shambles. A few of the crew escaped in a long boat. Gasparilla did not wait for the *Enterprise's* boarding party. Wrapping a heavy chain around his waist and neck, he leaped into the sea, in a final gesture of defiance. A surviving dozen of his crew were taken to New Orleans and eleven of them hanged. The cabin boy got ten years in federal prison.

Old Gaspar himself almost touched modern times. In Tampa in 1904, when Ye Mystic Krewe of Gasparilla was formed, there were men living who had known men who had actually known Gasparilla.

Source

Descriptive brochure, Greater Tampa Chamber of Commerce. Unsigned and undated, this brochure was written for the information of tourists.

José Gasparilla's Party

In a collection of "fragments of folklore" made by J. Frederick Doering, this anecdote was provided by Mrs. Frederick Webster, "a visitor to Tampa, Florida."

It is said that this famous Corsair made one particularly profitable raid down the Spanish Main. He determined then to return to one of his favorite retreats, the environs of Tampa Bay. Here he held a celebration which is famous for its splen-

The Pirate Who Became a Civic Legend

AMERICA   CELEBRATES

THE GASPARILLA PIRATE FESTIVAL

dor. Determined to impress people with his power, the pirate's train outshone that of any European monarch of his day. After the festivities, José returned to his predatory raids on merchantmen plying the waters of the Spanish Main.

Source

Southern Folklore Quarterly, II (1938), 218.

The Pirate Who Became a Civic Legend

Gasparilla's Golden Woman

J. Russell Reaver, a professor of English and Folklore at Florida State University, collected this item:

The best story I know about the Gasparilla Festival concerns the competi-tion among the floats of the Tampa elite in the parade. The story goes that a beautiful Cuban woman who worked in a Tampa cigar factory around 1930 allowed her nearly naked body to be covered with gold paint to win a prize, and she died a couple of days later, leaving her family without her income and in debt because the cigar factory would not even pay for funeral expenses.

Source

Collection of J. Russell Reaver.

February

14

ST. VALENTINE'S DAY

This day is dedicated to lovers who, according to custom, express their affection for each other through messages and gifts. Originally the choice of a lover was made by lot or by rhyming and riddling, and it was part of spring rituals during which unmarried couples were paired before their participation in orgiastic ceremonies. Such pairing might prove to be permanent, but that was not its initial purpose. Later, in some places on this holiday, the first persons of opposite sex to see each other by chance became valentines, thus encouraging a sportive and intimate relationship. Today cards and candy and affectionate rhymes are sent to one's valentine, sometimes anonymously and sometimes not.

Valentine's Day Wedding en masse

St. Valentine's is a day in honor of two Christian martyrs of the same name who were persecuted under the Roman Emperor Claudius II (A.D. 214–270) and who were buried on the Flaminiian Way on the same day. A church was built over their graves in the fourth century. Since the Middle Ages the day has been dedicated to romantic love, probably because it is the date on which the birds are supposed to start spring mating.

Scholars have thus related the customs of choosing a Valentine's Day sweetheart to a primitive game symbolizing the selection process and mating season of birds in the spring. In any event, birds, love birds particularly, are associated with Valentine's Day.

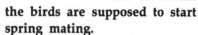

ST. VALENTINE'S DAY

Antique Valentines

Jean Caldwell wrote of a special valentine collection:

If Nancy Fletcher sends you a valentine, she may very well include a note asking you to send it back.

The director of public information at Mount Holyoke College has hundreds of valentines, some dating from as far back as 1848—most from a collection of antique valentines given to her when she was 10 by Marion Winslow Emerson, a distant cousin who was a founder of the Valentine Collectors of America.

Except for one—an elaborately framed shadow box with an intricate 1876 valentine depicting the four seasons that her mother kept in the family room of their Connecticut home—the valentines languished in the family attic for nearly 20 years. Fletcher didn't open the boxes until 1977, when a New Britain, Connecticut, museum whose officials had heard about the collection from a relative asked if she would display it.

In her attic she discovered valentines large and small, frilly and simple, sentimental and saucy. "It was like moving into another world," she said.

At first, Fletcher said, she thought valentines were frivolous. But she has come to realize, she said, that they "have to do with people and relationships. They chronicle how people relate. They are the expres-

sion of what love is, so they end up being central to life...."

Fletcher's oldest valentine, the 1848 specimen, is a beauty once sent to Elizabeth Rockefeller, a cousin of tycoon John D. Rockefeller. Some in the collection were made by Esther Howland, a graduate of Mount Holyoke who in 1848 became the first maker of valentine cards in the United States....

Turn-of-the-century valentines often were hinged so they would stand up, and many incorporate two to seven layers of flowery detail, Fletcher said. She has valentines that open like fans, others bordered in silk fringe, many with movable parts—such as the cherubic girl of the 1930s whose eyes move when a tab is pulled.

Source

Boston Globe, February 14, 1989.

Gingerbread Valentines

This recipe comes from a collection of recipes for "valentine cookies in the Victorian style."

In Victorian times lovers declared their affections in a veritable froth of words, songs, pictures and foods [such as] gingerbread "life cakes" in the shape of hearts....

2½ cups unsifted flour
2 teaspoons cinnamon
1½ teaspoons ginger

½ teaspoon ground cloves
¼ teaspoon salt
½ cup margarine
½ cup packed dark brown sugar
⅓ cup dark corn syrup
1 large egg

In large bowl, sift together flour, cinnamon, ginger, cloves and salt.

Blend together margarine and brown sugar until smooth. Add corn syrup and egg; beat well. Add dry ingredients, about one-third at a time, mixing until smooth after each addition. Chill dough one hour.

Roll out half of dough on lightly floured surface to one-quarter-inch thickness. (Reserve other half for decorations or for a second batch of cookies.) Using heart-shaped cookie cutter, press out cookie shapes or use knife to cut around a pattern. Place hearts on cookie sheet. Decorate as desired. Bake at 350 degrees for 15 to 20 minutes until golden. Remove and place on wire racks to cool. Store in covered container. Makes about eight 4½-inch cookies.

Source

Philadelphia Inquirer, February 11, 1981.

St. Valentine's Weather

Vance Randolph collected this information in the Ozark region of Misssouri:

Nearly all Ozark people say that the 14th of February, and not the 2nd [Candlemas], is the real Ground Hog Day, and are firmly convinced that if it is cloudy and cold on the 14th there will be six more weeks of winter weather.

Source

Journal of American Folklore, XL (1927), 87.

Goodheart's Court

Judge Goodheart Plays Cupid

Reporter Sergio R. Bustos described a Valentine's Day tradition in Philadelphia:

There was really nothing unusual about Courtroom 1105 yesterday afternoon [February 14, 1988] unless you count the four-piece band stationed next to the jurors' box and the fact that it was Sunday.

Then again, maybe the throng of reporters and camera crews that jammed the inside of the courtroom was just a little strange. And, perhaps, it seemed odd that all of those going before the presiding judge came in pairs—usually a man dressed in a handsome suit with a carnation pinned to his lapel accompanied by a woman wearing a beautiful dress and holding a bouquet.

OK. So the scene may have seemed out of the ordinary, but it wasn't necessarily uncommon.

For the last 12 years, Common Pleas Court Judge Bernard J. Goodheart, a King Cupid if you will, has joined in matrimony hundreds of lovesick couples wanting to wed on this most cherished of days—St. Valentine's Day.

Yesterday was no different. More than 30 couples wanting to tie the knot

AMERICA   CELEBRATES

ST. VALENTINE'S DAY

came to Goodheart's courtroom in Center City [Philadelphia] to do just that.

The first couple was joined in holy matrimony at 11:45 A.M. and the long assembly line of lovers didn't end until about 2:30 P.M., when the last couple kissed and marched arm in arm from the courtroom.

Goodheart's Court

It was definitely a day to remember, and Goodheart didn't let any couple walk away from his bench without dispensing a few words of wisdom.

"You are each separate individuals. You were each raised in different homes with different families and different values. So don't try to impose yourself on one another because nobody likes to be told what to do," the judge would say over and over again throughout the day to the parade of brides and grooms.

Afterward, Goodheart would stick a small, bright red Valentine heart on each of their marriage certificates and bid them farewell. As the couples would make their way to the elevators, the band would strike up such tunes as "Love Is a Many Splendored Thing," "All the Things You Want," "Make Someone Happy" and "My Funny Valentine."

The band ... has played previously for Goodheart on Valentine's Day.

"By doing 30 some weddings in a day, we fill out our quota for the entire year," said ... the band-leader.

The music and Goodheart's words of wisdom provided just the right touch to make the ceremony special for everybody.

When asked why they chose Valentine's Day to wed, Pugliese simply replied: "Why not? This is the best day of the year to get married."

Source

Philadelphia Inquirer, February 15, 1988.

Judge Goodheart Reties the Knot

A photo caption reported on the continuing tradition:

It's been a Valentine's Day tradition for 14 years now with Judge Bernard J. Goodheart, and yesterday [February 14, 1990] he again lived up to his name, joining couples in matrimony in his Common Pleas courtroom.... Among those enlisting his services on Cupid's day were Frank and Jeanne Matise of South Philadelphia, who were retying the knot after divorcing in 1986.

Source

Philadelphia Inquirer, February 15, 1990.

Safe Sex for Valentine's Day

A series of features compiled from wire reports rendered these new Valentine's Day observances:

America flirted with Valentine's Day this year with traditional weddings, flowers and a not-so-traditional barrage of warnings about AIDS and safe sex.

In the nation's capital, a florist capitalized on the acquired immune deficiency syndrome epidemic with the "Safe Sex Bouquet," a dozen roses spiced with baby's breath and a dozen condoms.

And some 10,000 Valentine cards containing condoms were distributed at bars across Connecticut to mark "National Condom Week."

Source

Providence Sunday Journal, February 14, 1988.

College Students Flunk on Origins of Valentine's Day

Students at the University of Rhode Island were interviewed by Angela Boffi, assistant news editor of the university daily, for this account:

If all goes as planned, Valentine's Day will be celebrated this coming Sunday. Some may be excited. Some may be depressed. How many know why we are celebrating in the first place? Where did this ambiguous holiday come from?

"Either from the French or the English," offered a pensive sophomore, "the French I think." Right hemisphere, wrong answer.

"I'd guess Italy," stated one junior, placing us on the right track.

A senior, scratching his head thoughtfully tried, "I used to know the story. Something to do with a guy named Valentino, I forget his first name." We are getting close.

"Probably has something to do with the Middle Ages," guessed another junior. He guessed correctly, but not completely.

"It's on the 14th. I have no clue where it came from," said one senior, obviously not losing sleep over his lack of historical knowledge.

Source

The Good 5¢ Cigar, February 12, 1988.

February

Mid-Month

PAUL BUNYAN BALL

The legendary Paul Bunyan is largely the creation of an advertising man, W. B. Laughead, who fleshed out a few lumbermen's jokes and allusions into full-blown tall tales and published them for promotional reasons in a trade journal. These tall tales gained popularity in the lumbering regions stretching west from Michigan. Huge in stature, Paul Bunyan is frequently pictured as a bearded fellow wearing a knit hat, a plaid flannel shirt, suspender pants, and a pair of stout boots. He was credited with collossal strength and

was said to preside over a gigantic lumber camp. His companion, Babe the Blue Ox, was also gargantuan; the span of his horns was calculated as "forty-two ax handles and a plug of tobacco." Even though by birth Bunyan might not be an entirely legitimate folk hero, he is certainly one of the most popular, endearing himself to lumberjacks, chambers of commerce, and generations of children. For forestry students in a state famous for its logging industry, he is accepted as a kind of secular patron saint.

Paul Bunyan College "Formal"

Clippings and background information on this holiday were supplied by John Carow, Professor Emeritus, School of Natural Resources, University of Michigan, who writes: "For the last two years we have not tried any so-called round dancing. It has been all square dancing.... As in earlier years there are a lot of displays and activities going on in other rooms besides the dance floor and we have had an ongoing sawing contest with male and female partners at one end of the dance floor that has attracted up to 100 pairs of sawyers... My experience has shown that there is a revival of some of the old-time college

traditions such as dancing and fraternity living, so that I look for a long continued success of this school's Paul Bunyan Ball."

Old Paul, Paul Bunyan, the patron saint of all lumberjacks, who, according to legend, had an irreconcilable aversion to the society of women, might not have looked with favor on the "formal" dance staged in his honor by the Michigan Foresters, Friday, November 20, [1943], in the Michigan Union Ballroom. But, Old Paul,

being a true American, would probably have consented wholeheartedly to the dance had he known that one couple received a grand prize of two United States War Bonds.

But if he had been here to object, he would have found himself a minority of one, for everybody who could get a ticket was on hand when Bill Sawyer's orchestra swung into the first number and the "would-be-lumberjacks" began dancing. Paul Bunyan and Babe, his great blue ox, attended the dance in person and both stood silently at one end of the ballroom, towering above the surrounding pines. Paul's huge ax hung directly above the band stand. Carefree informality prevailed throughout the entire evening.

This was not the first Paul Bunyan "Formal." 1938 saw the beginning of this campus favorite. It started as a barn dance at the Saline Valley Farms with only a small group of Foresters attending. The following year the real Paul Bunyan "Formal" was started....

Informality prevailed unanimously at the dance. Nearly every person wore a plaid shirt, and levis were far more common than pants. Girls wore slacks or old skirts; one lumber jill even came attired in a skirt made of burlap. Bill Sawyer gladly agreed to dress the entire orchestra just as informally as the dancers so that none of the Paul Bunyan atmosphere would be lost.

From 9 'til 12, dancers swayed gayly to fox trots and waltzes, jitterbugged, and had a grand la conga line. Everyone left the ballroom feeling that it had been an evening well spent. Praises for the dance were many. Bill Sawyer, who leads the campus' most popular band, said, "The Paul Bunyan 'Formal' is the most popular dance of the year."

After a lapse of ten years SNR [School of Natural Resources, University of Michigan] students this winter [February 16, 1979] revived an old School tradition, the Paul Bunyan Ball. The Natural Resources Club and the committee in charge did such a good job that its success rivaled that of any of its predecessors.

Led by "Bull of the Woods" Doug Boor and an active committee, the old format of the ball was thoroughly researched and in many cases followed. The affair was held in the Michigan Union Ballroom with an adjacent room for a cider bar and School displays.

The ballroom, decorated with Douglas fir trimmings (*Pseudotsuga menziesii* to the initiated) from Stinchfield Woods, held a massive sculpture of Paul Bunyan built from the ground up. Local merchants and restaurants contributed so many prizes, through committee urging, that contests were held throughout the evening to give them away. Very popular was a continuous Jack-and-Jill sawing event.

The main program was square dancing. The beginners were given a short instructional period before a full-size country band appeared on the scene. A jug band

AMERICA CELEBRATES

PAUL BUNYAN BALL

supplied intermission entertainment with conventional dancing at the evening's end.

Source

Michigan Forester Yearbook, 1943, 19, 21; *School of Natural Resources News*, University of Michigan, 1979, 4.

And that's not all:

For additional background and tales of Paul Bunyan, including an account of a "Paul Bunyan Winter Carnival" formerly held at Bemidji, Minnesota, see *Parade of Heroes*, 485-97.

February

29

LEAP YEAR DAY

Calendars provide a practical means of figuring time units so that past events can be recorded and future dates planned for. Natural occurrences such as the seasonal solar cycle and the phases of the moon supply logical bases for the compilation of calendars. The moon accomplishes a cycle of phases in about twenty-nine and one-half days. Some early calendars were based solely on the lunar year, made up

of twelve lunar cycles, or months, totalling more than 354 days. This method of reckoning was not easily reconciled with the solar year, in which the sun completes its cycle in a little over 365 days. Because months and years cannot be divided exactly by days, and years cannot be divided exactly into months, a method of inserting extra days, or intercalation, was devised. Thus, since the Earth takes five hours and forty-eight minutes longer than 365 days to complete its cycle of the sun,

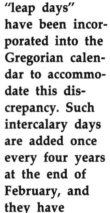

"leap days" have been incorporated into the Gregorian calendar to accommodate this discrepancy. Such intercalary days are added once every four years at the end of February, and they have evoked superstition, humor and confusion in popular tradition. February 29 is also known as "Ladies' Day," because of the tradition that women are free to propose marriage on that day, and as "St. Oswald's Day" after a tenth-century archbishop of York who died on February 29, 992.

Leap Day

David O'Reillly supplied this account of Leap Year Day:

Well, it has happened again. The Earth has circled four times around the sun, astronomers have designated this a leap year and anxious bachelors won't answer their telephones until midnight.

AMERICA CELEBRATES

LEAP YEAR DAY

It's Leap Year Day—the one day in four years when, by ancient custom, shy women may propose marriage. For women who have been wanting to pop The Big Question to the dawdling men of theirs—or who simply want to ask that hunk in algebra class out for a milkshake—now's the time. . . .

But sometime back in the Middle Ages women indeed acquired the "privilege" of proposing marriage during a leap year. In 1288 the Scottish Parliament even codified the tradition with a law that read: "For [each] year known as lepe yeare, any maiden ladye of both highe and lowe estait shall hae liberte to bespeke ye man she like." If he refused to make her his wife, he was fined one pound, "except . . . he can make it appear that he is betrothed to another woman." . . .

Since leap year is the result of man's efforts to adjust the calendar to the movements of the sun, it is not surprising that it is known in folklore as a disruption of the natural order.

Source

Philadelphia Inquirer, February 29, 1984.

February-March

Moveable

SHROVE TUESDAY OR MARDI GRAS

Shrove Tuesday immediately precedes Ash Wednesday and is the last day before Lent. Also called *Fastnacht* (German: Eve of Fast), *Mardi Gras* (French: Fat Tuesday), and Carnival, it has been noted for the elaborate mumming parades and boisterous parties that characterize its celebration in New Orleans, Mobile, Galveston, Trinidad, Brazil, France and, Italy. The name comes from the custom of "shriving," or purification through confessing one's sins, prior to Lent. The holiday is related to the coming of a New Year. On Shrove Tuesday in England, wild football games become ritualistic contests embodying the conflict between winter and summer, darkness and light, death and rebirth. Traditional food for this holiday—after which the Lenten period of abstention begins—includes thick soups of pig's feet, beans, peas, and pancakes. In fact "Pancake Day" is another name for Shrove Tuesday, and "Carnival" comes from Latin word roots meaning "farewell to meat." Carnival season begins on Twelfth Night and ends at midnight on Mardi Gras.

Mardi Gras in Galveston

Mardi Gras

New Orleans Mardi Gras

Marvy Evelyn Hill prepared this account in 1961 for a course in folklore at Wayne State University. Her informants were Mrs. R. L. Sherwood, age 55, and Mrs. M. Lemarie, age 60, both of New Orleans French background, and she cites Harnett T. Kane's Queen New Orleans, *for supportive information.*

Around 1820 a group of Creole youths, returning to New Orleans from Paris, decided to liven things up in the continental style with masked processions of substantial size. They appeared in the streets in every variety of costume while women leaned over galleries to throw roses and bonbons.

In 1857, the date usually given as the beginning of the Mardi Gras, a new organization was formed. It was to present a parade with floats and torchlights. The

SHROVE TUESDAY OR MARDI GRAS

organization called itself "The Mystick Krewe of Comus," and it put on a parade of two floats—one carrying a king, the other showing Satan in a blazing hell. Since that time only major conflicts have interfered, the Spanish American War not having been considered "major."

Mardi Gras owes its present day exuberance to a twenty-two year old Russian Grand Duke, who was present only by chance. In 1872 Alexis Alexandrovich Romanov, brother to the Tsar's heir apparent, was in America traveling. While in New York he became enamoured of an actress, Lydia Thompson, who was then appearing in "Bluebeard." As she sang the song "If Ever I Cease to Love," Alexis found himself completely lost to her charms. He trailed her on a tour south, and caught up with her in New Orleans. It was almost Mardi Gras and when the local inhabitants discovered a real Grand Duke was to be among them, they sat up and took notice. A new Carnival krewe was being planned and the project was elaborated.

A new king was named—Rex, Lord of Misrule. An official holiday was announced and street maskers were bidden to form a united procession. Carnival colors were chosen—purple, green, and gold. At the City Hall a thronelike chair was erected for Alexis.

Alexis arrived on the scene and the parade ensued. Since all the bands knew of his great liking for the song "If Ever I Cease to Love," band after band played it. The song has remained an integral part of Mardi Gras.

Alexis Alexandrovich had helped to fix the pattern that Mardi Gras would thenceforth follow: official holiday, Rex, and "If Ever I Cease to Love" as its song.

At the present time the number of krewes had increased to encompass nearly every conceivable group of people, from common work interests to nationality groups. The krewe captain is unpaid for his labor but wields vast influence. One of his major responsibilities is the preparation of the krewe's annual parade. Work begins for the next year at the close of the current season. The captain also chooses the king for the krewe. It must be a person of some wealth for he must provide his own costume, jeweled train, and accessories, give suppers and parties, buy presents for the queen and her maids, meet a hundred obligations.

The men rather than the women rule around the Mardi Gras time. The question of who shall be chosen queen for each of the older krewes—Comus, Rex, Twelfth Night, Atlanteans, and a few others is a seriously important issue.

To be queen of one of these older krewes a girl must usually belong to the well-defined group of the season's debutantes. A man may be quite old to be king, but a girl must be chosen at the debutante stage and this leads to acute tension.

The choice of queen is governed by a number of factors: family traditions, general social standing, wealth, business affiliations, and political obligations. When a candidate's mother has been a queen it is understood that the daughter will reign in her turn. The same girl may be queen twice, or even (though rarely) three times, or she may be queen at one ball and maid at others.

Christmas is the momentous day when the news is brought (or isn't). A male friend calls with a box of roses and a scroll that bids the girl to the court.

The persons to be invited to the ball given by a particular krewe can pose a serious problem. Committees work for weeks to pass on lists sent in by krewe members, each of them being allowed a limited number of invitations. The chairman of the committee often wishes he had not been granted the honor for he has to watch women cry, has alienated friends and has made permanent enemies.

At last comes the night of the parade. The warehouses, called "dens," near South Claiborne Avenue and Calliope Street, begin to fill with members arriving to don costumes and mount floats on which each has been assigned a specific position. According to the rules no one under the influence of liquor may ride. A generous buffet supper is provided for the participants.

Bands blare along the route and slowly floats move along, their path being cleared by policemen on horses and motorcycles. As each float passes, its maskers reach into bags holding the throw-outs: beads, whistles, and other trinkets for the crowd. "Throw me something!" "Gimme something, mister!" are the cries heard as the floats move by.

The parade route leads up St. Charles Avenue to Washington or Louisiana Avenue, then down the other side of St. Charles Avenue to Canal Street and along it or into the French Quarter for its destination, the Municipal Auditorium at Beauregard Square. Here the audience moves through closely guarded doors for the approaching ball. Each person must show an invitation in his own name to be admitted.

A visitor will not see a ball unless he is a relative or good friend of a member of the organization. Certain celebrities have had arrangements made and two of the krewes, Rex and Hermes, have invitations available for out-of-towners. However, these are in considerable demand.

Inside the auditorium the participants are dividing off. An invitation entitles a guest merely to look on from a seat upstairs. But various women have received call-outs, permitting them to sit below and be called forth for dances with members of the masked krewe. Each member is allowed a limited number of call-out cards and, understandably, they are major prizes. At the beginning of each dance committee members go about calling the names and finding the faces that match them.

AMERICA CELEBRATES

SHROVE TUESDAY OR MARDI GRAS

On the dance floor the lady pretends that she does not recognize her partner. She always receives a favor, some handsome trinket of durable value. Some gifts have been silver cigaret urns, dresser sets and silver card trays. These are engraved with the crest of the krewe and the year of the ball.

Always there is the more public part of the Carnival. The week before Mardi Gras parades multiply. Thursday and Friday two major organizations, Momus and Hermes, have night marches which all the city comes out to see. On Saturday there is a child king of the Krewe of Nor with a line of princes riding Shetland ponies, floats with older boys to pull them, and a queen awaiting His Majesty. Older monarchs stop at City Hall to toast first the Mayor, and then at one of the social clubs to toast the queen. Nor does much the same with hot chocolate or lemonade in place of champagne.

On Sunday a comparatively new organization, Venus, reverses the order: ladies wearing masks pick the king and dukes, whose names are given out while the ladies' identities supposedly remain secret. Sunday also sees Alla, King of Algiers, chugging down the river with a procession of tugs and ferries. Monday night Proteus of the Sea has his march through the streets.

Tuesday morning—Mardi Gras itself—finds the children up soon after dawn scrambling into their costumes and trying to hurry up the elders. On the streets trucks

are being loaded with masked youths. Along St. Charles Avenue for 35 blocks the banquette or sidewalks are filling with early arrivals, for it is here that they will see the main parade.

The first king on the scene is Zulu from Africa. His every act is a satire on self-conscious whites and their pretensions. He wears a rabbit skin and a grass skirt. He generally arrives on the float snorting audibly. His floats are decorated with moth eaten palm trees. His knights strut in the guise of medicine men and black face Keystone cops. Zulu does not salute the Mayor, but stops to toast bars which in return give him bottles of free stuff. He visits the Japanese Tea Room in the heart of the Negro section, and his queen awaits him at the Geddes and Moss Funeral Home. Zulu has a route which is seldom followed and he may be found all day rambling through the town.

About eleven A.M. Rex, chosen by the captain of the krewe, rides out with a procession of pastel floats. Mardi Gras has reached fever pitch and one finds people dressed in all manner of costumes.

The last parade of the year, Comus, takes place in the evening of Mardi Gras. The parade passes along Orleans Street toward the auditorium. Comus prepares to alight for his own tableaux and ball. Near midnight Rex, the other king, leaves with his court to go and salute Comus, the older monarch. Following a grand march, with a promenade of the two courts, there is a supper and officially Mardi Gras ends.

Source

Wayne State University Archive, 1961.

Cajun Country Mardi Gras

Andy Wallace gives a composite description of Mardi Gras customs in the Cajun country based on his observations:

If you want to see what old-style Cajun Mardi Gras is all about, you should go to the area around Praire Mamou or Eunice [Louisiana], right in the heart of what is called Cajun country, an area a hundred miles or so square extending from the Atchafalaya Basin to the Texas border down to the Gulf. There are perhaps a dozen towns in the area that still *courir le mardi gras* (run the Mardi Gras), with Mamou's being the biggest and best known. It features an all day street celebration with continuous live music to coincide with the traditional festivities described below. The following account is based on attendance at the Mamou, L'Anse Megre, and Eunice Mardi Gras runnings.

About 6:00 A.M., the Mardi Gras revelers start gathering at a central meeting place in their neighborhood to prepare for the day's excursion. At the Mardi Gras I've attended, several hundred people have participated. Of this group perhaps forty or fifty formed the hard core, mounted on horseback and wearing homemade costumes and masks, with some in blackface, others dressed as women or clowns. These were followed by a couple of flatbed trucks full of maskers, a truckload of musicians, then wives and families following in cars. To this day only males actively ride out on Mardi Gras, though women may tag along behind.

After an hour or so of milling around eating hot *boudin* (sausage), getting primed on beer and "trop d'antifreeze," the procession moves out and begins making the rounds of all the farms and houses in the neighborhood, led by a captain and three assistants on horseback. The captain is always a respected member of the community, someone who's capable of keeping his troup in order as the rowdiness progresses. At each house the captain, who is never masked, and who alone drinks no alcoholic beverages during the ride, dismounts, goes up to the master and mistress of the house, and asks if they will receive *les Mardi Gras* (the maskers). If the answer is "Ouais" (yes), as it always is, then the maskers come into the yard, clown around, and sing a haunting modal melody that is, as far as I know, unique in contemporary Cajun music.

There are minor variations in text from singer to singer, but the melody always seems to be the same....

Of course, the entire song is no longer sung at each house; instead the captain usually asks for a gift for the group. The household then obliges by offering food, usually a sack of rice, a few feet of sausage, or a chicken on the hoof, tossed in the air. Several frantic minutes ensue while some more-or-less inebriated maskers chase the fowl around the yard, finally capturing and dispatching it by whirling it over their heads with a shout of tri-

Mardi Gras

SHROVE   TUESDAY   OR   MARDI   GRAS

umph—*oh, ye yie!* Once dispatched, the offering is sent back to the gathering place to become part of the evening's gumbo.

The procession continues on for several hours, sometimes covering thirty or forty miles. Between stops, the revelers consume plenty of cold beer, hot *boudin*, and dozens of boiled eggs. In Mamou, the entire procession then parades down the main street of town, where several thousand folks are gathered for the festivities, and a riotous street dance ensues.

Around five, everyone adjourns a few blocks away to the spot where a huge gumbo is being prepared from the day's catch, and the last big feast before the Lenten fast commences. Gumbo is a Cajun stew, consisting of a base of *roux* (flour browned in oil) added to a stock of water laced with onions, garlic, scallions, parsley, salt, and pepper, in which pieces of meat, poultry, or seafood are cooked. The gumbo is served over rice. Mardi Gras gumbo is traditionally a chicken gumbo. After supper comes the *bal Masque* or dance party, the final fling until Easter lifts the Lenten restrictions. By midnight, everyone has retired to their homes for some much-needed rest.

Source

Tradition, XVII (Winter 1978), 1.

Carnival in Galveston

The carnival season and Mardi Gras, celebrated in Gulf Coast communities for generations, have always combined elements of Christian piety, folklore, social

pretension, commercialism, and the capacity to adapt to the times. In Galveston, Texas, Mardi Gras pageants and processions were first dominated by community leaders, but when they could no longer bear the expense, ordinary people, in the best folk tradition, continued to hold "impromptu parades" and street revels. Then businessmen took over again, sponsoring "cotton carnivals" and reviving Mardi Gras as a civic and social festival. Meanwhile, there was a locally hallowed spring rite, "Splash Day," which signaled the opening of the beaches, and incidentally, a profitable tourist season. It eventually superseded Mardi Gras, but after one riotous celebration, it was transformed into a "shrimp festival" which features an ecumenical blessing bestowed upon the fishing fleet. It is usually held in April, but like Easter is a moveable feast.

The Old Days

A Galveston historian, Ben C. Stuart, provided this background on the old days:

In the old days the celebration of Mardi Gras in Galveston [Texas] took place on an extended scale, and during the 1870s the street pageants at night, as well as the tableaux and balls, were both gorgeous and brilliant, attracting thousands of visitors to the city from the interior. Before these annual demonstrations were abandoned they were the event of the year, but the financial burdens resulting from their elaborate portrayal became too heavy for the exchequer of the majority of the residents of Galveston upon whom devolved the duty of meeting them, and the custom finally fell into disuse. In this sketch it is proposed to allude briefly to some of the principal demonstrations of this character in the city, the themes portrayed and the principal persons engaged in presenting them. The first celebration took place in 1867, when a dramatic entertainment and masked ball took place in the old Turner Hall on Avenue I, near Center street now occupied by the marble works of Charles S. Ott. The dramatic entertainment was a scene from "King Henry IV," where Alvan Reed, a Justice of the Peace, who weighed 350 pounds, essayed the character of Falstaff, without padding. One of the local papers remarked that "he was certainly without padding but not without pudding, and certainly cut it fat enough." Justice Reed in his day was a noted local character and was termed by the reporters of the epoch "a prodigious judicial hogshead." . . .

The first time Mardi Gras was celebrated to any great extent was in 1871, when there were two night parades by separate organizations, one known as the "K.O.M." and the other as the "Knights of Myth." The former had a [procession] representing the following themes:

1. Punch and Votaries.
2. Ancient France.
3. Crusades.
4. Peter the Great and His Friends.
5. China.

After traversing the principal streets the procession entered Turner Hall, where a number of tableaux were presented, followed by "a grand ball."

The second procession, under the auspices of the "Knights of Myth," was composed of four cars, headed by a transparency bearing the legend, "Organized January, 1871," and represented:

1. Knights of Myth.
2. Pokehontas.
3. Bismarck's Grand Band.
4. Scalawag's Enemies.

This procession, after covering its route, entered the Casino Hall. . . . Many of the visitors from the interior were present and paid their attention to a huge bowl of champagne punch, into which some practical joker had poured a vial of croton oil. The result can better be imagined than described. . . .

During the early '80s the custom of celebrating Mardi Gras by a grand street pageant was abandoned, the expense bearing too heavily upon those upon whom the greater portion of the burden fell. One of the last displays was by illuminated cars which traversed the principal lines of the electric roads, shortly after the installation of that system which supplanted the old "hay burners," as the mules, long the motive power, were popularly termed. The large cotton sheds, which were numerous in the old days, were used for shelter in the preparing of the illuminated floats, and there was no little degree of skill displayed in fitting them up.

Source

Galveston Daily News, August 11, 1907.

Street Maskers and Cotton Carnivals

This information was published in a newspaper feaature section on the Mardi Gras:

While lack of money forced the discontinuance of the mammoth parades in

*Carnival
in Galveston*

SHROVE TUESDAY OR MARDI GRAS

Carnival in Galveston

the late 80s, the Mardi Gras spirit was carried on by a secret organization known as the F.F.F. or Forty Funny Fellows.

This group specialized in staging impromptu parades which were participated in by thousands of maskers who filled the streets during the gala season.

Following the year 1900 the Mardi Gras events were discontinued for several years. The celebrations were gradually revived, but not on an extensive scale, backed by a strong organization, until about 1914.

In the period from 1910 to 1914 there were impromptu parades. Some fun-loving citizen or a small group would hire a band which would march around the streets. Groups of revelers in fancy costume would join in.

In 1910 the Galveston Business League announced that a plan would be worked out for Mardi Gras celebrations on an extensive scale, but records indicate this idea was not carried out to any great extent. It is believed that in this period the old cotton carnivals overshadowed attempts to put the Mardi Gras celebrations back into the picture in a big way.

In 1914, however, the old K.K.K. or Kotton Karnival Kids took over the Mardi Gras events. The name was originated by Ed Kauffman, state senator at that time from this district and secretary of the Galveston Business League.

Source

Galveston Tribune, January 30, 1932.

King Frivolous

This account of King Frivolous is taken from a daily series of historical background stories preceding the carnival season. The dynasty established by King Frivolous I reigned until well into the 1930s.

Mardi Gras, as it is staged in Galveston today [1924], had its premiere February 19 and 20, 1917, when R. M. Tevis was crowned as King Frivolous I at the city auditorium.

The king and his two pages, E. R. Cheeseborough Jr. and R. Starloy Tevis, arrived on the launch Colonel of the United States engineering department on the morning of February 19. Then followed the parade to the city hall, where the king was presented with the key to the city by Judge Lewis Fisher, then mayor. The king then went into seclusion.

The parade that night of sixteen floats, the first given as a part of Mardi Gras, depicted characters of the comic sheets.

The first children's party was held between Twenty-third and Twenty-fifth streets on Avenue J, with Miles Kirk Burton and Miss Alice Mamie Cavin as prince and princess of the affair. Dances of different kinds had been arranged and prizes were given for the best costumes in the various divisions.

The ball that night was a thing of splendor, and revealed Frank C. Briggs as the queen. Rear Admiral A. W. Grant of the United States navy was made an honorary member of the organization. The grand march that year passed in front of the royal party, instead of being led by them, as is the custom now.

The U. S. S. Columbia was in port for the celebration, and the members of her crew, along with soldiers stationed at Fort Crockett, took part in the parade.

Source

Galveston Daily News, February 23, 1924.

Splash Days and Bathing Beauties

Ann Abshier wrote this feature on Splash Days:

There will be quite a bit of difference between the scantily clad bathing beauties adorning the beaches these Splash Days, May 2-6 [1957], and those well-covered ones who appear in the first bathing revue here thirty-seven years ago.

Bathing beauties paraded in revue on Galveston beaches for the first time Sunday, May 23, 1920. . . .

The summer season in Galveston was ushered in about Easter time with Splash Day and was formally opened with the Bathing Girl Revue, an event given countrywide attention. The revue was conceded to be the "most artistic and spectacular display of feminine beauty seen anywhere in the country." It became a Galveston institution which many cities later adopted.

In 1926 the revue went even further than usual and became an international pageant held in May. Plans were made to change and improve the methods of pre-

senting the beauties by the sponsors, the Galveston Beach Association, Chamber of Commerce and Merchants Association.

A tremendous publicity campaign began to attract the interest of the nation to Galveston and its beauty show and beaches. Managing Director Willett L. Roe put wheels in motion for the campaign.

A card printed in six colors of oils, showing a bathing beauty riding an aquaplane, and with inserts of beauties from Mexico and Canada, was one of the advertising methods adopted. These cards were sent to city ticket offices of every railroad running into Galveston. The railroads cooperated in every way possible.

Trailers showing scenes of former revues, both in motion picture and slide form, were sent to more than 100 theaters. And a newspaper advertising campaign was carried on in every major city in the Southwest. . . .

It was assured that women of high moral standing as well as physical attraction would be present by a rule making it necessary for all contestants to be elected by contests conducted in home cities and sponsored by the chamber of commerce or other reliable agency.

Willett Roe announced that this contest was the "first beauty contest ever staged with an International feature" and "the first contest where the four essentials of beauty of face, grace, perfection of figure and personal charm will be considered equally by the judges."

Carnival in Galveston

SHROVE TUESDAY OR MARDI GRAS

Carnival in Galveston

The old Venus De Milo standards of judging were to be discarded in favor of modern standards. Ned Wayburn, then famous Broadway theatrical man and Ziegfeld follies producer, assured this when he accepted the chairmanship of the board of judges for the first international pageant.

The 40 cities, Mexico and Canada sent entries from large contests conducted in their areas. Their candidates were introduced to the pageant committee by telegrams and letters saying they were sending "sure winners who had captivated their city or nation."

And the entries were sent to Galveston in high style.

The *Omaha Daily News*, in connection with the trip to Galveston of Miss Omaha, arranged a "sunny South Special" to run over the Missouri Pacific Lines with stops in Hot Springs National Park, New Orleans, and other points of interest. A fare of $49.95 for the 2950 mile round-trip was charged. All along the route the special picked up entries and parties from other cities.

Miss New Orleans was sent in a special train with a large illuminated picture of her on glass displayed on the observation platform. Huge banners on each side of the cars announced the purpose of the trip and the name of the beauty inside....

The pageant, witnessed by 150,000, was climaxed with the elaborate coronation of Miss Universe, chosen after a final judging of the girls in evening gowns and bathing suits.

The first Miss Universe, Miss Catherine Moylan, Miss Dallas, received the grand prize of $2000 in gold and a "beautiful and valuable plaque suitably inscribed."

Source

Galveston Tribune, April 25, 1957.

Blessing the Galveston Shrimp Fleet

This account of the shrimp festival was filed by Kitty Kendall:

Galveston's first "Blessing of the Shrimp Fleet" as a Splash Days event Saturday seemed to have won the hearts and captured the imagination of hundreds of spectators.

Clergymen of three faiths blessed 65 shrimping boats in Galveston Ship Channel at Pier 20 in a two-hour ceremony.

The Reverend Lionel T. DeForrest, rector, Grace Episcopal church; the Rev. A. Daregas, pastor of the Assumption of the Virgin Mary Greek Orthodox church, and the Reverend Walter Montondon, assistant pastor of St. Mary's Cathedral, each blessed the gaily decorated vessels in the language of the respective churches—English, Greek and Latin.

The three clergymen, wearing vestments identified with the respective churches, were accompanied by acolytes carrying flags, crosses, candles, fans and other symbols of the churches....

The U.S. Coast Guard directed traffic in the channel as the shrimp boats formed a graceful and colorful aquatic procession as they passed before the clergymen to be blessed.

Source

Galveston Daily News, April 29, 1962.

Parade of the Shrimp Boats

Bob Parvin wrote this article on the "two-week Shrimp Festival held in late April" in Galveston.

The blessing of the fleet is carried out in both a serious and festive manner. Commercial and private boat owners and their immediate relatives hold strongly to the religious significance of the blessing. But they also take an active part in competition for the most elaborately decorated boat.

Preparations for the event begin weeks in advance when boat crews and family members secretly plan and produce the decorative themes for their crafts. Not until the morning of the blessing are the boats' full dress unveiled. It is only then that the pre-made adornments are brought from under wraps at home and taken down to the pier and lashed onto the boats.

Drab commercial vessels are transformed within hours into vibrantly colorful and fanciful arks done up in crepe paper, banners, flags, balloons and theme stylizations. Private yachts, sailboats, motorboats and inshore trawlers become floating mirages of colors and patterns.

Most vessels taking part in the competition are decorated to themes which are made known to judges only on the morning that the blessing is to take place. The procession this year [1973] featured nearly 60 vessels, about half of which were dressed up to such diverse themes as: "Alice in Wonderland," "Traveling Texas," and "Texas: Industrial Giant."

Many of the undecorated commercial boats had steamed into the channel in time only to receive the blessing and steer back out into the Gulf to resume fishing.

Each entry in the parade is given a Saint Christopher's Medal which is blessed to ensure safe passage. The blessing of the fleet usually begins in midafternoon. As the parade fleet begins to circle into position in the lower channel basin, the water is ablaze with rippling reflections cast from the gaudily rigged vessels. The crew and passengers aboard each boat shout and clap as they are applauded by the crowd ashore.

Then, on cue, they steam around and form a line down the channel. Each craft passes beside a barge upon whose upper deck stands a row of priests and altar boys who cast holy water in the direction of the boats and offer the awaited blessing.

"My Boat is so Small and the Seas are so Vast," reads the hastily drawn inscription painted along the gunnel of a dirty, wood hull shrimper, just arrived for the procession.

Source

Texas Highways, July 1973, 28.

Carnival in Galveston

SHROVE TUESDAY OR MARDI GRAS

Pennsylvania Dutch Shrove Tuesday Lore

Beliefs and Customs

Literally, Fasnacht or Fasenacht (Pennsylvania Dutch) and Fastnacht (German) mean "fast night." Alfred J. Shoemaker, a Pennsylvania Dutchman, cites his sources in this report on Fasnacht lore:

Fasnacht—the dialect word for Shrove Tuesday—and Christmas have one thing in common in the Dutch country: they are the two days in the year when the kiddies get up unusually early. On Christmas it is to see what the *grischtkindel* [Christ-child] has brought; on *fasnacht* morning the children get up early because the last one out of bed becomes the *fasnacht* and is teased unmercifully all day long, not only by the members of his family but by his schoolmates as well.

In the past few years I have collected several variants to the name *fasnacht*—all of them in the York-Adams County area, however. Dr. Colsin R. Shelly tells me the last one out of bed in his family on Shrove Tuesday was called the old cluck and the first one the little *peepie*. Mrs. Anna Trimmer, who grew up in the Dover section, says she used to hear the word *faws-gloock*.

Mrs. William E. Werner of Jefferson, who is in her 80s, told me some months ago that the last one up was *die faws* [Fasnacht] and the first one *die alt asch* [the old ash]. Mrs. Harry Senft of the same place says in their family the first one up was called *der gansert* [the gander]. And Mrs. Willis Burns also of Jefferson relates how her mother

came to her rescue when her brother teased her overmuch. Her mother told her to call him, the first riser on Shrove Tuesday morning, *der schpeel-loombasoockler* [the dishrag sucker].

As on the other religious holidays in the Dutch country, there is a work taboo on Shrove Tuesday. William Reinert of near Fredericksville, Berks County, tells me if you sew on *Fasnacht* you will sew up the hens' cloacae and prevent them from laying eggs. Victor C. Dieffenbach of Bethel used to hear the old-timers say if a woman sewed on Shrove Tuesday the snakes would come in her house in spring and summer.

The most welcome thing about Shrove Tuesday was the special kind of doughnut, called a *fasnacht*, which was baked only at this time of year. It has a shape all its own, rectangular with a slit in the middle. To the traditionalist, the shape of the *fasnacht* is more important than the age-old debate in Dutch country: raised versus unraised dough for the *fasnacht-koo-cha* [cake].

Of course, *fasnachts*, like all other cakes in the Dutch country, must be dunked to be good. In Lancaster and Lebanon Counties—our saffron belt—they are dunked in saffron tea. Mrs. J. R. Cresswell of Morgantown, West Virginia, wrote us at the Folklore Center some years ago, "The most delightful use we put saffron to was on Shrove Tuesday when we put it in tea. For supper on that day we always had *fasnachts*—big, rectangular ones, with lots of air holes inside them. You split the *fasnacht*, filled the holes up with molasses and then dunked them in the saffron tea. The only time I get really homesick to be back on the farm is on Shrove Tuesday evening.''

Saffron tea may be all right for someone who has his roots in the western section of our Dutchland. As for me, there is nothing that can compare with good old blue balsam tea. Naturally, the *fasnachts* must be dripping molasses before they are really dunkable.

In some of our Dutch families the first *fasnachts* that were baked were always fed to the chickens. Mrs. John Beaver of Kratzerville, Snyder County, tells me the old-timers used to lay a *blucks-line* [plow line] in a circle and then they crumbled the first three *fasnachts* in it for the chickens. The folk-belief was that if one did this the hawks would not fetch the chickens or chicks in spring. Mrs. Amelia Hildenbrand of the Mount Carmel area of Northampton County says her mother cut up the first three *fasnachts* for the chickens because she believed this would make them lay more eggs.

Then, in fine, there was the custom of barring out the teacher on Shrove Tuesday. (In most areas of the Dutch country barring-out-day was always on Christmas.) J. Steffy of near Red Run, Lancaster County, told me recently that when he attended the White Hollow school between Red Run [*Die Roat Koo* or the Red Cow in Dutch] and Terre Hill they locked out the teacher John

Mentzer on Shrove Tuesday afternoon. That was about the year 1888 says Steffy.

Source

Pennsylvania Dutchman, V (February 1, 1954), 3.

Genuine Fasenacht Kuche

Raymond E. Hollenbach of Saegersville, Pennsylvania, in the Dutch Country, first published this account in 1948 in the Reading (Pennsylvania) Eagle.

The shape of the *fasenacht kuche* [cake] has nothing at all to do in determining whether the product is genuine or not. The determining factor is whether or not it is baked with yeast. If it is baked with yeast it is just an ordinary doughnut, regardless of whether it is round, square, triangular, or whatever the shape may be. The hole in the center is also immaterial. That is merely put there to insure thoroughness in baking.

A genuine *fasenacht kuche* is made WITHOUT yeast. This is important. Shrove Tuesday is a religious holiday and the absence of yeast was considered very important by our ancestors. Another thing, *fasenacht kuche* are baked only once a year—on Shrove Tuesday or on the Monday before. The important thing is that they be eaten on Shrove Tuesday, although a sufficient quantity is generally baked to last the rest of the week, providing the family appetite is not too large. Anything baked with raised dough is NOT a *fasenacht kuche* regardless of when it is baked or how it is shaped.

For future reference, I am giving you herewith a recipe for genuine *fasenacht kuche:*

Penn-sylvania Dutch Shrove Tuesday Lore

AMERICA CELEBRATES

SHROVE TUESDAY OR MARDI GRAS

¾ cup of thick sour cream
¾ cup of thick sour milk
¼ cup of sugar
1 egg
1½ teaspoonful baking soda

Penn-sylvania Dutch Shrove Tuesday Lore

Stiffen with enough flour to roll. Roll about ¼ inch thick and cut into desired shape and size—two-inch squares are preferable. Fry in deep fat. The amount of sugar may be made larger, but this is not necessary if eaten in the approved manner.

To eat, split the *kuche* in half and fill the inside with *gwidde hunnich* (quince jam). To use anything as ordinary as common as molasses on a genuine *fasenacht kuche* is an abomination. In the absence of *gwidde hunnich*, crab apple jelly may be substituted, but in our house we always have the foresight to have on hand at least one jar of *gwidde hunnich* just for this occasion.

This recipe has been used in our family, to my own knowledge, for four generations, and tradition says it was brought from Europe. Surely there must be Berks County homes where it is still used. My mother's family (Metzger) originated in Maxatawny, and old Mrs. Miller (wife of Dr. A. S. Miller) in whose kitchen I was privileged to eat *fasenacht kuche* many years ago, came from Albany in Berks County. My wife's family, which originated in Maidencreek and Richmond townships, were not acquainted with the recipe, but I have introduced it and anyone coming to our

house on Shrove Tuesday will find the genuine product.

Source

Pennsylvania Dutchman, V (February 1, 1954), 3.

Last One out of Bed on Shrove Tuesday

A Shrove Tuesday sleepyhead was called "Fasenacht" for the doughnutlike cake prepared for this holiday. On Ash Wednesday the nickname was "Ash-puddle," meaning covered with ashes, a name by which Cinderella was also known. On Holy Thursday the late sleeper was called "Seven Sleeper," a reference to the Christian legend of the Seven Sleepers of Ephesus. To escape persecution they hid in a cave where they slept soundly for two hundred and thirty years.

Just a word about the last one out of bed, or the last one to arrive at school, during the *Fasenacht* season. On Shrove Tuesday the last one out of bed, or at school, was *die fasenacht*. Similarly, on Ash Wednesday that person was *der eschepudl*, and on the Thursday morning following, *der siwweschlaefer*. In industrious Pennsylvania Dutch families, where late rising was considered almost a crime, there was of course some opprobriumn attached to these names. However, since the last one out of bed was often the youngest member of the family, I am wondering if in the original custom the use of these names was not merely a gentle reproach and that they were used with a genuine feeling of affection.

Source

Pennsylvania Dutchman, V (February 1, 1954), 3.

Shrove Tuesday Dance

W. J. Hoffman collected this item:

Dances were held on Shrove Tuesday [in the Pennsylvania Dutch country] "for a good yield of flax for that year," or, in other words, the host's crop of flax would be tall in proportion to the height to which the dancers raised their feet from the floor.

Source

Journal of American Folklore, II (1889), 25.

International Pancake Race

Race History

Virginia Leete, publicity committee, of International Pancake Day of Liberal, Inc., wrote a "History of Pancake Day" for the official program of the "29th Annual Event" from which this description is taken. Featured events include pancake-eating contest; amateur talent competition; Shriving Worship Service; Trans-Atlantic Telephone Call with Olney, England; parade.

What a footrace! The annual Shrove Tuesday race between housewives of Liberal [Kansas], and those of Olney, England. They dash 415 yards through the main streets of the two towns, and winners' times are clocked with stopwatches, then compared by Trans-Atlantic telephone to determine the International Pancake Racing Champion.

This has gone on since 1950. R. J. Leete, then president of the Liberal Jaycees, saw a picture in *Time* magazine of women racing in Olney. For over 500 years it had been the custom to race to the church when the shriving bell rang. The story goes it all started when a housewife was using up cooking fats (forbidden during Lent) to bake pancakes on Shrove Tuesday. When the bell tolled calling all to the shriving service, in her haste she forgot to remove her apron, and ran to the church with skillet still in hand. Her neighbors, not to be outdone, got into the act the next year, and carried their skillets to church, so it became a contest to see who could reach the church steps first and collect a kiss from the bell-ringer. He gave the greeting, "The Peace of the Lord be always with you," so the prize became the "Kiss of Peace," still bestowed in both the Liberal and Olney races.

Leete cabled Ronald Collins, then Vicar of Olney and manager of the race there, and challenged the English to the first race. They readily accepted and it has grown into an internationally known event.

The score now [in 1978] stands at 15-11, in favor of Liberal. The 25th anniversary race was run for goodwill only, and the score did not count. The race is run according to Olney rules. The course is laid out in an "S" shape. In Olney the race starts at the village well, at the sound of a centuries-old bell. Over cobblestone streets, it goes past thatched roof cottages and the Old Bull Inn. In Liberal, a pistol shot signals the start, and we run over brick and asphalt streets.

Traditional garb is housedresses, aprons, and headscarves (the head coverings necessary for the church ceremony following the race in England). Three local wins disqualify a winner. A pancake

AMERICA CELEBRATES

SHROVE TUESDAY OR MARDI GRAS

dropped during the race does not disqualify, but the racer loses valuable time in retrieving it. The pancake must be flipped when the race starts and again after the runner crosses the finish line, to show she still has the pancake. Racers must be at least 16 years old and a resident of their respective towns. The only time this rule was set aside was in 1974 when Mrs. Leete was invited to run in the Olney race after Liberal had sent the Leetes to England as its representatives.

Source

International Pancake Day Program, Liberal, Kansas, February 7, 1978.

And that's not all:
See "Bastille Day Wine Glass Race."

Inter-national Pancake Race

A Recent Pancake Race

This item appeared in a newspaper column:

Louise Fitzgerald, 17, of Olney, England, flipped her pancake and took off running yesterday [March 6, 1984] while Mona Canaday, an aerobics instructor in Liberal, Kansas, did the same thing.

When it was over, the British had defeated the Americans by two seconds in the 415-yard race. Miss Fitzgerald's winning time was 1 minute, 4.1 seconds....

It's a bizarre race because contestants must flip pancakes while running....

The series now stands at 19-15 in favor of Liberal.

Source

Philadelphia Inquirer, March 7, 1984.

Pancake Race Superstitions

Leland Agan, Pancake Day Chairman for 1979, provided this information:

Listed below are a few superstitions that have sprung up [in Liberal] around the race:

It is considered good luck to carry a past winner's skillet in the race. Also to wear a past winner's apron.

One year, the stack of pancakes marking the starting point of the race, were stolen. This was considered a bad omen. The stack of pancakes (concrete) were later returned.

Although the women practice running 415 yards, it is considered bad luck to run the official race course during these practice sessions.

It is against the rules for entrants to run the official race course any time after midnight the day of the International Pancake Race.

All entrants have strong feelings about the traditional blessing bestowed on the winner of the race. This blessing, "The Peace of the Lord be alway (spelling correct) with you," is given by, in England, the Verger or Bell Ringer, in Liberal, the British Consul representing England in this area.

Source

Letter to T. P. C. dated November 10, 1978.

Paczki Day

This item was reported from New York Mills, New York, by Robert Maziarz, whose grandparents were born in Poland.

The day before Ash Wednesday is called [in Polish] *Paczki* day. *Paczki* are jellybuns. This is a day of feasting and merrymaking. (We still [in 1968] have jellybuns on the Tuesday before Ash Wednesday in our family.)

Source

New York Folklore Quarterly, XXIV (1968), 303.

Shrove Cakes, Pancakes, Cross-buns

J. Hampden Porter collected this information from unspecified "mountain whites" in the Allegheny mountains.

Shrove cakes on Shrove Tuesday, pancakes on Ash Wednesday, cross-buns at Easter, bring good luck. The first should be round and have a hole in the centre. If the grease used in frying them be preserved and applied to the axles of wagons in which the harvest is hauled home, mice will not eat the grain. One cross-bun must be kept during the year if the good influence is to be continued.

Source

Journal of American Folklore, VII (1894), 112.

February-March

14th Day of Adar
PURIM

Purim is a feast day celebrated on the fourteenth day of Adar, the sixth month of the Jewish calendar. It commemorates the escape of the Persian Jews from a massacre planned by Haman, minister of the King, Ahasuerus, through the intercession of Esther, the queen. This story is recounted in the Old Testament Book of Esther. Haman's anger had been provoked by a Jewish leader, Mordecai, who, for religious reasons, refused to bow in homage to him. Haman persuaded the king that the Jews were disobedient and seditious, and obtained a decree permitting their destruction. Lots were cast to determine when this should take place. Unknown to the king or Haman, Esther was the cousin of

Mordecai, and she revealed Haman's machinations and Mordecai's past services to Ahasuerus. The king could not legally alter his decree, but he granted the Jews the right to defend themselves, thus forestalling an attack, and had Haman hanged. Purim, also called the Feast of Lots, is characterized by frivolity—feasting, dancing, masquerade, playacting based on the story of Esther saving her people from Haman, and in more recent times, beauty contests for the selection of a "Queen Esther" who reigns over this Jewish carnival. The Purim observance usually begins with the reading of "the *Megillah*" or Book of Esther, a parchment scroll often kept in a handsomely ornamented case.

A Purim Reading

Marilyn Silverstein wrote this account of the Purim story and its observance:

The stage is set for the happiest holiday of the Jewish year—Purim 5748 [1988]. The characters assemble in the wings, awaiting their entrances: the powerful King Ahasuerus, the beautiful Queen Esther, the righteous Mordecai, the evil Haman.

The scene is Persia, the time some 2,000 years ago. The curtain will go up on Purim as the sun goes down Wednesday, ushering in the 14th day of the month of Adar. The drama of the deliverance of the Jews will unfold as the script—the scroll of Esther, known as the Megillah—is unrolled.

Let the play begin!

Ahasuerus has just banished his queen, Vashti, for refusing to dance before his assembled guests at a seven-day revel in the city of Shushan.

A search begins to find the most beautiful woman in the land to become Ahasuerus' new bride and queen. The king chooses Esther, unaware that she is a Jew and the cousin of his court Jew, Mordecai.

At the same time, Ahasuerus elevates his court adviser, Haman, to the position of vizier, chief among all the king's men. The vicious vizier immediately decrees that all men bow down to him.

The righteous Mordecai refuses. Enraged, Haman vows to destroy the Jewish people. He whispers into the king's ear: "There is a certain people scattered abroad and dispersed among the peoples. . . . Their laws are different from those of other people, they do not obey the king's law and the king should not tolerate them."

The king listens to Haman's malicious words and agrees to permit the destruction of the Jews. Haman casts lots, known as *purim,* to set the day of destruc-

tion. The chosen day is to be the 13th day of the month of Adar.

When Mordecai learns of Haman's evil intentions, he goes to his cousin Esther and appeals to her to come to the aid of their people.

Knowing that she risks death, Esther goes unsummoned to the king and requests that he and Haman come to a banquet in their honor.

Unable to sleep that night, Ahasuerus calls for his scribes and asks them to read to him from the history of his reign. As the scribes read, the king discovers that Mordecai once saved his life by foiling an assassination plot. But the court Jew has never been rewarded.

Ahasuerus sends for Haman and asks his advice: "What should be done for a man whom the king wishes to honor?"

Thinking that he himself is the man to be honored, Haman replies, "Such a one should be dressed in royal garb and led in a procession throughout the streets of Shushan, while a servant of the king walks beside him, crying, 'So it is that the king treats a man to whom honor is due!' "

The next evening, Ahasuerus and Haman attend the queen's banquet. As the feast is served, Esther points an accusing finger at Haman. Haman's plan to destroy the Jews, she tells the king, would mean the destruction of *her* people and the people of Mordecai.

AMERICA CELEBRATES

PURIM

Holding onto his three-cornered hat, Haman flees the banquet hall.

Later that night, Haman appears in Esther's chambers and throws himself at her feet, begging for mercy. But just at that moment, Ahasuerus bursts into the room and finds Haman alone with the queen in her chambers—an outrage punishable by death.

Haman and his 10 sons are hanged from the very gallows that the evil vizier had constructed to take the life of Mordecai. It's curtains for Haman as the curtain comes down on this ancient tale of deceit, deliverance and triumph over evil.

This is the whole Megillah, and it is considered a mitzvah [good deed] to hear every word of it. Everyone is called upon to hear the reading of the scroll of Esther—women and children as well as men.

It is a reading marked by revelry, for as the story is read, the assembled children traditionally hiss and boo and twirl their noisy groggers [rattles] every time they hear the name of the evil Haman.

It is also considered a mitzvah to partake of the joy of Purim—the feasting, drinking, noisemaking, parades and masquerades.

As it is written in the book of Esther, ''The Jews of the villages that lived in unwalled towns made the 14th of the month of Adar a day of gladness and feasting, a holiday and an occasion for sending gifts to one another.''

The Purim feast, *seudat Purim,* is a feast of victory over evil, as the merrymakers eat *hamantashen,* or Haman's hats: three-cornered pastries filled with sweet prunes or poppy seeds.

The customs of Purim include *shalach manot,* the exchange of small gifts of food, and *matanot l'evyonim,* the gift of charity to the poor.

It is also customary to celebrate Purim with carnivals, games and costume parades of pint-sized Esthers, Mordecais, Ahasueruses and deliciously evil Hamans.

On Purim, Jews are encouraged to get literally drunk with the joys of deliverance. One is instructed to drink wine until incapable of distinguishing between blessing Mordecai and cursing Haman.

This tradition is the source of the name given to the Israeli Purim celebration—*ad lo yadah,* until you do not know.

Let the play begin!

Source

Jewish Exponent, February 26, 1988. An article by religion editor Marilyn Silverstein.

Purim Recipes

These traditional recipes come from a mimeographed booklet on the history and lore associated with Purim for the use of the Detroit, Michigan, Jewish community.

Hamantashen (Haman's Pockets)

1½ cups boiling hot water
¾ cup milk

1   tsp. salt
2½ cups flour
¼   lb. poppyseeds
2   tsps. baking powder
2   eggs
¼   lb. melted butter
1¼ cup sugar
½   cup of seeded raisins

Scald the poppyseeds with boiling water and let stand until the seeds sink to the bottom of the bowl. Pour off the water and let poppyseeds drain in a fine strainer until all the water has dripped off. Then grind with the finest knife or food chopper. Fold in an egg, and work in ¾ cup sugar until mixture is well-balanced. Add raisins if desired.

Mix egg, milk, butter, salt, flour, ½ cup sugar and baking powder thoroughly and knead well. Roll out the dough ¼-inch thick and cut into four-inch circles with a cutter or glass. Then put a tablespoon of the poppyseed mixture in the center of each circle. Draw up three sides, and pinch in for sides of triangle. Place on greased pan and bake in medium oven until brown. Recipe makes twelve good-sized *hamantashen*.

Kichlach (Poppyseed Cookies)

1   cup sugar
1   cup salad oil
4   eggs
4   cups sifted flour
3   tsps. baking powder
½   tsp. salt
½   cup lukewarm water
¾   cup poppyseeds

Cream sugar and shortening. Add one egg at a time, beating or stirring well after each addition. Sift dry ingredients, adding poppyseeds. Combine both mixtures, adding a little of the water to form a stiff dough. Roll out on a lightly floured board—¼-inch thickness. Cut with a cutter into 2½-inch triangles. Brush cookies with an egg yolk diluted with a tablespoon of water. Sprinkle the cookies with a mixture of poppyseeds and sugar after arranging the cookies on a greased cookie sheet. Bake at 350°F. for 12 to 15 minutes.

Source

Purim: A Workbook and Guide, Jewish Community Center of Detroit, undated, 11.

More Purim Recipes

Anna Goldberg has requested Purim recipes for traditional hamantashen and kreplach. It is also customary to eat cooked beans in remembrance of Queen Esther's diet while she lived at King Ahasuerus' court.

Pareve Hamantashen

3   eggs
1   c. sugar
1   c. oil
1   navel orange, juice and rind, ground
1   lemon, juice only
4   cs. flour
2   tsps. baking powder
1   tsp. salt

Mix in order given. Chill.

PURIM

Roll out in small amounts on well-floured board. Cut in 2- or 3-inch rounds. Fill rounds of dough with about ½ tablespoon of filling.

Shape dough into triangle. Pinch openings together.

Bake on a greased cookie sheet at 375° for 30 minutes or until browned. Yields 40.

Pareve Filling
for Hamantashen

3   cs. prune or apricot lekvar or a combination of both
1   c. seedless dark raisins or currants
1   c. walnuts, coarsely chopped
    grated rind of 1 orange
1   apple, unpeeled and grated (optional)

Combine filling ingredients.

Kreplach

Dough:

2   cs. flour
2   eggs
1   tbsp. water
½   tsp. salt

Place unsifted flour on a board and make a well in the center. Drop in eggs, water and salt. Work into flour with one hand and knead until smooth and elastic.

Roll out and stretch dough as thin as possible. Cut into 3-inch squares and place a tablespoon of filling on each.

Fold dough over into a triangle. Press edges together with a little water. Pinch together two points. Drop in boiling salted

water. Cook for 20 minutes or until kreplach rise to the top. Drain.

Cheese-filled kreplach can be fried and served with sour cream. Meat-filled kreplach go well in chicken soup. Makes about 24, depending on how thinly dough is rolled.

Cheese Filling

1   c. dry cottage cheese
1   egg
½   tsp. salt
    dash pepper
2   tbsps. fine bread crumbs

Blend together with a fork and place on dough.

Meat Filling

1   tbsp. oil
½   lb. ground beef
½   c. minced onion
¾   tsp. salt
¼   tsp. pepper

Heat oil in a skillet; add meat and onion and cook for 10 minutes, stirring frequently. Add salt and pepper. Cool before placing on squares of dough.

Tomatoed Lima Beans

1   c. dried lima beans or 2 cs. canned
2½ cs. water
2   tbsps. margarine
4   tbsps. minced onion
3   tbsps. chopped celery
1   tbsp. minced dill or parsley (optional)
½   c. tomato sauce
    salt, pepper to taste
¼   c. cold water

Wash dried beans, cover with cold water and soak overnight. Cook in 2½ cups water until tender (about 1 hour) and drain. If using canned beans, simply drain.

Saute onion and celery in margarine until tender. Add remaining ingredients, mix well and heat through. Serves 4.

Source

The first two recipes are from *Purim: A Workbook and Guide,* Jewish Community Center of Detroit, undated, p. 11. Additional recipes are from the *Jewish Exponent,* February 26, 1988, from a food column, "Fannie's Favorites," by Fannie Fertik.

A Purim Tour

Ari L. Goldman wrote of forthcoming Purim celebrations in New York and New Jersey sponsored by Jewish religious, cultural, social, and labor organizations.

On Sunday [February 27, 1983] Hasidic families in Brooklyn's Crown Heights [New York] section will open their homes to visitors who want to share with them the joys of the Jewish festival of Purim. The excursion, sponsored by the 92nd Street Y, will provide a rare glimpse into the way Hasidic Jews live, worship and celebrate. Visitors will share a festive family meal, look in on a Hasidic synagogue, view a parade of costumed youngsters and they may join in singing and dancing in the streets. With Purim falling on a Sunday this year, the Crown Heights tour is but one of an unusually large number of holiday celebrations. . . .

The start, at 2 P.M., is from a Lubavitcher girls school, with the reading of the Purim story from the hand-lettered parchment scroll known as the *megillah.* The reading will be followed by a walking tour of the neighborhood, where some of the *megillah's* principal characters may be encountered.

Purim is a time to dress up and parade through the streets. In Hasidic communities, where sexual stereotyping is alive and well, every girl wants to be the beautiful Queen Esther. . . .

Visitors will stop at the area's major attractions, including a Jewish art gallery and the *mikvah* (ritual bath), and at bakeries, where there will be trays and trays of fresh *hamantashen,* the three-cornered pastry with prune or mohnseed filling. But visitors are urged not to eat too much along the way because at 5:30 the tour breaks up into smaller groups for holiday dinner at private homes.

"It is a chance to see Hasidic life beyond the black garb," said Batia Plotch, organizer of the Y's walking-tour series. "They are normal people, with warm and open homes."

Visitors are asked to respect Hasidic tradition. Women should not wear pants and men should wear yarmulkes, which will be available.

The Purim meal is often a boisterous occasion that includes an extended family of neighbors, friends from out of town and distant relatives. The meal is inevitably interrupted by a Purim tradition known as *m'sloach manot,* in which families send one

AMERICA   CELEBRATES

PURIM

another baskets of fruit and wine. Young Hamans and Esthers often make the deliveries.

When the meal ends, at about 9, those on the Y tour and their host families will walk to the main headquarters of the Lubavitcher movement for the major event of the day. It is the *"rebbe's fabrengen,"* a celebration at which the chief Lubavitcher rabbi, Menachem M. Schneerson, presides and addresses his followers. The speech is in Yiddish, but headsets for simultaneous translation are available.

Source

New York Times, February 25, 1983.

February-March

Late Winter/Early Spring
RATTLESNAKE HUNTS

The rattlesnake is a poisonous member of the pit viper family native to the Western hemisphere. It is characterized by a rattle located at the end of its tail, consisting of dried, hollow segments of skin that make a percussive sound when shaken to warn off attackers. Toxic to humans, the rattlesnake's venom is delivered via hollow fangs. The folklorist who describes the annual snake hunt at Wiggam, Georgia, calls it "a folk custom," and he is certainly correct. To explain its origin he relates a story (fragmentary and undocumented as folktales usually are) about the death of a schoolgirl who was bitten by a rattlesnake.

A lonestar rattlesnake roundup

This custom has become almost a ritual, each year commemorating a local tragedy and purging the community of a potential danger. It is also something more: a sport calling for skill and courage, a festival attracting outsiders characterized by "a carnival atmosphere," and a source of social coherence and pride. The same is true of a rattlesnake roundup at Sweetwater, Texas, each year in the second week of March. One also wonders whether these hunts would have survived had there not been professional handlers from commercial snake farms to provide instruction and financial encouragement.

Rattlesnake Roundup at Wiggam

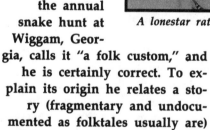

Douglas S. Button described the roundup and provided material on its origin and function:

In southwest Georgia lies the sleepy little town of Wiggam. It is approximately ten blocks long and two blocks wide, the largest building in town being the school-house. Excitement rarely touches Wiggam. Life there is normal; the pace is slow.

Three hundred and sixty-two days a year this is an accurate description of Wiggam. The other three days of the year are devoted to the annual Wiggam Rattlesnake Roundup. People travel to Wiggam

AMERICA CELEBRATES

RATTLESNAKE HUNTS

from as far away as Kansas City to watch and to participate in this event. Even the Associated Press supplies national coverage.

The roundup is held in late winter or in the early spring of each year because the temperature is still fairly cold outside and the rattler, being cold blooded, stays in his hole in a semi-conscious hibernating state. If the hunt were held during a warmer season, considerably more participants would be endangered because of the snake's increased mobility.

The participants, usually long-time friends, walk the fence rows, fields, and forests in search of gopher holes. When they find one of suitable size, they insert a three or four foot piece of garden hose part way into the hole. Next, one of the team pours two or three tablespoons of gasoline into the hose and blows the fumes down through the tube and into the hole. If the team is especially lucky, the fumes will bring out a fairly large rattler, angered by this unwanted inspection. While the rattler is coming out, the team prepares a snake stick or snag loop for him. When the snake emerges, the team hesitates until the snake's head is completely out of the hole. Then the rattler is snagged in the narrow section of his body, just behind the head. The next step, and the most dangerous, is to transfer five to eight feet of supple, writhing death from the hole to a burlap bag. One of the team members holds the sack open while another inserts the snake and capture stick.

The next step is to release the snake in the bag and to withdraw the stick without being bitten or losing the captive snake. If this is the last snake of the day, the team will collect and transport their catch to the schoolyard in the center of town. When the team arrives at the collection point, they will be greeted by a carnival atmosphere. Tents, concession stands, medical exhibits, and the snake cages are spread out across the schoolyard. Pick-up trucks loaded with rattlers are lined up by the cages waiting for their turn to display their snakes. Professional snake handlers are there to receive, sort, and cage the reptiles. Open chickenwire cages of varying sizes await the snakes. The larger ones are held up to the crowd who express their approval through great cheers.

At this point there are probably fifteen hundred rattlers in the cages with their rattlers all roaring like the sound of a jet engine at full throttle. The cages are open but roped off, so that only the handlers have immediate access to the snakes. The handlers move through the cages, counting, weighing, and sorting out the snakes by size as they are taken off the trucks. These handlers are employed by and furnished to the town by two snake farms, one in Florida, the other in Louisiana. Together with Wiggam these farms sponsor the roundup. The farms also supply two bounties: a one hundred dollar prize for the largest snake captured and a seventy-five dollar reward for the largest number of snakes.

Why does this event take place in Wiggam, and why is the schoolyard the main area of interest? I participated in the 1972 roundup with a knowledgeable friend who now lives in Chattanooga, Tennessee. We talked it over for some months before we actually left. Our reasons for going were not as personal or community minded as those of the local citizens I talked to after the hunt was over.

It seems that about twenty years ago a young schoolgirl, around seven years old, was walking alone in the schoolyard when she was struck by a fairly large rattler. The child died later that day. The story continues that the local parents were ready to lynch the town council if some immediate action was not taken. A group of Wiggam's young men was organized to avenge speedily the young girl's death. The mob went through the town killing a large number of rattlers. They did not, however, kill them all; and, in fact, more rattlers came into town. Threatened by this danger, the young men needed help and asked for it from neighboring towns. They organized a massive five-county hunt co-sponsored by the town and the previously mentioned snake farms. The snake farm handlers, skilled in snake capturing, taught the teams how to catch the snakes without taking too many risks and how to do it quickly and efficiently.

At the present time the surrounding towns are relatively snake free, and the snake population of the local countryside has decreased to safe levels again. It would

appear that these hunters have taken the place of the snakes' natural predators to keep the snake population at reasonable levels and are doing quite well. The hunt is an annual affair, and each year it gains more attention and more spectators.

Why the massive local participation? Perhaps the local citizens are trying to do more than just eliminate a few snakes. They are still in some way trying to clear their collective conscience for what they feel was the useless death of a little girl, a tragedy they might have averted through careful pest control. Hence, the Wiggam schoolyard is still used as the collection point for the hunt rather than the larger town square. The scene of the original "crime" becomes the place for its annual punishment.

Source

Mississippi Folklore Register, VIII (1974), 207–09.

Rattlesnake Round-Up at Sweetwater

Round-Up Features

A mimeographed information sheet supplied by the Chamber of Commerce, Sweetwater, Texas, describes the "World's Largest Rattlesnake Round-Up":

This area [Nolan County, Texas], since the days of its earliest pioneers, has been plagued by the harmful and dangerous rattlesnake. Countless numbers of valuable livestock have been killed by the bite of the rattlesnake. Numbers of humans, particularly young children, have

AMERICA CELEBRATES

RATTLESNAKE HUNTS

been bitten by these snakes, resulting in lost limbs and lost lives.... Since the Round-Up began in 1958, approximately the same number of snakes are captured each year. This shows that while the hunt helps to control the snake population, it is by no means exterminating them.

The snake hunt begins with wide-spread hunting and collection of the poisonous reptile. The captured snakes are brought to our huge Coliseum. The weigh-in operation can be viewed by the public only through heavy screen partitions. The snakes are placed in doubly lined and floored pits for public viewing.

Safety and handling demonstrations come next. False tales and rumors concerning rattlesnakes are discussed and explained by a professional rattlesnake handler, hired for this event. The public then leaves with a respect for the rattler based on understanding rather than fear. He also leaves knowing the proper procedures to follow in case of rattlesnake bite.

Rattlesnake Roundup at Sweetwater

The snakes are milked by professional handlers. The venom is made available for public and private research....

Two types of tours are also provided for visitors. The first is a bus tour for interested people and photographers who only wish to see the snakes caught and not to participate in the actual hunt. Another tour is provided for people who wish to hunt with the assistance of experienced hunters. Hunters are also able to hunt on their own on certain specified ranches in the area. All hunters who wish to participate in any of these tours or hunts must register with the Sweetwater Jaycees. The registration fee covers their hunting permit, insurance and hunting instructions. Equipment is available for rent or purchase at the registration table. All captured snakes turned in at the Round-Up become the property of the Sweetwater Jaycees.

A part of the Round-Up each year is the Miss Snake Charmer pageant. Young ladies from the Sweetwater area participate. This contest, held in the 1400 seat capacity Sweetwater High Auditorium, is held on Friday night. A dance is scheduled for Saturday night.

Source

Annual Sweetwater Jaycee Rattlesnake Round-Up, undated.

What You Need to Know about the Sweetwater Roundup

The Sweetwater Jaycees provided this further information:

When and how did the Sweetwater Jaycee Rattlesnake Round-Up get started?

The first Sweetwater Round-Up was held in 1958. Some enterprising young Jaycees thought it would be a good idea to help ranchers rid themselves of some snakes and make some money doing so. That first year, 3,100 pounds of snakes were turned in. The Jaycees made about $500.00. This year is the 21st annual Round-Up.

What is the largest amount of snakes brought in?

In 1960, 8,989 pounds were turned in.

How long do rattlesnakes get to be?

The longest turned in to the Sweetwater Round-Up was 74″ and was turned in by Tom Keene and Jay May in 1970. The longest recorded length is 84″.

When was the last snake bite victim?

In 1971—three people were bitten during this event.

What does snake meat taste like?

It's finger lickin' chicken/fish taste.

Why isn't the meat poison?

The venom glands are in the head and are not cooked.

How long do you cook the snake?

Deep fry it like chicken for a few minutes.

What does it cost to hunt snakes?

In order to sell rattlesnakes, you must be a registered hunter. The registration fee is $10.00 and includes insurance.

How do you determine when the Round-Up is to be held?

The Sweetwater Jaycee Rattlesnake Round-Up is always held the second weekend of March.

Where is the Sweetwater Rattlesnake Round-Up held?

It is held in the Nolan County Coliseum at Newman Park in Sweetwater, Texas.

Where can I obtain additional information?

You may call or write the Sweetwater Chamber of Commerce: P. O. Box 1148, Sweetwater, Texas 79556; (915) 235-5488.

Source

Sweetwater Jaycee Rattlesnake Round-Up Program for 1979.

And that's not all:
For another civic festival sponsored by the Jaycees, see "International Pancake Race."

March

3

DOLLS' OR GIRLS' FESTIVAL

Hina Matsuri, or Dolls' Day, is a highly symbolic holiday on which young Japanese and Japanese-American girls receive new dolls and display their doll collections. The holiday is sometimes called the Peach Festival since the dolls are often decorated with peach blossoms, the emblem of peace and mildness. Almost a thousand years ago, Lady Murasaki, author of the Japanese classic, *The Tale of Genji*, described

doll-playing as an almost ritualistic pastime that employed "diminutive stands, dishes, chopstick rests, etc." This practice evolved into a festive family ceremonial which expresses loyalty to the emperor, visualized in the five-step shelf with the two principal dolls at the top, and the lesser ranks on shelves below. The dolls also serve as models of decorum, their calm smiling demeanor presumably inculcating like qualities in the young girls honored by this festival. The dolls are exhibited for several days, and the festival provides occasions for family reunions and visits to admire the often extravagant displays. The boys' counterpart, *Tango-no-sekku* , on May 5, similarly involves the elaborate display of dolls dressed as samurai and adorned with weaponry, and is the occasion for family celebrations.

Dolls' Day

This observance is described by "Miss N. I." who, in 1934, collected information on Japanese holidays for a study of customs and beliefs of Asian minorities living in the San Francisco Bay area. She used "older," Japanese-speaking informants. Her research director and editor was Paul Radin.

A holiday which is a source of great delight to the girls in Japan is the Dolls' Festival of March 3rd, well-known in American circles. On this day all the Japanese who have daughters set up a little table in the corner of a room on which to display all the dolls owned by the girls in the family. Boxes or boards are arranged in

step-formation and covered with a bright red cloth. On the top row are the miniatures of the Emperor and Empress in antique court costume—dolls perfect in every detail of clothes, headgear, hairdress, and accessories—each seated on a lacquered dais. Below them are the ladies-in-waiting; on the next step, the court-musicians, each with his instrument, and so on until as complete a picture as possible is given of court life in the feudal days of Japan. Besides these dolls, there are numerous others of every description, large and small, new and old, and heirlooms which have been preserved from many years past, less aristocratic perhaps but more lovable. Little lanterns, pine trees and branches of cherry blossoms, in addition to tiny house furnishings in silver, lacquer, and porcelain scattered here and there, tend further to enhance the display. A table set in front of all the dolls is heaped with food which might appeal to them and their fostermothers—sweet wine, white wine, candies, cookies, and pretty tricolored diamond-shaped rice cakes.

All the little Japanese girls on this day don their holiday attire and visit their friends' homes to view the doll exhibits. "Oh-ing" and "ah-ing" over the "little babies" is accompanied by much admiring, caressing, and flattering. The dolls are offered hot tea, and various luxurious refreshments are placed before them, and it is only after they are served that the girls themselves join in the party. Besides thus feasting their eyes and palates, Japanese girls are given gifts of dolls by parents, relatives, or friends. These are added to the collection they already possess.

Source

Southwestern Journal of Anthropology, II (1946), 169.

March
15
BUZZARD DAY

The curious fact that a flock of turkey buzzards return annually on March 15 to Hinckley Ridge, near Hinckley, Ohio, has given rise to legend, speculation, and a local festival. Turkey buzzards are so called because their featherless red heads resemble those of wild turkeys. The buzzards, also known as carrion crows but officially called Cathartes aura, are scavengers, living on dead animals such as raccoons, opossums, skunks, snakes, turtles, frogs, and fish. They soar on warm updrafts, using keen eyesight to perform their function as nature's garbage collectors. The buzzards' winter range stretches from Kentucky, Tennessee, and Virginia to South America. The area around Hinckley Ridge, with its combination of rock ledges, open fields, and forests, offers an ideal nesting ground for the buzzards, who can live up to twenty years. They return to the Hinckley area with almost clocklike precision. Various local legends account for this long-lived natural phenomenon. The Hinckley Buzzard Day Festival takes place on the first Sunday after March 15. It features a pancake breakfast, the sale of such souvenirs as T-shirts and bumper stickers, and a bird walk to the south end of Hinckley Lake, the favored habitat of the vultures.

Hinckley's turkey buzzard

The Buzzards of Hinckley

The Hinckley, Ohio, Chamber of Commerce supplies this account of the event:

The uncanny clock-like return of 75+ turkey vultures to Hinckley Ridge each March 15 has been the subject of folk legends dating back nearly 150 years.

But few other than local historians paid much attention to the return of these birds—until recently.

That is, 1957, when Robert Bordner, a *Cleveland Press* writer, became interested in a claim by Metroparks patrolman Walter Nawaleniec. He told the reporter that he

had personally observed the buzzards' arrival to Hinckley each March 15 for the past 6 years and that his predecessor, the late Charlie Willard, had kept a personal log of their arrival for the past 23 years!

The reporter's interest was aroused. He wrote and printed in the February 15, 1957, issue of the *Cleveland Press*, the longtime legend of the Hinckley Buzzards. He further predicted their return in exactly one month—March 15.

Excitement mounted as the month progressed. Naturalists, ornithologists, reporters repeated and embellished the original story—and suspense mounted.

To make a long story short, March 15 arrived and so did the buzzards—right on schedule. News travelled fast and the weekend brought throngs of media and sightseers from Ohio, Pennsylvania and Indiana.

The township was unprepared for the 9000 plus visitors that flocked to participate in the biggest bird walk in history....

A normally hospitable Hinckley community was dazed by the volume of people and embarrassed to be caught "with its manners down." Plans to prevent such a reoccurrence began almost immediately.

Carl and Catherine Neu, Edward Spatz and other members of the Hinckley Chamber of Commerce teamed up and made arrangements for a pancake breakfast at Brongers Park, the first Sunday of Spring

(the first Sunday after March 15). This day was declared "Buzzard Day." ...

Over the years, the fame of the Hinckley Buzzards has spread—today their legendary return rivals stories of the "Swallows of Capistrano!"

As more learn of the buzzards never failing to return to Hinckley, more and more ask—why?

Theories are plentiful.

Some believe that the buzzards were first attracted by the tons and tons of butchered refuse and unwanted game after the "Great Hinckley Varmit Hunt" of December 24, 1818. At that time, 475 men and boys lined up along Hinckley's 25 mile square perimeters and began moving inward, in one of the largest drives in history to rid an area of predatory animals destroying local farm stock.

An old manuscript account by William Cogswell, one of the first white men to set foot in the township around 1810, makes several references to "vultures of the air" at the gallows of the Big Bend in the Rocky River where the Wyandotes had hung an Indian squaw for witchcraft two years earlier.

The finding of this manuscript indicated that the buzzard had made its home in Hinckley before 1810, so the "why Hinckley" question remains a mystery.

Source

The Buzzards of Hinckley, Ohio, a brochure published by the Hinckley Chamber of Commerce, Inc. Informa-

AMERICA   CELEBRATES

BUZZARD DAY

tion also supplied by Reg Slater, secretary of the Chamber of Commerce.

And that's not all:
Though hardly a folk festival, Clarksville, Missouri, and other small towns in that state have had "Ea-gle Days" in late December and January since 1978, when bald eagles fly south from Canada and the Great Lakes. They attract ornithologists and wildlife enthusiasts and are encouraged by conservation authorities.

March
17

ST. PATRICK'S DAY

St. Patrick, born near the Severn in Britain probably in A.D. 389, is the patron saint of Ireland. When he was sixteen, he is said to have been stolen from his home by Irish outlaws and sold as a slave. After six years as a slave in Antrim he escaped into Gaul. He returned to Ireland as a bishop in order to convert the land of his captivity to Christianity. He was highly successful, and by the time of his death in 461,

Piping on St. Paddy's Day

Ireland was well on the way to being a Christian nation. He is reputed to have driven all the snakes from Ireland, although biologists have assured us there were none there at the time, and his name is always associated with the shamrock because he was in the habit of using its three leaves to explain the Trinity. Irish-Americans in New York City have made their annual Fifth Avenue Parade on his feast day a major American event.

In Ireland, St. Patrick's Day is a religious day accompanied by church ceremonies, much like Christmas and Easter. The Irish do not drink green beer, wear shamrocks, or march in festive parades except as a means of meeting the expectations of tourists. Nonetheless, the enthusiasm for this ethnic celebration in America has had its effect on the old country. For example, Galway does hold a full-scale parade, even if it is paid for by shopkeepers and local hotel owners.

St. Patrick's Day Parades

Charles J. O'Fahey's descriptions of St. Patrick's Day parades of the past are from personal recollections and contemporary newspapers which he cites in his study of traditional oratory associated with this celebration:

Although the St. Patrick's Day parade may be the largest ethnic spectacle in the United States, many Irish-Americans feel ambivalent about it. On the one hand, the green lines painted on the parkways and the green paper hats appear vulgar and

ST. PATRICK'S DAY

trite in contrast to the joyous array of symbols in the Italian *festa* or the Spanish-speaking community's fiesta. What Irish-American does not feel anger at the sight of a donkey cart bearing "The World's Worst Irish Tenor" or a pudgy young woman in a green T-shirt inscribed "Erin Go Bra-less"? How many of us are not weary of hearing the strident sounds of "Sweet Rosie O'Grady" and "When Irish Eyes Are Smiling" lunge out at us from the crowded bars along the parade route? Every year on March 17 I want to swear off clay pipes and blackthorns.

But then I see in my mind's eye my grandfather in top hat and morning suit, adorned with a sash across his chest proclaiming that the Country Galway was his ancestral home. He always marched with a unit of the Ancient Order of Hibernians—like so many other AOH stalwarts who graced the parades in New York and Chicago and San Francisco 30 years ago. In Boston there are still memories of Mayor James Curley riding in the parade in a fur coat, piously shaking hands with priests and nuns along the way; of Grand Marshall Knocko McCormack (brother of former House Speaker John McCormack) heaving his 300 pounds onto a dray horse that hauled the ashcart for the City of Boston; of Up-Up Kelly, a Curley lieutenant, punctuating the mayor's St. Patrick's Day speech by jumping up every minute to applaud Curley's excoriation of the British and urging the audience to do likewise; of thirsty marchers thronging into P. J. Connelly's Bar for a "one and one"—a half-glass of blended whiskey and a dime glass of draft beer for a chaser. In those days the St. Patrick's Day parade had style and verve, and gave you a sense that the Irish had come from the docks and the railroad construction gangs to win a measure of acceptance in America.

In the nineteenth century, the Irish in America had no ambivalence about their enthusiasm for St. Patrick's Day parades. By the late 1840's the annual turnout in New York had dramatically increased with the coming of the Great Famine emigrants. In 1846 the *New York Herald* reported that during the St. Patrick's Day Mass at St. Columba's Church on 25th Street, the Reverend Joseph Burke preached on the life of the saint in the Irish language. The reporter commented: "The oration was all Greek to us; but to judge from the breathless silence which prevailed during its delivery, we saw that the audience was delighted with it." The New York press described the burgeoning parades of the 1850's and 1860's with increased detail. By 1870 the line of march looked like this: a platoon of policemen; the Sixty-Ninth Regiment; the Legion of St. Patrick; Men of Tipperary; 21 divisions of the Ancient Order of Hibernians; numerous parish benevolent societies and total abstinence units (e.g., "Father Mathew T.A.B. Society No. 2 of New York, 400 men" and "St. Bridget's R.C.T.A.B. Society, 1300 members"). Thirty-thousand men walked in the procession of 1870.

The parades of that day sometimes drew complaints from certain quarters. The *Irish Citizen* protested in 1868 that because so many German bands were hired, there weren't enough Irish airs in the parade:

> We are aware that there are but a few Irish bands in the city, but if those who hire the German bands insisted on having Irish music ... their demands would be attended to. We feel confident that nearly every man in the procession would prefer marching to one of the spirit-stirring airs with which they are familiar in the old land—if only played by a fife and drum—than to have their ears dinned with the *chef d'ouvres* of some foreign composer, which could never awaken a responsive throb in their hearts, or impart a spring to their step.

But generally the Irish-American press praised the manly bearing of the marchers and the enthusiasm of the spectators or pointed out parade highlights. In 1863 the *Metropolitan Record* told of a group of boys, 10 to 16 years old, who in green jackets and black pantaloons carried two banners. One was inscribed "The Temperance Cadets of the Visitation of the Blessed Virgin" and the other read: "All's Right: Dad's Sober." In 1871 the *Irish Citizen* described "a triumphal car" drawn by 10 white horses "covered completely with green drapery, fringed with gold and ornamented with mottoes in gold." Surmounting this car was a huge bust of Daniel O'Connell and seated in front of the bust a certain Mr. McClean, "harp in hand,

to represent the Irish minstrel." McClean was described as a man

> who stands six feet four in his stockings and is splendidly proportioned. Flowing white locks fell over his shoulders and on his head was a wreath of oak leaves, with acorns of gold. A long white plaited beard fell down on his breast. He wore a jacket and skirting, with a heavy cloak and drapery of saffron, trimmed with gold and green. About his waist was a red belt with a gold buckle. His tights were of saffron and his sandals scarlet. With golden bracelets, a large Tara brooch, set with jewels, and a small harp, which rested on his knee—his attire was complete.

To the rear of the bust rested in *papier-mache* an ancient Irish wolfhound "as large as a colt," bearing the legend "Gentle When Stroked; Fierce When Provoked." The car was preceded by a six foot seven inch "Irish Chieftain," with "his long-haired, herculean retainers and trumpeters." Obviously the Irish of that time in America revered symbols with origins in a distinctive, ancient culture.

Source

Ethnicity, II (1975), 244-46.

St. Patrick's Day Oration

A St. Patrick's Day oration by the Reverend D. W. Cahill is cited by Charles J. O'Fahey as typical of a genre popular during the last century. Using Ernest Bormann's definition of "fantasy themes," meaning "a recollection of something that happened to the group

AMERICA CELEBRATES

ST. PATRICK'S DAY

in the past or a dream of what the group might do in the future," O'Fahey explains that such orations gave the audience "a sense of participation in a social drama" vital to their self-identification and hence their ability to survive as a group.

At the conclusion of the St. Patrick's Day parade in New York in 1860, the Reverend D. W. Cahill spoke for two and a half hours to an overflowing crowd at the Academy of Music. His speech was filled with fantasy themes vividly describing British perfidy in Ireland. Referring to the seventeenth century, he said:

> I remember the history of the priests of those days, and when the poor priest, with brogues upon his feet, with his vestments in a bag on his shoulders, went from house to house, and there was five pounds upon his head but no one ever betrayed him. He stole to meet his flock in a lonely valley, and many a day the sun rose on their devotions ... and they celebrated the Mass under the broad canopy of the skies in the sight of God and the angels of heaven.

Cahill told his audience how he often visited in Ireland the ruins of monasteries destroyed by the invader. He declared:

> How often have I stood where the altar was, and at the priest's grave and said, O God, if I could wish to make a speech, this is the place where I would like to stand, on the martyr ashes of the dead ... and say, will you send me up some of the warmth of spirit you had when

living, and teach me speak in the defense of my country and religion.

And all this to Irish-Americans who, five or six years earlier, had encountered Know-Nothing hatred of Irish Catholics on the streets of New York.

Cahill, a professor of history in Ireland who had come to New York to help in the Catholic Church's ministry to Irish immigrants, moved his hearers with accounts of his experiences as a priest during the Great Famine. That the priest and his audience—many of them Famine emigrants themselves—were caught up in the painful memories of this disaster is evident in this passage:

> The potato crop failed and that was the heaviest curse—I won't say curse, I will say trial—that ever fell upon Ireland. The churchyards were red and are red yet with the blood of the dead buried without coffins. How can a man paint hell to please the fancy? How can a man describe damnation in pleasing colors to amuse you? How can a man walk over the graveyards of the uncoffined dead and speak with politeness?

In another part of his speech he described the effects of the Famine in the County Clare:

> No one could believe, in going through Clare, the fearful extermination that took place in those days. During the famine fever I saw little children with not a smile on their faces. The little children starving

and fever in their house, in place of seeing them playing in the green fields, their father and mother dead, and the little things sat by the walls and crept about without a smile in their faces. Lamentation covered the country like a dark cloud: the churchyards were brimful, and the coffins appeared above the surface.

It was the practice of these Irish-American orators to balance the tales of persecution and suffering with humorous anecdotes and asides. The editor who printed the text of Cahill's address indicated in parentheses many reactions of laughter to the priest's wit and stories. Even when he talked of the Famine emigration, Cahill could be comical:

Many a time I have gone to the custom house in Dublin to see a ship off for America. I recollect on one occasion of seeing on board an old man with a little child on his back. He had a few scattered hairs on his head, and the poor little fellow had hold of his grandfather's coat behind. This poor old fellow was kissing a dog. "What on earth," said I, "is the reason you are kissing the dog?" Not knowing me, he said, "O sir, it's no matter to you what I am doing." I insisted upon knowing the reason, and he explained that, having been driven from his lands by his landlord, he was obliged to go to America, and that his dog "Brady"—who was born on the same day with the child on his back—persisted in following them. At the solicitation of his children, he was

going to take the dog along with them; and so they were paying ten shillings for his passage. In the meantime Brady began to bark and I said, "What is the dog barking for?" "O," said the old man, "doesn't he hear us talking of the landlord, sir?"

The Irish detestation of British landlords was proverbial, and in the Ireland of that day even the dogs knew who the enemy was.

Source

Ethnicity, II (1975), 247-48.

Irish Coffee

Is drinking Irish coffee on St. Patrick's Day a traditional folk custom? Probably not, or at least not in the same way that eating hog jowl and blackeyed peas on New Year's Day is in rural Georgia, Carolina and Tennessee. Irish coffee doesn't go back as far in time, is not as closely linked to the holiday, and is not found in the oral tradition of the folk (as folklorists conservatively define the term) but in the gourmet columns of urban newspapers. But drinking something had always been part of St. Patrick's Day custom, and given the power of the press and the fact that its sophisticated readership needs folk tradition too, Irish coffee on St. Patrick's Day might well be on its way toward becoming traditional if it isn't there already. This discussion comes from Bill Collins, who observes that "It is meant to end controversies, but is written, with all humble pedantry, in full awareness that it will only start new ones."

Irish Coffee was invented either 34 years ago in the Shannon Airport bar in Western Ireland, or 27 years ago at the Buena Vista Cafe, not far from the bottom of the Leavenworth Street cable car line in

ST. PATRICK'S DAY

San Francisco. The weight of evidence lies with Shannon.

The story is that on St. Patrick's Day 1946 a bartender, coming to work at the airport after observing the hallowed eve, poured a shot of whisky into his coffee to ease his post-operative condition. He liked it. He tried it on some of his customers. They liked it. And so on.

Seven years later, Stanley Delaplane, travel writer and columnist with the San Francisco Chronicle, became one of those customers. When he got home he gave the recipe to an accommodating barkeep at the Buena Vista. The Buena Vista started promoting the drink, so successfully that pride and the mists of time wiped out the memory of Delaplane's gift. At any rate, the "B.V." now claims sole authorship and at last report was selling a Buena Vista Irish Coffee Set—stemmed glasses, a recipe and San Francisco's version of the Irish Coffee Story—as well as a rather inferior Irish Coffee.

How is it made? A thousand ways, 998 of which are wrong. The only proper ones are my way and yours. My way is as follows:

The ingredients: boiling water; 5 ounces hot, strong coffee made from fresh ground beans with a drip filter, preferably with untreated spring water; 1 teaspoon brown sugar; 1½ ounces Irish whisky; *softly* whipped cream. Absolutely nothing else.

The proper vessel is a clear stemmed glass of eight-ounce capacity. One with a handle is preferable; it makes holding the hot glass easier and eliminates unsightly smudges.

Put a spoon in the glass to keep it from cracking and carefully fill it halfway with boiling water. Remove the spoon and pour out the water.

Quickly now, pour in the coffee, the fresher and hotter the better. (There is leeway here in the type of coffee. A dark Vienna blend roast is good on very cold days, while the mellower mocha java seems best when the drink is being served in lieu of dessert; any good coffee will do.) Next the brown sugar. While white sugar was in the earliest Irish Coffees, it has been found that brown sugar better augments the burnished, boggy flavor of good Irish barleycorn.

And now the whisky, which brings up another argument: Which whisky? A roving Associated Press correspondent reported some years ago on a serious argument between supporters of Jameson's and James Power's, the "Catholic" whiskies of Dublin, and backers of Bushmill's, the "Protestant" distillation made in Ulster. The question is moot, because all Irish whiskies are now made by Irish Distillers Ltd., which is partly owned by an American company, Seagrams.

Lastly comes the cream. The Shannon recipe calls for plain, unwhipped cream. This would be all right if we could still find real cream in our markets—the kind that used to pop the cap off the bottle in winter, thick enough to eat with a fork. We can't and so we whip what we have, but lightly. We are looking for a consistency thick enough to float neatly on the coffee, soft enough to let the coffee be quaffed *through* the cream, thus cooling and enriching the hot brew. This can require experimenting; cream so thick that it floats like a wee iceberg away from the lips when a sip is taken, or rides up into your nose, is one of the commonest flaws in Irish Coffee. You have it just right when the first taste leaves you with a thin, evenly distributed, white mustache.

Source

Philadelphia Inquirer, March 14, 1980.

An Old Irish Neighborhood

Ethnic holidays, as here, also provide occasions for political expression and solidarity with the country of origin:

"Que buen dia para un desfile!"

In Spanish, Italian, Cambodian, or Gaelic, it all means the same thing: What a day for a parade!

But yesterday's [March 10] St. Patrick's Day Parade through Smith Hill [Providence, R.I.] was as much a celebration of the Irish patron saint as it was a statement of this neighborhood's ethnic and cultural diversity.

Of course this was a day for the Irish. The streets of Smith Hill were filled with a sea of green hats and green banners and politicians wearing green carnations. Mayor Joseph R. Paolino Jr. and his family were there. So was Governor DiPrete.

Where the cool breeze wasn't blowing, plenty of unmistakably Irish, freckled faces basked in the warm sun.

"We're still here. We've still got our St. Patrick's School and our St. Patrick's parish," said Robert Reynolds, standing on his door stoop.

Reynolds, who said his grandfather came to this country from County Cavan, stared down at his friends and family, sitting on blankets on the sidewalk in front of him. They were drinking green beer and eating homemade Irish soda bread.

"Smith Hill used to be about 90 percent Irish," Reynolds said. "But if you look around now, you'll see how it has changed. You'll see the people from places like Peru and Colombia and Cambodia and Nicaragua. Their kids are in the parade now, too. That's all part of it. This is like a neighborhood function."

A smiling man stepped out of Reynolds's house. He wore a button on his sweater that said: "You Betcha Culo, I'm Italian."

Down the street, at Walsh's Pub, the last place on Smith Street where you can still buy a pint of Guinness stout on tap, patrons drank beer and munched on corned-beef sandwiches....

"I'm an American Indian," said Walter Proffit, raising his voice to be heard over the sound of a bagpipe band moving past

AMERICA CELEBRATES

ST. PATRICK'S DAY

outside. "But I'll bet you I've been to Ireland more times than most American Irish—four times."

As the parade went by, people looked on from their porches, their front steps or an open window.

Next door to Walsh's Pub is the Asian Place, a Laotian restaurant. Inside the little five-table restaurant, two men sitting below a picture of John F. Kennedy ate noodle soup with chopsticks.

Next door to the Asian Place is V. V. Vorasanes Oriental Food Market; next door to that is Albert's Grocery Store for Spanish and American foods; next door to that is the Mikangelo Clothing Shop; next door to that is Dr. F. Mushnick, podiatrist.

But what would a St. Patrick's Day parade be without all the symbols of the things that matter most to the Irish?

Those messages were there, too.

More than a few people wore buttons that said: "26 + 6 = 1," a phrase used to show that if the 26 counties of Ireland merged with the 6 counties of British-ruled Northern Ireland, they would make one Irish nation.

Source

Providence Sunday Journal, March 11, 1990.

And that's not all:
See "Tet."

March

On or About the 21st
VERNAL EQUINOX

The word *equinox* is derived from Latin word roots that combine to mean "equal night." The term is used to refer to the point at which the sun appears to cross the celestial equator, seeming to shine directly on earth's equator.

The equinox happens twice per year, on or about March 21 and on or about September 23; on the date of the equinox night and day each last twelve hours all over the world. The autumnal, or fall, equinox occurring around September 23 refers to the point at which the sun appears to cross

the celestial equator from north to south, and is considered the official start of fall in the Northern Hemisphere. The vernal, or spring equinox occurring around March 21 refers to the point at which the sun appears to cross the celestial equator from south to north and signals the beginning of nature's renewal in the Northern Hemisphere. For this reason the equinox has long been a significant event for agricultural peoples. Emphasis is placed on fertility, growth, and new life, as another planting cycle begins again.

Upright Eggs and the Spring Equinox

Eggs have been associated with divination and fertility since time immemorial. There are literally thousands of superstitions connected to breaking them, puncturing and draining them, burying them, decorating them, reading their shells, and, as here, balancing them. If an egg balances as the day and night balance in length at the equinox, things are in harmony as they should be.

The *New York Times* on March 21, 1989, had a photograph captioned "Balancing Eggs: A Spring Tradition" taken at the World Trade Center. It shows "participants in a vernal equinox tradition" attempting, often with success, to stand eggs on end. It explains that "Folklore has it that eggs will balance more easily during "equinoxes . . . when the forces of the solar system are in special alignment" but adds that not many scientists take this notion seriously. The following account was written by Eddie Olsen:

Thirty dozen well-trained eggs stood eggs-actly balanced on end for 15 minutes

AMERICA CELEBRATES

VERNAL EQUINOX

in New York yesterday [March 20, 1984] to announce the arrival of spring.

No kidding.

"They really do stand up on their fat ends and then about 15 minutes later, they all slowly roll off their axes," Terry Savage said.

About 100 people gathered at a city park at 5:25 A.M. to see the balancing act. It's the only time you can get an egg—not to mention 360 of them—to stand upright.

"I don't really remember how all this works, something about the sun crossing the equator and the balance of the season," said Savage, a director of the Lower Manhattan Cultural Council. "But it works. It was terrific."

It was the ancient Chinese who thought up the ritual; folks balanced eggs—the symbol of fertility—at the Spring Equinox for good luck.

Source

Philadelphia Inquirer, March 21, 1984.

March
21
PERSIAN NEW YEAR

No Rooz and related celebrations of the Persian New Year are pre-Islamic. They are rooted in Zoroastrian tradition, which appears to have originated among the peace-loving and sedentary peoples of north Iran, once known as Persia. A quasi-dualistic religion, Zoroastrianism posits a struggle between good and evil spirits in which Ahura Mazdah, or sovereign knowledge, ultimately triumphs. The god Mazdah was represented in Zoroastrianism as the elements he created—fire, water, and earth—and fire was specially venerated in religious ceremonies, to the extent that Zoroastrians were sometimes mistaken for fire worshippers. No Rooz reflects legends to be found in the Persian epic poem,

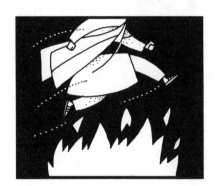

the *Shah nama* or "Book of Kings" by Firdausi, and is fundamentally related to the vernal equinox and therefore seasonal regeneration. In preparation for the Persian New Year, as in the instance of the spring festivals of Jewish Passover and the Seminole Indian Green Corn Busk, houses are thoroughly cleansed and useless articles discarded. Traditionally, during the bonfire that precedes New Year's day, members of the family jump over the flames, chanting a rhyme, "My pallor to you, your ruddiness to me," signifying that winter paleness and cold is replaced by spring warmth and health. The holiday season ends with an excursion into the countryside and a picnic, again suggesting nature's annual renewal.

No Rooz

The No Rooz celebration is crucial to Iranian identity, aside from the political and religious persuasion of those who celebrate it, and it is known to have been observed in the United States at least since the beginning of the present century, according to Mary Martin, Coordinator, Middle East Center, University of Pennsylvania. One Persian New Year tradition is the exchange of gifts of eggs. The following information comes from an article on the adaptation of Iranian political exiles by Rick Lyman.

AMERICA CELEBRATES

PERSIAN NEW YEAR

Informants include Nasser Jahanbani, formerly an admiral in the Iranian Royal Navy, and Ahmad Ashraf, a University of Pennsylvania faculty member.

Last week [the week of March 20, 1989] marked *No Rooz*, the ancient Persian New Year, when families gather for a feast celebrated for centuries. A table is decorated with seven platters—apples, greens, candles, eggs, vinegar, sweets and goldfish—each representing one of the seven spiritual forces of the old religion.

In the center is a dish. On the dish, a colored egg.

It is the symbol of new life.

"Everyone watches this egg, and, at one moment, everyone sees the egg turning," said Mahnaz Afkhami, director of the Washington-based Foundation for Iranian Studies. "It is the exact moment the New Year arrives. Everyone sees the egg turn. At least, everyone claims to see it."

The *No Rooz* feast and other traditional events—such as the bonfires of *Chahr Shanbeh Souri* on the Wednesday before New Year, or the spring picnics of *Sizdah Bedar* 13 days after—have adopted a new meaning for Iran's exiles.

"They take them even more seriously now," Afkhami said. "When we were living in Iran, the traditions were becoming out of style. But now it's different, especially since the Islamic regime has banned them. To observe them, on the full scale, is kind of an act of opposition."

[Nasser] Jahanbani agrees: "If we lose our traditions, our history is lost."

Source

Philadelphia Inquirer, March 27, 1989.

And that's not all:
For related traditions involving eggs, see "Vernal Equinox" and "Good Friday Eggs."

March-May

Various Days
SPRING RITES OF COLLEGE STUDENTS

Rites of Spring are many and diverse on American college campuses. They indicate the end of winter but also the approaching end of the academic year. Final examinations are soon to come, to be followed by graduation—which means the end of collegiate life. So a kind of pre-Lenten carnival spirit prevails. In addition to customs peculiar to individual institutions, such as "Fountain Day" at Clark University or going barefooted on May 1 as was once the practice of students at the University of South Carolina,

there is the tradition of students converging at seaside resorts, the most notorious example being the annual "Spring Break" at Fort Lauderdale, Florida, which at its peak in 1985 attracted some 350,000 college students.

Student rites of Spring are cyclic events and parallel more ancient seasonal rites, sometimes even incorporating details from them. The importance of water in many of these rites recalls a Polish custom on Easter Monday when young people drench each other, said to be based on a Spring fertility rite.

Spring beach rites

Spring Begins

A Clark University press release provides these notes:

The tradition of cancelling classes and arranging social activities on a secret date began in 1903, when a spontaneous "spring festival" was organized in conjunction with St. Patrick's Day. In following years it became customary for Gryphon, the senior men's honor society, to proclaim the beginning of spring for Clark students

by running through the classrooms and declaring the end of the academic day. If the interruption was not a false alarm (which often occurred), students and faculty alike would put away their books. The faculty then would overlook both the classwork and the exams temporarily cancelled by the diversion and would join students for the day's festivities.

SPRING RITES OF COLLEGE STUDENTS

Eventually called Spree Day, this annual rite fostered a particular closeness between faculty and students.

According to ... newspaper accounts, for many years athletic activities like the greased pole climb challenged the Spree Day stamina. Other activities added to the light-hearted atmosphere such as the pie-eating contest, the canoe-jousting matches on University Park Pond, and the pushball contest, in which a giant ball was rolled around the campus green. The famed rope pull, which was originally a fall event, became a Spree Day tradition in 1942. The contest pitted the freshmen against the sophomores at University Park Pond. The students gathered at opposite ends of the pond, while faculty members judged the contest. The first struggle resulted in a victory for the class of '43 over the mud-soaked class of '42.

Source

Press release from the Clark University Office of Communications by Adam Peretz, prepared for the 1988 class reunions.

Fountain Day

This rite is described in the Albany State University of New York handbook:

Fountain Day has become one of the most popular spring traditions at the [Albany State] University [of New York]. On that special day everyone gathers on the podium to watch as the President of the University presides over the ceremony dur-

ing which the campus' huge main fountain is turned on for the first time of the year.

Subsequently, hundreds of students celebrate this rite of spring by wading and playing frisbee in the fountain's pool.

Source

Student Handbook, Albany State University of New York, 1989-90.

Splash Day in Galveston

A Galveston regional magazine carried this report:

Galveston had always been known for its April-May celebration which began in 1920 with "Aquatic Day." It was basically a beauty review and "Splash Day," as locals came to know it, served as the Island's official beach opening. The celebration was as much for the locals as for the tourists because every beachfront merchant knew that once Splash Day hit, those tourist dollars were just around the corner. Splash Day really became a big deal after World War II when local entrepreneur Christy Mitchell took over the reins of the tourist-promoting Greater Galveston Beach Association. By the late 50s the opening of beaches or Splash Day had become one of the biggest tourist promotions of the year.

The 1961 Splash Day was no different. A letter was purportedly drafted and widely circulated through "official" channels (the United States Mail). Colleges, Universities, Fraternities, Sororities, Glee Clubs, Pep Squads, Drill Teams, Marching Bands, Beauty Queens, all were told and asked to tell their friends of the upcoming "Meeting of the Collegiate Tribes" on Galveston Island for Spring Break and/or Easter Holidays, depending upon your persuasion. This also happened to coincidentally be the weekend "officially" designated as "Splash Day Weekend" by the powers at hand and also the "official" kick-off of the tourist season. After all, wasn't tourism the name of the game? What does it matter if the kid was spending *his* money or his *daddy's*, it was still *money* and he was spending it *here*! The drawing board began to wobble under the weight of student response. In distributing "The Letter" they had hardly anticipated selling every hotel room on the Island. . . . By midday Friday, the Causeway was a steady stream of incoming cars. At times, the line on the Port Bolivar side of the Ferry looked like it reached High Island. Law enforcement officials were becoming concerned. What are all these kids going to the same place at the same time for? Hotel management was becoming alarmed. Suddenly, a one-hundred-and-thirty-five pound room clerk was faced with a pair of two-hundred-and-ten-pound linebackers from A&M and a brace of two-hundred-and-fifteen-pound offensive tackles from UT, enthusiastically discussing the respective merits of their squads, and he must find a way to diplomatically explain that the hotel has been "over-sold" . . . that is to say, more reservations were taken than the available rooms on hand . . . How'd we know everybody was gonna show up? The tension builds. The weather doesn't seem to be helping us out much, either.

The air hung heavy and thick enough to cut with a broken beer bottle. The Buccaneer Hotel (present-day site of the Moody House) had no more rooms, but how were they to know that the two pert cheerleaders from Lamar Tech were going to meet the entire S.M.U. swimming team, whose rooms at the Jack Tar (present-day site of the Islander Beach) had been rented to the Baylor Offensive Backfield, and that now, their "double-occupancy" single room was being occupied by no less than (count 'em) nine people? The story was the same up and down the beach front. No room? Double up . . . Triple up . . . Sextuple up, aha . . .

Everyone you talk to has a different story as to who, why, what, when, where and how it all started . . . here goes. The traffic light had changed several times at Twenty-third Street (in front of the Buccaneer Hotel) with no progression of traffic. Horns began to honk. Hotel officials were beginning to get hot. All this noise outside, all this noise inside, and besides that, if there's nine people in that room, we ought to be able to charge extra *money*!. . .

People: in the streets, on the sidewalks, hanging out of hotel windows . . . waving at the cars below . . . exchanging words with the cars below . . . sharing libations with the cars below . . . Tossing half-empty quart beer bottles on the cars below . . . Bottles? Yes, bottles. . . .The first bottle thrown at the corner of 23rd Street at 11 P.M. was in response to a bottle dropped

SPRING RITES OF COLLEGE STUDENTS

from a hotel window above ... The fighting began.

The first police call went out at 11:04 P.M. and it was a report of "two boys fighting on the beach in front of the Buccaneer." At 11:12 P.M., a two-man unit was sent to the scene. Fifteen minutes later a call came ... for help ... then help began to call for help ... then more help called for help ... "There's a million crazy drunk college kids out there ... half of 'em the size of Water Buffaloes."

Five hundred students arrested ... that's the figure released to the press at the conclusion of the weekend-long ordeal ... Charges were made for Drunk & Disorderly, Possession of Alcohol by a Minor, Sale of Alcohol to a Minor, Resisting Arrest, False Identification, and Assault on a Police Officer. Assistance had been received from Law Enforcement Agencies within a one-hundred-and-fifty-mile radius. It seemed as though the back of the revolution had been broken by 2 P.M. ... What brought it under control? Was it the combined efforts of City, County and State Police? The appearance of the Fire Truck on the scene? The arrival and omni-presence of Texas Rangers (plural)? None of the above, I'm afraid. If there is to be any one faction that can be attributed to having effectively dealt with the type of rambunction exhibited that Splash Day Weekend, my bet would ride with the amazingly efficient K-9 Corps that was sent by the Houston Police Dept. Certainly, by Saturday, and throughout Sunday you could see officers totin' riot

guns, and even Thompson sub-machine guns, but that didn't seem to present a real threat ... you're not supposed to shoot somebody that doesn't have a gun ... but those dogs ... that was a different story. So still, the legend grows. Some may ask, "What happened to Splash Days?" As one Native Son so aptly put it: "They had it for a couple more years, and then they changed the name to the Blessing of the Fleet, or somethin'."

Source

Galveston County's In Between, February 1979, 38-40, 42. From an unsigned article titled "Whatever happened to ... Splash Day?"

And that's not all:
See "Splash Days and Bathing Beauties."

Who Came to Fort Lauderdale and How Much They Spent

Florida's Broward County Tourist Development Council released this information:

Due to frequent requests for statistical information pertaining to students who come to Fort Lauderdale for spring break, a survey was undertaken this year [1984] to gain information about this important market segment of our tourism industry in Broward County.

(1) Over the period March 9 through April 6, 324 students from 133 different colleges and universities responded to the survey. These schools were located in the following states, Pennsylvania, Georgia, Rhode Island, Ohio, Florida, Massachusetts, Minnesota, New Jersey, New Hampshire, Wisconsin, Virginia, New York,

Washington, D.C., Michigan, Connecticut, Tennessee, Maryland, South Carolina, Missouri, Iowa, Alabama, Texas, Indiana, North Carolina, Maine, Kentucky, Vermont, Illinois, Mississippi, Delaware and California. A few schools from the province of Ontario Canada were among those responding in addition to the 32 states listed.

(2) The average age of all respondents was 21. Males accounted for 64.2% of all respondents while females accounted for 35.8%. On the average students were in their junior year ready to graduate in 1985.

(3) 62.7% of all respondents came to Fort Lauderdale by auto or van. The next most popular means of transportation was by scheduled or chartered airline (32.6%). The least popular transportation selection was by bus or train (4.7%). Of all means of transportation, the average number traveling together as a group was ten.

(4) On the average each respondent spent 7.4 nights in the area. The greatest number of students stayed at hotels or motels (68.1%); friends and relatives occupied second place with 17.6% followed by condo or campground with 12.1%. Other accommodations which consisted of either car or boat was the selection of only 2.2% of the students. Of all types of accommodations selected, the average number of students staying together in the same place was five.

(5) The average daily expenses of all respondents for lodging, food, beverages, entertainment, local transit, taxis and sight-seeing was $45.77. Based on an average stay of 7.4 nights, each student spends $338.70 on his or her spring break vacation to Fort Lauderdale. An estimated 300,000 students yields over $100 million in revenue to the Broward economy during spring break.

Source

Memorandum of the Broward County Tourist Development Council, by Bruce H. Laster, research analyst, dated April 17, 1984.

Breaking the Spring Break Habit

The Orlando Sentinel *ran this item:*

What started out in the '50s as good, scrubbed, all-American fun—spring break in Fort Lauderdale—had, by the mid-1980s, become an annual time of dread for our area's residents, business people and city officials.

This annual rite of passage had sprung from the collegiate swimming forums of the 1930s and was spurred on by the 1960 movie *Where the Boys Are,* which painted Fort Lauderdale's beaches and weather in their rosiest hues, local law enforcement as benevolent but bumbling and populated this enticing canvas with plenty of attractive young people of both sexes, all enjoying themselves away from the cold winter climes.

Who could resist? Fort Lauderdale—willingly or not—quickly became the "spring break capital." By 1985, some 350,000 college students were cramming our area during a spring period that

SPRING RITES OF COLLEGE STUDENTS

stretched to six weeks and longer, spending some $140 million in the process. At the same time, these crowds were becoming increasingly raucous and more destructive, packing beaches, overwhelming facilities, causing massive traffic tie ups, and becoming more and more unmanageable.

Fort Lauderdale had gridlock, beach-lock and kidlock.

It also had enough: While $140 million generated in six weeks is nothing to sneeze at, untold revenues were being scared off each year by spring break's distinctly negative image—which masked our real visitor attractions and attributes. Hordes of visitors, anxious to avoid "rowdy" Fort Lauderdale, poured into other areas of Florida.

It was at this point that city and county officials made a dramatic and much debated decision—get rid of the students. Move beyond spring break and refocus on a totally new tourism marketing strategy aimed at families and a more upscale market. . . .

Yes, college students still vacation here in the spring—but in greatly diminished and totally manageable numbers. This past spring, we welcomed fewer than 20,000 well behaved college students.

Source

Orlando Sentinel, July 30, 1989. Edited from a special article by Richard D. Weaver, president of the Greater Lauderdale Convention and Visitors Bureau.

March
25

GREEK INDEPENDENCE DAY

Ancient Greek culture flourished in the fifth century B.C., and it was there that political democracy developed. Greece's independent city-states, however, ravaged each other with internal warfare, and Greece fell into Roman control in 146 B.C. Beginning in the fourth century A.D. Greece was part of the Byzantine empire and was subject to frequent invasion. By the beginning of the 15th century the Ottoman Turks had seized control of Greece, which they ruled for approximately four centuries. Then, inspired by the success of the American and French revolutions, the Greeks began a rebellion in 1821. On March 25, 1821, Germanos, Bishop of Patras, raised the Greek national flag at the Aghia Lavra monastery in

the Peloponnese. This flag-raising signalled the Church's official blessing on the Greek uprising against the Ottoman Turks, and is now recognized as the rebellion's symbolic beginning. The ensuing Greek War of Independence was led by Alexander and Demetrios Ypsilanti. With British, French, and eventually Russian aid, Greece became an independent monarchy in 1832. In Greece Independence Day is celebrated nationwide with flying flags, dancing, and church services. Buildings are decorated with branches of myrtle and bay, patriotic artwork, and banners. The week-long celebration also incorporates the spring festival. It is believed that on March 25 the swallows return to Greece from their winter range.

Greek Independence Day Parade

Martha Woodall filed this report:

Konstantine Sioutis, 5, of Upper Darby [Pennsylvania], may have been born in the United States, but he was caught up in the excitement of the Greek Independence Day parade yesterday.

AMERICA CELEBRATES

GREEK INDEPENDENCE DAY

Clutching bright blue-and-white Greek flags tightly in both hands, he waved them happily as the city's Police and Fireman's Band marched down Chestnut Street followed by scores of Greek-Americans dressed in traditional folk costumes.

Konstantine grew tired several blocks east of the staging point at City Hall and had to be carried a few blocks by his father, Paul. But he was revived by the time they reached the speaker's platform at the terminus at Independence Mall and was energetically waving again as the parade wound down.

In all, 31 colorful groups marched, and city police estimated that more than 10,000 observers turned out for the parade commemorating Greece's independence from the Turkish Ottoman Empire on March 25, 1821.

Sponsored by the Philadelphia Federation of American Hellenic Societies, the annual, daylong celebration began with a church service at the St. George Greek Orthodox Cathedral on Eighth Street and concluded with speeches and Greek folk dances in a Greek Freedom Celebration at the Civic Center. Similar celebrations took place in Greek communities across the country....

Peter Psihogios of Havertown, who operates Olympia II Pizza & Restaurant in Center City, emigrated from Greece 19 years ago. He said he attended the event every year "even if it's raining."

Near the speaker's platform at Independence Mall stood another regular, Peter Apostolos of Mount Holly, who was holding three small cloth flags representing Greece, Cyprus and the United States. Born in Greece, he came to the United States in 1920.

Apostolos said he and his wife, Maria, made it to the celebration in Philadelphia every year. Why? "Because it is an ethnic holiday and we are patriotic," he explained. "Why do you celebrate July Fourth?"

Source

Philadelphia Inquirer, March 28, 1988.

March-April

Begins 15th Day of Nisan
PASSOVER

The Hebrew word *Pesach* means "pass over" and refers to the eight days beginning on the fifteenth day of Nisan, the seventh month of the lunar year. It alludes to the story in the Old Testament's Book of Exodus about the angel of death who killed the firstborn children of the Egyptians but "passed over" the houses of the children of Israel which had been marked, by God's command, with the blood of a lamb slaughtered in preparation for their redemption from slavery. On the anniversary of this date, the Israelites were required to slaughter a lamb, and in the days of the temple at Jerusalem, pour its blood on the altar and eat its flesh. Later a ceremonial meal, the *Seder*, assumed ritualistic primacy. During this meal, the *Haggadah,* a book containing the liturgy and the story of deliverance, was read and symbolic food served.

This food includes meat of the paschal lamb; *matzo* or unleavened bread, unfermented and sun-baked because of the hasty departure from Egypt; bitter herbs recalling the harsh life of slavery; and wine symbolizing the fruitfulness of the earth. *Seder* means "order" or "narration," and suggests the order of the service and the ordering effect of ceremonially narrating the biblical story through the generations. Passover absorbed an older Semitic festival of spring renewal. Today it is essentially a household holiday—a reaffirmation of familial, religious, historic and seasonal traditions that have continuing significance. It is ongoing also in another sense, for its culmination is seen as the presentation of the Ten Commandments and the Covenant between God and Israel at Mount Sinai. This is celebrated at the festival of Shavout.

Preparing for Passover

The Jewish Community Center of Detroit published this background material:

A few days before the holiday a transaction is carried out through the Rabbi wherein a sale of a *Chometz*—any matter of leaven which is unfeasible to discard, is made to a non-Jew. This is known as *M'Chiras Chometz*, "sale of the *chometz*," and is comparable to a contract of bailment in law wherein possession is transferred for a period of time.

Also, in the weeks before the holiday, the community is busy in the collection of *Ma-os Chittim*—literally, a measure of grain. Nowadays, monies are collected so that the poor of the community may be supplied with the necessities of Passover.

On the night before Passover a ritual is followed called *B'dikas Chometz*; it is the searching out of any *chometz* that might have been overlooked in the intensive cleaning of the house. To make sure that some *chometz* will be found, it is customary to place crumbs of bread in advance in certain corners of the house. These are collected to be burned the next morning (*bi-ur chometz*) when an Aramaic formula is said renouncing any *chometz* which may have been overlooked.

The morning of the eve of Passover is a fast day for the first born as an expression of thanksgiving for the sparing of the Israelite firstborn. However, to avoid the fast, the last portion, a tractate of the Talmud is studied and finished.

This completion—*Si-yum*—demands a religious feast, and all participants are thereby exempted from fasting.

Source

Passover: A Workbook and Guide, Jewish Community Center of Detroit, 1953. Traditional material on the celebration of this holiday from a mimeographed booklet "assembled" by Max Chomsky, in the archives of YIVO Institute for Jewish Research, New York.

The Maxwell House Haggadahs

Carol Cott Gross supplied this information on an American aspect of Passover:

For 56 years, 33 million Maxwell House haggadahs have been distributed free of charge in markets across the United States. They have been mailed (upon request) to American servicemen stationed the world over, and to anyone else who has asked for them.

The haggadahs, which are used to promote Maxwell House coffee, have often become prized family possessions handed down from generation to generation. Early editions, from the 1930s and '40s, are nostalgic reminders of the immigrant experience, when Jews couldn't always afford to buy them.

It was the late Joseph Jacobs, founder of the New York City advertising and marketing firm that bears his name, who dreamed up the concept of the Maxwell House haggadah to use as an advertising promotion. According to Richard Jacobs, current president of the Joseph Jacobs Organization, Inc., his father had a hard sell.

"The executives of General Foods, the non-Jewish company that owned Maxwell House coffee, were quite reluctant, and understandably so, to use a Jewish prayer book written in English and Hebrew to advertise one of their products," says Jacobs.

Joseph Jacobs finally was able to convince General Foods to go ahead with the haggadah project. He pointed to the increased sales of Maxwell House coffee in Jewish neighborhoods during the holiday of Passover, which resulted after Jacobs had suggested that Maxwell House have its coffee certified kosher for Passover in 1923.

"My father was a marketing genius," says Richard Jacobs. "He knew that many Eastern European Jews mistakenly believed that coffee beans were like lima beans and green beans, not 'legal' Passover food," he explains. (Eastern European Jews traditionally do not eat peas or beans during Passover.) "When Maxwell House coffee was certified kosher for Passover by Orthodox rabbis, my father knew that Jews would buy the product during the holiday."

The elder Jacobs' ideas did not stop there. "My father thought that a haggadah compiled by Orthodox rabbis and imprinted with the Maxwell House logo would make coffee a legitimate Passover item— one that would encourage the Jews who used the free haggadahs to buy Maxwell House coffee."

And he was right on the mark. Sales of Maxwell House soared during Passover. The haggadah, imprinted with advertising copy and illustrations of the coffee, was the first of its kind, and a model for similar haggadahs distributed by other food companies.

Except for two years during World War II, when paper was scarce, the booklets have been used as a sales premium every Passover season since 1934. As a result, the Maxwell House haggadah is believed to be the oldest promotional item in continual use in the history of modern advertising.

The haggadah will also be included in an exhibit, "The Making of the American Jewish Home: 1870 to 1950," this fall [1990] at the Jewish Museum in New York City. According to Dr. Jenna Weissman Joselit, guest curator of the exhibit, the Maxwell House haggadah has instant recognition and is a "cultural icon and a resonant text imbued with memories of seders past." The exhibit will include a typical 1940s-style seder table, complete with mismatched haggadahs, wine goblets and the glass dishes most Jews of that era used for Passover.

AMERICA CELEBRATES

PASSOVER

Source

Inside: The Quarterly of Jewish Life and Style (Spring 1990), 183-84. From an article by Carol Cott Gross entitled "Coffee & Custom."

Dayenu

This chant occurs during the reading of the Exodus story which precedes the ritual Passover meal. The phrase Dayenu *means "It would have been sufficient," and it refers to the "manifold favors" bestowed upon the Children of Israel during their deliverance from Egypt. It is chanted to a traditional tune by the company at the supper table in response to the recitation of these favors by the reader. After each favor is recited, the company sings out, "Dayenu!"*

Ilu hotsi, hotsianu, hotsianu mi Mitsrayim,
Hotsianu mi Mitsrayim,
Dayenu:

[If he had delivered us from Egypt,
Delivered us from Egypt,
It would have been sufficient:]

Dadayenu,—
Dadayenu,—
Dadayenu
Dayenu, Dayenu

Source

YIVO Institute for Jewish Research Archives. From *Passover*, p. 48, an undated pamphlet issued by the Labor Zionist Organization of America, New York, and affiliated organizations.

Games for Passover

The Jewish Community Center of Detroit provided these items:

The majority of games for *Pesach* [Passover] are played with nuts. . . .

"Passover Polo": A small circle is drawn on the floor. Nuts are thrown into a circle. If an even number go in the circle the player receives from the banker the same amount of nuts plus the original nuts. All nuts falling outside the circle belong to the banker.

"*Pesach* Golf": Various places or holes are marked on the floor. Each player flips the nut with his thumb and forefinger to move it from hole to hole. As in golf, the player who finished the course with the least amount of strokes is the winner.

"Logging Nuts": A line is drawn ten to twenty-five feet away from the players, who stand on a throwing line. Nuts are thrown by the players. The one whose nut is nearest the line wins all the other nuts. . . .

"Shpitz Tzi Kopp" (Heads or Tails): The players sit in a row. The person beginning the game approaches the first person in the row, shows him a closed fist in which is found a nut and asks him to guess the position of the nut, whether it is head up or point up, saying "Head or tail?"

Source

Passover: A Workbook and Guide, Jewish Community Center, Detroit, 1953, 10.

One Kid, One Kid

This chant is widely known and usually included in the Haggadah, the narrative of the Exodus and associated materials, read at the Seder, or Passover supper ceremony.

The cumulative form of this chant is old and has many parallels as a song, rhyme and tale. The traditional tune and Yiddish text provided here are from *Passover, an undated pamphlet; the commentary is provided by Leah R. C. Yoffie.*

Chad Gadya
(One Kid)

Perhaps the most interesting survival in the Passover ritual is the use of the cumulative chant of the kid.

"One kid, one kid, which my father
bought for two zuzim,
One kid, one kid.

And a stick came and beat the kid,
which my father bought for two
zuzim,
One kid, one kid.

And a fire came and burned the stick,
which beat the kid, which my
father bought for two zuzim,
One kid, one kid.

And a water came and quenched the
fire, which burned the stick, which
beat the kid, which my father
bought for two zuzim,
One kid, one kid.

And an ox came and drank the water,
which quenched the fire, which
burned the stick, which beat the
kid, which my father bought for
two zuzim,
One kid, one kid.

And a butcher came and killed the ox,
which drank the water, which
quenched the fire, which burned the
stick, which beat the kid, which my
father bought for two zuzim,
One kid, one kid.

And the angel of death came and
killed the butcher, who killed the
ox, which drank the water, which
quenched the fire, which burned the
stick, which beat the kid, which my
father bought for two zuzim,
One kid, one kid.

AMERICA CELEBRATES

PASSOVER

And the Holy One, blessed be He,
    came and slew the angel of death,
    who killed the butcher, who slew
    the ox, which drank the water,
    which quenched the fire, which
    burned the stick, which beat the
    kid, which my father bought for
    two zuzim,
                    One kid, one kid."

How this verse crept into a solemn religious ritual, it is hard to say, and it is equally difficult to make conjectures as to its source and date. The words are Aramaic, not Hebrew; and the tune is a peculiar, monotonous chant. It occurs at the very end of the service. Of course, the Jews have given a religious and allegorical significance to this simple song. To some it means a glorification of the power and strength of God, to whom all things must come back for solution. To others the kid represents Israel, whom God the Father saves from all his enemies.

In spite of the spiritual interpretations given to the song, the Chasidim, a sect among the orthodox Jews, exclude it from their service altogether, saying that it is childish and silly. Since this sect is very old and is especially noted for its piety, and because the rhyme is at the very end of the ritual, it is perhaps possible that the song is a later addition. The fact that the name of God is not given, but that he is referred to by one of his attributes—the Holy One, blessed be He—is an indication that the chant is of secular origin, since the Jews never use the name of God in non-religious songs or proverbs.

Source

Journal of American Folklore, XXIX (1916), 416-17; issued by the Labor Zionist Organization of America, New York, and affiliated groups in the archives of YIVO Institute for Jewish Research, New York.

Carry-out for Passover, Yet

Joan Nathan filed this special feature:

There was a time when the Jewish housewife had to put forth titanic energies to produce a massive *seder* meal. After cleaning her home for the springtime festival that features unleavened bread (matzo) she would change dishes, then with only hours to spare, make gefilte fish, matzo ball soup, brisket or chicken, *hareset* (a sweet relish), compote and macaroons. Finally, scrambling to set the table, she would miraculously complete her preparations minutes before the seder meal. Many men and women still work this way.

Even with the assistance of modern mass marketing, food processors, meat grinders and blenders, the job is still an enormous one.

What could be more logical than carry-out food for Passover?...

Except for the ceremonial seder plate with *hareset,* the typically chopped apple and nut combination, reminding the Jews of the mortar with which they built pyramids in Egypt, caterers will provide entire Passover packages. On extreme urging they will even provide the seder plate.

Locally, for example, David Yegher's Caterers of Silver Spring [Maryland] prepares three types of carry-out dinners: Chicken, brisket, and prime ribs. The meal includes chopped liver or gefilte fish, matzo ball or vegetable soup, carrot *tzimmes* and potato kugel. Dessert will have to come from elsewhere.

Schleider and Shabat, Baltimore caterers, are providing Washingtonians with identical Passover packages with homemade gefilte fish, horseradish, chicken soup, matzo balls, roasted stuffed caponette, potato kugel, *tzimmes*, *knaidlach* and fruit compote.

Both caterers have homemade Passover foods to go, including such items as chopped herring, chopped liver, *kishka* and fruit compote. Shabat is featuring a special potato knish for Passover this year with a potato and matzo meal crust filled with meat.

For those who do not think about ordering in advance, Shalom Market in Silver Spring will carry Schleider's matzo rolls, apple *schalet* and potato and noodle kugels. In addition, Shalom will make roast turkey, brisket and rotisserie chicken strictly for Passover.

The other constant on most Washington menus is matzo ball soup. Again, those who do not want to make their own can go to the above-mentioned caterers or even ask Duke Zeibert. He makes at least 300 extra matzo balls for many of Washington's more illustrious seder dinners. Names were not available, as some hostesses would prefer that the accolades stay in the family. Duke used to make his own gefilte fish at Passover, but feels that it is too expensive today and that the bottled varieties, doctored up, do quite nicely.

Other than the traditional Manischewitz and Barton's macaroons and candies, Four Corners market has brought in a line of European jam and honey cookies made with potato starch from Montreal.

Even Bloomingdale's bakery will be catering to the Passover crowd with daily freshly baked honey cakes, strawberry shortcakes, sponge cakes and coconut and almond macaroons for Passover.

The range of compliance with Orthodox dietary law and customs varies from the kosher-style restaurants and caterers that do not make a pretense of Rabbinic supervision, to caterers who employ rabbis in supervisory rules. The same is true of prepared products. If in doubt of whether the dietary laws are being followed (*kashurt*), consult your local rabbi.

Source

Washington Post, March 27, 1980.

March-April

Moveable

EASTER WEEK AND EASTER

The most important holy day in the Christian calendar, Easter commemorates the Resurrection of Christ, but its celebration incorporates pre-Christian rites of seasonal regeneration. The Council of Nicea in 325 determined that Easter should be observed on the Sunday after the first full moon on or following the vernal equinox, a range of thirty-five days. This set the date of Lent and determines the dates of Shrove Tuesday and Ash Wednesday; of Palm Sunday and the Holy Week immediately preceding Easter; and Ascension Day, Whitsunday, Corpus Christi Day afterwards.

A White House egg hunt

In many countries Easter is a time of fairs, fiestas, bonfires, promenades, and pilgrimages. The Easter parade and the wearing of bright, new clothes to church exemplify some of these customs. The flowers and eggs associated with Easter are fertility symbols, reflecting ancient spring renewal rites and beliefs that have been absorbed into paschal tradition. The fact that the eggs are brought by a rabbit, another fertility symbol, underscores the pagan elements that remain part of Easter. The rabbit was the escort of the Germanic goddess Ostara who gave her name to a holiday which fell at the time of vernal equinox.

Good Friday Eggs

Nell Henderson supplied the following information:

The ancient Persians, among others, believed that the earth was hatched from a cosmic egg. Perhaps from this lore comes the belief in eggs laid during the Easter season, particularly on Holy Thursday and

Good Friday. The Holy Thursday egg, or *antlassei* [German: Holy Thursday Egg], was supposed to stay fresh all year.

According to one lady, a Mrs. Bosworth of Long Beach, Mississippi, the Good Friday egg has even greater power. She says that the yolk of an egg laid on Good

Friday will turn into a diamond if it is kept for a hundred years. One such egg she has is more than thirty years old. According to Mrs. Bosworth, eggs laid both before and after Good Friday will rot, but the Good Friday egg, stored alongside it, will not rot. Further, foods prepared with Good Friday eggs will remain fresh longer than those prepared with eggs laid on other days.

Source

Mississippi Folklore Register, X (1976), 37-38.

And that's not all:
Henderson was given a Good Friday egg by Mrs. Bosworth, laid in 1973 and at the time of her report still "clear and untainted."

Easter Eggs at Tiffany's

Albert Scardino provided information on this retailing tradition:

Gene Moore is leaning back in his chair this morning in his seventh-floor office at Tiffany & Company dreaming about Easter 1989. "Eggs," he is thinking, as he has every Easter for the 53 years since he began to dress windows in the stores along Fifth Avenue. "What can I do with eggs that I haven't done before?"

Mr. Moore, the dean of display art in American retailing, works a year ahead on his designs for the Tiffany windows, the most expensive display space in the world. "You wouldn't want to think about Easter in November," he said, waving an ever-present cigarette. "I have to be in the mood along with everybody else." [Gene Moore rose from a $14-a-week prop builder to a top window-display designer for such stores as I. Miller, Bergdorf, and Bonwit-Teller, as well as Tiffany's. A Vice-President at Tiffany's, he also designs sets for the Park Taylor Dance Company.]

Every year since 1955, he has used eggs to represent the arrival of spring and the joy of Easter. That makes 34 different egg-based displays, so at the moment he is trying to invent new interpretations for this common symbol of creation. He has scrambled them, painted them and strung them into necklaces, some years piling hundreds of them in each window.

Now, at the age of 77, as he approaches the end of his legendary career, he has entered a minimalist phase. This year [1988], in one of Tiffany's five windows, he has suspended a single egg in midair as if by magic and hidden a Tiffany diamond-and-turquoise pin in the clover beneath it.

It is a classic Moore design, the fragile egg ready to drop, the pin camouflaged among the clover and tucked beneath an azalea bush in full bloom. It represents a contrast so full of energy that shoppers cruising past the most important retail corner in the United States pull themselves up short to gaze through the window, then break into a smile as the joke leaps through the glass to grab them....

Source

New York Times, March 28, 1988.

AMERICA   CELEBRATES

EASTER WEEK AND EASTER

White House Egg Roll

Bands played and balloons bobbed as President Bush, accompanied by his wife, Barbara, and six of their 11 grandchildren, blew a whistle yesterday [March 27, 1989] to open the traditional White House Easter egg roll on the South Lawn. About 40,000 youngsters and parents attended. The President hung in for 15 minutes of the four-hour event before slipping back to the Oval Office. Before leaving, he asked one girl if she knew who lived in the White House. "The Easter Bunny," she said. "Who else?" he asked. "I don't know," she said....The American Egg Council gave 5,000 eggs to this year's roll while the White House contributed 23,000 wooden ones as prizes and souvenirs.

Source

Philadelphia Inquirer, March 28, 1989.

A Country Egg Hunt

Carol Farish of Decatur, Mississippi, described this rural observance:

At the White House children roll eggs on the lawn. On Fifth Avenue New Yorkers parade in their spring finery. In Lawton, Oklahoma, the citizens present a passion play; and on Easter Sunday in Stallo, Mississippi, people hunt eggs in a meadow.

Stallo is located on Highway 15 near the northern edge of Neshoba County and is one of the few communities where an egg hunt is still an annual event. Earlier in this century egg hunts were quite common; but with the shift of population from rural to urban areas, egg hunts have, in many rural communities, disappeared.

It is difficult to pinpoint the beginning of a folk activity such as the Stallo egg hunt. One citizen who has lived in Stallo since 1925 says the hunt was not being held when she moved to the community as a bride, but she remembers accompanying her own small children to the event. The hunt seems to have been well-established by the early 1930's, which fact leads to the interesting speculation that perhaps it was an outgrowth of the Great Depression when, although money was scarce, eggs were plentiful, and the people of rural East Mississippi felt a need for an inexpensive diversion.

The Stallo hunt was first sponsored by the two churches in the community and was held for several years in an oak grove behind the Methodist Church. Much of the settlement, including the churches, was then situated near the Gulf, Mobile and Ohio Railroad, some three-fourths of a mile off Highway 15. In 1940 the highway was paved, and many people hesitated to drive their cars on the sometimes muddy and always ill-tended county road, so the egg hunt was moved closer to the "hard road." For three or four years the hunt was held in a grassy plot beside the Snow Family Cemetery, just west of the highway. It was at this time that the hunt lost, for no apparent reason, its connection with the churches. It is still held after the church service in the afternoon (services being moved from morning to afternoon for this one day each year), and the one remaining church is now also located on Highway 15, a mile and a half from its original location. The church, however, makes no pretense of sponsoring the egg hunt, and a majority of the hunters are not members of the local church.

Perhaps the adults hunting eggs (and there are as many adults joining the hunt as there are children) found hunting eggs next to the cemetery fence incongruous, for after only three or four years, the hunt was moved 200 yards east of Highway 15 to a meadow, where it is held today. The meadow provides an ideal setting with gently sloping sides leading down to a flat grassy bottom some 100 yards long. The brown needles under the pines at the top of the slopes, the thick grass in the meadow, and an old fence row on the western edge provide ample hiding places for the more than three hundred eggs hidden each year. The pasture being in use to graze cows, someone with an earthy sense of humor usually hides an egg under a dried disc of cow manure.

The men of the community hide the eggs while the women and children wait at the church or on the porch of Snow's Store. After the hiding is completed and the hunt is in progress, it is not uncommon to see a father who has hidden the eggs helping his children and others who have not been successful in the hunt fill their baskets. In years past, a careful count of the eggs was made; and if all were not found, children and their dogs would spend the next day searching out the missing eggs. Recently, however, an exact count has not been kept.

In earlier years, and in fact until the past eight or ten years, participants in the hunt wore their new "Easter outfits." The dresses of the women and girls were especially important, and their color and pattern were kept secret until Easter day when they were worn to church and afterwards to the egg hunt. A lifetime resident of the community remembers the importance of her Easter outfit. "It was white organdy with many ruffles, and I had new white sandals to match. It had rained the night before, and of course the roads back then were very muddy. I remember walking barefoot and holding my dress up around my thighs. About a hundred yards from the church, I stopped, washed my feet in a rainpuddle, put on my shoes, and entered in style."

Although everyone had eggs during the first years of the hunt, not everyone had the money to buy commercial egg coloring. Some people simply brought eggs undyed; others colored them with bits of crayon; while others boiled their eggs with a scrap of new cloth to receive the benefit of fading. Some hunters also had conventional Easter eggs dyed with "store bought" dye, but there seems to have been no social significance attached to the type of colored eggs a family brought.

One unusual aspect of this particular egg hunt is the hiding of a "Queen's Nest." Traditionally, at egg hunts, the person who

AMERICA CELEBRATES

EASTER WEEK AND EASTER

finds the most eggs is given a prize. At the Stallo hunt, however, a group of four or six of the brightest eggs are hidden together. The person finding this "nest" receives a small prize, usually candy bars and soda pop from Snow's Store....

Residents agree that during the past forty years the egg hunt has been canceled fewer than five times. Three or four times it poured rain all day, and one Easter afternoon a funeral was held in the Snow Cemetery. Otherwise, not even World War II prevented the egg hunt.

The people of Stallo do not know that by holding an Easter egg hunt each spring they are carrying on a tradition which was begun in Western Europe in the fifteenth century. Neither do they know that the practice of coloring eggs was brought back to England by the Crusaders. They have no concept of the cosmogenic ideas connected with eggs, nor of the fertility powers the ancient Egyptians attributed to eggs in their spring festivals. Many of the residents would not be aware of the tradition of rolling eggs at the White House, but they know that barring torrential rain or community tragedy the Stallo Easter egg hunt will be held on Easter afternoon.

Source

Mississippi Folklore Register, VIII (1974), 183-85.

Easter Begins to Look Like Christmas

Henry Scarupa noted these recent trends:

Is the Easter Bunny becoming another Santa Claus?

While some observers assert that Easter's strong religious tradition keeps it from being transformed into a national folk festival and commercialized in the same way as Christmas, others say that in its secular guise, Easter in recent years has taken on many of its winter counterpart's trappings.

Seen more and more often in front yards, for instance, is the Easter tree or egg tree, usually bare of leaves at this time of year and gaily decorated with colored eggs. This practice is "growing by leaps and bounds," says Jack Santino, professor of popular culture at Bowling Green State University in Ohio and a specialist in folklore. "Special Easter decorations are becoming more prevalent, and we're seeing such things as plastic bunnies on lawns."

The marketing specialists at Hallmark Cards, who closely watch the ways Americans observe holidays to detect new trends, have this season [1990] brought out 229 articles for the Easter market in response to the public's increasing interest in decorating and gift giving. Among them are "trimmers"—plastic eggs, ducks, bunnies and other decorations to be hung on Easter trees and attached to Easter wreaths.

"People today are interested in a fuller holiday experience," said Barbara Miller, marketing media relations coordinator for the Kansas City, Missouri-based company.

"They go to family gatherings, have family dinners, do more things together. It's the baby boomer generation having children. Some have waited, and now that they have children they want to provide them with a full experience, either the kind of Easter they had as children or the kind of holiday they feel their children should enjoy. They want their children to have an Easter they'll remember."

That desire has resulted in a number of growing traditions. Miller says that the Easter wreath is one of them. People usually fashion the wreaths themselves, using grape vines or woven twigs, spray-painted white, or they buy straw wreaths from a florist that they decorate. The wreaths are hung outside on the door or inside over the mantel, or placed flat on the table as a centerpiece, ringed with small candles or with a single large candle stuck in the middle.

Also new is the windsock, adorned with a rabbit design, and hauled up to dance in the wind, heralding the season, Miller says.

Gifts, similar to the items stuffed into Christmas stockings, are tucked into Easter baskets along with jelly beans and chocolate eggs, destined mainly for younger children. Typical gift items include decorated bibs, caps and T-shirts, she adds.

Another growing custom is a direct play off the Santa Claus custom: dressing up as the Easter Bunny to entertain young children. According to Shayna Doll, costume and rental clerk at Party Time, a costume shop in Baltimore, the demand for rabbit outfits has exceeded last year's, and the shop has had to order more of the white, furry suits. The cost is not slight. The suits rent for $50 a day and sell for up to $225. Hotels and shopping malls make up the bulk of the customers.

Santino points out that costumed bunnies now appear more and more frequently at stores and malls.

Despite these changes, some observers believe the religious focus of the holiday remains paramount.

"Easter is still holding tight to tradition," says the Rev. Marion C. Bascom, paster of Douglas Memorial Community Church in Baltimore. "I'm sure it's going to last. There hasn't been the same kind of commercialization as with Christmas."

Santino agrees. "Christmas is both a holiday and a religious holy day," he notes. "Easter is basically a religious day, so there's been less effort made to push it down people's throats."

Indeed, recent Gallup and Roper polls indicate that religion and traditional values are becoming more meaningful to Americans, and Hallmark has found interest in religious cards gaining over the past three years.

But the company also features a "contemporary Christian" card, which depicts a spring scene or motif in soft pastels

144

rather than such traditional symbols as the cross, stained glass window and Bible.

"The contemporary card doesn't highlight Christian symbols as much as it emphasizes shared beliefs," Hallmark's Miller says.

Source

Providence Sunday Journal, April 15, 1990; reprinted from The Baltimore Sun.

The Penitentes

Los Hermanos Penitentes, *the Penitent Brothers or Penitentes, is a lay religious brotherhood related to the Roman Catholic Church with a membership mainly in northern New Mexico and southern Colorado. Its purposes are spiritual, and its practices emphasize penitence, including flagellation and other mortifications of the flesh, but it is also a charitable association, and an institution which informs the social and political structures of the Mexican-American communities in which it has existed for perhaps one hundred and fifty years. It seems to have grown up in remote villages at a time when members of the church were without the regular services of the priesthood. It is a folk religious sect in the sense that it adapted itself to local circumstances, and for a long time was unsupervised by the Roman Catholic Church. It has tended to be secretive. Religious confraternities for penitential purposes, which practiced corporal penance,were not uncommon in Spanish and Hispanic America in the sixteenth century and thereafter.*

Practices of a Lay Order

Cosette Chavez Lowe supplied this background on the Penitentes:

Self-inflicted punishment and torture as a means of atonement is probably as old as the history of civilization. However, it was not until the early years of the thir-

teenth century that flagellation as penance became a recognized practice. Under Saint Anthony of Padua, an Italian monk of the Franciscan Order, the lash became an instrument of grace, and for centuries following, solemn processions of flagellants were seen throughout Latin Europe.

Saint Anthony of Padua was dearly beloved as a miracle worker. So pure and humble of heart was he that God bestowed upon him the blessed privilege of holding the Infant Jesus. Hence he is pictured with shaven head, wearing the robes of a Franciscan monk, holding the Infant Jesus in one hand and the Bible in the other. It is not surprising that a religious order, so firmly established in Catholic countries of the Old World, was introduced, by missionary priests and Spanish colonists into the New World. Nevertheless, it is surprising that nearly four hundred years after the Spanish conquest, flagellation is practiced today by the Penitente Brotherhood in remote mountain villages of New Mexico.

With the conquest also came a lay order, "The Third Order of Saint Francis," and as brought from Spain, the group was a gentleman's society purely for religious study and purification, with flagellation as merely a gesture. In the wills of many Spanish Grandees is expressed the desire to be buried in the brown robes of a Franciscan monk, a privilege granted to lay members of the Third Order.

Colonization in New Mexico spread slowly. Early settlers isolated in high mountain villages and cut off from the outside world intermarried with Indians in neighboring pueblos. Religion took on a mingling of pagan ceremonies with the forms of Christian worship, and the Penitente Brotherhood became the heritage of the masses, with flagellation practiced in stark, bloody reality.

The reasoning of the Penitente is very simple. Christ is Our Saviour and our example. Through His love for us He bore the mortifications, the lashes, curses, and tortures of the Crucifixion; so he too (the Penitente) must atone by means of such punishment, if he is to enjoy the fruits of heaven as promised by the Savior.

The Penitentes have their own meeting house or chapels, called *"moradas."* These small adobes are built to blend into a hillside or in the bend of a lonely canyon, to be unnoticed from the road. If built in a little settlement, they are indistinguishable from the adobe houses about them, although some may have a cross above the door.

The Penitente Brotherhood is active throughout the year. They minister to the sick, help the more unfortunate members farm their land or herd their sheep, and they hold *"velorios,"* or wakes, when a member dies. During the year personal misbehavior or violations of the law by members of the order are brought before a committee dealing with waywardness....

It is during the Lenten season that the Penitentes are most active. Weeks before Lent *"los Hermanos de Luz"* (the Broth-

ers of Light) meet in their little chapels, spending hours in prayer, fasting, and listening to instructions by their elders. Lent is rigidly observed. On Ash Wednesday confessions of sins and flagellation in the seclusion of their moradas signal the beginning of active penance. A *"Cristo,"* or Christ, is chosen by drawing lots with straws, or named by a vision made known to *"el Hermano Mayor"* (the Eldest Brother). Often a *Cristo* has been secretly chosen at the August fifteenth meeting.

At this meeting novices are accepted by the order and branded with the Penitente's seal, three slashes cut into the flesh of the back with a sharp flint. Then with a whip, often made of prickly pear or Spanish bayonet (types of cactus) or of rawhide, the novice will receive three lashes on one side the length of his spine and three on the other. He will then ask, "For the love of God, bestow on me the five wounds of Christ," and receive five lashes. Again he will ask, "For the love of God, bestow on me the seven last words," and receive seven lashes. And again he will request forty lashes for the forty days Christ spent in the wilderness. By now his lacerated back will be covered with blood and will be washed with a strong tea of Romero weed, a healing mountain sage. Then the novice will be allowed to go home.

During Holy Week one will see heavy wooden crosses leaning against the *morada* wall or planted upright by the *morada* door. One cold night in March we hid our car in a clump of scrub piñon and

AMERICA CELEBRATES

EASTER WEEK AND EASTER

with Penitente friends from the mountain village walked up the slope of a lonesome canyon in which a *morada* was hidden. Soon outlined against the frosty, starry heavens was the little mud chapel. Feeble lines of light emanated from the *morada* door and now and then mournful voices accented the mystery of its interior. We were admitted and picked our way through kneeling figures to a mud bench along the wall. As our eyes became accustomed to the dim light we found we were in a fairly large room. A black-draped altar stood at one end and in the rear a door stood open into the secret chamber or discipline room. The earthen floor was packed with kneeling people. Black-shawled women and children knelt or squatted on the left, the men and boys on the right.

On the altar were three objects: a candle, an open Bible, and a crudely carved image of Christ on the cross, gruesome, with human hair, a crown of thorns,and blood-spotted body. On the floor before the altar was a black, wooden candlestick holding thirteen candles. A man with a lighted candle emerged from the back room and came forward to stand by the altar and turn the pages of the Bible. As he turned the pages he chanted a litany in Spanish and the kneeling figures responded in mournful, flowing murmurs.

In a few minutes the chanter at the altar was replaced by another, and he, in turn, by another, reminding me of solemn children playing priest. As one chanter replaced the other, the candles burned lower and lower, until those at the foot of the altar finally flickered and went out— one by one. When at last the candle on the altar, beside the Bible, burned out we were told that all visitors and all women and children must leave. The outside door opened and the chilling frost of a mountain night swept in.

We stepped into the half-moonlight. The silence of ages had settled over the valley and the mountains disdained the folly of men. Snow still lingered under the piñon trees; so we huddled in our sheepskin coats and blankets, in the black shadows of a rocky ledge. After what seemed hours, though I am sure it could not have been more than thirty minutes, the morada door opened and again candle light shone within. A man with a reed fife, or *"pito,"* stepped out and sent forth a piteous wail. Dim figures emerged and a procession following *"el pitero"* (the piper) passed not far from where we were hidden. Now several dim lanterns seemed to swing from invisible arms, and in their thin rays we saw the flagellants. Five black-hooded figures, naked to the waist, white cotton drawers rolled to the knees,bare feet stumbling on stones and frozen earth, took a few steps, and then we heard and saw the lash of whips on their bare backs.

Again the five took a few steps and again the slap of whips. Steps and whips, steps and whips—seemed to move in measured rhythm. We knew blood oozed, although we could not see it. Unschooled male voices chanted hymns of penance.

The harmonious chords arose like mist through the rugged canyon and somehow conformed to the stark misery of these half-naked, self-made martyrs. The Penitente procession passed and we arose, stiff and cold, and returned to Santa Fe.

Source

New Mexico Folklore Record, XI (1963-64), 18-20. From an article entitled "A Lash for the Grace of God."

The Death Cart of the Penitentes

Tracing its origin to religious floats used in Holy Week processions in Spain and Latin America, Louisa R. Stark discusses the Easter procession of the Penitentes:

During their Easter procession, the Penitentes of New Mexico and Colorado engage in physical penance including self-flagellation with whips or chains, the dragging of enormous crosses, and the dragging of the *Carreta de la Muerte* (Death Cart). In 1935 the pulling of the *Carreta* was described as follows:

> The Penitente dragged the *Carreta de la Muerte* by a horse-hair rope passed over his shoulders and under his armpits. The axles of the cart were stationary and where there was a turn in the path, the entire cart and its inflexible wheels were dragged by main strength.

Riding in the *Carreta* is a figure of Death. In some areas the figure is merely called *La Muerte* (Death); in others it is called *Nuestra Comadre Sebastiana* (Our Comadre Sebastiana) or *Doña Sebastiana*. In the latter case, Death is treated as a female as often happens in Spain. This may be because *Muerte* is a noun of feminine gender. *Comadre,* in New Mexico as in most other Spanish-speaking areas, is a term generally used to express kinship between mother and godmother. And the name *Sebastiana* is probably due to a confusion in iconography. That is, the naked Saint Sebastian, riddled with arrows, was confused with the naked skeleton holding a bow and arrow.

Nineteenth-century figures of the *Muerte* that survive fall into two categories: those of the Sangre de Cristo Mountain area of New Mexico, and those of the San Luis Valley of southern Colorado. The *Muerte* from the Sangre de Cristo area is a skeleton, usually about thirty-six inches in height, and is in a sitting or kneeling position holding a bow and arrow. It is carved of wood and usually covered with a light coat of gesso. Generally it is unpainted, although there are a few rare exceptions when a design is placed on the body. When not decorated, the figure is dressed in a black robe with a hood that covers its head.

The Sangre de Cristo *Muerte* generally has large hands and a tiny head, adding to its rather grotesque appearance. Gray and white horsehair is often attached to the crown with animal glue. This is then arranged in such a way as to give the figure the appearance of having a bald spot fringed with hair that forms a braid at the back of the neck. Occasionally eyes of obsidian are added, although the sockets are usually left empty. The mouth of the skeleton is always in a grimace, showing

EASTER WEEK AND EASTER

wood or bone teeth. A great deal of attention is paid to the anatomy of the body. The ribs are prominently displayed and the limbs seem to billow at the joints. But the number of ribs is usually inaccurate and the limbs are out of proportion to the rest of the body.

The second type of *Muerte* comes from the San Luis Valley of southern Colorado and is usually dated later than its Sangre de Cristo counterpart. The first Penitentes in the San Luis area migrated from New Mexico in the mid-nineteenth century. The isolation of the area preserved their activities, although the figure of the *Muerte* changed.

The Penitentes

The San Luis *Muerte* is a more personalized conception of Death than the Sangre de Cristo figure. Although the same size, the San Luis figure assumes a crouching position in the cart, while holding a bow and arrow. The figure is usually made of wooden blocks which are later covered with outer garments. Only the hands, feet, and head of the figure are carved in any detail. And in the case of the head, only the face is carved; the rest of the block is covered with a hood. Generally the head is large in proportion to the rest of the body. All the extremities are gessoed and then painted with white house paint. The eyes of the figure are painted black and then covered with window glass. The nose is generally quite long and broad, and the mouth is opened showing teeth of bone or wood. The expression of the face is achieved by a hood which, when placed on the head, shades the eyes and gives them a menacing expression. The hood is attached to the brown or black robe covering the figure, the latter cinched at the waist by a rope or chain from which hangs a bunch of keys.

In general, the major difference between the Sangre de Cristo and San Luis *Muertes* is in technology. The Sangre de Cristo figures exhibit a great deal of craftsmanship and care in execution. On the other hand, the San Luis *Muerte* is an example of true expediency in technique with only visible parts of the body executed in any detail. But, notwithstanding these differences in execution, both types of *Muertes* function similarly in the Good Friday processions.

Source

Journal of American Folklore, LXXXIV (1971), 304-07. From a paper on "The Origin of the Penitente 'Death Cart.'"

The Darkness

Las Tinieblas—in Latin Tenebrae, meaning darkness or Hell—were rites conducted on Holy Thursday, Good Friday and Holy Saturday. From the Middle Ages they took place in darkness. The extinction of a series of candles, except for one, symbolized the burial of Christ. The sole remaining candle suggested the promise of resurrection. The noise and tumult after the candles were put out is said to represent the darkness and the earthquake which, according to the Gospels, occurred when Christ died. Mary Marta Weigle brought this information to light:

Las Tinieblas, or Tenebrae, services are always held on Thursday evening. They follow the praying of the rosary conducted by the members. Immediately after the

Rosario [rosary service], the brothers file out and return to the *morada* [chapel or chapter house]. Those who wish to stay for the Tenebrae await their return. They are very prompt in this second appearance and with them will be many members practicing penance....In some cases, two or three of the penitents will throw themselves face down in front of the door of the church, thus signifying that they wish the people to walk on them as they enter. There is little squeamishness in complying with this request, young and old alike stepping firmly on the bare backs of the prostrate figures. In later years, women wearing high-heeled shoes executed cruel punishment on backs already sore and wounded by the scourge.

When all are inside, the doors are firmly closed. The brethren kneel in front of the altar, inside the rail, except the partly-clothed penitents; these lie prostrate before the altar throughout the ensuing ceremony.

All candles ... are extinguished, leaving only a row of some thirty candles across the front of the altar to light the whole church. There is a subdued sound of shuffling feet and suppressed nervous giggles from the young girls as the villagers kneel in segregated groups on the floor, the women taking most of the space in the center of the floor while the men kneel towards the back of the church and near the side walls. There is an instinctive move towards one's neighbor....

One lone singer from the *morada* takes up his position near one end of the row of candles on the altar and starts a hymn of a peculiarly haunting quality ... As he concludes each verse, he reaches out and pinches a yellow candle flame ... The singer has a carefully shaded lantern under the protecting folds of his coat, so shaded as to throw light only on his song book. Having extinguished the last light, he makes for the low door of the sacristy, which opens off from the altar space to the left. Passing through this door the dim light afforded by his shaded lantern is cut off also,leaving the church in utter and appalling darkness. Suddenly a voice calls out *"Ave María,"* whereupon a deafening tumult breaks out; it is the clapping of hands added to that of the clattering racket of the *matracas* ... in the hands of the brethren. When the noise dies down, some one is heard saying *"Un sudario en el nombre de Dios por l'alma del difunto José"* (a prayer for the repose of the soul of the deceased José—, for the love of God). A subdued murmur is heard as most of the assembly join in a semi-whispered response to the request. Another name is called out, and the request is complied with. Perhaps three or more requests for prayers are called out and complied with when the same voice again calls out *"Ave María,"* and the clapping of hands is resumed with the accompanying sounds as before. As from a great distance, the voice of the lone singer is heard from the sacristy above the tumult of the clapping hands, the *matracas*, and the rattling of heavy chains.

This darkened service continues for nearly an hour, but the time seems longer to eyes that strain to glimpse a ray of light

AMERICA CELEBRATES

EASTER WEEK AND EASTER

and to ears deafened by the tumult raised to scare away the evil spirits.

Some of the children in the crowd get out of hand, but subside when sternly admonished. The whole service is awe-inspiring, with a touch of the uncanny, and to many it is a great relief when the door of the sacristy opens and the faint light of the lantern signals the end. The brethren form a line and shuffle backward toward the door, with the huddled blood-caked figures in the white drawers in their midst. As they reach the door, they make a genuflection towards the front of the church and pass into the churchyard. Heavy crosses are lifted onto benumbed backs and scourges swing again; the sound of the *pito* [primitive flute], as it grows fainter and fainter, marks the painful progress of bare feet back towards the *morada*, doubtless a welcome abiding place, which the name implies.

Source

Mary Marta Weigle, "*Los Hermanos Penitentes*: Historical and Ritual Aspects of Folk Religion in Northern New Mexico and Southern Colorado," Ph.D. Dissertation, University of Pennsylvania, 1971, 545-47. Quoted in an appendix to the dissertation. Weigle's source is an undated, anonymous manuscript entitled "Lent in Córdova" [New Mexico], pages 81-84, W.P.A. Project Files, New Mexico State Records Center and Archives, Sante Fe, filed as "Social History: Penitentes."

The
Penitentes

The Discipline

Father Persone, an Italian Jesuit missionary, was assigned to the parish of Our Lady of Guadalupe at Conejos, Colorado, in 1871, and periodically sent letters and reports to his order. This one was written in August 1874. In it he writes about "the customs of this place."

The *Morada* [chapel or chapter house] is always outside the village. About half a mile from the *Morada* can be seen a cross. Towards mid-night although there is snow on the ground, and the temperature low, the penitents emerge from the *Morada* for a procession. The brethren of the light wear costumes and chant the rosary; they are accompanied by the brethren of the mask who proceed naked except for white pants, shoe-less and shirtless. Some carry a heavy cross on their shoulders, while others discipline themselves to blood. This discipline lasts during the whole time it is necessary to go from the *Morada* to the so-called Calvary or cross which I mentioned before, and all during the return journey. Each brother is recognized by three scars which are made on the shoulders. These scars consist of three slight vertical cuts which each member receives on the day of entrance to the society. And these three cuts are about four inches long. Every time that a brother disciplines himself, the scars are opened with a small sharp stone. When the blood begins to flow, the discipline commences; such discipline must intensify the wounds. I assure you that when such a spectacle of fifty, sixty, or two hundred men disciplining themselves is seen for the first time, it is shocking. On returning to the *Morada* the men find prepared for them hot water and something else (I don't know what); they wash themselves, and everything seems over. Sometimes there are brethren of a *Morada* who make a vow to visit one, two, three, or more other *Morada* nearby. And three or four join a brother of light who serves as their companion. Some carry a cross, others discipline themselves; all this goes on for six, or eight miles; they are naked, as I said, wearing only some short pants in the deep of winter. The things they do during Holy Week are incredible. One of these is the crucifixion. A poor brother is tied to a huge cross by his hands and feet; and the cross is then lifted. The brother hangs from it God knows how long. This year, one of these crucified brethren died, I was told, from sheer pain. This happened in a parish seventy miles away from ours [at Conejos, Colorado]. And it is a wonder how these intense colds do not kill off fifty or more every year. On the contrary, only a few take sick; this they ascribe to a special help from heaven. Poor simple people! Some of them count on buying heaven with such indiscretions, and maybe they do, because they do it in good faith. The chiefs do it for political reasons. They use these simple brethren for their votes in the elections.

One more item, and I shall finish. A brother who renders himself unworthy of belonging to the organization is expelled. But before the expulsion, he is obliged to appear at the *Morada* where three horizontal wounds are made over the three vertical wounds in the back, of which I spoke earlier. These horizontal wounds announce that the person who bears them no longer belongs to the organization and has, therefore,no right to enter a *Morada*.

Source

Colorado Magazine, XXXI (1954), 178-79. Excerpt from a letter from Father Salvatore Persone, first printed in Italian in the *Lettre Edificanti,* 1874-75, of the Neapolitan Province of the Society of Jesus. The translator and editor is E. R. Volmar, S. J.

Penitentes Ghost Story

The Penitentes

Aurelio M. Espinosa retold this tale he heard from "my father, who lived in Taos when the tale was current."

A certain evening during holy week the Penitentes entered the church in Taos [New Mexico] for the purpose of flogging themselves. After flogging themselves in the usual manner, they left the church. As they departed, however, they heard the floggings of a Penitente who seemed to have remained in the church. The elder brother (*hermano mayor*) counted his Penitentes, and no one was missing. To the astonishment of the other Penitentes, the one in the church continued his flagellation, and they decided to return. No one dared to reënter the church, however; and while they disputed in silence and made various conjectures as to what the presence of an unknown Penitente might mean, the floggings became harder and harder. At last one of the Penitentes volunteered to enter alone; but, as he opened the door, he discovered that the one who was scourging himself mercilessly was high above in the choir,and it was necessary to obtain a lighted candle before venturing to ascend to the choir in the darkness. He procured a lighted candle and attempted to ascend. But, lo! he could not, for every time he reached the top of the stairs, the Penitente whom he plainly saw there, flogging himself, would approach and put out his candle. After trying for several times, the

EASTER WEEK AND EASTER

brave Penitente gave up the attempt, and all decided to leave the unknown and mysterious stranger alone in the church. As they departed, they saw the mysterious Penitente leave the church and turn in an opposite direction. They again consulted one another, and decided to follow him. They did so; and, since the stranger walked slowly scourging himself continuously and brutally, they were soon at a short distance from him. The majority of the flagellants followed slowly behind; while the brave one, who had previously attempted to ascend to the choir, advanced to the side of the mysterious stranger and walked slowly by him. He did not cease scourging himself, though his body was visibly becoming very weak, and blood was flowing freely from his mutilated back. Thus the whole procession continued in the silence of the night, the stranger leading the Penitentes through abrupt paths and up a steep and high mountain. At last, when all were nearly dead with fatigue, the mysterious Penitente suddenly disappeared, leaving his good companion and the other Penitentes in the greatest consternation. The Penitentes later explained that this was doubtless the soul of a dead Penitente who had not done his duty in life—a false Penitente—and God had sent him back to earth to scourge himself properly, before allowing him to enter heaven.

Source

Journal of American Folklore, XXIII (1910), 407-08.

April

1

ALL FOOLS' DAY

On this day of license, practical jokes may be played with impunity: sending people on foolish errands, crying wolf, putting salt in the sugar bowl. The custom which is called "hunting the gowk (cuckoo, hence fool)" in Scotland and *"poisson d'avril"* in France may well reflect spring sexual license (for instance, there is the traditional play on the words "cuckoo" and "cuckold") and the efforts to deceive evil spirits which might interfere with fertility at the time when planting and sprouting are occurring. It is also associated with civil and church rebellion such as the Lord of Misrule

and Boy Bishop ceremonies.

The origin of the custom is uncertain, but it seems to have come about in France as a result of the change to the Gregorian calendar in 1582 when New Year's was moved from March 25 to January 1. Thus, the first April fools may have been people who failed to make the proper adjustment. In Mexico, where the borrowing of trivial items and the failure to return them is a feature, a similar day is celebrated on December 28, and some countries like Germany and Norway have two such days on the first and last dates in April.

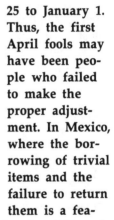

April Fool's Tricks

Annie W. Whitney and Caroline C. Bullock collected these items:

The first of April has always been celebrated as All Fool's Day.

The April-first greeting of a teacher who taught about 1864 was invariably,

"Oh, come out and see the flock of wild geese!"

The little children would catch each other by calling, "Oh, look at that little bird," "It's snowing!" "You have a black mark on your face," etc. Tying a rag on the back of the dress, and pinning a label on the back were popular.

ALL FOOLS' DAY

Filling the sugar bowl with salt, stuffing a biscuit with cotton and offering an empty egg shell at breakfast, were good old tricks.

Glueing a penny on the pavement, stuffing an old purse with paper and dropping it, tying handkerchiefs to strings and dropping them, then pulling them back when almost to be picked up were favorite performances. Some sent false orders or April Fool messages through the mails.

Source

Memoirs of the American Folklore Society, XVIII (1925), 119, from "Folk-Lore from Maryland." Informants not given.

April Fools

Edwina B. Doran collected this information in White County, Tennessee:

Make up any kind of story such as "Your shoe is untied," and when the person looks, greet him with, "April Fool." If it is a later day, he says,

> "Ha, ha. April Fool's gone and past;
> You're the biggest fool at last."

Put coffee sacks filled with dirt in the road. Hide and see who picks them up.

Fill a paper sack with manure and set fire to it outside someone's door. Knock. Then watch the person stamp out the fire.

Source

"Folklore from White County, Tennessee," Ph.D. Dissertation, George Peabody College for Teachers, 1969, 194. Collected in 1967-68. Doran's informants were residents or former residents of White County, but she does not always indicate her specific sources.

Adult April Fool

April Fool tricks are not, it seems, confined to children. Catherine Harris Ainsworth published a number of accounts of pranks played by adult factory and office workers in the Buffalo area of New York in her book *American Calendar Customs.* One involved bakery employees in collusion with the manager telling a girl who had just finished her shift that she was to substitute for the next shift as well. One involved putting red pepper in a worker's coffee thermos. He took the prank seriously and thought the boss had done it. The trick resulted in an argument. The man quit, and ultimately he ran off with the boss's secretary. Such childish tricks as taping down telephone hooks so the phone will continue to ring after being answered, taping filing cabinets closed, and stapling folders together seem to have been common, as were more elaborate pranks such as faking phone calls, issuing tickets for nonexistent parties, and creating bomb scares. We recorded these anecdotes during an interview with an insurance salesman in a Providence, Rhode Island office in the summer of 1984. The informant wished to remain anonymous. The pranks, in his words, "were played a while back."

Yeah, they play April Fool tricks in the office. I remember a couple that were pretty bad. One, the guys all park out on the street and run up a lot of parking tickets. Mostly, this is ignored. I mean the city's lax about it and some of the guys know the cops. They even come up and get coffee from the girls. But still those tickets are there. One guy had run up a real lot, maybe $500-600. So April Fool we got this cop to come up to the office and pretend to be looking for him. When he found him, he said that there'd been a big crackdown on traffic tickets and he'd have to come along to the Police Station. The guy nearly died, turned white as a sheet, and nobody let on it was a trick till just as they were going out the door. Then we all yelled "April Fool."

But the worst one . . . I don't know if it ever happened. I just heard about it. I wasn't in on it. One of the salesmen had been fooling around with a secretary. He was married and everyone in the office knew about it, though I guess his wife didn't. The girl was a bit crazy, a real screwball, and one of the other salesmen persuaded her to tell her boy friend she was pregnant as an April Fool joke. I guess she went in his office and left the door open so everyone could hear. Finally, it got bad enough she had to tell him it was a joke. You know, most guys would have really been pissed off, but I guess this guy was a little crazy too. He thought it was a big joke. Maybe he was just happy it was an April Fool joke. But he just laughed and kept right on going around with her.

Source

University of Pennsylvania Folklore Archives, undated.

April Fool Computerized

This item proved to be an "April Fool"; such warnings were widely circulated but the virus did not materialize:

An especially destructive computer virus set to "go off" on April 1 was recently discovered in West Germany. This virus attaches itself to ".com" files on IBM and IBM-compatible micro-computers. The only way currently known to detect it is by using any popular utility program . . . to search for the virus's "signature" in the first 7 bytes of a ".com" file.

The virus destroys all data on hard drives and diskettes inserted into the computer. A precaution for users of microcomputers is to backup their data files.

Although no current information has surfaced on the worldwide virus alert list about Macintosh or UNIX-based computers, all users should be aware that April 1 may bring out the worst in virus terrorists. Be alert for any unusual system behavior.

Source

An official notice by the University of Pennsylvania Computing Resource Center published in the *Almanac*, the university's internal newsletter, of March 27, 1990.

April

First Monday
TATER DAY

Little did Christopher Columbus know that in bringing to the Old World the funny-looking orange tuber called *batats* by inhabitants of the New World, he would provide the roots for what has become the nation's oldest trade day.

Cultivated long ago by the Aztecs, the sweet potato is native, in two varieties, to Peru, Central America and the West Indies; it was first introduced in Europe and then to Asia, where it

'Tater Day festivities

has become a dietary staple. The many sweet potato varieties are distinguished by their leaf shape, and are primarily a southern crop in the United States—where they are as "rampant as the kudzu vine"—although they are to be found as far north as Massachusetts. Rich in vitamin A, sweet potatoes are mostly grown for human consumption in the form of

flour, starch, alcohol or glucose, and they are also grown to be used as livestock feed. Originally a market fair where sweet potato slips for spring planting could be bought, Tater Day has been revived as a country carnival, with the usual games of chance, side shows, and rides. In Benton, Kentucky, Sweet Potato Day— replete with horse and mule pulling contests, beauty pageant, quilt show and flea market—has been celebrated since 1843, making it the oldest trade day in the nation. Any Benton resident would be quick to point out that the yam, another orange tuber, is not to be confused with the sweet potato, which belongs to an entirely different family. And don't ever forget that 'Tater Day is not to be confused with the annual Yambilee Festival, which awards prizes to the best yam recipes in the South.

Sweet Potato Day

This information and the accompanying recipes were obtained from members of the Kentucky Federation of Women's Clubs. The glazed sweet potatoes recipe is from Lummie Taylor of Beaver Dam; the potato pudding recipe from Mrs. Carl Jones of Clinton:

Tater Day, held in Benton [Kentucky] on the first Monday in April, was organized in 1843 and has been revitalized. Originally Tater Day was the time when farmers came to Benton to sell or buy "sweet tater" slips for planting and to visit with friends and relatives and maybe do a little mule swapping or knife trading. Nowadays you might have difficulty in finding a sweet tater but the crowds come—an estimated 15,000 in 1974. In honor of the day you might want to try one of our sweet potato recipes.

Glazed Sweet Potatoes

9   large sweet potatoes
1   tbsp. water
1   tbsp. sugar
4   tbsp. butter

Boil potatoes 50 minutes. Pare them, cut in halves lengthwise, and sprinkle both sides with salt. Place them cut side down in a dripping pan. Put sugar and water in a small pan; stir until sugar is dissolved. Add butter and stir over low heat until it melts. Baste the potatoes with this liquid and bake in a 400⁰ oven 20 minutes. The potatoes should be glossy brown when they come from the oven. Serves 12.

Sweet Potato Pudding

1   egg
½   cup sugar
¼   cup melted butter
1   cup grated sweet potatoes
1⅓ cups milk
¼   tsp. allspice
¼   tsp. nutmeg
      pinch of salt

Beat egg and add remaining ingredients. Pour into a greased baking dish. Bake at 400⁰ for 30 minutes or until thick, stirring occasionally. Serves 4.

Source

Kentucky Hospitality (Kentucky Federation of Women's Clubs), 1976, 176.

April
8

BIRTHDAY OF THE BUDDHA

The founder of Buddhism had the given name, Siddhartha; the family name, Gautama; the clan name, Shaka; and he is commonly called the Buddha, which in Sanskrit means "the enlightened one." He is also called the Tathagata (he who has come thus), Bhagavat (the Lord), and Sugata (well-gone). He is thought to have lived in India from c. 563 B.C. to 483 B.C. In his youth Siddhartha lived the sheltered and luxurious life of a prince. At age twenty-nine he left the palace grounds and for the first time encountered suffering, poverty, and death. From that moment he dedicated his life to the pursuit of enlightenment. At age thirty-five he reached enlightenment, becoming a Buddha. For the next forty-five years he was a travelling teacher. His teachings, called Buddha's Dharmas, advocate a way of life patterned after his own path to enlightenment. The process is accompanied by four *jnanas*, or holy states: compassion, joy, peace, and equanimity. Buddha's birthday is celebrated by millions of Buddhists in Sri Lanka, Tibet, Nepal, Burma, Vietnam, Korea, China, Japan, and elsewhere in Asia, and by Buddhists in the United States.

Buddha's Birthday in California

This description comes from material collected by "Miss N. I." in 1934 on beliefs of Asian minorities in the San Francisco Bay area:

Among the Buddhist holidays [the] celebration on April 8th, the day of the birth of Shaka [a name for the Buddha] ... is the most important celebration of them all. . . . To commemorate the birthday anniversary of Shaka, ... the Buddhist temples in Japan and America alike construct [in 1934] a temporary platform, the roof of which is covered with flowers, in keeping with the traditional story that flowers rained at the birth of Shaka. On this platform is placed an image of the infant Buddha in a tub filled with licorice tea. The

members of the church then take part in the ritual of pouring licorice tea over the figure of Buddha with bamboo ladles to signify the act of bathing him. They then drink some of the sweet tea themselves, an act which is supposed to effect the purification of their souls, and cause them to become Buddha-like in thought, word, and deed.

Source

Southwestern Journal of Anthropology, II (1946), 177. The research director and editor of this material was Paul Radin. Informants were "older residents of Oakland and Berkeley" and the interviews upon which this description is based were conducted in Japanese.

April

Third Wednesday
SHAD PLANKING

Outdoor political rallies at a time conveniently preceding elections were common when America was more rural and less under the sway of the mass media. They were highlighted by flamboyant oratory, hard liquor, and regional food prepared out-of-doors, such as barbecue, fish stew, and chicken bog, usually cooked according to a traditional recipe by a local specialist. Their number and political importance have diminished, but they are still much enjoyed for their food, drink, and good fellowship. For more than thirty years, when the shad and the politicians are running, the Wakefield, Virginia, Ruritan Club has served them up in its own distinctive way. The shad are cooked as much by the hot sauce in which they are basted as the bed of wood coals over which they remain for many hours. The festivities begin with informal drinking, followed by political oratory, usually supplied by a senator or governor, or at least a congressman. Then comes the eating.

Shad plankers and politicians

The Wakefield Shad-planking

Getting Ready

This background was supplied by James W. Renney, a Wakefield attorney, master of ceremonies for the shad planking since 1959:

The work will get under way at the [Wakefield] Sportsmen's Club on Tuesday, April 19, [1977] at 3:00 P.M. when a truck arrives with over a ton and a half of shad and rock fish. The rock are mainly eaten by the workers and the shad are planked for the guests.

Men from Wakefield farms, business establishments and offices will meet there, and, according to the usual schedule, the entire lot of fish will be scaled, dressed and iced by 6:00 P.M. Then a supper of shad roe and fried rock will be served the workers.

At 5:00 A.M. the following morning, a 150-foot long fire will be lighted and

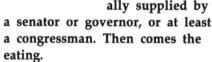

coaxed into a slow bank of coals. At this state the "nailing committee" will take over and tack the shad to planks which will be lined up on each side of the fire. The cooking process is underway by 9:00 A.M. and will continue throughout the day. The fish will be basted no less than 15 times with a special "secret" sauce prepared by Dr. E. C. Nettles of Wakefield. The cooking will end shortly before the address by the Honorable Robert W. Daniel, Jr., at 4:30 P.M. There will be approximately 100 workers assisting in the preparation and serving of a ton and a half of shad, a half ton of slaw, and many hundreds of pounds of cornbread cooked by Lyle Pond and his crew of expert cookers.

Plankers

Blaine Harden filed this report from Wakefield:

The gentlemen of Virginia, with politics on their minds and whiskey in their hands, assembled here [Wakefield, Virginia April 16, 1980] this afternoon in the piney woods for the 32nd annual shad planking, a one-day festival of boney fish, speechmaking and the search for ice.

The barriers that for years kept women, blacks and Republicans away from the picnic supposedly have fallen. But women today were as scarce as abolitionists: blacks mostly tended the fish, and the Republicans, according to many longtime shad plankers, now sound so much like old-time Virginia Democrats that they are indistinguishable from the regular.

A shad planker is a man, a member of the local Ruritan Club in this town of 1,000 located about 60 miles southeast of Richmond, who got up early this morning, took a galvanized, sheet-metal nail and a hammer, and stuck a cleaned shad to an oak board. The shad then was smoked for nearly six hours over an oak fire.

The salty taste of that bony fish— along with the appeal of Virginia's top elected officials and a sunny afternoon— drew nearly 4,300 people, almost all white males.

The record crowd that paid $7.50 per person for a ticket to the picnic, impatiently listened to the traditional patriotic speech that briefly interferes with the drinking here. Virginia Lt. Gov. Charles S. (Chuck) Robb of McLean, considered the likely Democratic nominee for governor next year, even prefaced his speech by saying, "Nobody comes to shad planking to hear speeches. We come here to quench our thirst.". . .

When the shad-planking picnics began more than three decades ago, political control of Virginia was in the hands of Sen. Harry F. Byrd, Sr., and his political machine. Conservative political power in the state, for the most part, is now held by the Republican Party.

Gov. John N. Dalton, who spoke briefly at today's picnic, didn't let the opportunity of promoting his party's strength slip away.

The Wakefield Shad Planking

AMERICA CELEBRATES

SHAD PLANKING

"When I first came here in 1969," said Dalton, as the afternoon sun filtered through the pine trees, "I bet more than 100 people told me I was the first elected Republican figure ever seen at the shad planking."

Up until this year attendance at the picnic was by invitation only. But 4,000 tickets went up for sale to the general public late this winter, and they were all purchased within a month.

Despite changes in the political labels of the politicians who run Virginia, one thing that has remained constant at the shad planking is the sauce.

Dr. E. C. Nettle, a 78-year-old Wakefield physician who stands 6 feet 5 and today wore a bright red sweater, plaid slacks and a tan wool coat, is in charge of the sauce. It is said here that the best way to know the sauce—which is poured over the shad several times—is to stick your finger in it, that is, if "you got a finger you don't much care about."

Dr. Nettle, who knows the sauce better than any Virginian, enumerated the potent ingredients:

"We got eight gallons of Worchestershire sauce, 45 pounds of butter, 18 quarts of lemon juice, 13 pounds of black pepper and four pounds of red pepper." Nettle said there was also about 18 pounds of salt in the sauce. When the sauce is poured on an open fire it bursts into flame.

Before most of the men had a chance to taste Dr. Nettle's sauce on the 700 pounds of flounder, 400 pounds of rockfish and 2,900 pounds of shad, they sampled some of their own—mostly out of the tailgates and trunks of their cars.

Spencer Perkins, 72, an optometrist from Petersburg, parked his green 1972 Dodge in the pasture parking lot about one-half mile from where the speech-making took place. He and three of his friends broke out a fifth of Jim Beam bourbon, opened an ice chest and gathered around the rear of the car for some conversation. "When you come out here and have two or three drinks, you love everybody, everybody is your friend," said Perkins.

Source

Washington Post, April 17, 1980. From an article datelined Wakefield, Virginia, April 16.

And that's not all:
See "Labor Day Politicking" and "Return Day in Delaware."

April

Usually 4th Friday
ARBOR DAY

Arbor Day is celebrated in various states across the nation, in various ways and at various times, in accordance with planting seasons. Although the planting of trees for memorial and ritualistic reasons is an ancient custom, J. Sterling Morton, a Nebraska newspaper publisher, is sometimes given credit for starting formal Arbor Days in the United States in 1872. That year more than one million trees were planted, and the day has been a public holiday in Nebraska ever since. At the Morton Orchard and Tree Farm in Nebraska City, Morton's home town, Arbor Day events include a carnival, musical contests and festivals, an arts and crafts show, educational programs, and

sports competitions, in addition to the tree-planting activities. Elsewhere across the country Arbor Day observances often involve schoolchildren in tree-planting ceremonies. Recently, with media reports on deforestation and global warming from the greenhouse effect, tree-planting has assumed greater importance. Earth Day, first observed on April 22, 1970, is often celebrated in conjunction with Arbor Day and promotes a broader environmental message. The twentieth anniversary celebration of Earth Day in 1990 revealed a tremendous cultural upswell of environmental concern, in which the more traditional Arbor Day continues to have a place.

Observing Arbor Day

William E. Schmidt reported on Arbor Day activities:

While city workers passed out 1,500 honey locust seedlings today in small plastic bags, schoolchildren, politicians and

officials gathered downtown in fog and drizzle for Chicago's annual celebration of trees.

A bake sale and poster contest, speeches and poetry all marked Arbor Day,

AMERICA CELEBRATES

ARBOR DAY

celebrated in most states on the fourth Friday of April....

In Wisconsin, Gov. Tommy G. Thompson urged planting a million trees this week to replace those lost in the drought and forest fires last year. In one project, 130 seventh grade students from Shawano, Wisconsin, planted 5,000 seedlings in an area burned out by a forest fire last summer.

In New Jersey, there were tree-planting ceremonies in 37 communities marking Arbor Day, and in New York trees were planted on the grounds of the Governor's Mansion and in a park at Binghamton....

A volunteer group in Chicago, Neighborwoods, has planted more than 800 trees on vacant lots and empty city land since it began two years ago.

On Friday, in a ceremony at a Roman Catholic high school, Neighborwoods planted a 6-foot sapling that is a direct descendant of the Stelmuze, a 2,000-year-old, 30-foot-wide English Oak in Lithuania that is revered as a national monument.

Source

New York Times, April 29, 1989.

And that's not all:
See "Tu B'Shevat."

Memorial Trees for Children

Kristin E. Holmes noted this special observance:

Spindly, yet graceful, the trees stood only a few feet apart in Upper Southampton [Pennsylvania], wrapped in ribbons of pink and blue.

A warm breeze slightly tipped the branches of the Tall Red Maples, rustling the 8-inch-by-11-inch signs attached to each of them.

Dianilou. Tierra. Aubrey. Jamil. Celise. One name was written on each of the signs. One name was for each of five sick children who had died—of AIDs, sudden infant death syndrome or other maladies—while in foster care.

The children were remembered yesterday [April 28, 1989] at a special Arbor Day memorial ceremony at Bethanna, a social-service agency in Bucks County that helps children who are abused, neglected or who suffer medical problems.

Before 80 guests and staffers, members of the nonprofit Christian organization planted a tree for each of the five "medically needy" children who died between December 1987 and December 1988.

"There is a fear that these children will die forgotten ... and that would be a second tragedy," said Scott Eldredge, a foster care supervisor at the agency. "We had to do something to remind the community of their responsibility to take care of these children."

Planting the trees was a gesture that the Bethanna staff hopes will spread beyond their 40-acre grounds to places where people want to commemorate the lives of sick children who have died. It is a gesture they hope will become as synonymous with Arbor Day as planting a tree.

Source

Philadelphia Inquirer, April 29, 1989.

April
30
BELTANE

Much Western European folklore owes a debt to the Celts, a group of peoples whose presence dates as far back as the second millenium B.C., and whose roots reach from southwest Germany and eastern France all across the British Isles.

The Celts believed in a demonic universe and submitted to the ministry of the Druids, a priestly upper class. The Druids worshipped a pantheon of nature deities in an ex-

tremely ritualistic manner, and their religious ceremonies are believed to have taken place primarily in tree groves and at river sources and lakes. Beltane, the Celtic name for the first day of May, has long been celebrated among the Celts; among the Druids of Britain, Beltane divided the year in half and was observed by kindling hill-top "beltane fires" to honor the sun god. In fact, "beltane" is popularly believed to be derived from a Gaelic word meaning "bright fire." In Scotland two fires were built close together and cattle driven between them to ward off disease before putting them out to pasture for the new season. The fires were lit on May Day Eve in keeping with the belief that each day begins with the setting of the sun the night before. Also in Scotland, Beltane was one of the quarter-days or term days when rents were due and debts were settled, along with Lammas (August 1), Hallowmas (November 1) and Candlemas (February 2).

A Beltane Fire

Urban Anderson of Knoxville, Tennessee, collected this information as part of a study of survivals of "older beliefs," this one associated with the hilltop bonfires lit during the Druid festival of Beltane, which marked the beginning of summer:

There are few, or no, examples of midsummer or Beltane fire festivals in the folklore of East Tennessee. However, it was recently reported by an informant who lives in Marion County that it was once customary for people in her neighborhood

AMERICA CELEBRATES

BELTANE

to pile up all brush and undergrowth cleared from new ground and to leave this in stacks until May Day Eve, at which time it was set on fire. May Day Eve was, of course, the date on which one of the more important of the fire-festivals was held, but my informant had never heard any explanation given for the custom.

Source

Tennessee Folklore Society Bulletin, III (February 1937), 7.

And that's not all:
See "Halloween Bonfires" and "Persian New Year."

May

1

MAY DAY

A spring festival common in Europe and North America, May Day is celebrated by the gathering of knots, branches, and flowers on May Eve or early on May Day morning; by the crowning of a May Queen; by choral performances at daybreak; by dancing around a May bush, pole or tree; and by mumming from house to house carrying blossoms and soliciting gifts and food. The sports of May Day symbolize spring, relating human fertility to crop fertility and rebirth. Once it was common for young couples to pair up, often by lot, and "may together" in the woods all May Eve night. Similar celebrations occur on Whitsunday and Midsummer's Day. Such goings on, to say nothing of the phallic symbolism of the May Pole, horrified British Puritans. In his history of the Plymouth colony William Bradford reports that in 1628, when the nearby Anglican colony at Mount Merry "set up a maypole, drinking and dancing about it ... inviting Indian women for their consorts," the Pilgrim Fathers sent a military party to cut it down and punish the offenders. Since then in America maypole dancing has been, on the whole, a tame affair. In some countries, particularly Socialist countries, May Day is a labor festival honoring industrial and military might.

A May Day maypole dance

Maypole Dance and Woman Power

Stella M. Eisele filed this special report:

Elizabethan pageantry and chivalry were the heralds of spring yesterday as Bryn Mawr College held its annual ... May Day celebration.

"I proclaimed, against all odds, that this would be a perfect day. And it is," said Mary Patterson McPherson, college president.

MAY DAY

Spirits were high as students cavorted across the sun-splashed campus, many wearing the customary white dresses and May Day crowns of fresh flowers....

After the maypole dancing, the crowd of about 2,000 quieted to listen to McPherson make brief remarks.

The ceremony then took a feminist turn, when about 100 women took part in what organizer Deborah Rowan, a graduating student and wandering minstrel for the day, called the "mayhole dance." The antithetical event began in 1984, said alumna and participant Denise Tuggle, one of the founders.

The dancers' arms were bound to their bodies with tissue paper, symbolic of the bonds of oppression which they believe bind women, Tuggle said.

Rowan and fellow organizer Cheryl Kim freed one woman from her bonds to begin the 1990 dance. When all 100 women were free, the women shook a lavender parachute in the air, freeing a cascade of colorful flower petals.

"This is about women getting together and empowering themselves through sisterhood," Kim said.

Source

Philadelphia Inquirer, May 7, 1990.

Planting on May Day

Past Practices in Tennessee

Urban Anderson of Knoxville, Tennessee, provided this background:

It seems quite a step from the Dionysaic revels to relatively modern East Tennessee, but in folklore remoteness is, more often than not, a rare thing. A survival of these ancient rites—or, again, if not a survival, at least a custom based on similar philosophy—existed in Tennessee only about sixty years ago [1877] near a little settlement, then called Phebe, on Powell's River, some twenty or thirty miles above the government dam at Norris. It has been reported to me by four or five informants who lived in the region, that at one time the farmers of the neighborhood thought it necessary in planting turnips to hang a long-necked gourd between their legs to symbolize the male organ of generation. They would march through the plowed fields sowing the seed and chanting as they went an admonition to the turnips-to-be to equal in size the gourds they wore—and employing an obscene term to designate the gourds which they actually identified with their own organs. Two walnuts were sometimes placed inside the gourd, adds one informant.

Apparently, the masculine element of sex was thought necessarily predominant in the planting of turnips. This may be inferred from the fact that a woman was thought completely incapable of having any success at all in raising turnips unless she wore an unusually large gourd-phallus.

And yet woman, because of her position with reference to birth and care of the child, is usually thought to be able to impart fertility to the field and orchard. It was partly due to this feeling that the

Indian squaws were permitted to take care of the agricultural interests of the tribe, states Sir J. G. Fraser in *The Golden Bough*. This belief, too, is found at Phebe. Mrs. V. V. (I was asked to withhold the name) was once taken to task for having walked through a neighbor's field, whereat she replied with some heat, "Don't you know corn grows best where I walk?"

Cucumbers were supposed to grow much better when planted by women than when men planted them, and there is some reason for thinking that they were to be planted on May Day in a manner similar to that in which turnips were planted. You will remember that it was supposed to be very unusual for a woman to have luck in raising turnips. Perhaps, the very shape of the two vegetables may explain this belief.

In one community near Phebe, Blue Springs Hollow, it is said that when turnips were sown it was the custom to tie weights, such as bullets and nails, to the male organ before entering the field. My informant tells me it was believed that the more weights the sower could support the greater would be the crop of turnips. In this case, as well as that of the gourd-phallus, tremendous size and weight of the phallic symbol is sought in order that the crops will be quickened. We shall note below other instances of weights used in fertility rites.

The first day of May, Walpurgis Day, or Beltane, as it has been variously called, is ostensibly in recent conception, a date on which languishing young maidens may augur the coming of their princes charming, but its past history is at times unprintable. It was, of old, a vernal festival intended to promote the growth of vegetation and attended by such obscene rites as we have mentioned above in connection with the early history of the phallus. In the course of the ages, it has been purified by asceticism, Platonism and what-not, but just the same, survivals of the old pre-Christian beliefs cling with the tenacity that characterizes folklore in certain parts of the Old World.

In East Tennessee, there was a custom observed rather recently which seems to be a survival of the old spring festivals, although it is just as likely to deserve another interpretation. Many farmers thought it necessary when planting watermelons to go to the fields before sun-up on the morning of May Day, usually without speaking, and, after removing trousers, plant the watermelon seeds in shirt-tails. This may very conceivably be a vestige of an older and more obscene usage in which it was perhaps necessary that the male organ be uncovered. My mother tells me that farmers of yesteryear had a habit of doffing underclothes on May Day, and if we may legitimately add one usage to the other we may infer that removal of the trousers entailed appearance "in the nude" from waist down.

Source

Tennessee Folklore Society Bulletin, III (February 1937), 3-4. From an essay titled, blandly, "A Comparative Study of Some of the Older Beliefs and Usages of East Tennessee."

AMERICA CELEBRATES

MAY DAY

And that's not all:
See "To Grow Cabbage" in *Folklore in America*, 137-39; and *Journal of American Folklore* LXVI (1953), 333-37.

Planting on May Day

It Takes a Man to Plant Cucumbers

Vance Randolph collected this information from "people who live in the Ozark country" Missouri.

Most farmers believe that cucumbers should be planted "when the sign's in the arms," which means that the moon is in Gemini. But many old-timers think that the main thing is to get the seed covered before daylight on May 1, by a naked man in the prime of life. It is believed that the quality of a cucumber depends upon the virility of the planter. Cucumbers grown by women, children, or old men never amount to much. There are several vulgar jokes and stories about this. To say that a girl "ought to be raising cucumbers" means that she needs a vigorous young husband.

Source

Journal of American Folklore, LXVI (1953), 34. Printed in *Folklore in America*, p. 139.

Lehigh Corn

W. J. Hoffman reports:

In Lehigh County, the first day of May was set apart for planting corn [by the Pennsylvania Dutch].

Source

Journal of American Folklore, I (1888), 130.

May Day Marriage Predictions
Carolina Mountains

James Mooney reports:

If a young girl will pluck a white dogwood blossom and wear it in her bosom on May morning, the first man met wearing a white hat will have the Christian name of her future husband. Her handkerchief left out on the grass the previous eve will have his name written upon it in the morning, and from analogous beliefs in Ireland and elsewhere it is presumable that the writing is done by a snail crawling over it. If she will take a looking-glass to the spring on May morning, and, turning her back to the spring, look into the mirror, she will see the figure of her lover rise out of the water behind her.

Source

Journal of American Folklore, II (1889), 98. From "Folklore of the Carolina Mountains." Informants not given.

Kentucky

Betty Craft of Morehead, Kentucky, collected these items:

If you take a mirror on the first day of May and hold it over a well, you will see your future husband reflected in the mirror.

If you find a snail real early on the first day of May and lay it on a board, it will make your future husband's initials when it crawls.

Source

Kentucky Folklore Record, X (1964), 13. The first item comes from Mrs. Mazella Rhodes and the second from Mrs. Dot Mack, both of Frenchburg, Kentucky.

Southeastern Illinois

Lelah Allison turned up these items in the Wabash region of southeastern Illinois:

On the last day of April put a handkerchief where dew will form on it. Get up early and you will find the initial of your future mate on it.

On the night before May 1 a girl should place a snail on a plate of meal under her bed. The initial of her future mate will be on the plate.

On May 1 at 12:00 o'clock hold a mirror over a well to see your future mate.

On the morning of May 1 look out of the window and count the number of live things you can see. That will be the number of years before you marry.

On May 1 look for birds' nests. The number of eggs you find will be the number of years you will be single.

Source

Journal of American Folklore, LXIII (1950), 314-15. Informants not given.

Mid-Tennessee

T.J. Farr identified these beliefs from "the Cumberland section of middle Tennessee."

Get up on the first morning of May and before speaking to any one, look out of the window. The number of chickens you see will represent the number of years before you marry.

On the first morning of May a girl should rise without speaking and turn around under a cedar tree three times and listen for noises. If she hears singing, she will be happily married. If she hears knocking, it is the driving of nails in her coffin and she will die before she marries. If she hears no sound at all, she will never marry.

If a handkerchief has been left outside over night before the first day of May, the next morning the initials of your future mate will be written on the handkerchief.

If you walk around a wheat field on the first day of May, you will meet your mate.

If on the first day of May at sunrise, you look into an open well, you will see the reflection of your future husband or wife.

On the first morning in May, place a glass of water in the sun at sunrise and let it remain all day. At sunset, look into the water. If you are to die an old maid or bachelor, a coffin will appear in the water.

Source

Southern Folklore Quarterly, II (1938), 165-74. Informants not given.

And that's not all:
For more marriage predictions, see " New Year's Beliefs" and "To See Your Future Husband on Halloween."

May Day Marriage Predictions

May Morning Love Charms

These items were collected by James Mooney from mountaineers in western North Carolina who were farmers.

The sparseness of population and the roughness of the country [western North Carolina] prevent frequent gatherings for social enjoyment, and the result is seen in the scarcity of holiday customs and obser-

AMERICA   CELEBRATES

MAY DAY

vances. The few which survive from earlier days are mainly love charms pertaining to May morning....

The girls have a number of love charms ... most of them being practiced also in Europe on Hallow Eve, a celebration which appears to have dropped out from the mountain calendar. If an egg, placed in front of the fire by a young woman, be seen to *sweat blood*, it is a sign that she will succeed in winning the sweetheart she desires. By giving to a number of mistletoe leaves the names of her several suitors, and ranging them in line before the fire, she can test the affection of each sweetheart. The leaf which the heat causes to pop over nearest to where she is standing will indicate which lover is most sincere in his professions, and in the same way will be shown the relative ardor of the others. If a girl will take out the yolk from a hard-boiled egg, fill the cavity with salt, then eat the egg and go to bed, her destined husband will appear in the night and offer her a drink. Another way is to eat a mixture of a thimbleful of meal and another of salt, and then, being careful always to observe a strict silence, walk backwards to bed with the hands clasped behind the back, take off the clothing backwards, and get into bed. The apparition of the future husband will come as before and give her a drink of water.

Liverwort is known by the appropriate name of "heart leaf," and the peculiar shape of its leaves has suggested their use as a love philter. A girl can infallibly win the love of any sweetheart she may desire

by secretly throwing over his clothing some of the powder made by rubbing together a few heart leaves which have been dried before the fire. She may, if she wish, have a score of lovers by simply carrying the leaves in her bosom. It is to be presumed that the recipe would be equally efficacious if used by one of the opposite sex.

Source

Journal of American Folklore, II (1889), 98-9. The name of the informant, the place of collection, and the date are not given. Printed in *Folklore from the Working Folk of America*, 179-80.

St. Tamina's Day

Taminend, a Delaware Indian chief who figures in American legend and literature, is said to have befriended William Penn with whom he signed a treaty. During the pre-Revolutionary strife, groups of American patriots took the name "St. Tammany" to ridicule and counter the traditional British patriotic societies honoring St. George and St. Andrew and celebrating their days. They adopted what their members believed to be Indian titles, rites and ceremonies. Tammany Societies, notably in New York, have lingered on as political clubs of a Jeffersonian, and later Jacksonian, persuasion. This information was collected by Annie W. Whitney and Caroline C. Bullock:

In and around Annapolis [May Day] was long known as St. Tamina's Day, for it was the date set apart by the St. Tamina Society to celebrate the memory of the ancient Delaware Chief, Taminend, "whose equal was never known." Both Pennsylvania and Maryland selected this day on which to honor the Chief. In the Journal of a southern girl visiting in Philadelphia, is the following item under date of May 1, 1771.

"This morning was ushered in by the ringing of bells in memory of King Tammany as he used to be called; but now I think they have got him canonized, for he is now celebrated as St. Tammany."

[William] Eddis, in his *Letters [from America]* writing from Annapolis, in 1771 says,

"The Americans on this part of the continent have likewise a saint whose history is lost in fable and uncertainty. The first of May is however set apart to the memory of St. Tamina, on which occasion the natives wear a piece of buck's tail, etc." The St. Tamina Society seems to have been founded first in Maryland and to have been in existence there until 1841. In Pennsylvania it practically died out during the revolution, with spasmodic resurrections from time to time afterwards.

Why Taminend should have been honored first in Maryland, it is difficult to say, for he is associated with the people of Pennsylvania, and is said to have been under the elm tree with William Penn. His signature to a deed giving property to the latter is still in existence and is "a snake not tightly coiled."

Various legends are told of this great "chief of many days"; he had a hand-to-hand encounter with the devil; had personal intercourse with good spirits; performed miracles, and when his time came to die, set fire to his wigwam, but being too pure and good to perish in the flames, was translated.

The May pole was a feature in the celebration of St. Tamina's Day in Annapolis. It was erected in a public place and garlanded with flowers, the members of the St. Tamina Society, forming a ring round it, danced the Indian war dance "with many other customs which they had seen exhibited by the children of the forest." All citizens who chose to take part in this wore a piece of buck's tail in their hats. There was an evening entertainment to which general invitations were issued. In the midst of the dancing, the members of the Society, dressed like Indians, rushed into the assembly with a war whoop which was followed by war songs and dances of the Indians.

Before the evening was over, a collection was taken up.

The celebration of the day in Philadelphia differed from this, a wigwam outside the city taking the place of the May pole. To the Indian dances and war songs, was added the calumet of peace.

Source

Memoirs of the American Folklore Society, XVIII (1925), 119-20. From "Folk-Lore from Maryland"; data on sources incomplete.

May
5

CINCO DE MAYO

The Fifth of May is the day on which the Mexicans and Mexican-Americans commemorate the defeat of the French by General Ignacio Zaragoza at the Battle of Pueblo in 1862. His defense of this city was an important blow to Napoleon III's attempt to establish a permanent French colony in Central America and led toward their eventual expulsion from Mexico by Benito Juarez five years later. It is a national holiday second in importance only to September 16, Independence Day. Even as early as 1863, the day was celebrated by Mexicans living in American cities such as San Francisco, and it has been considered *"la gloriosa fecha"* (the glorious date) in the Bay Area ever since.

In San Francisco, *Cinco de Mayo* has developed into a festival to perpetuate Mexican nationalism in a foreign land. The language of the associated events (the pageants, speeches, songs, parades) is Spanish, and while

the American flag is flown alongside the Mexican flag and while both national anthems may be sung, the celebration is thoroughly Mexican.

For Chicanos today, *Cinco de Mayo* is symbolic of a bold stand against outside forces, against oppression, and against interventions into their lives by the United States and its culture. The celebrations stress such terms as *"La Raza"* (the Race); the "Mestizo Nation" (Bronze Culture); and the homeland of Aztlán (a mythical Aztec domain covering northern Mexico and the southwestern United States). Recently, and perhaps surprisingly, other Latin groups such as Puerto Ricans and Nicaraguans have joined with the Chicanos in celebrating *Cinco de Mayo*. Still, the Chicanos jealously believe that the Fifth of May is their day, and, though joining with other Hispanic peoples when Latin-Americans feel threatened by the host culture, they resent intrusions on their celebrations.

Cinco de Mayo: The Celebration in Aztlán

Ilene Linssen provided this information from the Oakland, California, Office of Bilingual Education:

To be clearly understood, the Chicano celebration of "Cinco de Mayo" must be viewed in the context of a struggle for social justice.

In the last decade, the Chicano movement has shattered the false mirror that was blinding the Chicanos' clear vision into his soul. The term Mexican American died and was replaced by Chicano. The solitude was broken. The Chicano was born from the suffering of the people that had come before. As he looked into his own mirror, he began to retrace the footprints left on the road that his ancestors had traversed. La Raza students have made "Cinco de Mayo" a very important celebration in all the schools. Chicano celebrations of "Cinco de Mayo" have been culturally heavily adorned experiences accompanied by mariachi music and speeches relating the important lessons of the French Intervention. The Chicano yell, "Viva La Raza!" is very significant in that it affirms his faith in the people. The Chicano finds his face in his heritage. He does not deny the past but embraces it. He utilizes these celebrations like a shield to guard against the forces that would erase his roots. The celebration communicates this message to the hearts of La Raza: "We know where we come from. We know where we are going."

In 1969, Chicanos proclaimed "El Plan Espiritual de Aztlán" in all Cinco de Mayo celebrations. The following is the original text of this important document:

In the spirit of a new people that is conscious not only of its proud historical heritage, but also of the brutal gringo invasion of our territories—we the Chicano inhabitants and civilizers of the northern land of Aztlán, from whence came our forefathers, reclaiming the land of their birth and consecrating the determination of our people of the sun—declare that the call of our blood is our power, our responsibility and our inevitable destiny.

We are free and sovereign to determine those tasks which are justly called for by our house, our land, the sweat of our brows and our hearts. Aztlán belongs to those that plant the seeds, water the fields and gather the crops—and not to the foreign Europeans. We do not recognize capricious frontiers on the Bronze Continent.

Brotherhood unites us, and love for our brothers makes us a people whose time has come, and who struggles against the foreigner gabacho who exploits our riches and destroys our culture. With our heart in our hands and our hands in the

CINCO DE MAYO

soil, we declare the independence of our Mestizo Nation. We are a Bronze People with a Bronze Culture. Before the world, before all of North America, before all our brothers in the Bronze Continent—we are a Nation, we are a Union of Free Pueblos, we are

Aztlán.

Por la Raza Todo—Fuera de la Raza Nada

(All for the Race—Without the Race Nothing).

The Chicanos have added a new dimension to their celebration of this Mexican holiday. Chicano theatre does not reenact the Battle of Puebla on Cinco de Mayo but rather places on stage all of the contradictions of the cultural life of La Raza in its struggle for survival within the political boundaries of the United States. The theatres have demonstrated a strong inclination to present the lives and struggles of the Indigenous Gods. A return to our religious roots to become strong in our struggle is the Chicano's celebration of Cinco de Mayo. This new perspective signifies a return to our past to understand our present to determine our future.

Source

Cinco de Mayo, a booklet printed by the Oakland, California, Unified School District, Educational Department Services, Office of Communications, n.d., 26-7.

May
5
BOYS' FESTIVAL

Like the Japanese Dolls' or Girls' Festival (*Hina-no-sekku*) on March 3, the Boys' Festival (*Tango-no-sekku*) is a family-centered holiday. It, too, is intended to instill a sense of tradition and a respect for traditional roles.

Dolls are displayed, but unlike the Girls' Day ceremonial dolls, which are decorated with peach blossoms—the symbols of mildness and peacefulness— the Boys' Festival dolls are costumed as samurai, the aristocratic warriors of feudal Japan whose martial prowess and indifference to physical suffering make them symbols of manliness. The ceremonial dolls often reflect the elaborate medieval costumes and weapons of these feudal knights (samurai were permitted to wear two swords), and implements of battle are sometimes displayed as well. While girls during the Peach Blossom Festival (Girls' Day) quietly sip tea and eat sweets, boys emulate the qualities represented by their samurai dolls, engaging in mock warfare and tests of their prowess. Red and black banners in the shape of carp, also associated with masculine virtues, are flown from a bamboo pole, one for each boy in the family. Because of this, the holiday is also designated as the Feast of Banners or the Feast of Flags. The Boys' Festival coincides with Children's Day (*Kodomo-no-hi*), a Japanese national holiday set aside to honor children.

Japanese Boys' Festival

"Miss N. I." studied the holiday customs of persons of Japanese descent living in the San Francisco Bay area in 1934 under the direction of Paul Radin, and provided this account:

Corresponding to [the] Dolls' Festival, the happiest day of the year for Japanese girls, there is a Boys' Festival—often called the Festival of Flags or Banners—which takes place on May 5th, in honor of male children. On this day, dolls

BOYS' FESTIVAL

are again displayed, but this time they are images representing soldiers, warriors, and heroes; swords and bows and arrows are also carefully laid out on exhibit. Outside the house, in addition to variegated colored flags and banners, there is the special feature of a long bamboo cane, representing a fishing rod, from which are suspended one or more paper carp. These vary according to the number of little boys in the family. Instead of being occupied in the effeminate pastime of caressing dolls and sipping tea, the boys, on the contrary, spend the day in great glee, fighting mock battles in imitation of the warriors of the glorious feudal days.

The history of the observance of the Dolls' and Boys' Festivals by the Japanese in America has undergone an interesting series of fluctuations. Before the year 1910 or so, there were, strictly speaking, . . . not many Japanese families in America. This, added to the . . . lack of proper equipment, explains the relatively late beginning here of the celebration of these children's holidays. Since the increase in the number of families and therefore of children, and the appearance of large Japanese stores, however, both March 3rd and May 5th have become gala days for Japanese youngsters in America.

Source

Southwestern Journal of Anthropology, II (1946), 169-70.

May

First Saturday

KENTUCKY DERBY

America's most famous horse race, the Kentucky Derby, is modeled on England's Epsom Derby. Limited to three-year-old thoroughbreds, it was originally run at one mile and a half (now at a mile and a quarter), and has been held continuously since 1875 at Louisville, Kentucky. *Aristides*, the winner of the first Derby at Chuchill Downs, Kentucky, brought his owner a purse of $2850. Colonel Meriwether Lewis Clark, who organized the first race, wanted it to be a festive occasion, and he gave a Derby breakfast for his friends before the first running—a custom that he continued through his life and that many others have followed.

Derby Week festivities

Parties, dances, and carnival-like gaiety have long been a feature of Derby Week. The Derby's emergence as an event of national note is due largely to Colonel Matt Winn, a shrewd promoter who cultivated wealthy eastern horse owners and such sports writers as Damon Runyon and Grantland Rice. He had seen his first Derby as a lad, and he directed the event from 1902 until his death in 1949. The Kentucky Derby is one of the country's largest civic celebrations, and is the first event in the "Triple Crown" series. Traditionally, the Derby is followed by the Preakness (the second Saturday after the Derby), and the Belmont Stakes (the fifth Saturday after the Derby).

The One Hundredth Derby: Its Mint Juleps

John Ed Pearce tells here "how a two-minute horse race, abetted by colorful people and odd events, grew into a legend in only one century":

Sometime around five o'clock on the afternoon of the first Saturday in May, a dozen or so horses will charge around the track at Louisville's Churchill Downs in the 100th running of the Kentucky Derby, a mad but mellow mixture of horses, hysteria

AMERICA CELEBRATES

KENTUCKY DERBY

and hoopla. A band will play "My Old Kentucky Home," tears will flow like mint juleps, people will scream and jump about. And in the process, a three-year-old Thoroughbred will win the first leg of the Triple Crown, horsedom's biggest biggie. . . .

Considering that it lasts only two minutes, give or take a couple of seconds or fractions thereof, it is a tribute to the race that it has become the country's premier sports spectacle. The Indianapolis 500 may draw more on-the-site spectators: the Super Bowl may engage a larger television audience. But those events last for long and often tedious hours. The Derby boils it down to one frantic burst, and for its brief life-span it pulls them in as does no other event. This year [1974], 125,000 ticket buyers are expected to cram themselves into the Churchill Downs enclosure, built to accommodate half that number, while 75 million others watch it more comfortably on television.

Of course, the Derby is not just a horse race, any more than Mardi Gras is a parade. It is more a kind of fit that seizes the Bluegrass state each May, a fine spring madness with betting windows. The festivities, which last the better part of a week, include a Pegasus parade in honor of the mythical winged horse (who did not win a Derby and therefore is not highly regarded by Kentuckians), a steamboat race on the Ohio River between two surviving sternwheelers, a massive dance thrown by ladies calling themselves Colonettes, and a dinner

given for, by and at the expense of Kentucky Colonels. . . .

Why does the Derby arouse emotions and excitement unique in horse racing? It is not the oldest race in the country. The Travers Handicap (begun in 1864) and the Belmont Stakes (1867) have years on the Derby, which was not begun until 1875. Even older is Keeneland's Phoenix Handicap, first run in 1831. Neither is the Derby, a $125,000-added contest, the richest race. Several pay more. . . .

[However,] the other races have lapsed from time to time. Neither war nor flood nor gasoline rationing has kept the three-year-olds from their appointed round of the Downs since Aristides won the first Derby on May 17, 1875, loping the mile and a half (Derby distance is now a mile and a quarter) in the respectable time of 2:37¾. And while the prize money is not the biggest in the business, it is not hay. More importantly, winning it usually leads on to greater things. A Derby winner may command handsome fees as a stud after his racing days are done. And while few Derby winners go on to capture the Triple Crown (Derby, Preakness, Belmont), the fact remains that a horse must win the Derby first to become a Triple Crowner and take his place alongside the likes of Secretariat, Citation, Whirlaway and Gallant Fox.

Still, some owners prefer not to risk burning out their hayburners with a premature race, and some of the great stakes winners of the American turf never touched hoof to Downs on Derby Day. For example, Man o' War, probably the greatest American Thoroughbred, not only did not run in the Derby but also never raced in Kentucky, a fact Kentuckians prefer not to discuss. And there was Bubbling Over, who never raced again after taking the 1926 Derby.

What sets the Derby apart is that it is, as someone once said (or should have), the right race in the right place at the right time. Kentucky is, after all, the home and heart of the horse industry. Its weather in winter and summer can be foul, but in the first weeks of spring nature blesses it with magic. It is a place of blooming tulips and dogwood, soft-greening trees, warm sun and colts prancing across white-fenced bluegrass acres. Louisville, basically an industrial Midwestern town, takes on an aura of Southern charm. Colonels sprout like mint twigs, and residents only recently arrived from Schenectady or Pittsburgh develop Southern accents and serve mint juleps to their Yankee guests.

"The whole thing," said Wathen Knebelkamp, late president of Churchill Downs, "is corny as hell in some ways. But it's hard to beat."...

As a social event, the Derby is something of a mixed bag. Proper hostesses insist that the whole thing is a bore and just a bit tacky, but they compete tensely for distinguished guests, especially for the traditional Derby-eve parties and Derby-morning breakfasts. The customary Derby party begins graciously with mint juleps in frosted glasses and every man a colonel, and winds up, shortly before daybreak, with bourbon and water and every man for himself. Derby breakfast is a strict ritual at which eggs and other staples must be accompanied by country ham and beaten biscuits which look and often taste like the center cut from a cueball. And, of course, mint juleps.

It is also considered good form to take one's guests to breakfast or lunch in the clubhouse dining room at the Downs, where one can view the preliminary races with casual disinterest while downing the same fare and the inevitable juleps. The great majority of spectators, however, could care less about good form. By the thousands they sprawl on the grass of the infield, eating from picnic hampers and getting sozzled on beer, while others swarm through the stands hoping to catch a glimpse of the rich and/or famous....

The first Derby was different only in degree. There were three races then, instead of today's nine, and there were 10,000 people on hand rather than 100,000. They drove out from Louisville in hacks and surreys, or rode the horsedrawn trolley. They could enjoy the whole thing for a dollar, and for some the tab was even less. What is now called the infield was then the "free gate area," and several hundred viewers drove their wagons in, ate a home-packed lunch and watched standing up in wagon beds....

Kentucky, though, was still small potatoes in the horse world, and when the Jockey Club of New York was formed in

KENTUCKY DERBY

1891, its members tended to view Churchill Downs, like all other Southern tracks, with disdain—not the place, really, where a gentleman wanted to race his horses. Horse racing, they decided, belonged in the East, where gentlemen could afford it. After all, it had started in New York where, in 1668, the governor, Col. Richard Nicolls, had presented the winner of the first organized race with a silver porringer.

Matt Winn [President of Churchill Downs] turned the thing around. Until he took over, the Derby had attracted scant notice from the national press. The Downs had a good plant, but its finances depended heavily on the one big event—the Derby. And while crowds were good, they weren't good enough to pay the bills the rest of the year. A natural and tireless promoter, Winn spruced the place up, planted the grounds with banks of tulips and other spring flowers, timed to bloom around Derby week, pioneered the $2 pari-mutuel bet, and began a dogged courtship of the two groups he needed to turn the Derby into a national event—horse owners and newspapermen.

Early on, he got two big breaks. In 1913 a long shot named Donerail came in and paid $184.90 for a $2 ticket in the Derby. This price—and the Derby—got a lot of national attention. Then, in 1915, Harry Payne Whitney, among the bluest of Eastern bloods, agreed to enter his filly, Regret, in the Derby. Regret won, the only filly ever to take the race [until 1980], and

again reaped a golden crop of news headlines.

Winn saw to it that Whitney was treated royally during his stay in Kentucky, and the hospitality paid off. "I don't care whether she ever wins another race," boomed Whitney, patting his victorious Regret after the Derby. "She's already won the greatest race in the world." Winn made sure this statement got wide circulation.

Exactly when the mint julep and the Derby got together is not clear. The julep has been a Bluegrass tradition since before the Civil War, and few Kentuckians of any prominence have gone to their graves without having, at one time or another, produced their personal recipe. Henry Clay, John Campbell Breckinridge, and Irvin S. Cobb went into ecstasies describing the delights of a julep and instructing the uninitiated in the mysteries of its concoction. On the other hand, Marse Henry Watterson, famed Louisville editor, offered this recipe:

"Pluck the mint gently from its bed just as the dew of evening is about to form on it. Select the choicer sprigs only, but do not rinse them. Prepare the simple syrup and measure out half a tumbler of whisky. Pour the whisky into a well-frosted silver cup, throw the other ingredients out the window and drink the whisky straight."

But Winn managed to weave the julep into the richening legend of the Derby, along with bluegrass, colonels and Southern hospitality. The effect of all this was to make Louisville sound as though it were nestled on the banks of the Suwannee River rather than on the Ohio. . . .

Thousands of bad mint juleps will be consumed by drinkers who would not know a good one if they got one. Visitors will complain about room and meal prices and cab fares. Most of them will eventually get to the Derby, and they will eat and drink and gawk and bet, and squeal at each other and make sure that they are seen. And they will find that, as the afternoon goes on, they are getting very excited, for reasons hard to explain, as slowly the legend and myth and glamour and ballyhoo that surround the Derby build to the awaited climax.

Suddenly a bugle will blow, and out onto the track will come the horses, sleek, beautifully shaped animals, their jockeys crisp in their bright silks. And as they prance by the stands the band will begin the soft strains of "My Old Kentucky Home," and there will be tears in the eyes of people who couldn't tell Kentucky from a corncake. Then the music will die and the horses will be led, one by one, into the starting gate. A hush will fall over the throng until it is swept by the magic shout, "They're off!"

Hokum? Perhaps. Corny? Probably. Manufactured glamour? Maybe. But still the Kentucky Derby, the greatest race of them all.

Source

Louisville *Courier-Journal & Times Magazine,* April 28, 1974.

Chancy Gambling and Surefire Fun

Colleen Ballard Hayes provided the following account:

"Lady, don't you know there ain't no telephones at a race track?" an incredulous New Yorker asked me as we stood among bettors at Churchill Down's pari-mutuel windows. New to horse racing, I had never considered that public telephones could be used to spirit race results to off-track bettors in time to wager on the winner before official postings.

I was baptized in the sport—and the chancy gambling and surefire fun that attends it—at the world's greatest thoroughbred horse race last May [1987] in Louisville, Kentucky.

To be sure, the Run for the Roses (as the Kentucky Derby is commonly called) is more than just a great race. Since the first Kentucky Derby in 1875, the race—which some sports writers say constitutes the greatest two minutes in sports—and its preliminaries have evolved into perhaps the world's biggest adult game.

Throughout the 10-day Derby Festival that begins a week before the Derby, movie stars, great athletes, Wall Street tycoons, politicians and con artists descend on Louisville, which becomes an interna-

AMERICA CELEBRATES

KENTUCKY DERBY

tional city during its brief season in the spotlight.

Along streets that converge on Churchill Downs, I passed vendors selling home-cooked meals, fuchsia-colored stuffed giraffes, raincoats, sunglasses and lawn chairs to racegoers—all jammed into parking lots and front yards. I was on my way to see the Kentucky Oaks, a race for thoroughbred fillies held the day before the main event.

Entering Churchill Downs—that mecca of thoroughbred horsedom whose white turreted walls resemble those of Bavarian castles—the first thing I saw were tipsters hawking tip sheets predicting the day's winners. Vendors sold souvenirs and official programs with each day's lineup of races. Inside the clubhouse or amid the clubhouse garden's 10,000 imported Holland tulips, the general-admission patrons had set up folding chairs. Both groups had to be content watching races on TV monitors since the track was not visible from there.

Sophisticated bettors buy the *Daily Racing Form* with its section entitled "Past Performances" that includes a listing of each horse's bloodline, trainer and past race results. Two tote boards—each 15 by 200 feet—serve as scorecards in Churchill Downs' infield, posting the results of each race: win, place, show and fourth place, race times and mutuel payoffs on $2 bets.

Between races, nine to 10 a day during Derby week, patrons have 30 to 50 minutes to place bets, collect wins, buy refreshments, and see and be seen. Dressed to the nines on Millionaires' Row on the clubhouse's top floors, celebrities and near-celebrities looked down on the more casual crowd of 75,000 along the track's infield, many in T-shirts and jeans. Socialites flaunting extravagant, broad-brimmed hats and designer clothes paraded in aisles between reserved boxes along the track. Vendors shouting "mint julep" hawked that legendary southern drink of Kentucky bourbon with a little mint, crushed ice and sugar thrown in.

While Kentucky bourbon and betting are a potentially volatile mixture, the mint juleps (sold in elegant souvenir Derby glasses) are a tame Derby tradition.

Another is the sewing of the roses, a tradition since 1932. On Derby eve, a crowd at Louisville's Kroger Company grocery store watched three women sew 600 rosebuds into a blanket of roses that adorns the Derby winner. From eight o'clock that night to eight o'clock the next morning, the women stitched together the red Kentucky rosebuds timed to open just before the blanket's presentation.

Newer Derby-related events number more than 80, scheduled as part of the Kentucky Derby Festival that began simply as the Pegasus Parade in 1956. The festival has mushroomed into civic celebrations of balls, barbecues, concerts and parades, a sort of Louisville Mardi Gras. Among last year's activities were stern-wheeler and hot-air balloon races, a mini-marathon and the Run for the Rosé, in which local waiters and waitresses carrying trays of wine-filled glasses raced over an obstacle course. . . .

Estimates put Derby-weekend parties as high as 10,000, of which some of the most glamorous (including the winner's party) are catered by Steve Clements at the adjacent Kentucky Derby Museum. But the biggest party happens at the track's front rails. On the day of the Derby, I had a great box seat, but wanting to get closer to the horses, as do many spectators, I moved to a spot across from the tote board near the track's finish line. In one hour, I met an Atlanta, Georgia, investment banker; a Buffalo, New York, couple who attend annually; a Tennessee native who drives up each May; and a former disc jockey from Cleveland whose scientific study of thoroughbreds didn't seem to beat the odds in this year's running.

Rumor has it that bets that pay off are often the result of hunches, superstition or beginner's luck. I had one omen: Only an hour before the Derby I got the autograph of trainer Jack Van Berg, whose colt, Alysheba, soon won the race.

Experienced bettors scrutinize the field for Kentucky-bred entries. Since 1875, when Aristides won the first Derby, three-fourths of all the race's winners have been bred in Kentucky.

In the final analysis, the real Derby pull is the horses. The three-year-olds that race in the Derby are the choicest of the choice, thoroughbreds bred and trained almost from birth to finish first in the Run for the Roses. They are the most spirited, determined, high-strung, beautiful horses in the world—as well as the fastest.

Source

Travel-Holiday, March, 1988, 62-65.

Kentucky Derby Carnival

Sports columnist Red Smith filed this account from Louisville in 1980:

A few yards beyond the pedestrian tunnel to the Churchill Downs infield, a young man standing on a cooler held up a handlettered sign: "Don't you love smut?" Propped up at his feet was a more elaborate message. "Girls," it read, in red block letters, "get naked here. Expert assistance. Ask for Joe."

He was finding no takers, but it wasn't yet noon. He remained at his stand, confident that as the summery day wore on toward post time for the 106th [1980] Kentucky Derby, the true carnival spirit would take over.

More and more noticeably in recent years, the Derby's center-field picnic has become a "happening" for the college crowd. Seats in the grandstand and clubhouse and the bleachers outside the clubhouse turn are always sold out, so the only area where attendance varies from year to year is the grassy plain enclosed by the bridle path. That crowd swells or shrinks according to the weather, which has never been more promising than it was this morning.

So they came swarming in by the tens of thousands, toting coolers and ice buckets and hampers and blankets and

AMERICA CELEBRATES

KENTUCKY DERBY

folding chairs. They set up pup tents and hammocks, laid out their goodies and stretched out at ease until the whole broad meadow, seen from above, heaved and pulsated.

Here came a girl in halter and shorts pulling a red wagon loaded with comestibles. There ambled a bearded young man bare to the waist except for red galluses supporting blue jeans, which were rolled up to the knees.

By comparison with his fellows, he was overdressed. Standard attire for males was blue shorts, with or without shoes; for females, a few additional threads. The sun's rays, dazzling in the morning, were strained through a filmy overcast by 1 P.M., but by that time acres and acres of skin had turned a painful pink.

Strollers had to pick their way among bodies. Hour by hour as the throng grew, less and less grass remained visible until there was more to smoke than to walk on. The unmistakable bouquet of burning pot, rather like the scent given off by an overheated electric motor, hung on the still air like incense.

It was a merry crowd, relaxed and friendly and mostly young. There seemed to be no shortage of potables, though management discourages carrying stimulants through the gates. At the clubhouse entrance about 11 A.M., security guards were seen to relieve a customer of assorted bottles which they pitched into a trash can.

"That was a pretty good haul," a bystander said.

Frisbees sailed about the infield scene. Inside the clubhouse turn a volleyball game went on without pause. For the third year in a row, a young entrepreneur worked his basketball grift. He had a basket set up on a standard and charged 50 cents for two shots from the free-throw distance, paying $1 if both throws went in. Maybe one player in 20 hit twice and collected. For its proprietor, the game was a surer thing than any horse.

Admission to the infield is $10 and anyone who has heard that you can't see horses from there has been misinformed. The second race started from the six-furlong gate in the backstretch. Crowds pressed against the tall cyclone fence surrounding the infield could see the field leave the gate and proceed 40 or 50 yards before disappearing beyond the multitude.

State troopers patrolled outside the fence, lending a touch of Dannemora to the happy scene....

"Welcome to the rodeo," a ... sign read, and this could have been editorial comment on the Derby's informal riding tactics. In 105 runnings of this cavalry charge, there has never been a disqualification for rough riding, making the Derby easily the most cleanly contested sports event in America.

Source

New York Times, May 4, 1980.

May

When Corn Ripens

FLORIDA SEMINOLE GREEN CORN DANCE

Ceremonies involving the planting, ripening and harvest of corn were particularly widespread, practiced by the Indians of the Prairies and Southwest as well as by those of the Eastern Woodlands. The Green Corn Dance or busk, as it was usually called by early white observers, took place when the corn had ripened. It was a first fruits ceremony, marking the beginning of a new year. Thus William Bartram in his *Travels* (1791) among the southern Indians in the 1770s notes that "every town celebrates the busk separately, when their own harvest is ready." He adds: "When a town celebrates the busk, having previously

provided themselves with new clothes, new pots and other household utensils and furniture, they collect all their worn-out clothes and other despicable things, sweep and cleanse their houses, squares and the whole town of their filth, which with all the remaining grain and other provisions, they cast together into one common heap, and consume it with fire." Quoting from Bartram's account in *Walden*, Thoreau remarks approvingly, "I have scarcely heard of a truer sacrament, that is, as the dictionary defines it, 'outward and visible sign of an inward and spiritual grace.'"

The Corn Dance

Robert F. Greenlee made these observations in 1939:

The Green Corn Dance is the principal ceremony among the Florida Seminoles and affords them recreational diversion once a year. Although many of the customs are of recent origin, the Green Corn Dance

by way of contrast, is a very old observance. It is not confined to the Seminoles and has constituted an intimate part of the ceremonial life of the Creek Indians, the Alabama tribe, as well as the Cherokee and Natchez, who took on the dance late in their existence. The Seminole dance is derived from the Creek busk ceremony.

FLORIDA SEMINOLE GREEN CORN DANCE

The word busk is derived from *boskita* meaning to fast, and is an integral part of the ceremony which marked the old Creek new year. Variations of the Green Corn Dance have been given year in and year out among the Florida Seminoles as well as among the Timuquans, who preceded them on the Florida peninsula.

The separate rites which compose the dance are both old and widespread among the original peoples of the Southeast. One such practice is the taking of an emetic. The well-known cassine or *ilex vomitoria* is employed as emetic at the Green Corn Dance. This shrub, which is none other than the familiar holly, is found along the sea coast of the two Carolinas, Georgia, and northern Florida. The French writer Bossu speaks of the use of cassine among the Alabama tribe, who roasted the leaves to make a tea and drank the infusion in the ritual of many ceremonies. The Creeks, also, were inveterate cassine drinkers. They referred to it as *asi* instead of the usual popular expression "black drink." The Creeks likewise had a religious belief that the *asi* used at the busk had the following properties: It purified them from all sin and left them in a state of perfect innocence. It exalted them with invincible daring in war and was a means of cementing friendship.

Another important feature of the Green Corn Dance is the ceremonial scratching which occurs just before the Feather Dance on the second day of the ceremony. Scratching of this sort was known among the Cherokees, Creeks, Seminoles, Yuchi, and Catawba tribes in particular. In the Cherokee instance ball players are scratched on their naked bodies with a bamboo brier having stout thorns. This left broad gashes on the backs of the victims. Among the Seminoles snake fangs are inserted into a wooden holder and is used to scratch the assembled members. Different purposes for the scratching are as punishment of children, relief of fatigue, and the cleansing of the body from impurities as in the case of the Green Corn Dance ceremony.

Aside from its purely ceremonial purpose the Green Corn Dance is a time for council meetings. All the troubles of the old year, with the exception of murder and any serious infraction of the marriage rules are forgiven. One rule, that of marrying into the clan of one's mother, since the Seminole count descent not from both sides of the family as with us but only on the mother's side, is particularly guarded against. Any infraction here cannot be simply wiped away by the repentance at the Green Corn Dance.

An additional function of the meeting is the naming of youths who have come of age. Remember that an Indian name is more than a label, it is a distinct part of his personality just as much so as are his eyes or his teeth. He believes that injury will result from the wrong handling of his name just as readily as a wound inflicted on some part of his body. Thus the small rites accompanying the dances which occur on the last night of the Corn Dance serve to give the young members of the tribe their ceremonial names. This clan name they then bear for the remainder of their lives. Only medicine men or other important personages receive further honorary names.

The ball game at the Corn Dance which I witnessed in the Big Cypress swamp in May, 1939, had little definite form. It was played in the quiet periods between the ceremonies of more serious import. The object was to send the ball hitting against an indented mark cut some six feet up on a twenty-foot pole. Making a charcoal mark on the pole for each hit registered constituted the method of scoring. Most of the time the boys and girls just played in a formless and desultory fashion—tossing the buckskin ball around aimlessly. On several occasions when the game assumed a more serious character the boys played with small gut-thonged racquets while the girls used their bare hands.

In the evening the so-called stomp dances took place. They had little form and were mere survivals of dances which probably had much significance earlier in Seminole history. The first dance was the Catfish Dance, which was soon followed by the Hair Dance. The latter is probably a survival of the scalp dance which was given earlier in the Southeast when Indians referred to the scalp as "hair." The Alligator Dance and the Buffalo Dance were also given. Other dances often rendered at the Green Corn Dance are Rattlesnake Dance (*cinti chobi talellwi*), Switchgrass Dance (*pahi loci talellwi*), Redbug Dance (*waski talellwi*), and Rabbit Dance (*cokfi talellwi*).

While dancing the women wear rattles made out of tin cans punctured and filled with pebbles. The rattles are tied to the leg just above the ankle. The men carry palmetto fronds in their hands and a few merely held sprigs of bush which they carried in a similar manner.

During the evening dances one Indian acted as fire tender and announcer. He stood within the bough-decked ceremonial lodge on the east end of the ceremonial grounds and called out the names of the dancers who were to participate in a coming event.

Of all the dances the Feather Dance is the only one which merits special notice. It is danced in the morning and immediately after lunch on the last day of the ceremony. Each participant held white egret feathers attached to a long thin pole. The pole thus adorned was carried over the left shoulder. No women were allowed to take part in the Feather Dance.

The Men went around the ceremonial grounds making four steps, one at each corner. They stopped at the corner, shook their rattles and then let out a short piercing whoop. The ceremonial ground was occupied in the following manner to give this dance:

.

AMERICA CELEBRATES

FLORIDA SEMINOLE GREEN CORN DANCE

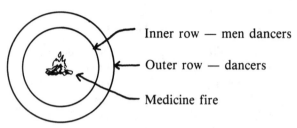

Inner row — men dancers

Outer row — dancers

Medicine fire

At three o'clock the same afternoon the men retired to the same ceremonial grounds near the ball game pole to take the "black drink." This emetic is now composed of six ingredients. Without warning the ceremonial scratching with snake fangs set in a scratching instrument resembling a pocket comb began. First the men pulled up their trousers to the knees and rubbed medicine on their legs. After this they hastily went into the nearby sawgrass to inflict another series of scratches upon their legs just below the thigh and in the shin

region as well. Boys received scratches on their fore and upper arm. After the scratching the men went further into the sawgrass. Vomiting ensued for such was the instantaneous effect of the emetic they had taken so soon before.

The Green Corn Dance had little else to recommend it to the visitor. There was a feast, participated in by all, in which large slabs of beef were eaten. Another event was the eating of *kumpti,* a food made from a root resembling cassava. It was also rather interesting to see the women grind the new corn meal in the old stump grinders which the Seminoles and other Southeastern Indians used for so many years.

Source

Southern Folklore Quarterly, IX (1945), 147-50.

And that's not all:
See "Seneca Green Corn Dance." For a discussion of the "black drink" (an effusion of *ilex vomitoria*) as a beverage and as used on ritual occasions by southeastern Indians, see *Black Drink: A Native American Tea,* edited by Charles M. Hudson, Athens, Georgia, 1979.

May
30
MEMORIAL DAY

By federal law, Memorial Day is now celebrated the last Monday in May. The origins of Memorial Day, or Decoration Day as it was first known, are remote and mixed. In rural America, the custom of cleaning the cemeteries and decorating graves, usually in the late summer, was an occasion for reunions, revivals, and picnics. But more ancient and widespread are the festivals of the Dead, such as the Japanese Obon or

Memorial Day at Indy

Festival of Lanterns or the Zuñi Indian All Souls' Day which occur at the end of a season or before a new year begins, a time when the boundaries between the living and the dead were believed to thin out. Historically speaking, the immediate origin of the American legal holiday is confused by a number of claimants to priority, as the discussion below shows, and the fact that several states, especially those of the former Confederacy, observe the holiday on different dates. What this seems to indicate is that Memorial Day grew up almost spontaneously from ancient tradition; American folklife; American history; and, as sociologists suggest, from the American need for a secular, patriotic ceremony honoring its military dead. Memorial Day, at the beginning of the summer, like Labor Day at its end, is a convenient open space on the calendar for less somber events, and has become a traditional time for family cookouts in the backyard or sporting events like the Indianapolis Speedway automobile race.

Origin of Memorial Day

General Order No. 11 from General John A. Logan, dated May 5, 1868, begins: "The 30th of May, 1868, is designated for the purpose of strewing with flowers, or otherwise decorating the graves of comrades who died in defense of their country during the late rebellion, whose bodies now lie in almost every city, village and hamlet churchyard in the land...." In 1966 by Congressional resolution and presidential proclamation Waterloo, New York, was designated the "birthplace" of Memorial Day. Here Ernest C. Klein provides the historical data and summarizes the priority of claims regarding the origin of Memorial Day:

For more than ten years, I have been researching the origin of Memorial Day. It began as a hobby when I was a pastor in Boalsburg, Pennsylvania, where it was claimed that the decoration of some graves July 4, 1864, made that village the "Birthplace of Memorial Day." As a matter of record, a total of 25 places have been named in connection with the origin of Memorial Day. One of the oldest claims is that of Jackson, Mississippi, where Sue Landon Vaughan, a descendent of President John Adams, put out a call to decorate Confederate graves on April 26, 1865. Her act is commemorated in stone on a monument erected 1888 on the old State Capital grounds at Jackson, now known as Confederate Park.

Perhaps the most beautiful "claim" is the event at Columbus, Mississippi, where four women in Friendship Cemetery on April 25, 1866, decorated the graves of their fallen soldiers. It was here that the additional act of decorating the graves of 40 Federal soldiers buried there brought about the writing of the poem, "The Blue and Gray" by Francis Miles Finch. Mr. Finch, an attorney in Ithaca, New York, had read of the act in a New York newspaper and included a historical note with his poem, which was published in the *Atlantic Monthly* in 1867. This poem, no doubt, did much to make the Columbus event the best known of all celebrations of Memorial Day.

Hopkinton (Delaware County), Iowa, dedicated a monument on Nov. 7, 1865, to the 44 soldiers from Lenox College who served in the Civil War. Although believed to be the first monument to Civil War soldiers, and thus establishing the basis of Hopkinton's claim to have been the first town in the nation to celebrate Memorial Day, earlier monuments were erected at Kensington, Connecticut, and Stones River National Battlefield, Murfreesboro, Tennessee.

An even earlier event is the decoration of graves by Mrs. George H. Evans (maiden name, Sarah J. Nichols) in a cemetery in Arlington Heights which is near Washington, D.C. Arlington National Cemetery received its first Union soldier for burial in May, 1864. When Mrs. Evans' husband, from Hudson, Michigan, enlisted in the Union Army, Mrs. Evans served as a nurse. On April 13, 1862, with the wife of Chaplain May of the Second Michigan Volunteers and two other women, Mrs.

Evans decorated 17 graves of soldiers who died in the defense of the capitol. The decoration was repeated in 1863 and 1864. Mrs. Evans was recognized in 1873 by the G.A.R. Post 12, Des Moines, as "Originator of Memorial Day."

Richmond, Virginia, has several variations; one is that Cassandra Oliver Moncure decorated, or had a part in decorating, graves in the Hollywood Cemetery. Another is that early services were held on Belle Isle in James River near Richmond. Winchester, Virginia, had a Women's Memorial Society and observed June 6, 1866, the anniversary of the death of Gen. Turner Ashby. But, many southern women established Memorial Societies to organize the return of their dead soldiers to a burial place near home. Petersburg, Virginia, observed June 9, 1866, the anniversary of the assault of 1864. In Blandford Cemetery, the stone of the grave of Nora Fontaine Maury Davidson credits her as "originator of Memorial Day which was inspiration for the National Decoration Day."

Mrs. John A. Logan, wife of the commander-in-chief of the Grand Army of the Republic recounted more than once of her trip in March, 1868, to see the battle fields around Richmond and Petersburg. Because the General, who was serving in Congress at the time, was busy with his legislative duties and thus unable to make the trip, Mrs. Logan described the trip to him, giving him the details about the decorated graves and tiny flags. According to Mrs. Logan, General Order Eleven was written at that time.

Another version credits Mrs. Henry S. Kimball of W. Philadelphia, Pennsylvania, for suggesting the custom to Gen. Logan in a letter she wrote after her return from a southern tour. Yet a third version is given by Logan's Adj. Gen. of the G.A.R., N.P. Chipman, who claims that a comrade of German background, from Cincinnati, suggested the custom of decorating the graves with flowers. According to this version, Chipman wrote most of General Order Eleven.

Carbondale, Illinois, the home area of Gen. Logan, held a service on April 29, 1866, in which returned veterans planned and participated in decorating graves of their buddies who had fallen in battle. Significant is the fact that the speaker was Gen. Logan, who so heartily sponsored Memorial Day services throughout the nation. It was reported by several of Gen. Logan's friends, and repeated in his funeral sermon, that he considered General Order Eleven the "proudest act of his life." One historian writes that no one act did more to remove public prejudice against the G.A.R. than did the inauguration of Memorial Day.

Lloyd Lewis, a newspaperman and friend of Carl Sandburg, suggested that Memorial Day was established in the wild delirium following the funeral of Abraham Lincoln. Another newspaper reporter, James Redpath of Charleston, South Carolina, told of the decorating of 257 graves of Union soldiers by the families of former

AMERICA   CELEBRATES

MEMORIAL DAY

slaves on May 1, 1865. However, this was, properly speaking, a cemetery dedication.

As a result of the meeting of some women in Columbus, Georgia, Mrs. Mary Williams wrote a letter in the local newspaper there on March 12, 1866, which was reprinted throughout the south. She appealed to the women to cover the graves of their soldiers with flowers. April 26 was chosen as the date for the event because that was the anniversary of the surrender of Gen. Joseph E. Johnston, the last of the forces of the Confederate Army. In Linwood cemetery, a tombstone marks the grave of Lizzie Rutherford Ellis, crediting her with the suggestions for originating Memorial Day.

In Waterloo, New York, Henry C. Welles and Gen. John B. Murray are given credit as the originators of the day. Their first observance was May 5, 1866. Their claim is qualified as the "first formal village-wide ·observance of the day." By a Joint Resolution of Congress, Waterloo has been recognized "The Birthplace of Memorial Day."

Source

Annuals of Iowa, XXXIX (1968), 311-14.

Memorial Day Carnival at the Indy Speedway

Car races, like horse races in earlier times, have become a feature of various holidays in America. The "Indy 500" is the major Memorial Day event for a large number of Americans who gather in Indianapolis or around television sets to see it. First run at 500 miles on May 30, 1911, the event has become the premier automobile race in the world with a purse of more than four and one half million dollars, $500,000 of which goes to the winner. The grandstand, which is unique, holds a quarter of a million spectators. This account was written by Diane Ackerman:

Seven drunken, bare-chested teenage boys drape themselves across the windshield of my car as I wait for the light to change. Squirming, they relayer themselves like slabs of bacon, and their mirrored sunglasses send blinding jets of light in a dozen directions. The stoplight probably changed some minutes ago, but all I can see is flesh tanned to the color of walnut oil, cans of beer, hairless chests, and lascivious leers. A rhythmic pounding on the car roof tells me that at least one young man is trying to get in feet first. Out of the back window, I watch six more trying to lift the car by its bumpers and cart it away. Another, with a video camera perched like a falcon on his shoulder, zooms in for a close-up of my chest. Just as I begin wondering if this can possibly be for real, I decipher what they have been chanting maniacally for the past few minutes: "Show us your tits! Show us your tits!"

When the light changes, they melt off the car and surge around a young woman reckless enough to take a stroll in a bikini through what appears to be the largest fraternity party on earth, which begins miles from the Speedway in all directions and now, the day before the race, is building to a crescendo that only tomorrow's auto-eroticism will satisfy.

Sixteenth Street, the main drag that leads to the Speedway, looks like a war zone. At the doorway to one trailer, a large papier-mâché sculpture of a woman, naked from the waist up, wears a sign that says OFFICIAL INSPECTION STATION. Unhinged by the sight of females of all ages and body types, the men chant until they're hoarse and then make breast-juggling motions with their hands. At odd moments a girl will leap atop a trailer and pose with her blouse held open, turn, then button up and disappear into the rowdy mob.

Radios blare, people caterwaul, engines rev, and the combined smear of low drama and teeth-rattling noise becomes fiercer the closer you get to the Speedway itself, that sacred arena, the still center of the carnival. Carnival, from the Latin *carne*, "flesh," and *levare*, "to take away." A tub-thumping, earthy, hell-for-leather orgy before life's fun has to stop.

By 6 A.M., when the gates open on race day, people are already in line to find the seats they purchased last year the morning after the race. Next to them stand fans from all over the country and all over the world: shoe salesmen from Switzerland tired of the Grand Prix circuit, bartenders from Phoenix and autobody workers from Detroit who will leave with their first sunburns, carloads of young men, families with small children, women dressed in brightly colored flame suits that hug the body tightly and suggest that they might, at any moment, be called upon to leap into the pits and take charge.

Souvenir stands are already hawking Indy 500 air fresheners, place mats, Frisbees, coffee mugs, miniature cars, black-and-white checkered victory flags, pot holders, and T-shirts. I can't resist buying a turquoise-and-pink T-shirt with an Indy car zooming off the chest, which vows LIFE BEGINS AT 220 MPH. As I slip it on over my sundress to check the size, and then off again, a platoon of men yell from their girl-watching spot. By now this is old news, and I've learned that the men don't touch you; their assaults (or compliments, depending on your point of view) are strictly verbal.

Inside Gasoline Alley, where the cars are stabled, wide boulevards of combed cement separate rows of garages, and life is as serious as a bank balance. The winner will zoom off with half a million dollars, and just being in the race guarantees about $90,000. Companies donate dozens of miscellaneous awards from $5,000 to $75,000 to the oldest driver, fastest qualifier, leader of the first ten laps, best chief mechanic, driver with the least pit time, and so on.

Bustling around the tense streets of Gasoline Alley, young men dressed in Flash Gordon jumpsuits make sure their cars are fit. A high-wing Cessna airplane flies overhead, towing a banner that reads OLD INDIANA FUN PARK—ZOW! It recalls the Kenneth Fearing poem in which he describes a man's brief, highspeed cartoon life with "Zowie did he live and zowie did he die."

The cars emerge from their garages, some towed by long blue canvas ribbons

that look like the long lines trainers use when exercising Thoroughbreds. Parts of the cars are often wearing black blankets to keep their flanks covered. A low-slung sulfur yellow car belongs to Al Unser, whose son will be racing against him today; it contains the power of over seven hundred horses, though it's only fifteen feet long and weighs only about fifteen hundred pounds. Unser climbs inside the car, which has been molded to the eccentricities of his bottom and back, and stretches his legs far into the nose. He will race practically lying down.

Enclosed entirely in armor, with only a narrow visor open across their eyes, the drivers are all modern knights, riding horsepower. Speed is their lance. Despite the crews, this is not a team sport. Everyone else out on the track will be an opponent. Medieval knights had allegorical names, like Sir Goodheart or Lancelot; these latter-day knights walk around the grounds and drive cars plastered with slogans. Some call them the fastest billboards on earth. But how eerie it is to see a man with "Living Well" emblazoned on his helmet and "Die Hard" stamped on his back. On his shoulder may be the words "Goodyear" or "Champion" or "Sound Design" or "True Value."

What are you to make of a glossy red car driving toward you with "Sleep Cheap" (the slogan of the Red Roof Inns) on both sides of its nose?

Cars, drivers, and pit crews all push through the crowds and take their places on the racetrack. At some point the crews and officials withdraw a little, and the men are alone with their machines. The steering wheels often have been put in *after* them. Sealed up in their narrow cockpits, they adjust the knitted Ninja masks over their faces, fix the rub of the helmet strap, and check the buckles that hold helmet and flame suit together so that their necks won't sprain in the terrible g [gravity] forces of the turns. You can see the loneliness in their eyes, the squinting concentration with which they erase every one of the half million people from the raceway. They hear nothing, see nothing, but track....

The national anthem is followed by a Memorial Day invocation by clergy, and it's no coincidence that the race takes place on Sunday at 11 A.M., church-service time, with a somewhat previous prayer for the dead and injured, and then "Taps" while the stands fall silent. Jim Nabors sings about going back home to Indiana. Thousands of multicolored balloons spiral like DNA into the blue. "Gentlemen," the frail voice of the Speedway's chairperson ritualistically intones, "start your engines." "The magnificent machines," the announcer cries, "are ready!"

A heaving and soughing of engines. Pace cars roll away to lead a warmup lap, then there's a pace lap that reaches a speed of one hundred miles per hour as the crews sprint back to their pits to get ready for action. On the electronic scoreboard, silhouetted fans leap and cheer. The crowd stretching thickly around the two-and-a-half-mile oval twitches and yells, rising like the prerace balloons as the cars roar around the far turn and into sight again. The pace car peels off and the drivers take flight. . . .

Three cars collide, metal parts arcing high into the air, and the race stops for a short while. The cars pause at speed and aren't allowed to change position relative to one another until the debris is cleared from the track and the yellow flag is lifted. Suddenly the race restarts. . . .

The speed at which the cars pass is sense-bludgeoning. Whining, they catapult around a corner into the straight-away while their engines growl and gnaw in a thirty-megaton buzz. You need peripheral vision to see the cars arrive, flash past, vanish around the next turn. They move so fast that unless you fix on one car and track it, a loud blur of color whizzes past. Fans shake their heads no, no, no, no, thirty-three times as the field rushes by. People dropping empty beer cans into the scaffolding underneath the bleachers make a constant drizzle of tin. When cars pull into the pits, the crews come alive, changing treadless tires ("skins"), filling the forty-gallon tanks with methanol, tinkering, adjusting, putting out small fires, handing the driver a drink, then shoving him back—all within ten or twenty seconds.

Not only mechanics and engineers but also aerodynamic specialists work with each driver. As the orange wind sock atop the tower reminds you, this is really an air race. How do you keep a light piece of metal going over two hundred miles per hour on the ground? Though the men and occasionally women inside are called drivers, they sit in a *cockpit*, they worry about the car's *wings*, and they are obsessed with *wake turbulence*. Small canard fins at the *nose cone* up front pay homage to Burt Rutan's *Voyager* and all the other canard designs he's made famous over the years. The rear wing functions like an upside-down airplane wing, producing *down force*. An airplane wing is rounded on top, but car wings are rounded on the bottom. Air whooshes all around the wing, but it has farther to travel along the bottom, becomes thinner, and produces a low-pressure area. On top, the higher pressure bears down and keeps the car on the ground. The car's underside holds the ground, too. But these effects combine to churn up small tornadoes, and the swirling whirlpools of wind that each car trails behind it put the next car in peril. . . .

Beating, banging, fighting the steering wheel, pulling g's, the furious cars slide in and out of corners. Drivers need to be aggressive but at a controlled pace. They must be mentally relaxed, but there is constant battering to their neck and muscles. Few sports stay right on the edge of life from start to finish. Exhaust pours from the cars, and, from the drivers, exhaustion. A passion for the extreme must be what fuels drivers and fans alike: a dizzying, all-out, pedal-to-the-metal, death-defying effort for as long as life allows. . . .

I don't believe most race fans come to see crashes. They come to see their gods

MEMORIAL DAY

parading at speed before them. Accidents happen, but they are described as "spectacular," and the spectators just confirm how gripping the element of sheer spectacle is. You can't really love cars without disowning the preindustrial world. But the scorpion of progress has a wicked sting in its tail. Nature may thwart us at every turn, but the machines we've created and endowed with superhuman power sometimes terrify and thwart us even more. When men are injured in crashes, the fans sound truly aggrieved. When men walk away from devastating smashups, the fans shriek with joy. They have come partly to see Man vs. Machine, urgently hoping that man will prevail.

Source

Traveler, May, 1988. From an article in "The Traveling Spectator."

June
13
MINERS' UNION DAY

Miners' Union Day was the annual rally and celebration of Local #1 of the Western Federation of Miners which had its headquarters in Butte, Montana, where the local was founded on June 13, 1878. The militant Western Federation of Miners considered itself the toughest union in America. The International Workers of the World, better known as the Wobblies, an equally tough and violent union, was at-

tempting to gain control of the federation, and the flames of the dispute were reportedly being fanned by the bosses who were glad to pit the two unions against each other. On June 13, 1914, during a strike by the federation, a parade of 10,000 miners was broken up by Wobblie agitators and the Union Hall was blown up by dynamite. This act brought about the declaration of martial law in the town, broke the strike, and forced the miners' union to leave Butte. Miners' Union Day was revived in 1934 during the time of the NRA.

Copper Camp: Stories of the World's Greatest Mining Town, Butte, Montana (New York, 1943), compiled by the Writers' Program of the Works Projects Administration, states that "according to the old time miner's calendar there are three regular legal holidays and four *Butte* holidays—St. Patrick's Day, St. George's Day, Miners' Union Day and Election Day." The importance of St. Patrick's Day and St. George's Day reflect the preponderance of Irish and Cornish miners in Butte at that time.

AMERICA CELEBRATES

MINERS' UNION DAY

Butte Miners' Union Day

In an article on the folklore of the Butte, Montana, hardrock miners, Wayland D. Hand assembles information on holiday observances. Here he draws both from the popular verses of Joseph H. Duffy who evokes the color and tradition of this miners' celebration and from Duffy's book, Butte Was Like That, *which contains a prose account of the same celebration. He also cites the Federal Writers' Project memoir of the period:* Copper Camp: Stories of the World's Greatest Mining Town.

Of all the entertainments and holidays in a miner's life in Butte [Montana] in the old days nothing bulked as large as Miners' Union Day, celebrated annually on June 13 from 1878 until 1914 and resumed again in 1934. More was made of the holiday in the days now almost beyond recall than at any time since the first World War, when a whole day's entertainment, including speechmaking, contests of various sorts, picnicking, and all the other things that go with an outing at an amusement park, was held at Columbia Gardens in a canyon east of Butte at the foot of the Continental Divide. The ballad "One Miners' Union Day," by Joe Duffy, gives an unforgettable picture of what happened at Columbia Gardens on one such gala occasion:

The old Butte Miners' Union, one 13th day of June,
   Held a picnic at the "Gardens," where nature was in tune.
The sun was shining brightly and a happy crowd was there;

The Gardens used to advertise: "Fun, Flowers and Fresh Air."

Each street-car stopping at the gate, had passengers galore
   And when a car was empty, it went back to town for more.
The miners took their families, each mucker took a "frill"—
   The 10-day men took bottled goods to help ward off a chill.

The babies played upon the grass, the girls played on the swings,
   The hobby-horses galloped 'round, their riders grabbing rings.
The young folks all were dancing, the old folks watched the games;
   To mention each feat by itself, would take too many names.

The Sullivans and Harringtons, the Murphys and Malones,
   Richards, Williams, Thomases, Trevithick and Treglowns—
Take-a-hitch and Six-year-itch, Olson, Johnson, Thor
   Were the names of some contestants when they had the tug-o'-war.

The next four stanzas treat the speech of the orator of the day who tells of a baby boy in Dublin who grew to manhood, emigrated to Butte City, joined the union, and, starting from outside guard, "wint thro' all th' chairs—" at which "The audience applauded like they do at County Fairs."

He waved them down to silence—of water took a drink—

"That ould couple back in Ireland—little did they think
That on this 13th day of June, nineteen an' ought, ought,
    An educated audience would be upon this spot."

"We have a dhrillin' contest an' a thry at muckin' rock
    An' th' street-cars will be runnin' afther 12 o'clock;
There's a lot here to amuse ye, for this is a day av joy—
    An' in closing let me mintion, that I was that baby bhoy."

Written much in the same vein, and once more featuring an Irish hero, Bill Burke's "Miners' Union Day in Butte," with a descriptive subtitle, "In the Good Old Days," takes one to a typical parade held in the city proper, with five bands playing, and all the rest.

Call me early in the mornin'
And press me other suit,
For tomorrow is the greatest day
Of all the days in Butte.
Pluck a posy for me frock coat,
Put some lard upon me shoes,
Look in me union stamp book
To be sure I've paid me dues.

'Tis Miners' Union Day, dear,
I'm to wear a white cockade.
I'm fourth assistant marshal
In the Miners' Day parade.
I'm to ride a fine big bay horse;
Sure your heart will burst with pride
Whin you see me ridin' down on Park
    Street
Like a mounted Lord asthride.

I'll be marchin' with the mayor;
The cops 'll all be there.
Lay out me brightest necktie,
Me new, green shirt I'll wear.
Six thousand miners will be marchin'
While I ride in stately ease,
Just like a Celtic warrior
As handsome as you please.

Five bands will all be playin'
Sammy Treloar at their lead,
While I ride in time to music
Asthride me prancin' steed.
I'll arise at dawn tomorrow
Long afore the whistles toot,
Sure, I wouldn't miss a minute
When 'tis Miners' Day in Butte.

There'll be shots and scoops and
    Shawn O's,
And big cigars galore;
There'll be dancers, fights, and frolics,
And then we'll drink some more.
There'll be arguments a-plenty,
And perhaps a broken snoot;
For anything can happen
When 'tis Miners' Day in Butte.

The pièce de résistance of any Miners' Union Day was the drilling contest, and this more than anything kept alive memories of working conditions in the mines in the early days of the camp. Mike McNichols and Walter Bradshaw were Butte's greatest drilling team, Bradshaw alone winning $13,000 over the years in prize and wager money at contests all over the West. Joe Freethy, another Butte hammersmith and a Cousin Jack, teamed with Bradshaw at Spokane in 1901 to drill fifty-five inches in fifteen minutes for a world's record. The contests were held not only in Columbia

AMERICA CELEBRATES

MINERS' UNION DAY

Gardens but at other places in town and at the mines themselves; and granite boulders around town, notably one in Mrs. Globich's yard in the McQueen addition, provided training grounds for aspiring hammersmen. *Copper Camp*, from which I take much of my material, lists the names of other famous teams, including those of a couple of blind men, Harry Rodda and Mike Davey, and gives an excellent description of how short steel is replaced by longer rods without the loss of rhythm in the blows of the double jacker. I am informed that a variety of granite found in Silver Plume, Colorado, was much in demand throughout the West for drilling contests because of its unusual hardness, but all that is changed now that the sport has almost died out. Although drilling contests are occasionally still held in a few camps in the West, no one seems to recall any in Butte for a decade or more. On Labor Day, 1941, I witnessed an exciting drilling contest in Virginia City, Nevada, with three or four crack teams performing. Machine drilling contests are sometimes held, as for example on Miners' Union Day in Park City, Utah, but these have never gained wide favor.

Because of the fact that no special skill was needed, mucking contests were very popular also, and prodigious amounts of rock were mucked from metal "turn sheets," or slabs of iron, brought to the Gardens from the mines in trucks. As in mucking, strength and weight, rather than skill, counted in the tug of war and provided a good means of stimulating group rivalries. Duffy relates one such contest in which Serbians were pitted against the Irish, and after a see-saw battle appeared to be winning, when the wives and sweethearts of the Sons of Erin grabbed the end of the rope and saved the day for their team. What happened after that belongs to the apocryphal lore of the camp. The bull and bear fight, a favorite divertisement of miners in California and elsewhere during the gold-rush period, was revived as late as July 4, 1895, in Butte; and rat baiting, which never was especially associated with the mines, enjoyed a perilous illegal existence, along with cock fighting, dog fighting, and the like.

Source

California Folklore Quarterly, V (1946), 169-72.

June
19

JUNETEENTH

January 1, 1863, the date of President Lincoln's Emancipation Proclamation, is solemnly commemorated in many American black communities. It is, however, only one of a number of "freedom day" celebrations held on various dates, for the end of slavery was a gradual process and often a local one which evoked local observances. Thus the date on which General Gordon Granger arrived in Texas—June 19, 1863—with the avowed intention of enforcing Lincoln's

proclamation, is commemorated as "Juneteenth" in eastern Texas and beyond, and a considerable body of tradition and lore has grown up about it. Why is it called "Juneteenth"? Mrs. E. B. Tollette, who lives in a rural black community of Tollette, Arkansas, has this to say: " I was talking with a friend about it today and he said, jokingly, 'You know how we name things,' and said 'was the nineteenth' and says, 'then we began to call it "Juneteenth,"' said, 'we nickname these things.'"

Juneteenth in the South and West

William H. Wiggins, Jr., based this account largely on the "oral records and lifestyles of the many members of the black masses," supplemented with "written records":

June 19, 1865, was freedom day for slaves in east Texas and portions of the surrounding states. It was on this day that General Gordon Granger landed with federal troops in Galveston, Texas, with the

expressed mission of forcing the slave owners to release their slaves. Many of these slaves had been brought to east Texas from other southern states, such as Tennessee, Georgia, Virginia and "all over the south" by slave owners "because the abolitionist had talked freedom for the Negroes and they were afraid that their slaves would be freed and all that investment that they had [made]...." [Legends of three types] soon arose explaining the date of the celebration ... : (1) the news withheld to

JUNETEENTH

make one last crop, (2) the news delayed by mule travel, and (3) the news delayed by the murder of the messenger. The most frequently collected legend was the one which explains the date in light of the master's need to make one more crop. Versions of it were used to explain the observance in east Texas and southwestern Arkansas.

Although none of the informants told the legend of the slain messenger, there were several versions of the mule legend collected. The most stylized account was included in a letter sent by Haywood Hygh, Jr., a high school teacher in Compton, California, who attended Juneteenth celebrations as a lad in Karnack, Texas. He wrote:

> One [story] is of paramount importance to us. How Juneteenth got started. The story is legendary in nature. However, my eighty-six year old father swears that it is the truth; that an ex-Union soldier (Negro) rode a mule from Washington, with a message given him by Abe Lincoln, Yessuh, all the way to this section of the country. And when he got to Oklahoma, he informed the slaves that they were free. From there he went to Arkansas [sic] and Texas. It was the nineteenth of June when he arrived in Oklahoma. My father swears it, and he says if his father was still alive, he would do the same swearing without batting his eyes. Many of the old-timers are with him one hundred percent.

Only two informants indicated that they knew the mule legend. Artis Lovelady said he had heard it, but confessed that "I don't know the whole story."

Juneteenth was also originally celebrated in Louisiana. Rupert Secrett, retired barber and former sponsor of the celebration in Brenham, Texas, mentioned friendly "hurrahing" among blacks of Louisiana and Texas as to which state was the first to celebrate emancipation. Louisiana blacks often said: "The people in Texas didn't know they was free until the people from Louisiana came over and told 'em." David Johnson, Dean of Students at Texas College, Tyler, Texas, and a native of Louisiana, recalls the celebration being observed "... all over the state of Louisiana." He specifically recalled the celebration being strong around the New Orleans area, the city from which General Granger began his historic voyage to Galveston. And U. T. D. Williams, Steward in the Ebenzer AME church, Tyler, Texas, attended Juneteenth celebrations in the northwestern town of Grand Bayou, Louisiana, where "the white folks" furnished all the food.

Southwestern Arkansas was another area of an adjoining state into which the Juneteenth celebration spilled over. This southwestern area of Arkansas, like the adjoining east Texas, is heavily populated with blacks. Mrs. E. B. Tollette lived in the all-Negro town of Tollette in this rural southwestern section of the state. Tollette, Arkansas, "was a large community" of "farmers" and "home owners." She also recalled, with pride, that it also had its own post office. The black farmers in Blevins, Paraloma, Nashville, Tollette, etc. "had great big picnics on the 19th of June." . . .

In the late 1800s many ex-slaves began to migrate out of the tri-state area into the territory which was soon to become Oklahoma . . . and took their precious freedom festival with them. Like the blacks who would take part in the great northern migration of the early 1900s, the ex-slaves who took part in this westward movement of the 1880s were close enough to the end of physical slavery to still have a deep appreciation for the day which signaled its end. Therefore, throughout Oklahoma, especially the newly formed all-black communities, they transplanted their Juneteenth celebrations. Mrs. Lillian Crisp, a public school teacher in Ardmore, Oklahoma, taught in the all-black Oklahoma town of Tatums and recalled Juneteenth being an all-day celebration of picnics, baseball games, occasional political speeches, square dancing and general socializing.

There was a second migration of blacks from the southwestern states of Louisiana, Arkansas, Texas and Oklahoma in the late 1930s and early 1940s. This time the move was further west to California, with the major attraction being good paying jobs in the war industries of the Golden State. So many blacks left the peonage of east Texas sharecropping, the unfulfilled promise of Oklahoma's all-black communities, and the rigid segregation patterns of Arkansas and Louisiana and headed west

to California in search of a better life. However, the Juneteenth celebration was one of the cultural casualties of this migration. The generation of blacks who made this trip were some seventy odd years removed from June 19, 1865, that day of days when their ancestors became free men.

These west coast offspring still honored Juneteenth, but not in a manner that would rival their forefathers. In California there were attempts to transplant the tradition once again, but the celebration had dwindled in scope to Juneteenth picnics sponsored by blacks from the same state. For example, an "Oklahoma Picnic" is held in Los Angeles' Lincoln Heights Park every June 19th. However, the biggest change in Juneteenth observances by blacks on the west coast has been homecoming. Like the swallows of Capistrano, each year many of them migrate back home on the weekend nearest the 19th of June. At the 1972 celebration in the all-black community of Branchville, Texas, blacks came back from Kansas, Missouri and California.

Juneteenth has also been celebrated in isolated areas of Alabama and Florida. Mrs. Minnie Lee Riley, an old member of Miles Chapel AME church, Little Rock, Arkansas, told, after church services, how Juneteenth was celebrated in her native home of Clark County, Alabama. And the 19th of June has been observed in the southern Florida town of Boynton Beach. . . .

JUNETEENTH

The most common type of Juneteenth celebrations was an all-day secular affair which began around 10 o'clock in the morning with a parade and ended around 1 o'clock the next morning with the breakup of the dance or "suppers." In the afternoon there were various activities, the biggest being the baseball game, "tie downs" [calf roping], individual games and eating. One of the biggest parades was annually held in Brenham, Texas.... Brenham's parades were routed through the heart of the downtown area and witnessed by very large mixed crowds. Holsey Johnson, a sixty year old farmer, regularly attended these celebrations in Brenham and recalled that it was so crowded "you couldn't walk on the streets."

The parade was composed of blacks from the surrounding communities who would prepare their own floats. Mrs. Eloise Holmes, a retired school teacher who grew up in Brenham, Texas, recalled that "each community would decorate floats and they would select children from that community to ride on these floats." Accompanying these ten or twelve floats were men on horseback and a brass band.

The parade had a king and queen. The queen wore the title, "The Goddess of Liberty," and was selected by a money raising contest, in which several "nice looking girls" would solicit donations. Each one carried shoeboxes for this purpose and raised sums which ranged from $600.00 to $1,000.00. The king was selected by the queen.

Source

" 'Free at Last!': A Study of Afro-American Emancipation Day Celebrations," Ph.D. Dissertation, Indiana University, 1974, 82-85, 88-91. The quotations, unless otherwise indicated, are from interviews, tape recordings, and correspondence which appear in an appendix to the dissertation.

And that's not all:
See "Emancipation Day."

June
24
ST. JOHN'S OR MIDSUMMER'S DAY

The Feast of St. John the Baptist is unusual in that it is celebrated on the day of his death rather than on the day of his birth. John was sanctified before he was born. He has been called the saint of the summer solstice because his feast has long been associated with Midsummer's Day and solstitial rites. Thus round dances, men and women bathing nude together, predictions of death, and bonfires are common to the

St. John's festival. Fire, a symbol of the sun's power, is central to Midsummer rites, and hilltop blazes through which people leap, drive their animals, and hurl objects cleanse evil from the community and renew reproductive powers. Torches from such fires are carried through fields and even applied to them. On Midsummer's Eve witches, fairies, and ghosts range abroad, evidence of its association with ancient beliefs about the dead. The day is also sacred to lovers. The mingling of these themes, pagan and Christian, are nowhere better seen than in William Shakespeare's *A Midsummer Night's Dream*. They are also echoed in the phrase John is supposed to have uttered while preaching in rivalry with Jesus: "He must increase while I decrease"—after St. John's Day the days shorten; after Christmas they lengthen again.

St. John's Eve Calinda

The "kalinda" were the songs of braggadocio sung by the stick-fighters of Trinidad. The stick-fighters, who represented various black "yards" or districts, were so quarrelsome that their stick-fights and bragging bouts often ended in riots. When stick-fighting was banned in 1881, the kalinda was also banned. In its place, a new kind of song emerged based on the "cariso," lyric songs which the women had sung in the intervals or recesses between kalinda singing. These the men transformed into erotic and politically satiric songs, which in turn developed into the modern calypso. This account is from "The Dance in Place Congo" by George Washington Cable, the New Orleans local colorist:

The true Calinda was bad enough. In Louisiana, at least, its song was always a

ST. JOHN'S OR MIDSUMMER'S DAY

grossly personal satirical ballad, and it was the favorite dance all the way to Trinidad. To dance it publicly is not allowed this side of the West Indies. All this Congo Square business was suppressed at one time; 1843, says tradition. . . . One Calinda is still familiar to all Creole ears. It has long been a vehicle for the white Creole's satire; for generations the man of municipal politics was fortunate who escaped entirely a lampooning set to its air.

In my childhood I used, at one time, to hear, every morning, a certain black *marchande des calas*—peddler-woman selling rice croquettes—chanting the song as she moved from street to street at the sunrise hour with her broad, shallow, laden basket balanced on her head.

In other words, a certain Judge Preval gave a ball—not an outdoor Congo dance—and made such Cuffees as could pay three dollars a ticket. It doesn't rhyme, but it was probably true. "Dance, dance the Calindá! Boujoum! Boujoum!"

The number of stanzas has never been counted; here are a few of them.

> Dans l'equirie la 'y' avé grand gala;
> Mo cré choual la yé t b'en étonné.

Miché Preval, li té capitaine bal;
So cocher Louis, té maite cérémonie.

Y avé des négresses belle passé maitresses,
Qui volé bel-bel dans l'ormoire momselle.

....

Ala maite la geô li trouvé si drôle,
Li dit, "moin aussi, mo fé bal ici."

Ouatchman la yé yé tombé la dans;
Yé fé gran' déga dans léguirie la.
(etc.)

"It was in a stable that they had this gala night," says the song; "the horses there were greatly astonished. Preval was captain; his coachman, Louis, was master of ceremonies. There were negresses made prettier than their mistresses by adornments stolen from the ladies' wardrobes (*armoires*). But the jailer found it all so funny that he proposed to himself to take an unexpected part; the watchmen came down. . . ."

No official exaltation bought immunity from the jeer of the Calinda. Preval was a magistrate. Stephen Mazureau, in his attorney-general's office, the song likened to a bull-frog in a bucket of water. A page might be covered by the roll of victims. The masters winked at these gross but harmless liberties and, as often as any others, added stanzas of their own invention.

The Calinda ended these dissipations of the summer Sabbath afternoons. They could not run far into the night, for all the fascinations of all the dances could not excuse the slave's tarrying in public places after a certain other *bon-djoum*! (that was not of the Calinda, but of the regular nine-o'clock evening gun) had rolled down Orleans Street from the Place d'Armes; and the black man or woman who wanted to keep a whole skin on the back had to keep out of the Calaboose. Times have changed, and there is nothing to be regretted in the change that has come over Congo Square. Still a glamour hangs over its dark past. There is the pathos of slavery, the poetry of the weak oppressed by the strong, and of limbs that danced after toil, and of barbaric love-making. The rags and semi-nakedness, the bamboula drum, the dance, and almost the banjo, are gone; but the *bizarre* melodies and dark lovers' apostrophes live on. . . .

Source

Century Magazine, IX (February 1886), 527-28.

Seeing the Future on Midsummer Eve

This information was reported from family tradition by Ruth Howland Deyo, "a housewife living in Morehead City," North Carolina.

My mother used to tell tales handed down to her mother, whose forebears came from England, about fascinating pagan rites connected with Midsummer Eve (June 23). She also described divination rites which she and her friends practiced on Midsummer Eve. Some of these I have practiced with my friends.

Mamma said that in England young maidens gathered flowers and wove garlands to be worn around the neck on Midsummer Eve and Midsummer Day. In the villages great bonfires were built for Midsummer Eve. These fires were lighted with need fire, kindled by friction. The bonfires were votive fires. Into them the people threw herbs, gathered by moonlight, as charms against witchcraft. Salt, thrown in, warded off bad luck. The people ate Midsummer cake, drank wine, and danced around the bonfires, calling forth good spirits to render assistance in love. They also practiced all sorts of divinations.

When Mamma was a young girl, living in Morehead City [North Carolina], at Midsummer Eve she and her friends practiced a few divinations. I will describe them as they were told to me.

On Midsummer Eve, at 12 o'clock noon, you put a glass of water in the sun, leaving it there for one hour. During this hour you must not speak a word. If you speak, the spell is broken. If you have not spoken when the hour has passed, you take the white of an egg and pour it in the glass. In a few minutes the egg white has formed a figure indicating the occupation of your husband-to-be. I practiced this divination during my teens. One time the egg white formed a tree trunk; at another, a tent; and at a third, the spars and rigging of a ship.

If you pare an apple round and round without a break in the peeling and throw the peel over the left shoulder, it will

ST. JOHN'S OR MIDSUMMER'S DAY

form the initial or initials of your future husband.

When girl friends are spending the night together, let each one be given a bowl of water. Write all the letters of the alphabet on bits of cardboard and place the cards, letters down, in the water. Next morning the initials of the beloved will be face up.

If you have a well, take a mirror at noon of Midsummer Eve and reflect the sun's rays into the water. (Remember, the spell is broken if you speak.) In a few minutes you will see the reflected image of your husband-to-be.

Mrs. Mamie Murdock Tolson (Mrs. Cornelius Tolson), whose daughter, Mrs. Jesse Bell, lives in Morehead City, told me she saw her future husband in this way. She and some friends were flashing their mirrors in the well at Wildwood, where they lived as young girls. It was Miss Mamie's turn. The others knew whom she was to marry—she was engaged. They were a little frightened when the water began to boil, but no one said a word. The ripples spread out, wider and wider. Then a man's face appeared. But it wasn't the face of her betrothed. It was the face of a neighbor, Mr. Cornelius Tolson, a man forty-four years older than Miss Mamie.

Another interesting tale was one that Mamma's grandmother told her children. When she was a girl my great-grandmother lived in Beaufort. One Midsummer Eve Night she and girl friends spending the

night with her were performing their magic rites by roasting eggs in the shell in the fireplace. At midnight the husbands-to-be were supposed to walk into the room through the unlatched door. It was a calm moonlight night. All of the girls were silent and shaking with excitement. Suddenly, a roaring, rushing wind was heard, and a mighty gust shook the house. Smoke billowed forth from the fireplace, stinging the eyes of the girls and making them cough as they sat in a semicircle around the fireplace. The door blew open, and two men entered. They carried a pine coffin. One of the girls screamed and fainted. She died before the year was out.

Source

North Carolina Folklore, VIII (1960), 29-30.
And that's not all:
See "To See Your Future Husband on Halloween."

St. John's Day and the Summer Solstice

Peter J. Hamilton of San Juan, Puerto Rico collected this information:

[In Puerto Rico, saints'] days are observed at least by not working, and often by large attendance at church services. On Corpus Christi the sacred image is carried to slow music through the streets, but in the capital, as in Spain, the greatest celebration is on St. John's Day. This is of interest, because really reminding of the primitive celebration at the Summer Solstice. The Church has appropriated the season, but some customs point back of church usages. On that morning throwing salt on the palm flowers will ensure a crop of cocoas, and a relic of sympathetic magic is seen in the custom of planting a bit of hair at the root of a banana tree—hair and bush growing and helping each other. In Spain, but less often in Puerto Rico, one can see his or her future fate the midnight before St. John's by ceremonies similar to those [poet John] Keats has associated for us with St. Agnes' Eve.

Source

Folk-Lore, XXXVIII (1927), 64.

Parada San Juan Bautista

Laura Quinn provided this background on a St. John's parade:

There was dancing in the street outside Rosa Santiago's house in South Camden [New Jersey] last week. Everyone was memorizing steps.

Yesterday, Santiago paced in front of a trailer packed full of children, some wearing oversize straw hats and flouncy skirts. No one was sitting still and the trailer heaved back and forth.

"We want to teach the children about the culture," Santiago said, shouting directions to the children. Moments later, Camden's 37th Annual St. John the Baptist Day Parade (Parade San Juan Bautista) began and a chain of beauty queens, salsa dancers and jazzed-up Toyotas headed down Cooper Street. . . .

"The Spanish like to have one day to be recognized," said Santiago, who moved to Camden from Puerto Rico 33 years ago and has participated in the yearly parade ever since. The event is billed as the only organized parade in Camden and is cherished by many of the city's 15,000 Hispanic residents.

More than 600 people lined the parade route and then gathered in Wiggins Park to eat ice cream, sip cold drinks and watch as awards were given to the top floats. Folk dancers performed the *tuna* and *cumbia* in the hot sun.

The parade culminated a week of festivities—including a banquet, art exhibits and a flag-raising ceremony—recognizing Hispanics in the city.

For some, yesterday's parade was an occasion for nostalgia. Felix E. Montes, president of this year's event and a city administrator, was born in Mayguez, Puerto Rico, and came to Camden in 1944 at age 7. He pointed to the Campbell Soup Co. factory where his father got his first job in this country.

Elena Morales, 17, emigrated just 10 years ago. Yesterday, Morales, wearing a bright red floral skirt, danced *La Plana* in the parade. "It's nice to show people what our country has," she said. "It's not a rich country, but it has it's own [culture]."

The parade is named after the patron saint of Puerto Rico—St. John the Baptist. Christopher Columbus, who historians say discovered the Caribbean island in 1493, christened it St. John the Baptist, which was later changed to Rich Port, or Puerto Rico.

AMERICA   CELEBRATES

ST. JOHN'S OR MIDSUMMER'S DAY

Puerto Ricans first migrated to Camden in the 1940s, many taking jobs at Campbell Soup. By the 1970s, about 7,500 Puerto Ricans were living in Camden, and the number had doubled by this decade....

One purpose of the parade, said Santiago, is to keep Puerto Rican traditions alive among the city's young. In her neighborhood, she is the official guardian of these traditions. "We want to teach the children about the culture," she said. "It's very important."

Santiago was up at 6 A.M. yesterday preparing the float, festooned with red, white and blue crepe paper. "It's very important for me to get involved with the kids," she said, moments before her dancers—a few barely old enough to walk—headed down Cooper Street.

Source

The Philadelphia Inquirer, June 26, 1989.

Running the Rooster on St. John's Day

Captain John G. Bourke collected these items in the Rio Grande Valley:

Chicken fighting is freely indulged in by the Mexicans, as it was by the Arabs, but it was probably played by Romans and Carthaginians in Spain long before the Arabs landed; therefore not much stress need be laid upon its existence. The Romans caused to fight both chickens and quails.

There is another form of diversion with fowl which must, however, be mentioned, although it too, in one shape or another, has spread over much of the surface of the earth, and that is the great sport of *correr el gallo*, or "running the rooster," which strictly speaking is more frequently an old hen. The victim selected is buried up to its neck in sand, and then horsemen dash at full speed up to the chicken, lean out from the saddle and try to grasp it. There are many failures, involving ludicrous mishaps and perilous tumbles, but finally some rider, bolder or more dextrous than his comrades, seizes the hen by the neck and gallops down the valley, followed by all the other contestants. The hen is usually torn to pieces in the struggle. This was the method observed at the Indian pueblo of Santo Domingo, New Mexico, in the month of August, after harvest, in 1881.

In the lower Rio Grande, on St. John's Day (June), the young men engage in *correr el gallo*, but instead of a living bird make use of an image of paper, ribbon, and feathers. In both cases the riding is superb, and there are not a few accidents.

Source

Journal of American Folklore, IX (1896), 101-02.

July

4

INDEPENDENCE DAY

England's colonies in the New World began armed conflict against British imperial power in April of 1775, after the famous midnight ride of Paul Revere alerted minutemen in Lexington and Concord, Massachusetts, to the impending arrival of hostile British troops. By July 2, 1776, the colonies voted for independence from Britain. A document stating this intent was subsequently prepared. Independence Day,

the most important American national holiday, commemorates the signing of this Declaration of Independence by John Hancock—president of the Continental Congress, July 4, 1776,

at Philadelphia—and its subsequent adoption by the delegates from the thirteen colonies. The holiday's observance increased in popularity as a sense of national pride and accomplishment increased, and by the 1880s Independence Day had become a major patriotic occasion. It is a political holiday and a community enterprise traditionally observed with fireworks, parades, band concerts, oratory, bonfires, picnics, block parties, public entertainment, and especially sporting events. Like Memorial Day, its celebration has always been affected by national crises, such as the sectional conflicts of the 1850s, the Civil War, and later wars.

July Fourth and the Rodeo

Mody Boatright documents his history of "The American Rodeo" fully with contemporary descriptions and newspaper accounts. He does not emphasize its association with Independence Day, being mainly concerned with the rodeo as "a professional sport ... that grew out of the daily labor of the cowboy" and contributed toward making him a "popular symbol of

the American frontier." Nonetheless, here he mentions some Independence Day rodeo observances:

In 1880 he would have been a hardy soul indeed who predicted that in the first half of the next century the cowboy would become the leading American folk hero. For at that time he was known, if known at all outside the region he frequented, at best as

a provincial rustic and at worst as a ruffian and a thief and a murderer. How he attained his present status is a complicated story, only a single chapter of which will be attempted here.

One of the most effective means by which the cowboy established a favorable image of himself was by the public exhibitions of his occupational skills, skills hitherto unknown to Europeans and Eastern Americans. The range cattle industry, out of which these skills developed, had been established in the southern tip of Texas by Mexican rancheros, from whom the Anglo Texans borrowed the equipment and techniques for handling wild longhorn cattle by men on horseback. Basic to this equipment was the rope (*lasso, lariat, reata*), and a strong saddle with a horn to serve as a snubbing post. A highly skilled roper, who could catch an animal by the horns, neck, forefeet, hindfeet or any single foot named, was much admired. Admired too was his horse, which knew exactly what to do when he found a steer or a bull on the other end of the rope.

These horses had not been brought up as pets. Whether they were captured mustangs or horses raised on the ranch, they had been allowed to run on the range until mature. When first ridden they invariably tried to unseat their riders by a series of violent movements called pitching (bucking in the Northwest). Since pitching was peculiar to the range horse of the Americas, the contest between horse and rider had a novel fascination for those

unaccustomed to range life. It has an equal (though not novel) fascination for the range men themselves, for whenever broncs were to be ridden cowboys and *vaqueros* gathered to see the show and to shout derision or encouragement. . . .

In a bronc riding contest held in Deer Trail, Colorado, on July 4, 1869, a cowboy named Gardenshire, lately from England, by riding a famous outlaw horse known as Montana Blizzard, won first prize and the praise of a newspaper reporter, who described the performance in some detail and called it "a magnificent piece of horsemanship."

Perhaps earlier than the Deer Trail competition was a more elaborate one held in San Antonio, and reported by John Duval in a book of which he says all the events happened, though not necessarily to the persons or in the sequence represented. Participating were "Comanche warriors, decked out in their savage finery," Texas "rangers" and "a few Mexican rancheros, dressed in their steeple crown, broad brim sombreros, showy scarfs and 'slashed' trousers, holding gracefully in check the fiery mustangs on which they were mounted.

Some of the events, such as picking up objects from the ground, shooting at targets from horses running at full speed, riding hanging by one leg from the saddle and firing under the horse's neck, were related to border warfare and the protection of herds. But it was the bronc riding that Duval found the most "interesting and exciting of them." Each contestant saddled his own horse in the ring without assistance. The winner was a ranger named McMullen, whose mount, "snorting and absolutely screaming with rage and terror, gave one tremendous bound, and then darted off at headlong speed across the prairie.". . .

In view of the enthusiastic admiration they elicited, as well as the business they brought to town, it was to be expected that roping and riding contests would be staged throughout the cattle country. Those held before 1890 include the following: Austin, Texas, 1883; Pecos, Texas, 1883; San Antonio, 1883; Galveston, 1883; Mobeetie, Texas, 1884; Miles City, Montana, 1885; Albuquerque, 1886; Denver, 1887; Montrose, Colorado, 1887; San Antonio, 1888; Prescott, Arizona, 1888; Canadian, Texas, 1888; San Angelo, Texas, 1889.

The Pecos contest, held on July 4, 1883, was staged to settle a long dispute among the ranch hands about which outfit had the best ropers. The news spread rapidly, and soon the town was overcrowded with people.

> Cash prizes were posted, and the leading ropers from each ranch were selected. Morgan Livingston of the NA ranch took first money, and Trav Windham second. There was a barbecue, and the town was crowded with people. Business was booming, especially around the saloons.

Exactly one year before the Pecos contest a celebration had been held at North Platte, Nebraska, that initiated a series of events that was to bring the cowboy and his skills before millions in America and Europe. The ranchmen of that region decided to celebrate the Fourth of July with an "Old Glory Blowout" and appointed William Cody to get it up. Under the name of Buffalo Bill, Cody was already famous as a scout and stage actor whose role was to play himself in a melodrama of variant forms, but always involving Indians, cowboys, scouts and frontiersmen, a lost maiden and comic relief. As he had long felt the need of a larger stage, he welcomed the opportunity. "I got out some handbills," he said later, "and sent them to all the ranches around for hundreds of miles and advertised in the papers that prizes would be given for some fancy cowboy stunts." He expected about a hundred cowboys and a thousand responded. To the cowboy events he added the attack on the Deadwood stagecoach by Indians (he had used real Indians on the stage), horse races, shooting contests and a drive of a small herd of buffalo. The attendance was gratifying. "North Platte had the biggest crowd it has ever had before or since." "I tried it out on my neighbors," Cody said "and they lived through it and liked it. I made up my mind I'd take the show East."

For three decades Buffalo Bill's Wild West Show was to tour America and Europe and to bring the cowboy before millions and to win approval of the ranking military brass of both continents, the sporting plutocracy and the peerage and royalty of Europe, that is, of the taste makers of the era.

AMERICA CELEBRATES

INDEPENDENCE DAY

Source

American Quarterly, XVI (1964), 195-98.

Homemade Fireworks

Katharine G. Ecob remembers homemade fireworks and noisemakers before "prudence, law, or inertia finally ended these unique demonstrations":

Well after the turn of the century the village of Gilbertsville, New York, was still celebrating the Fourth of July in an unusual way.

During the night of July 3rd there was a pandemonium of drums, bells, and every variety of noise. Rising above the tumult was the indescribable sound of a "horse fiddle." This was made by stretching a rope tightly across the top of an open barrel. A plank, serving as a bow and drawn vigorously over the rope, produced a screech that could be heard for miles.

More unusual were the "fireballs." A day in advance a few older girls, instructed by a very old man, would gather to make them. Candlewicking was twisted into loose balls about the size of a small grapefruit. With a long needle and string they were stitched through and through to hold the wicking together. The finished balls were left to soak overnight in pails of turpentine.

On the evening of the Fourth, as soon as it was dark, the balls were taken out and lighted with matches. They were then thrown up and down the main street of the village. Arching overhead with a blaze of two or three feet, they made an impressive display. Competition to throw them was keen, and there was a scrimmage over each ball as it fell.

Strange to say, the flaming balls did not burn the hands. Turpentine burns at a moderate temperature. The motion of snatching the ball from the ground carried the flame away from the hand. In the split second of throwing the only damage was to singe the hair on the back of the hand.

Source

New York Folklore Quarterly, XV (1959), 112.

July Fourth at the Front

This is a letter from Lieutenant Harry Kessenich, in France, to his parents, dated July 7, 1918:

The great and glorious Fourth [in 1918] has come and gone. The weather here was perfect. It was a gala day everywhere. It would have done your heart good to see the crowds of Englishmen, Frenchmen, Scotchmen, Irishmen, Australians, and Canadians mixing with our lads in a perfect realization of what July Fourth meant to America and what it means to the world today ....

And now, folks, let me tell you about the day's program in our own little camp. We had an afternoon of sports, track and field events and boxing contests that would be hard to beat anywhere. Two hundred English Tommies and their officers were with us. It was an afternoon of fun. The lads surely enjoyed the contests as it was a fight for supremacy between platoons. And they gave their guests some good, wholesome ideas of the strength, speed, and alertness of real Americans. . . .

As I have often written to you, the English officers at this place have made it their duty to do for us everything in their power to make our camp better and more pleasant. We have appreciated their kindness and resolved to do something for them on the Fourth. So I asked them for the privilege of their officers' mess that evening that we might give them a regular dinner. We have not as yet the facilities in our camp for staging such affairs. But they agreed with pleasure and with the aid of their English cooks and their school adjutant we went to work and staged a dinner, which for its completeness, its good fellowship, and its patriotism was the peer of any I have ever attended, and I would wager it had no equal in France.

The circumstances made it such. There we were, nine Americans and ten British officers, dining together in an English school, celebrating the day that gave America liberty from Britain, celebrating the fact that America and Britain are now allies in a common cause and all of us on foreign soil! It was a cosmopolitan gathering. We ranged in rank from second lieutenant to major. The major commandant of the British school is a famous athlete from Cambridge University. One of his instructor captains is from Oxford University, where he played on the football, cricket, and track teams. Other English officers attended the University of London-West.

Among the Americans the following universities were represented: Yale, Vanderbilt, Tennessee, Washington and Lee, Richmond College, Michigan, Georgetown, Marquette, and Wisconsin. Could you ask for a representation more varied among such a number of men?

The table was gorgeous in American and British flags, red, white, and blue flowers. I had the honor of being at the head of the table, with the major commandant on my right. At the other end of the table, acting as vice-master, was a Scotch captain. At the conclusion of the "oats" I said a very few words apropos the occasion and proposed a toast to His Majesty, the King of England. The major responded by lauding America's efforts, reading the official communique of the day, wherein it told of America's million soldiers in France, and of the launching that day of a hundred American ships. He praised President Wilson as the greatest statesman of the day and then asked a toast to "His Excellency, Woodrow Wilson, president of the United States." Toasts were then proposed to the English navy, which has performed one of the miracles of the war in keeping the English channel open, and in helping in the transport of America's army across the seas with the loss of less than three hundred lives. Then came words of praise for General Pershing, General Haig, and General Foch, and finally a toast to the English staff, who prepared the dinner. The bombardier, a quick-witted Irishman, McCarthy by name, said that while in his opinion the dinner with its fixings was the best they

AMERICA CELEBRATES

INDEPENDENCE DAY

had ever staged at the school, yet it was the easiest to prepare, "because your toastmaster came to me with a fistful of money, told me that the sky was the limit, not to bother about expenses, and that if I needed more money to come to him." It was the truth. We spared no effort to make the affair one which the guests would never forget, one which the hosts would always cherish as one of the most glorious "Fourth" celebrations ever.

When we went into the anteroom we sang "America" and "God Save the King," gave about a dozen yells for each university represented and a lot that were not represented. Then the party broke up. My throat is still sore.

Source

Wisconsin Magazine of History, II (1918-19), 298-301; first published in the Madison, Wisconsin, *Democrat* of August 6, 1918.

July Fourth Block Party

Margaret Robinson, an author and teacher at Widener University, covered this neighborhood observance:

For the last 12 years, the residents of the dead-end section of Dickinson Avenue in Swarthmore [Pennsylvania] have held an annual block party in the turnaround at the end of the street. This year's event is scheduled for Sunday [July 3, 1988] at 4:30 in the afternoon.

If things run true to form, the weather will be hot and sticky, and the party will start slow. The big plastic garbage cans often show up first. They're followed by a grill of coals for the hot dogs and hamburgers, a cooler of ice and soda, another of ice and beer. Watermelons float in another tub of ice water.

Other equipment arrives—a few long tables to hold the food, a volleyball net in the meadow down by the creek.

Some kids wander down with a dog, who doesn't even bother to sniff the watermelons. "Hey," the kids say to each other. "Where is everybody?"

But by 5 or 5:15 or 5:30, just about everybody will have turned up with their lawn chairs, plates and utensils.

Each household pays 50 cents per person and brings a main dish, salad or dessert. Once in a while someone gets carried away and makes a seafood mousse, but mostly it's macaroni, cole slaw and good old three-bean salad. Plenty for seconds and thirds. There are always brownies among the desserts and sometimes homemade vanilla ice cream.

Lots of greetings—"Hi, how are you, seems like I haven't seen you since the last block party!" Lots of talk—Iraq, Noriega, babies, aging parents, and of course, the local schools.

In recent years the egg-catching contest has been replaced by a water-filled balloon catching contest. The eggs were too hard to clean up. Later on, the vigorous play some volleyball and the sloths have another beer. At dusk, there might be sparklers for the kids.

When it gets dark, the moon may appear, and a mosquito or two. The children are gone, and the talk gets quieter and more personal. One person is grieving for a friend who just died of AIDS. Another describes a teenage daughter's resourcefulness in thwarting a would-be rapist.

Eventually, the diehards collect their gear and straggle home. They leave behind an orphan lawn chair and the big plastic garbage cans.

They like knowing that the chairman for next year's party has already been chosen.

Source

Philadelphia Inquirer, July 1, 1988.

July
12-16
OBON, FESTIVAL OF THE DEAD

Virtually every culture observes the custom of designating a day or days to honor the dead. The Buddhist festival of *Bon* or *Obon* may be compared with All-Hallows or All Souls' Day in the Roman Catholic calendar, which, in its turn, drew on the pagan Festival of the Dead. In Japan it is commonly believed that the spirits of the dead return to the earth during *Obon* (see Halloween), and preparations are made to receive and honor them. Family shrines are cleaned and special meals cooked for these spirits during this celebration, which is also known as the Feast of Fortune. Because lanterns are lighted in the cemeteries, and in some cases bonfires

made at doorways to welcome ghostly visitants, the holiday is also called the Festival of Lanterns.

Obon festivals are often sponsored by Buddhist religious congregations and are celebrated in Japan and in Japanese communities throughout the world. Although the dates of *Obon* are fixed, in many American cities public celebrations are held from July to early September. For instance, in Hawaii, with almost 100 Buddhist churches, an *Obon* festival is held almost every weekend during the summer. *Obon* festivities are sometimes combined with *Rokusai Nembutsu*, with danced prayer and folk-dance events.

Festival for the Spirits of the Dead

"Miss N.I." investigated holidays observed by Japanese-Americans living in the San Francisco Bay area in 1934 under the direction of Paul Radin, who edited this report. Informants were "older" persons and were interviewed in Japanese.

July 12th to 16th are the dates of the Festival of the Dead. Among the Japanese, the belief is held that the dead return once a year to visit their living relatives, and elaborate plans are made for the reception of these returning spirits. Fruit and other delectable foods, as well as gifts, are placed

upon altars in all the temples and private shrines. From time to time tea is poured out for the refreshment of the unseen visitor, while many prayers are recited. When night sets in, innumerable lanterns are hung along the streets and in the cemeteries to guide the footsteps of the souls, and everyone takes part in the large group dances conducted in the streets, in which, it is supposed, the spirits of the dead participate. On the 16th of July, the final day of the celebration, a picturesque ceremony is held. A few of the various things offered at the altars are placed on a lotus leaf, and with a lighted candle in the center, this is sent sailing into a nearby body of water. As each little "boat" bursts into flames, the spirit contained in it is supposed to rise and be on its way back to its heavenly abode.

In connection with this festival a curious evolution has taken place. Originally a religious celebration, specifically Buddhist, it became secularized and developed into a popular national holiday and an occasion for much merriment and exchange of gifts.

In America, the Festival of the Dead, or *obon* as it is called by the Japanese, has remained a religious holiday, observed for the most part only by the Buddhists. It has almost come to correspond to Memorial Day in America, with the services being held in church and the organization of groups to clean up and freshly decorate the graves in the various cemeteries where Japanese are buried. Even in America, the custom of offering food and gifts at private family altars to deceased members of the family has been preserved. About three years ago [1931], the feature of the group dances was, for the first time in America, added to the celebration of the Festival of the Dead. All indications point to the increasing popularity of these bon-odoni or bon dances, which are today held along one or two city blocks, temporarily roped off and illuminated by Japanese lanterns. These dances are participated in by groups numbering anywhere from one hundred upwards, composed of men, women, boys, and girls, all dressed in simple yet colorful one-piece Japanese garments.

Source

Southwestern Journal of Anthropology, II (1946), 173-74.

Obon in Rural New Jersey

Suzanne Gordon wrote about the Obon observance in Seabrook, a small rural town in southern New Jersey.

"It's a joyful remembrance of the lifetimes of our mothers and fathers and all of our ancestors, their contributions to our existence today," said Ellen Nakamura in explaining why Japanese-Americans gathered at the Buddhist Church in Seabrook, New Jersey, this weekend to celebrate the *Obon* Festival, a traditional ceremony honoring the dead.

The *Obon* Memorial Service, a Buddhist ritual honoring the dead—said in English and Japanese—was conducted yesterday [July 11, 1982] morning to conclude the annual festival held in the farming community.

AMERICA CELEBRATES

OBON, FESTIVAL OF THE DEAD

The night before, more than 100 dancers—from toddlers to the elderly, all dressed in colorful kimonos—participated in traditional folk dances at the *Obon* Festival, held each summer on the seven-acre grounds of the Seabrook Buddhist Church.

Mrs. Nakamura, a church member who served as a master of ceremonies for the Saturday night activities, said the *Obon* rituals are "a nurturing of our own joy in faith."

The dancers, who had been rehearsing the popular Japanese folk dances for several weeks, moved to the beat of the *Soh*

Daiko drum unit of the New York Buddhist Church, whose members participated in the Seabrook festival.

The resident priest, the Rev. Shingetsu Akahoshi, led the dancers and audience in silent meditation of thanksgiving.

The evening's entertainment, which was open to the public, culminated with the Japanese circle dance, called "*Tanko Bushi*" the Coal Miner's Dance. Everyone joined in to depict, through hand movements, the miner's work—digging, heaving coal, wiping sweat from their brows.

Source

Philadelphia Inquirer, July 12, 1982.

July
14

BASTILLE DAY

A patriotic holiday in France comparable with July 4 in the United States, it commemorates the seizure of the Bastille, a state fortress in Paris, in a popular uprising on July 14, 1789.

The Bastille (the word simply means a building) had been used to house political prisoners such as Voltaire and the mysterious "Man in the Iron Mask," and, as a symbol of royal absolutism, was hated by the French revolutionaries. Its guns protected one of the gates of Paris, and when the mob stormed it on July 14, they were hoping to obtain ammunition. The prison's commandant, the marquis de Launey, was forced to surrender and the revolutionaries mounted his head on a pike. The storming of the Bastille brought the lower classes into the French Revolution; the building's demolition on the first anniversary of its capture was a revolutionary gesture, and the date was made a national holiday of the French Republic. In the United States, Bastille Day has been observed especially by the descendants of French Canadians in Louisiana and New England, but even cities such as Chicago organize celebrations.

Cajun Bastille Day

Correspondent Lisa Belkin filed this special report:

This weekend [1989] the Bastille will be stormed once again, but this time it will be made of crayon and cardboard and glue and its bars will be the inner tubes of paper towel rolls covered with aluminum foil.

And its destruction will be the highlight of the year in this Cajun town [Kaplan, Louisiana] of 5,000 people about 75 miles southwest of Baton Rouge.

"The Bastille Day Festival is such a big part of what Kaplan stands for," said Janet Merritt, this year's festival chairman. "It's a very big deal."

AMERICA CELEBRATES

BASTILLE DAY

As in many other towns in southern Louisiana, many of the people here are descendants of Acadians (Cajuns), French colonists who migrated from Canada to this area, which was settled by Germans. Those of French heritage still speak a unique dialect of French; their English is often accented with Brooklynese.

There is no party in Kaplan on the Fourth of July. Here they celebrate Bastille Day.

Kaplan was named for a Jewish merchant, Abram Kaplan, whose great-great-nephew, Connie Kaplan, runs the local newspaper, *The Kaplan Herald*. Abram Kaplan never lived here; the town was officially founded in 1902. He did arrange to route the Southern Pacific Railroad through this area, then a collection of rice farms owned by Cajun and German farmers. Railroad officials named the depot after him.

In 1888 a young Frenchman, Eugene Eleazar, migrated to Louisiana. He was saddened that the Cajuns did not observe his favorite holiday, July 14.

He tried to arouse interest, first in New Orleans, then in a country town, but the residents were not enthusiastic. He moved to Kaplan in 1906, to find that farmers would travel for miles to attend an observance. It became a town ritual. . . .

Preparations were under way this week at the Kaplan Recreation Center, down the block from Abshire's Welding and across the street from LeMaire's Slaughterhouse.

Members of the Key Club and the Keyettes were draping the stage in purple and blue crepe paper and building a runway for the Bastille Baby Contest.

The club members were under the eye of Luddie Herpin, who has helped organize the event since 1976. Considering, he said, that "13 years is a long time," this year he brought with him the Broussard twins, Jerry and Terry, and is training them to take over his role.

"There are about 100 members of the Jaycees," said Kathy Touchet, director of advertising for the festival. She said those members might be happy to attend, but not always happy to work. "Maybe 20 of the hundred are active members and maybe 10 show up to help," she said. "It's a heavy load for us committed ones."

The committed ones coordinate the egg toss and the watermelon-eating and the beer-drinking contests. They must get the automotive grease and spread it over the entire length of a telephone pole for the greasy pole-climbing contest. They must place a flag atop the pole (American, not French, and that is the subject of a heated debate) and make sure $60 is available for anyone who reaches the top.

And they must set up the table outside Cher's Cajun Gifts where volunteers who work for the post office will give letters a special Bastille Day postmark.

And the committed ones must book the bands for the outdoor dancing. This year Echouffe, or Cajun National Orchestra, will play Saturday night; Mrs. Merritt says she is lucky to get the band. "The president of the Jaycees, her brother is in the group," she said, "so that helped."

There will be no band for the 10-block parade. "All the bands, they're playing at other festivals," said Mrs. Touchet.

Outside the recreation center, the grass is newly mowed. Mrs. Merritt's husband brought over the family rider-mower. Mrs. Merritt feared that a thick growth would bring mosquitoes. The field, used for softball practice, is the temporary home of a Ferris wheel, bumper cars and a small merry-go-round.

Standing near a patch of mud she hopes will dry in time, Mrs. Merritt said she wanted to make it clear that her town was not unpatriotic.

She likes the Fourth of July, she said, but she sees no reason to celebrate it in Kaplan. "If we want fireworks," she said, "we just drive over to Erath," another tiny town about 20 miles away.

"We don't cut into their festival and they don't cut into ours," she said.

"This is what we have that makes Kaplan special."

Source

New York Times, July 14, 1989; publication took place on the two hundredth anniversary of the storming of the Bastille. Copyright © 1989 by The New York Times Company. Reprinted by permission.

Bastille Day Wine Glass Race

Sue-Sun Yom covered this event:

It was a race in the best tradition of the bon vivant: shattered champagne glasses, spilled wine and a winner who sauntered into the red-ribbon finish with the élan of a Maurice Chevalier.

J.P. Smith from Clarke Cooke House in Newport sailed around the orange cones in Kennedy Plaza [Providence, Rhode Island] yesterday, outmaneuvering 40 competitors from 20 area restaurants to win the eighth annual Bastille Day Waiters and Waitresses Race.

The contestants had each paid $15 to race the sloped walkway while balancing trays of wine-filled glasses with one hand.

The Omni Biltmore hotel sponsored the event and directed all proceeds to the Journal-Bulletin Summertime Fund.

Smith finished far ahead of the six other waiters who had won their qualifying heats, and was rewarded with an awed "wow" from the sidelines.

After dealing with a barrage of accolades, he flopped down in shady seclusion to "rest my feet."

Representatives of Pot au Feu on Custom House Street turned out handsomely for the fete in tricolored bow ties.

AMERICA CELEBRATES

BASTILLE DAY

The standard-bearer carried the red, white and blue French flag.

Unfortunately, on the day before the 200th anniversary of the storming of the Bastille, the "French" representatives were shackled. Neither competitor from Pot au Feu qualified for the final heat.

Were they disappointed? "A little bit," but why cry over spilled wine, said Pot au Feu's Kevin McGavock, 26, last year's first-place winner.

"I have to stop coming back and beating these 21-year-old kids," said a laughing Smith, who won in 1987. Smith is 33.

Smith left the competition with a large bottle of Moët & Chandon and a trip for two to Lake George, N.Y.

Paul Dubuc, a waiter from the Sheraton-Islander Inn in Newport finished second and won a trip to Boston.

Rene Saulnier, a waiter at Cafè in the Barn in Seekonk, Mass., won a dinner for two at Stanford's American Bar and Grille for his third-place finish.

Source

Providence Journal–Bulletin, July 14, 1989.

And that's not all:
See "International Pancake Race."

July

Mid-Month
TURTLE DAYS

Snapping turtles commonly weigh ten or twelve pounds. Those in the mud-bottomed lakes near Churubusco, Indiana, a town of about 1,500 people in a prosperous farming region, are said to grow larger. Soon after he took the place, Gale Harris, a farmer with a reputation for integrity and seriousness of purpose, heard that an unusual turtle lived in the seven-acre lake on his farm. In the fall of 1948,

while patching his roof with the help of his Nazarene minister, he sighted the turtle at a distance, and within a few days they and others saw it often and at close range. It was agreed that the turtle was as big as the top of a dining-room table— maybe four or five feet wide and six feet long; in short, a monster. With notable persistence and help from his neighbors, Harris sought to capture the turtle, which he hoped to exhibit. He tried nets, grapples, homemade traps and pens, professional divers, and a female turtle as a decoy. Finally, he began to pump out the lake. The story was reported in the press, and high-spirited crowds came to watch the various efforts. Some of the attempts were almost successful, but the turtle, by now known as Oscar, always broke away. Efforts continued until January, 1950, when the dam retaining the pumped-out water collapsed, and the lake filled up again. At that point, Harris gave up. That spring the town needed to raise funds for a community meeting hall, and almost spontaneously decided to have a local festival on the order of a county fair that would exploit the fame of Oscar, the so-called "Beast of 'Busco." Among its attractions would be a parade featuring a turtle float and booths selling turtle soup. Socially and financially successful, it set the pattern for the Turtle Days that have been held ever since.

AMERICA CELEBRATES

TURTLE DAYS

Tall Tales about the Turtle

These windies (typical American tall tales) were first published in special "Turtle Editions" of the Churubusco Truth *dated March 10, 1949; March 17, 1949; and March 24, 1949:*

Frank Flowers Jr. declares that when the turtle was frozen in the ice this winter, it tried to walk to the bank and in doing so moved the whole lake twenty feet.

Ralph Shanabarger says the turtle, when he swims in the lake, pushes so much water ahead of him that he kicks up dust from the bottom with his hind legs.

Others say that Jake Jones, who formerly owned the farm, now knows what happened to the black Angus cattle that used to turn up missing and why a fence erected between the cattle and the lake stopped the loss.

Charlie Horner, the butcher, says that when a mule was used in an attempt to pull the "Fulk Lake monster" from the water, the turtle pulled the mule into the lake—ate him—and came out of the water picking his teeth with a singletree.

When two ministers from Kalamazoo stopped at the Harris farm for a turtle chat, Gale Harris told them he was surprised that they, as preachers, would be interested in the turtle, since so many lies had circulated about old Oscar. The ministers replied that they figured Churubusco, because of the number of liars, would be a pretty good spot in which to set up business.

Source

"American Folklore and the Modern American Festival: A Case Study of Turtle Days in Churubusco, Indiana," Ph.D. Dissertation, Indiana University, 1977, 113-14.

Turtle Hunter

Reported from Indianapolis in 1961, this is an example of a legend in the process of development; it is no longer simply a locally told story, but, probably due to the mass media, told at a distance from its place of origin:

The Beast of 'Busco is supposedly in a lake in Churubusco, Indiana. This town is 20 miles NE of Fort Wayne, Indiana. This animal is a turtle 19 feet in diameter. The story goes that a small boy was out playing on the lake and the turtle came up on the shore. When people came looking for the boy all that could be found were his shoes and a few pieces of clothing. There were turtle footprints about 6 to 8 inches. Residents nearby say they hear weird noises when the moon is out. No one has ever seen this animal. Some claim they have seen him or something that resembles him.

Source

"American Folklore and the Modern American Community Festival: A Case Study of Turtle Days in Churubusco, Indiana," Ph.D. Dissertation, Indiana University, 1977, 151. Quoted from the Legend Collection, Indiana University Folklore Archive No. 910.

July

Last Full Week
CHEYENNE FRONTIER DAYS

The first rodeos were held by the forerunners of the American cowboy, the Mexican *vaqueros.* They developed out of the normal tasks of the cattle ranch: roping, lassoing, bulldogging, and bronco riding. Contests between individual cowboys, outfits that ran into each other, and rival ranches served as entertainment and offered ample opportunities for betting and bragging. Known in the American Southwest short-

Cowboys and bucking broncos

ly after the Civil War and flourishing in Texas by the 1880s, they were nationally popularized by touring, circus-like extravaganzas such as Buffalo Bill Cody's "Wild West Show"

and formalized in celebrations such as Cheyenne Frontier Days, the Pendleton (Oregon) Round-up, and the Calgary Stampede. Before long they developed large followings and commercial possibilities. Today, aided by the long tradition of the cowboy novel, movie, and television show, the rodeo has a full "circuit" of events, corporate sponsorship, and professional performers who may earn large incomes.

Cheyenne Frontier Days, which originated in 1897, before the novels and the movies, is an elaborated folk event. It has, however, developed a tradition of its own.

Frontier Days Breakfast

Over 30,000 people were treated to a free breakfast of pancakes, ham and coffee or milk at the three free Cheyenne Frontier Days breakfasts last year [1987].

That, folks, is a bunch of flapjacks! More than 100,000 to be nearly exact.

Mixed in a cement truck (you heard it right), the pancakes are the focus of a breakfast which also includes ham, syrup, butter, coffee and/or milk—and no one waits in line more than 20 minutes.

Good food and good fun are served up with blue denim hospitality on Monday, Wednesday and Friday from 7 to 9 A.M. at

the City Center Parking Mall in downtown Cheyenne.

In true Cheyenne Frontier Days fashion, the free pancake breakfasts are a cooperative venture. The Frontier Committee provides the food with the help of donors and sponsors and the City of Cheyenne provides the facility and cleanup.

Food is prepared in traditional open-range style by the 390-member Cheyenne Kiwanis Club, who put in an estimated 2,300 man-hours getting breakfast prepared and served.

Planning to serve 30,000 for breakfast? A "typical" recipe calls for 3,600 pounds of pancake mix, 1,130 pounds of butter, 300 gallons of syrup, 2,800 pounds of ham, 9,000 pints of milk, 520 gallons of coffee, 125 pounds of sugar and 12 gallons of cooking oil.

People from all 50 states and more than 20 foreign countries enjoyed breakfast Frontier Days style last year.

Take a deep seat on a hay bale, enjoy your flapjacks and be entertained by various bands, the Southern Plains Indians, local talent and the Frontier Days royalty.

The Frontier Days pancake breakfast. It's fun ... it's tasty ... it's Western ... it's free!!!

Source

Program for the 1988 Cheyenne Frontier Days.

Cowgirls and Frontier Days

Mary L. Remley documents the unique participation of women:

The world of the rodeo is generally believed to be ... the rough, tough, rigorous competition of the western cowboy, a masculine domain of thrills, excitement and danger. Developed out of day-to-day ranch tasks, informal contests for entertainment at the close of the work day or for the social gatherings hosted by the ranch owners, these contests eventually became the major entertainment at county fairs. From these simple beginnings, the rodeo developed into highly organized and vigorous competition among men, "but, as in every other activity in the West, females quickly invaded their ranks as participants." ...

The early pioneer ranch women of necessity became accomplished equestrians. Horses provided their primary mode of transportation, and the far reaches of the sprawling ranches or the nearest neighbors were most easily accessible by horseback. Prior to the twentieth century, almost every woman rode "sidesaddle like a lady," but skilled horsemanship even in the "modest sidesaddle positions which twisted their spines askew" was a desirable asset to ranch life. By the late 1800s, however, some women were beginning to adopt the more practical attitude about riding of ranchwoman Agnes Morley [who wrote, in *No Life for a Lady*:]

My own great concession to a new age was to abandon the sidesaddle ... I recall the steps that led to emancipation. First, I discarded, or rather refused to adopt, the sunbonnet, conventional head gear of my female neighbors. When I went unashamedly about under a five-gallon (not ten-gallon) Stetson, many an eyebrow was raised; then followed a double-breasted blue flannel shirt. In time came blue denim knickers worn *under* a short blue denim skirt. Slow evolution (or was it decadence) toward a costume suited for immediate needs. Decadence having set in, the descent from existing standards of female modesty to purely human comfort and convenience was swift. A man's saddle and a divided skirt (awful monstrosity that was) were inevitable.

Many ranchwomen followed the example of Agnes Morley, and for some of them the transition from sidesaddle to rodeo was but a single step.

Long before the end of the nineteenth century women were giving public exhibitions of their equestrian skills. During the 1850s "one Mary Ann Whitaker made a career of her skill . . . under the title of 'First Female Equestrian Artist in America.'" Other women joined the ranks of the circus to display their skilled horsemanship. With the introduction of rodeo to the West, however, a new arena opened up for the skilled horsewoman. When the citizens of Cheyenne, Wyoming, set aside a festival day in 1897 to commemorate early life on the Western frontier, it is doubtful that the planning committee considered the possi-

bility of female entrants in the male world of cowpony races, roping contests, or pitching and bucking events. They failed to reckon with the interest and persistence of the Wyoming horsewoman, and within a short time, she, too, was a participant in Cheyenne's Frontier Days, the oldest continuous rodeo in existence.

The first scheduled event for women appeared in 1899 when "The Committee decided to have a half-mile ladies' race and will give as a prize a $45.00 saddle." The official program of events listed the race as the Ladies' Cow Pony Race, one-half-mile, prize, a ladies' sidesaddle to the winner. The sidesaddle prize was perhaps indicative of the masculine view of the female contestants; the sidesaddle was still more appropriate for women even though they were racing astride in a regular Western saddle. Although news reports described the race as unsatisfactory in regard to the starting, it was considered an interesting event and apparently paved the way for the continued inclusion of women's events in future years.

During the next four years of Frontier Days the Ladies' Cow Pony Race was the only competition open to women participants. No entry fee was required, but regulations were as strictly enforced as those for men contestants. No thoroughbred horses were allowed; only Wyoming cowponies could be ridden; and cowgirls' saddles, the conventional Western saddle for riding astride, were required. Beginning in 1900, prize money rather than a saddle

AMERICA CELEBRATES

CHEYENNE FRONTIER DAYS

was awarded to the first, second, and third place winners in the race. The amounts of $25, $15, and $10 were less than those for comparable men's races; however, a small "purse" in no way dampened the enthusiasm of the women riders nor that of their cheering supporters in the stands. [*Cheyenne Leader* of August 21, 1901 described the action:]

> The Ladies' Cow Pony Race was one of the most enjoyable features of the program and was as exciting as the most exacting could desire. Nowhere else in the world do women display the fearless horsemanship to be found on the prairies of Wyoming, and as the ladies came under the wire at break neck speed they were wildly cheered. There were eleven entries and the race was hotly contested owing to the great rivalry as to who is the best girl rider in the state. Those who have never seen Wyoming girls ride were amazed at the remarkable exhibition they witnessed. As the ladies started around the track the grandstand and bleachers went wild with excitement, and the interest taken in the race was greater than any of the running events of the afternoon.

In 1902 the Ladies' Cow Pony Races were scheduled on each of three days of the celebration. Prize money had increased to $75 a race ($40, $20, and $15) and the title "champion of the world" was bestowed on the winner of a final heat in which winners of two previous contests had qualified. The ladies had established themselves as bona

fide rodeo participants in at least one event and the cowpony race was popular with both participants and spectators throughout the years in which women competed in Cheyenne's Frontier Days.

One of the most unlikely rodeo events in which women might have been expected to participate at the turn of the century was bronco riding. But as early as 1902 "several lady riders ... expressed a desire to enter the bucking and pitching contests during frontier days ... "

Since no rough riding events were scheduled for women, one enterprising young woman, Bertha Kaepernick, entered the men's events in 1904. She was headlined in the [*Wyoming Tribune* of September 1, 1904] as

> the only (woman) rider to ever enter the championship bucking and pitching contest ... (she) drew a vicious mount and within a few seconds the girl was compelled to pull leather disqualifying her from the contest. After the animal had apparently been subdued, the crazy brute again seemed possessed of an evil spirit and began bucking in so wild and erratic a manner that Miss Kaepernick was thrown completely over the animal's head.

Even though disqualified from a chance to win the contest, the fearless Miss Kaepernick climbed back on the horse and rode him to submission amid the roaring cheers of the crowd. Though few women had either the interest or the inclination to risk life and limb astride a bucking bronco, the excitement generated by those who did led to the inclusion of the event as an annual exhibition. No prize money was awarded, but each year the ladies' bronco riding drew enthusiastic applause from the spectators. As numbers of entrants increased in the exhibitions, the Frontier Days Committee became convinced that a World Champion Ladies Bronco Riding contest would be a success, and in 1914 the event was initiated as a regular part of the scheduled program. Rules governing the event were the same as those for men. Riders had to stay on their mount for eight seconds; spur the horse at the start of the contest; and could not grab the saddle or horn to assist in staying on the horse. Women, however, had the option of riding with or without hobbled stirrups—stirrups hooked together by a cinch under the horse to avoid the wild flapping that occurred when the horse bucked. Ladies' bronco riding was extremely popular in Cheyenne for several years, but interest waned in the 1920s. The number of contestants was too small to provide a fair or interesting competition, and the judges found it increasingly difficult to determine a winner fairly. She was often either the person riding the most spectacular horse, or one who could tolerate the most punishment in the time allotted. Thus in 1928 bronco riding for women was discontinued at Cheyenne's Frontier Days.

Other events for women which began only as exhibitions in Cheyenne's Frontier Days were steer roping and trick and fancy riding; but these, too, became regularly scheduled contests as horsewomen became more daring and proficient. Steer roping was conducted under essentially the same rules as those for men. While riding at full speed the contestant had to rope the running steer, dismount and tie three of his flailing legs, as her horse held the rope taut. The winner was the person completing the tie in the shortest time. As numbers of entrants increased and times improved, the steer ropers were required to perform on three consecutive days with first place awarded to the "best average time for the three steers." Results were sometimes disappointing, however, when the ladies had difficulty in performing the various skills required in the event. On one occasion three of the four contestants were unsuccessful in catching their steers and the fourth caught hers, but could not "bust" him (throw him to the ground) and complete the tie. Even with such setbacks, steer roping continued to be one of the prize money events for women for a number of years.

In trick and fancy riding "the girls ride upside down, jumping on and off, at the horse's side, under it, and go through all manner of exciting stunts while the horse is on a tearing run." The event was essentially one of the showmanship and many women became adept at a large repertoire of tricks that displayed their riding abilities and their courage to greatest advantage. One championship rider of the 1920s, Lorena Trickey, was noted as "the only girl who can go entirely around under

CHEYENNE FRONTIER DAYS

her horse's neck and back up to the saddle on the other side while the horse is on the run.''

Perhaps the most spectacular of all the women's events in Frontier Days was the Ladies' Relay Race. Initiated in 1906 the relay drew a large number of contestants during most of its forty years' existence. The prize money was the largest purse of any of the women's events, and the winner also was awarded a large silver loving cup donated by *The Denver Post*, sponsor of the race [described in the *Wyoming Tribune* of July 21, 1906 as follows]:

> In this event each contestant is provided with three horses. When the word is given she mounts one of the animals, dashes around the half mile track, dismounts, leaps onto another cowpony and is off again. The race is one and one-half miles long, so that each lady must dismount and remount twice. As much time is either lost or gained according to the dexterity of the fair competitor to leap from a horse, often with the animal in full gallop, and spring on to her next mount, it can well be imagined that the contest is such as to excite the greatest possible enthusiasm and excitement in the spectators. The committee has decided that the riders need not use the same saddle for all three horses as in their great haste to be off again saddles are often put on in a careless manner and by using a separate saddle for each horse a great element of danger to the ladies will be

eliminated and the race lose nothing of its exciting nature.

The relay race became one of the most popular rodeo events, and various rules changes through the years were indicative of the skill attained by the riders. At one time the riders used only one saddle; one assistant held the waiting horse, but the rider had to saddle, unsaddle, mount and remount with no help from the assistant. Clearly, dexterity in handling the saddle became as important as riding skill and a fast horse in determining a winner. At other times when saddled horses were again used, regulations stated that the rider's feet must touch the ground in changing mounts. Prior to that rule, the fastest riders merely crossed under the half-mile wire, leaped out of one saddle and flew through the air on to another. There were obvious advantages for those riders skilled enough to change mounts in this manner, but the possibilities for accidents were surely decreased with the rule change barring such acrobatics....

Roman riding or racing two horses in a standing position with one foot on the back of each mount enjoyed some popularity with both men and women riders for a time. Since it seemed more appropriate for the circus ring as a spectacle than the rodeo circuit, where the most popular activities were outgrowths of ranch chores, Roman riding never held the interest of spectators as did some of the other events.

The stake race for women, introduced in Cheyenne in 1916, was probably the forerunner of the modern women's barrel race. Unlike the barrel race in which the riders weave around a barrel course in a cloverleaf pattern, the early stake riders raced down a straightaway, turned sharply around a stake at the end of the stretch, then sped back to the finish line. The race was a short sprint, and the speed of the horses and deftness in the turn generated great excitement among the spectators.

Trick and fancy roping also appeared as one of the women's exhibitions in the early 1900s. Though roping was not scheduled as a contest, some women developed the skill to a high degree. "A particularly difficult trick was to twirl the rope into a large loop catching several mounted men as they rode by."

During the early years of the twentieth century women entered rodeo contests across the country in increasing numbers. Some riders, like Lorena Trickey, developed rodeo skills out of necessity when ranch responsibilities were thrust upon them. Upon the death of their father, Lorena and her two brothers were left to run their ranch. She weighed barely a hundred pounds, yet she was known as one of the best "cowboys" on her home range and could handle a lariat and branding iron as efficiently as her two brothers. Bertha Kaepernick owned and operated her own ranch and developed riding skills comparable to those of any man in the day-to-day operation of the ranch....

Unlike Miss Kaepernick and Miss Trickey, many women never had to assume the full responsibility of the ranch owner, but they grew up on Western ranches and, in carrying their share of ranch chores, became proficient riders at an early age. The experiences that catapulted Mrs. Goldie St. Clair to the title of "Champion Woman Bronco Buster of the World" were probably typical of most early women champions. [The *Cheyenne State Leader* of August 21, 1909, notes:]

> Her parents were riders, her mother being a noted relay rider, and the children were given the run of the range. Mrs. St. Clair and one of her brothers herded cattle on barebacked horses as soon as they were able to toddle. As they grew older the children rode the horses to and from school and were such daring little experts that they nearly wore them out. At last the father restricted the children to some mules. They were small mules but could match with Steamboat or Rocking Chair (well known bucking horses) when it came to bucking ... As time went by they began to have bucking contests every Sunday afternoon. The exhibition ground was a wheat field, and the spectators were neighbors ... It was in this wheat field that Mrs. St. Clair got the training which was afterward to make her the champion of the world.

Cheyenne's Frontier Days had offered the first opportunities for women to participate in the colorful world of the rodeo, and it was perhaps fitting that the first state giving women the legal right to

CHEYENNE FRONTIER DAYS

vote in 1869 and hold public office should also pave the way for their entry into other activities generally considered the exclusive domain of men. As rodeo developed and expanded in other parts of the country, additional opportunities for women were made available, and they did not hesitate to take advantage of them. Two of the best known rodeos, other than Frontier Days—the Pendleton, Oregon, Round-up, originating in 1909, and the Calgary, Alberta, Stampede in 1912—both scheduled events for women in their early stages of development. Many smaller communities offered their own versions of the larger celebrations, and women along with men became "circuit riders," moving from one rodeo to another to test their skill and finesse in handling a horse, a rope, or a steer. On occasion the best women riders challenged each other to special contests to claim such titles as "champion rough rider of the world."

Lucille Mulhall, a champion steer roper who could rope eight horses with one throw of a lariat made a million dollars in silent westerns. [Such] women also had a profound effect on rodeo costuming. They soon tired of their tailored shirtwaists and long divided skirts of drab colors and exchanged them for shorter split skirts of red velvet and fancy silk shirts of equally brilliant hues. With this kind of colorful competition, men, too, discarded their denim jeans and work shirts and adopted the bright colored attire which women had made popular.

Women were involved in rodeo for almost half a century, and in the early years, "they attempted to do everything their male counterparts excelled at." The number of contestants decreased markedly in the 1940s, and women's events began to disappear not only from Cheyenne's Frontier Days, but from other rodeos as well. A number of factors probably contributed to the paucity of women contestants, but the prominent seemed to be these: (1) Prize money for women was relatively small and was always less than that for men competing in the same events. (2) The danger inherent in bronco riding and steer roping kept many women from competing. (3) Maintaining and transporting specially trained horses, particularly the three to six needed for the relay races, was very expensive. (4) Fewer rodeos were scheduling a wide range of events for women, and it was difficult for a rider to stay in top form with fewer contests. "With the demise of the ladies' relay race in 1946 female participation in (Frontier Days) ceased." Although all-girl rodeos were initiated at about this same time, and the barrel race was introduced as the only event in men's rodeo in which women could compete, the conclusion of women's participation in Frontier Days signalled the end of an era. Women had competed in almost every rodeo event and had tested their skills in the same arena as the best men contestants. For almost fifty years they had shared the limelight and "old timers remembered with regret the intense competition among the cowgirls and the excitement provided by them..."

Source

Journal of the West, XVII (July 1978), 44-52. Edited from a carefully documented article by Mary L. Remley entitled "From Sidesaddle to Rodeo."

And that's not all:
The book by Alice Morley Cleaveland, *No Life for a Lady,* was published in Boston, 1941.

July—August

Variable
CAPTAIN BRADY DAY

The eighteenth century in the Northwest Territories was a period of tremendous unrest: the French and Indian wars, Pontiac's uprising against the British and the exploits of ruthless fur traders gave rise to fantastic stories of courage, luck, and prowess among the frontiersmen; the best known of these featured Daniel Boone, but he was not the only subject of such stories. Brady Lake in Ohio is named for Captain Samuel Brady (1758-95), an American frontiersman who fought in the Revolutionary War and served as a scout in the Northwest Territory

under General Anthony Wayne. His legendary exploits include an escape from Indians by submerging himself beneath the surface of the lake and breathing through a reed. The Captain Brady celebration, first held in 1973 and since then on a date not yet firmly fixed, is an example of a folk festival in the process of evolving, since it reflects a profound sense of local tradition and at the same time shows parallels with practices of distant cultures. Re-enacting the frontiersman's miraculous escape from death, the festival celebrates life triumphant and the benificent power of nature.

Captain Brady and the Muskrats of Brady Lake

Richard Feinberg based this report upon data collected by his students, particularly Martin Bramlett. Their main interests are in the lake and the totemic muskrat as "collective representations" of the community, and in suggesting that Americans, as instanced by the residents of Brady Lake, may have more in common with nonwestern peoples than is generally recognized.

Anthropological literature is replete with descriptions of people who consider themselves related to one or another species of plant or animal. Often, members of a social group call themselves by the name of such a species, surround that species with an aura of respect or sanctity, and share a

prohibition against killing or eating members of that species. This phenomenon is commonly called "totemism." . . .

Brady Lake is a small community located in Ohio's Portage County, about midway between the city of Kent (home of Kent State University) and the county seat of Ravenna. Attention was first called to the lake during the late eighteenth century when Captain Samuel Brady of the Continental Army is said to have escaped a group of Wyandotte Indians by breathing through a hollow reed while hiding underwater. This event serves as a sort of origin myth for the community and focuses attention on the lake from a very early date.

For about a century following Brady's escape the area immediately surrounding the lake was mostly woods and farmland. In the 1890s the lake was made into a feeder reservoir for the Ohio-Pennsylvania Canal. In the waning years of the last century, a major tourist resort was developed around the lake, complete with waterfront cottages, a dancing pavilion, boating, swimming, and assorted other forms of entertainment. In 1927, the east side of the lake was incorporated as a village. . . .

Beginning in 1976 the level of Lake Brady began to drop precipitously. In a two-year period the surface area declined from 99 to 75 acres. Informants say the growth of algae, weeds, and the appearance of unsightly mud flats has impaired the lake's aesthetic quality. The appearance has deteriorated and it has lost much of its appeal to swimmers, fishermen, and boat-

ers. Simultaneous with the recession of the lake has been a decline in the water level of many local wells. Some wells have gone dry, and most have been to some degree affected.

Residents of Brady Lake were asked to identify the most important problems facing the community. They were unanimous in selecting the water crisis as one of the most pressing problems. Much time and effort has been expended in the search for a solution. Innumerable hours have been spent at meetings, conferences, and informal conversations. Studies have been conducted, plans drawn up, revised, and scrapped, and water is a constant topic of discussion.

Undoubtedly, the falling water table has created problems for the people of Brady Lake. Lack of water has affected activities ranging from cooking to washing clothes and flushing toilets, transforming everyday pursuits into tests of ingenuity and will. And people are concerned about the possible impact of the crisis on the value of their land and homes. Yet, the fact remains that people are getting along. Informants indicate that property values have kept pace with inflation. . . . As far as we could tell no one has moved out of Brady Lake because of the water problem, nor would anyone admit to contemplating such a move. And many residents assert the crisis has helped to bring them closer together, making them into more of a community. From a distance, the lake still looks almost idyllic, and from personal

CAPTAIN BRADY DAY

experience I can attest that it is still a pleasant spot to swim, while fishing is as good as that in any of the local lakes. Why is it, then, that everyone is so preoccupied with water and the falling level of the lake?

Evidently, water has more than a practical significance to people of the area. The lake is a shared symbol. People identify with the lake and are conscious of the lake as something that they hold in common, differentiating them from outsiders. . . .

The importance of the lake is evident in the very fact that the community is named for it. The "origin myth" involves the founding "ancestor" escaping death by hiding in the lake which offered him protection, and every year at Captain Brady Day this event is re-enacted. Physically as well as conceptually the community is centered around the lake, and the events of Captain Brady Day take place at the water's edge. Residents of Brady Lake describe themselves collectively as "Lakers" as opposed to nonresidents who are not designated by this term. Alternatively, they identify themselves as "Muskrats." The muskrat is a water animal, associated with the lake, and it appears to be symbolically isomorphic with the lake itself. The muskrat is an emblem of the community. In preparation for Captain Brady Day in August, 1978, signs were posted at close intervals within about a three-mile radius of Brady Lake. The signs encouraged people to join the celebration, and in the middle of each sign was printed a large

picture of a muskrat. A wide variety of objects were on sale at the festivities, but the most popular appeared to be T-shirts made especially for the event, printed with a picture of a muskrat on the front and the inscription, "Muskrats do it better," on the back. By mid-morning the entire stock already had been sold.

The term, muskrat, first appeared in conjunction with Brady Lake during the early 1950s, when a group of area youths formed a club and began trapping muskrats to sell the pelts for spending money. Eventually, they took the name, "The Muskrats," for the club.

The club quickly gained a reputation as a group of young toughs and were viewed with disapproval by the other residents. As they got older, however, the original Muskrats either moved away or settled down to become respected members of the community, and gradually the name came to be adopted by all residents of Brady Lake. As acceptance of the name spread through the population a sense of identification with the animal increased. During the study, when one informant complained of muskrats destroying her vegetable garden the interviewer suggested that she kill the pests. The informant's horrified response was that "We couldn't do that! Not now!" The sanctification was now underway. . . .

The community consists of dwelling houses distributed in a rough circle surrounding the sacred lake which constitutes the center. It is the lake upon which attention has always been focused. The lake symbolizes the unity and solidarity of the community. And it is at the lake shore that the sacred ceremony of renewal takes place annually. Beyond the periphery exists the outside world, seen as dangerous and often hostile, fraught with forces bent upon destruction of the way of life established by the Lakers and jealously guarded by them.

Brady Lake's concentric structure is cross-cut by a diametric one. The east side of the lake constitutes a formally incorporated village; the people on the west side reside in Franklin township. Although both sides see themselves as making up a joint community and there are many activities in which these boundaries are overridden, a sense of differentiation and competition between the sides remains. The township residents often disparage the village government and make such statements as, "They're too busy playing village to get anything done." The two bars of the area are frequented by members of the "moieties" in which they are located. The Club House, in the township, is the larger of the two, has fewer amenities, and has a down-to-earth appearance. The Chaparell Lounge, in the village, creates an image of a more refined, genteel establishment, with clientele to match. People in the village see

the other side as poorer, and I was warned by several village residents that if I should go swimming in the lake I ought not to approach the western shore because of sewage seeping down into the water. The village shore, I was assured, remained pollution-free and safe for swimming.

The moiety division is given ritual enactment each year at Captain Brady Day. A major event each year appears to be a tug-of-war between the patrons of the two bars, each team representing its moiety. Water mediates between the two opposing sides as it is sprayed between them with a hose. The first team to be pulled through the mud puddle in the center loses. True to cultural proprieties, for the past several years the Club House has emerged victorious from this test of muscle power.

Source

"Muskrats of Brady Lake: A Case of American Totemism," Research Report of a Field School in Cultural Anthropology, Kent State University, Ohio, 1978, unpublished. Excerpted from a field report by Richard Feinberg, director of the field school. A shorter version of Feinberg's report, with the same title, was published in *The Gamut*, No. 5 (1982), 20-26.

And that's not all:

The escape from Indians by hiding underwater and breathing through a reed is also told about other frontiersmen such as Tim Murphy and Daniel Boone.

August

First Weekend
THE CROW FAIR

The Crow Indians were a Siouan tribe, originally part of the Hidatsa. Legend has it that two equally powerful Hidatsa chiefs had a dispute late in the 18th century which resulted in one chief and his followers separating and moving west from the banks of the Missouri River to the vicinity of the Rocky Mountains. There they became a tribe of wandering hunters, superior in horsemanship, and extremely warlike. The modern Crow Reservation in eastern Montana covers about 2400 square miles of their original range, and the Crow Fair is held on the banks of the Little Bighorn River.

The Crow Fair seems to echo the Sun Dance ceremonies that were originally celebrated in late summer or early fall by almost all the Plains tribes. Probably a summer solstice rite at the start, it developed into a mixture of secret rites and public performances designed to unite the tribe and verify its traditions. Dancing, drama, parading, elaborate costuming, both fasting and feasting, sacrifices, self-torture, politics, and socializing were all part of this major event. Opposed by missionaries and the United States government, the Sun Dance was stamped out or greatly modified. The Crow Fair, embracing all Native Americans and open to tourist viewing, is a tribal and an ethnic spectacle, more suitable for the 20th century.

A Native American Fair

Constance Poten provided this background on the Crow Fair:

Crow Fair, which always begins on the [first weekend] in August, attracts Native Americans from all over North America. They come to compete in the All-Indian Rodeo, to sell beadwork, jewelry and T-shirts, to fry bread and Indian tacos, to dance and drum at the powwow and to greet friends they haven't seen for a year.

Tawny children race their ponies through the grass and swim in river shallows. Young men and women buckle on their chaps and spurs beside the rodeo stalls. Parents raise camps, throwing leafy cottonwood boughs over arbor frames, and exercise Thoroughbreds and quarter horses for the races. Elders paint the faces of their clan children, carefully outfitting them in traditional Crow dress for the parades.

Medicine man John Pretty On Top, never without the deerskin-wrapped medicine bundle on a thong around his neck, has participated in every aspect of Crow Fair. He says those morning parades are the vital center of the five-day celebration; they keep alive Crow arts, giving clan members a chance to use the precious artifacts held in their families for generations. "The parade is a good way to show young people the use, the value of these things," says Pretty On Top.

In tribute to their modern warriors, the Crows choose veterans from World War II, Korea and Vietnam to lead the morning parades. In uniform and medals, they carry the flags of the Crow Nation, of Montana and of the United States. Crows of all ages follow, dressed in the finest regalia of their ancestors. Young mothers cradling their babies ride on original high-backed Indian saddles; children wrapped up like teddy bears in buckskin and beads sit on the hoods of cars spread with buffalo robes and Pendleton blankets; clan members dance and drum on flatbed trailer floats. Montana politicians, the Christian Cowboys, local celebrities and Indian princesses from a

dozen other tribes are scattered through the procession.

It is a breathtaking sight, as it must have been 150 years ago when Crow bands streamed across mountains and prairies to their summer celebration. The fleet Crow horses, manes and tails woven with eagle feathers, wore ornate saddles, breast collars and bridles. Their long-haired riders wore buckskins quilled and tasseled with ermine tails and scalplocks; their eagle-feather head-dresses sailed on the wind.

"No part of the human race could present a more picturesque and thrilling appearance on horseback," wrote painter George Catlin in 1832, "than a party of Crows rigged out in all their plumes and trappings—galloping about and yelping in what they call a war parade." Catlin said that he and fur traders of the era thought the Crows ("beautifully clad, handsome and gentlemanly") surpassed all other Plains tribes for their high sense of honor and fearless pride.

Each August that graceful, bold Crow world of the buffalo days is resurrected—not for tourists, though they are welcome to witness the spectacle, but for the reunion of family and clan, and for the celebration of a culture still nurtured by the 7,000 Crow people.

Source

Travel and Leisure, Volume 19, #3, 127-28. From an article entitled "Powwow!" [Reprinted with permission from *Travel and Leisure*, March, 1989. Copyright © 1989 American Express Publishing Corporation. All rights reserved.]

August
16

ANNIVERSARY OF ELVIS PRESLEY'S DEATH

Elvis Aaron (he often spelled it "Aron") Presley was born to a truck driver and a sewing-machine operator in Tupelo, Mississippi, on January 8, 1935. By his late teens he was locally successful as a country singer, appearing at the Grand Ole Opry and on Louisiana Hayride. He got his big break in the mid-1950s with appearances on television shows, and with an RCA recording contract. Using a variety of styles

Elvis fans commune together

based on gospel singing, on black blues, and even on light opera, he had one smash record after another, defining a rock-and-roll style that became the symbol of teen-age rebellion and culture. A gifted performer with a versatile voice, and suggestively good-looking, he would, as one critic described it, "make love to the mike," gyrating and "un-huh-ing." In Bob Hope's words, he was "wearing his trousers out from the inside." Songs like "Don't Be Cruel,"

"Teddy Bear," "Love Me Tender," and "I'm All Shook Up"—along with a host of movies—made him a fortune.

Nevertheless, his private life was a confusion of drinking, drugs, indulgence, and unsuccessful love affairs. In 1977 at the age of 42 Presley died on a bathroom floor of heart failure. However, his commercial appeal and following were so great that a host of imitators, his old managers and associates, his wife Priscilla, and his old girl friends have continued to make money from his name. His lavish home at Graceland in Memphis has become a shrine. Each year a tribute week honoring his death brings thousands of tourists, fans, and other curiosity-seekers to the town. Elvis' followers and the people who make money from his name have given him the trappings of a true folk hero. Guarding his memory, they have created a modern, pseudo-religious festival.

Taking Care of Elvis

This article by Bob Kerr and the following one reveal that Presley's fans have treated his life and career in much the same way that they treat their heroes. The ideas that he may still be alive, that his end was a sort of martyrdom, that his mission was religious, distinguish him from other cult figures of the entertainment world such as Marilyn Monroe, James Dean, and John Lennon. The tribute week in Memphis has attained festival status within only a decade.

There is the woman from Paris who goes every morning to the Meditation Garden behind Elvis Presley's home to sit by his grave and cry.

There is the 7-year-old boy from Boone, Iowa, who wears a gold suit and walks among the boozey hard trade of a bottom-line barroom to sing "Blue Suede Shoes" and throw scarves to screaming ladies, just as Elvis did.

There is Sunny Burke, the man from New Orleans who paints cars for a living and admits he's broke because he's spent $17,000 turning his pickup truck into a rolling tribute to Elvis. The grill says "Elvis1" and the bug screen says "The King Lives On Forever" in quarter-inch steel.

And there are tens of thousands more who have come here, turned pilgrims and sometimes poets by a man who in his pathetic, lonely death gave them a warm and comfortable way to make a mean, crazy world stand still.

The people who have jammed Memphis for Elvis Presley Tribute Week—which climaxes today, the 10th anniversary of his death—are almost exclusively white and far from wealthy.

They do little else outside home, work and family but honor Elvis. He and Graceland, his home, are their Rotary Club, their trip to the Bahamas. They care not so much for the music as the man, who they believe handled fame and wealth as it should be handled and never got uppity.

As they wait in often-bored obligation to board the tours buses for yet another look at Graceland; as they move through the souvenir shops to consider Elvis beach towels, baby clothes, Love Me Tender Moisturizing Cream and clocks that feature pink Cadillac second hands; as they participate in the attendant rituals of trivia and impersonator contests, they seem united in an almost defiant willingness to forgive and, in many cases, forget.

They forgive Elvis his flabby death-by-excess on a bathroom floor. They forgive or refuse to acknowledge his slide from raw, greasy rocker to a paunchy self-parody who sang "My Way" in American Eagle jumpsuits.

But they do not forgive the transgressors. They do not forgive his wife, Priscilla, for leaving him. They do not forgive Lucy de Barbin, the Louisiana lady who claims to have been Elvis's lover for 24 years and

AMERICA CELEBRATES

ELVIS PRESLEY

wrote a book about it. "Lucy Lied" pins were big sellers in Memphis this week.

They say crude, nasty things about Albert Goldman who wrote a scathing Elvis biography that details bizarre sexual habits. Peggy Sue Sosebee of Atlanta, who teaches her grandchildren to say "Elvis" before they say anything else, says she wrote to Goldman to ask how many whorehouses he visited in order to be able to compare Graceland to one. He didn't write back.

Sosebee, who wears a jumpsuit covered in Elvis patches, owns some burned-out wires from Elvis's stove, a piece of carpet and a dimmer switch from Graceland, and the needle and thread used to sew up Elvis's pants when they split during a concert in Alabama.

"If you're not an Elvis fan, you can't understand," she said, reciting what has become a fairly typical response to the prevailing question, "What does it all mean?"

There is a reassuring "us against them" feeling in the blind love of Elvis that in some ways reflects the singer's own flamboyant rejection of how a rich man in America should live.

And the people who run the great money mill that Graceland has become do nothing to dispel it. Todd Morgan, Graceland's communications director and its bubbling, forever-up answer to Pat Sajak, told fans to be polite to reporters who ask them what it all means.

He told them reporters often just don't understand and end up spreading foul thoughts about The King.

As with anything that approaches a religion—and the worship of Elvis surely does—there is an accepted gospel and articles of faith.

The devoted know that Elvis was a good man who gave away Cadillacs and houses, loved his mother, had perfect Southern manners, contributed to charity, didn't go to orgies and didn't like liquor.

"And he brought together more people in love than anyone else in the world, including Jesus," said Grace Bledsoe of Adel, Georgia, whose Elvis fan club won the first Elvis window-decorating contest, in 1981.

But the fans, the true fans and not the tourists, know, too, that Elvis was vulnerable, that he was badly used, that he didn't have good people around him when he needed good people most.

"He was very vulnerable," says Professor Charles Wilson of the Center for the Study of Southern Culture at the University of Mississippi. "His talent was an intuitive talent, not intellectual. There was great feeling, sentiment, passion. But he was not a particularly shrewd or clever person who could have coped with the pressure."

It is in the vulnerability, in the real or imagined betrayal by those closest to him, that many who come to the Memphis shrine seem to forge their strongest link with Elvis.

There is the feeling that if only they could have been there to help, to undo the wrong done by others, one of rock 'n' roll's most bizarre tragedies might not have occurred.

So they wear bracelets, pendants and pins that say "TCE" for "Taking Care of Elvis." It is a loving, post-mortem variation on the "TCB," or "Taking Care of Business," motto that Elvis plastered on just about everything, including his two private jets, the Lisa Marie and Teddy Bear.

They take care of Elvis by pouring their money into Graceland to assure that it will always be there for them to come back to. They raise money for many of the same charities to which Elvis generously contributed. They fashion their hair into jet-black helmets with sideburns down to the jawline. Some even indulge in a bit of morbid resurrection.

"You'll probably think I'm crazy, but I don't think he's dead," said Sonny Burke, the car painter from New Orleans who has blown his savings on his pickup truck. "That could have been a dummy they put in that coffin."

Not too many agree with Sonny, but some do.

Artie Mentz, who comes from Dubuque, Iowa, and has been called "Dubuque's Own Elvis" because of his alleged striking resemblance to Presley, does not believe that Elvis is alive.

He also thinks some people put Elvis a little too close to Jesus. After all, says Mentz, those problems with the prescription drugs have been pretty well verified.

But Mentz, who works as a professional Elvis impersonator, believes he has a mission, and the mission is Elvis.

"An Elvis impersonator is like a priest to a church," he said. "He gives that performance Elvis can't give anymore."

Mentz was standing in the haze of Bad Bob's-Vapors nightclub, where he is appearing nightly and competing in a week-long impersonator contest. On stage was 7-year-old Jamie Kelley of Boone, Iowa. Jamie, in the gold suit, made the finals.

His father, who opted for black leather, got knocked out in the preliminaries. His mother wore a low-cut dress and handed him the scarves that he, in turn, handed to the dutifully frenzied women near the stage.

It was a week to flaunt it, to sneer the way Elvis sneered, to be an Elvis fan in the protective circle of other Elvis fans. They left behind the derision they admit they sometimes suffer at the hands of the heretics back home.

"To fans, Elvis is a martyr," said Michael Stern who co-wrote the book *Elvis World* with his wife, Jane. "That's one of the central themes to Elvis. When [televi-

AMERICA   CELEBRATES

ELVIS PRESLEY

sion host] Steve Allen made him put on a tux and sing to a basset hound, the fans hated it.

"That was one of the first attempts to put him down. The blinders the fans put on is a reaction to that. They feel an obligation and a duty to blindly defend him for all they got from him. When they say 'taking care of Elvis,' that's what they really do."

The Sterns, who have made careers out of writing about roadside food in America, think they know why Elvis lives on.

"He lived a life every poor boy dreams of," said Michael Stern. "He didn't get into a stock portfolio; he gave away Cadillacs. And fans love that house. It is to interior decoration what "Hound Dog" and "Jailhouse Rock" were to the popular music of the '50s."

At Humes High School, on Manassas Street, where Elvis graduated in 1953, black students dressed in blue shirts and ties are conducting tours of the rooms where Elvis sort of studied and of the auditorium that bears his name and where he sang "Old Shep" in a school talent show.

Still, Humes students know they belong to a different musical era.

Stephanie Tate, who will be a ninth-grader this fall, said that Elvis means a lot to the students at Humes because he went to the same school they do. But she said she likes [singer] Whitney Houston a lot more.

Source

Providence Journal Bulletin, August 16, 1987.

Did Elvis Fake His Death?

Columnist William E. Schmidt adds the following:

[If] Elvis Presley is alive, if the King faked his own funeral and has been hiding out somewhere for the last 11 years. Ann Dinsik figures he could do a lot worse than Vicksburg.

"He'd need a place like this, kind of out of the way and quiet where he wouldn't be bothered much," said Mrs. Dinsik, talking from behind the counter at the Malt Shoppe, an ice cream parlor in this town of 2,800 people in southwestern Michigan. "I mean, look at the way people are. They wouldn't even let the man be dead."

There has been a lot of talk like that over the last year in Vicksburg, ever since a local woman, Louise Welling, began telling people that she saw Elvis Presley—she says she is absolutely certain it was he—standing in checkout line No. 2 one Sunday at Felpausch's Supermarket.

He was wearing a white jumpsuit, she said, and paying for an electrical fuse. "I was so dumbfounded I couldn't speak," she said. She remembers that he seemed nervous, as someone might who had something to hide.

She went straight to the editors at *The Commercial Express,* the weekly newspaper in town, but they didn't believe her.

Neither did reporters at *The Kalamazoo Gazette*. But she found an ear at *The Weekly World News*, a supermarket tabloid published from Lantana, Florida.

"Elvis is Alive!" the newspaper bannered last May. "The King admits his funeral was faked and tells of secret life in Michigan!"

They printed it all, not only that Elvis shopped at Felpausch's, but was seen eating at a nearby Burger King and was probably living in an old hotel in downtown Kalamazoo, about 10 miles away....

Radio stations and disk jockeys from California to New York called Felpausch's, demanding interviews with clerks. In Kalamazoo, someone filed petitions nominating Elvis Presley as a Republican candidate for precinct delegate, and Mayor Ed Annen fielded telephone calls from reporters around the country.

Mr. Annen said, "I told them that everyone knows this is where he lives and that they should send their residents here to spend tourist dollars to find him."

With the news that Elvis had patronized Felpausch's, a rival supermarket put out its own sign: "Jimmy Hoffa Shops Here." The Main Street restaurant introduced "Don't Be Cruel" bean soup on its menu. Next door, a dentist advertised: "The King gets regular check-ups here."

As it turns out, what happened here was only an early symptom of a much wider mania that in recent months has resulted in a barrage of other sightings and dubious reports, circulated in the tabloid press: grainy telephoto pictures of a man said to be Elvis standing in a Las Vegas parking lot; the purported discovery by astronomers of a statue of Elvis on Mars.

Then there was the book published earlier this year by an Atlanta woman offering evidence that Elvis, exhausted and overwhelmed by his fans, staged his own death and funeral in 1977 and went into hiding.

Mrs. Welling says the book certainly persuaded her; she believes he still lives in the area, but has now adopted a beard as a disguise.

Source

New York Times, October 17, 1988. From the column, "Vicksburg Journal." Copyright 1988 by The New York Times Company. Reprinted by permission.

Elvis and an NFL Exhibition Game

Sports columnist Jim Donaldson noted this observance:

Forget about winning one for The Gipper.

The [New England] Patriots wanted to win this one for The King.

As the Pats kicked off here last night in the Liberty Bowl against the [Houston] Oilers, Elvis International Tribute Week did, too.

AMERICA CELEBRATES

ELVIS PRESLEY

Tuesday marks the 11th anniversary of the death of Elvis Presley, who is buried here at his mansion, Graceland. And, in memory of the King of Rock and Roll, a week-long series of events has been planned.

If you want to talk excitement, well, there is far more to be found during Elvis International Tribute Week than you ever could hope to see in an NFL [National Football League] preseason game.

You could attend the Aloha From Graceland Luau, inspired by Elvis' 1961 movie, Blue Hawaii, on Wednesday.

You could go see a "Visions of Elvis" art exhibit—don't you just loooove that velvet texture, Jim Bob—? or stop in at the Elvis Fan Festival being hosted by the Elvis Presley Burning Love Fan Club from Streamwood, Ill.

Not to be outdone, the Then, Now and Forever Elvis Presley Fan Club of Memphis is sponsoring an open house for Elvis fans at the Pizza Hut at 429 Elvis Presley Boulevard, which used to be plain, old Bellevue Avenue, Route 51.

You could tour Humes Junior High School, which was a high school when Elvis graduated in 1953, or attend the Elvis Memorial Service being conducted Tuesday at the Memphis State University Theater, or even take part in the fifth annual Elvis Presley Memorial Karate Tournament.

Then there's the "Elvis: Legacy in Light" laser light show at the Pink Palace

Planetarium, or you could tap your blue suede shoes while watching the Memphis State Pompon Squad dance to the music from Jailhouse Rock.

Last night's halftime show was a bowl-game type extravaganza, featuring Andy Childs, an Elvis impersonator—oops, ahem, an Elvis *stylist*.

The emotional highlight of the week, of course, is the candlelight vigil, which begins at 10 tomorrow night at Graceland and lasts until the last fan in the procession has walked up the mansion drive to Elvis grave in Meditation Garden. Last year, that wasn't until after sunrise.

Such devotion is understandable to Patriots guard Ron Wooten.

"I've been to Graceland," said Wooten, who grew up in North Carolina. "It was one of the high points of my life."

Asked if he was an Elvis fan, Wooten replied: "Elvis doesn't have fans. They're more like worshippers. He has an unusual, god-like status. That's part of the package when you're one of the chosen few, one of the immortals."

Does Wooten believe The King lives still?

"He's alive in my heart," said Wooten. "He'll never die."

There are many who believe Elvis isn't dead.

"I was on a radio show in San Diego," Oilers coach Jerry Glanville said one day last week, "and there were people who called up who said they'd seen him. They said he's trimmed his sideburns and doesn't look as heavy as he used to."

Just in case Elvis might still be around, Glanville left a ticket for him last night at the "Will Call" window.

"There'll be a pass for him, left under the name of The King," Glanville said. "I hear Elvis is living now in Michigan or Minnesota. Well, we'd like him to come and be on our bench. I don't care how much weight he's gained. We still love him."

So do Patriots coach Raymond Berry and his wife, Sally.

"Some of the first money I ever spent was on Elvis records," Berry said last week at training camp at Bryant [College]. "I really dug Elvis.

"He started his rise to fame traveling through East Texas in the '50s. My wife saw him then. We were in on his rhythm wavelength."

Source

Providence Sunday Journal, August 14, 1988.

September

First Monday
LABOR DAY

Peter J. Maguire, a labor union leader, was the originator of Labor Day. He suggested to the Central Labor Union of New York a celebration honoring the American working man. Acting on this idea, some 10,000 workers paraded in Union Square, New York, reviewed by officials of their fraternal society, the Knights of Labor. Afterwards there were political speeches, fireworks, and a picnic. The celebration became an annual event, made official by state proclamations. The date has no traditional or historic significance.

Labor Day on Fifth Avenue

It was simply convenient, chosen, according to Maguire, because it was "nearly midway between the Fourth of July and Thanksgiving, and would fill a gap in the chronology of legal holidays." In time, the significance of Labor Day as a trade union holiday declined, but it remains important because it marks the end of the vacation season and provides a good time for family picnics, sporting events, political rallies, reunions of various kinds, and festivals not necessarily tied to a fixed date.

Holiday for the Workers?

Sam Howe Verhovek filed this Labor Day report:

To many of the people marching in the parade up Fifth Avenue yesterday [September 5, 1988], the point of having a Labor Day holiday was clear.

"This is for the honor of the working class of this country," said Bob Zuzzolo, a member of Local 28 of the Sheet Metal Workers Union International. "This is our day."

True enough. Just as on Memorial Day Americans are supposed to pause and remember the nation's fallen soldiers, so Americans were supposed to pause yesterday to praise working men and women and contemplate the role of labor unions in the nation's history.

Many did, and perhaps rumors of the holiday's metamorphosis are a bit premature. But just as Memorial Day has largely become a time to gather 'round the barbecue and welcome the beginning of summer, so Labor Day has largely become a day to give the season a good send-off.

"The idea should be, 'Let's go out and march,'" said Francis Rodriquez, a cafeteria worker at Public School 31 in the Bronx. "Instead for a lot of people it's, 'Let's go to the beach one last time.'"

Indeed, just a few blocks away from the parade route yesterday, there was plenty of evidence, 106 years after the holiday's inauguration, that Labor was not the operative word in Labor Day.

"Independence Day, right?" was one response in Central Park to a question about what, exactly, was being celebrated.

"Somebody got killed or something," was another.

"The idea is to take a rest from your labor," ran a third.

"Let's face it," said Cynthia Salmons who was walking with a friend. "A lot of our holidays have lost their original meaning. I actually remember, when I was a kid, we'd go to the cemetery on Memorial Day. Sure we'd have a picnic afterward, but we'd always go to the cemetery to remember what the day was all about."

Are holidays not what they used to be? Or have they never been what they were intended to be?

Professors of leisure studies are taking a look at these questions. "I think you'd have to say that Labor Day is essentially celebrated as a three-day weekend rather than as a meaning-laden holiday," said Dr. John R. Kelly, a professor of leisure studies at the University of Illinois in Champaign-Urbana.

Dr. Kelly noted Americans' voracious pursuit of leisure has altered the traditional dividing lines between the week, the weekend and holidays. For the convenience of the three-day weekend, for example, Americans gladly take Washington and Lincoln's birthdays, put them together and celebrate them on a date that usually corresponds to the birth date of neither.

Source

New York Times, September 6, 1988. Copyright© 1988 by The New York Times Company. Reprinted by permission.

Labor Day and the Labor Movement

Michael L. Rozansky examined the labor movement's observance in Philadelphia:

The labor songs and speeches had nearly ended when Jim Moran took a final look at the departing crowd. He stood on a platform overlooking the Judge Lewis Quadrangle in Center City, his hands tapping his thighs to the catchy rhythms of the East Logan Drill Team.

A satisfied smile broke through his grizzled white beard.

LABOR DAY

"We feel we hit a grand-slam home run," said Moran, 50, a key organizer of the Philadelphia area's tri-state Labor Day march and rally. He faced another labor leader and said, "It looks like there's some movement back in the movement."

About 2,000 people paraded yesterday through nearly barren city streets and rallied at the quadrangle in what organizers said was the first such march in Philadelphia in 107 years, since a parade pressing for an eight-hour workday was held.

Morgan and others predicted that the strong turnout would herald a revitalized labor movement.

"Putting people on their feet one day of the whole year doesn't necessarily change the labor movement," said Morgan, director of the nonprofit Philadelphia Area Project on Occupational Safety and Health. "But it's one piece of what we have to do to bring back that spirit." ...

Veteran organizers and rank-and-file workers gathered under cool, crystalline skies. It was the first rally for 2-month-old Reed Frye, who bounced contentedly in a shoulder sling worn by his father, Chris, a Camden printer and member of the Graphic Communications International Union Local 14M. And it was one of many rallies for white-haired Sophia Jackson, a retired Philadelphia schoolteacher who remembered when May 1—now called national Law Day—was a day for labor, not lawyers.

"I'm proud to be a member of the union," said Chris Frye. "I think there's an all-out war against organized labor in this country. I'm afraid there's a plan to do away with unions in this country, and we're not going to let that happen.

"I want there to be good jobs for him when he grows up," he said.

Marches yesterday had villains aplenty. There was the Pittstown Coal Group Inc., whose Virginia and West Virginia mines have been the scene of a bitter, five-month-old strike. There was Amtrak president W. Graham Claytor, Jr., depicted on one sign as presiding over colliding toy trains and buses. One union official accused Claytor of attempting to cut wages 30 percent in contract talks.

There was, as always, former President Ronald Reagan, under whom labor "certainly took a beating," said Andrew Douglas of Mount Laurel, another member of Local 14M of the Graphic Communications Union.

There were the unnamed profit–driven "corporate pirates" and the foreign investors behind "the buying of America," said Edward J. Keller, executive director of Council 13 of the American Federation of State, County and Municipal Employees.

But the most often reviled corporate manager yesterday had to be Frank Lorenzo, chairman of Eastern Airlines' parent company, who appeared on buttons ("Weenie!") and on a sign as a vampire (held at bay by the Statue of Liberty's torch).

In the last year, Labor Day "sure took on a lot more significance than picnics and ballgames," said Phil Harris, 41, one of four area strike coordinators for the International Association of Machinists and Aerospace Workers, which along with the pilots is striking Eastern.

"I think all the members now realize what unscrupulous managers like Lorenzo are trying to take away from us," he said.

Keller of the AFSCME said labor today was seeking a different social agenda that includes raising the minimum wage, securing health benefits, and providing day care.

Moran's wife, Aggie, paraded in a red, white and blue Uncle Sam suit, with her 6-year-old grandson Jimmy, in a matching costume, as that "real-live nephew of my Uncle Sam."

"I think the labor movement's been on its knees too long, and it just stood up for the first time today," she said in a light Scottish brogue.

Source

Philadelphia Inquirer, September 5, 1989.

Joe Hill on Labor Day, 1971

This description of the Labor Day rally in Washington is by Archie Green, an authority on labor history and its lore. The "Will" mentioned here was actually written just before his death by Joe Hillstrom (Joe Hill), a labor organizer and poet-songwriter who was executed on November 19, 1915, for the murder of a Salt Lake City grocer. Convicted on shaky evidence, Hill emerged as a hero of the labor movement and sent a famous telegram from his death cell to IWW headquarters reading "Don't mourn for me: organize!" The "Will" was printed in the ninth edition of the IWW "little red songbook," Songs of the Workers, and has been famous ever since.

On Labor Day, 1971, while several AFL-CIO unions joined to present a colorful songfest on the National Mall in Washington, Jonathan Eberhardt performed the "Will" ["My Last Will" by Joe Hill], accompanying himself with a complicated guitar arrangement.

> My Will is easy to decide
> For there is nothing to divide
> My kin don't need to fuss and mourn
> "Moss does not cling to rolling stone."
> My body?—Oh!—If I could choose
> I would to ashes it reduce
> And let the merry breezes blow
> My dust to where some flowers grow—
> Perhaps some fading flower then
> Would come to life and bloom again.
>
> This is my Last and Final Will.—
> Good Luck to All of you.
> Joe Hill

Present at this songfest facing the Washington Monument, I was drawn to the moody rock treatment of Hill's poetry. In my mind I contrasted Eberhardt's "uptown" guitar with a faraway second instrument—the gospel mission piano in San Pedro where Joe Hill had picked out the tunes of his parodies. Despite my long interest in Joe Hill, as a figure in history and

AMERICA CELEBRATES

LABOR DAY

folklore, the meaning of his "Will's" proverbial imagery did not really come alive for me until this past Labor Day. When a "folk revival" guitarist used Hill's simple poem to bring together staid labor unionists and counterculture youngsters, new flowers did indeed take root and bloom.

Source

From the section on Joe Hill in *Folklore from the Working Folk of America*, 408-09.

Labor Day Politicking

These items are extracted from a news story on the 1980 presidential political campaign by Tom Fiedler:

Tuscumbia, Ala.—Jimmy Carter returned to his native South yesterday [September 1, 1980] to open his 1980 re-election campaign beneath a towering weeping willow tree.

Speaking near the edge of this picturesque small town, the President struck two major themes that his aides said he would repeat throughout the campaign—increased employment and strong national security.

Carter traveled from the White House to attend the Tuscumbia Springs Park Labor Day picnic, an annual event featuring barbecue, balloons and music—high school bands playing "Dixie" and the Charlie Daniels Band, a favorite of Carter's, playing bluegrass....

The Labor Day trip was deliberately fashioned as a reaffirmation of his roots and a reminder to the crowd of 25,000 that

they are the base on which he built his successful campaign in 1976.

"I have seen a lot of places and a lot of people the past four years," he told the crowd. "But I just want to say how great it is to be with folks who don't talk with an accent." ...

Carter returned to Washington after the speech here to host a more traditional Labor Day picnic on the White House lawn with labor union leaders, who constitute another cornerstone of his re-election effort.

Source

Philadelphia Inquirer, September 2, 1980.

And that's not all:
See "Shad Planking," and "Return Day in Delaware."

Portuguese Labor Day Festa
A Rhode Island Tradition

The Feast of the Holy Ghost, a Portuguese-American ethnic festival held on Labor Day, evolved from several sources: a dinner for the poor given by a Portuguese queen centuries ago, a religious devotion to the Holy Ghost as a symbol of charity, a desire to recall Old World customs in a new and changing environment, and perhaps most of all a reunion with family and friends of like background. Labor Day itself merely provides a suitable space in the calendar. One local authority, Mary Pacheco, suggests that the festa first appeared in Gloucester, Massachusetts, among fishermen who wished to express their gratitude after a voyage in particularly stormy seas. By 1911, it had spread to the Portuguese in West Warwick, Rhode Island. Charity and gratitude remain important elements of the festa. For example, children who have recovered from a serious illness are carried or walk in the festa parade, and a person who had regained the use of an injured leg might give a loaf of bread baked in the shape of a leg to be sold at the charity auction held in connection with the festa. Farmers who have prospered during the year likewise show thanks by donating produce for sale at the auction. This news article on the festa sponsored by the Sociedade Portuguesa do Spirito Santo was written by Bob Stewart:

More than 500 years ago, Queen Isabella of Portugal . . . honored the peasant poor with a feast in a rural village. The festival was climaxed when the Queen removed her crown and placed it on the head of one of the villagers.

This weekend [Labor Day weekend, 1975] the descendant of that feast of charity will be celebrated in West Warwick [Rhode Island], as the Portuguese Holy Ghost Society launches the 3-day festa it has sponsored for the past 64 years.

From early Saturday morning until late Monday night the Ventura Street neighborhood where the society is located in Lippitt, will fill with the sights, smells, and sounds of brass bands, rides, games, auctioneers and Portuguese food. Lots of it.

While the original feast was a strictly secular affair, this weekend's Feast of the Holy Ghost has a definite religious background.

According to Holy Ghost Society Treasurer Peter Furtado the religious element was introduced by Portuguese inhabitants of the Azore Islands. They worshipped the third member of the Trinity—the Holy Ghost, symbol of charity—and

incorporated their belief into the celebration of the feast.

Thus the symbol of the feast is no longer simply a crown, in remembrance of the queen, but a crown placed under charity's representative, a dove. That's the way that society secretary Steve Salois tells the story.

While the Feast of the Holy Ghost is central to the celebration it is by no means all of it.

Festivities begin Saturday morning, when Msgr. Hyacinth Moniz of St. Anthony's Church will bless the *oferta*—food to be given out to society members in recognition of payment of their *pensoa*—club dues. Society members will deliver that food all day.

At about 6:30 Saturday evening, one of the festa's many parades will proceed from Granfield Square along East Main and Main Street to Ventura Street. At the head of the parade will be society president Manny Ferreira.

When the parade reaches the society grounds, the festival begins. The rides will run, members of the women's auxiliary will sell the *casouila*—barbequed beef sandwiches seasoned with Portuguese spices—they have prepared, and two bands will battle for the crowd's attention.

Sunday morning features the big event. An eight division parade will leave Ventura Street around 10:00 A.M., headed for St. Anthony's Church on Sunset Ave-

AMERICA   CELEBRATES

LABOR DAY

nue. A Coronation Mass will be celebrated at 11:00 A.M. Then the parade, to be composed of representatives of the Portuguese Citizens Club, the Portuguese Sports Club, the West Warwick Police, the Coventry Fire Department and various veterans' organizations, will head back towards Ventura Street, to the accompaniment of the Tiverton, Bristol, and Washington Independent bands.

Then comes the Feast of Charity. To everyone present, members of the Holy Ghost Society will distribute portions of a specially prepared dish. In Portuguese it is called *Soupas do Espirito Santo*. In English it means the soup of the Holy Ghost. Rides, games and bands are to follow.

Monday—Labor Day—will be occupied by the *migalha*, the collection of food and livestock for the auction Monday night. Funds from the auction go to defray the costs of the festa, treasurer Furtado explains.

Finally, on Monday night, a special ceremony is held. At the conclusion of the festa, lots will be drawn to see which six families will have custody of the Crown of the Holy Ghost during the coming year.

Source

Pawtuxet Valley (Rhode Island) *Daily Times*, August 29, 1975.

Portuguese Labor Day Festa

The Festa Crown

The word domingas, *hosts of the crown, is apparently derived from the verb* domingar, *meaning to dress up for a special occasion such as for church on Sunday.* Domingo *means Sunday.*

When the sterling silver crown topped with a golden dove is carried through the streets of West Warwick this weekend [Labor Day weekend, 1978], close to 500 years of Portuguese tradition and symbolism will be carried with it.

The annual week-long Festa of the Holy Ghost began centuries ago as a social event, gradually took on a spiritual meaning, and now ranks as the largest ethnic religious celebration of its kind in the state of Rhode Island.

The festa traces its roots back to 15th-century Portugal, during the reign of Queen Isabella, who was known for her generosity toward the poor. Each year she threw a lavish feast for the village peasants. During the feast, the Queen would place her crown on the head of a peasant child.

In the modern-day festa, the Queen's gesture is re-enacted with the crowning of a local child. This year's choice is Gina Andrade of West Warwick, who will be crowned after each of the processions and parades during the festa.

The sterling silver filigree crown she will wear is not just a reminder of Queen Isabella and a symbol of charity. It has religious meaning as well. The small golden dove on top of the crown symbolizes the protection and guidance of the Holy Ghost. . . . This religious aspect of the festival was incorporated by the Portuguese residents of the Azores, who worshipped the Holy Ghost as a symbol of charity. . . .

The crown used in the festival is developing a history of its own. It was originally brought here from the Azores in 1911 by the Holy Ghost Society. But over the years, as it was carried through the streets and placed on the heads of dozens of awed children, the crown began to show its age. About 12 years ago, the Society ordered a new replica of the crown from the motherland and retired the old one from active duty. The original crown now rests in permanent display in the Society's hall on Ventura Street, surrounded by fresh flowers.

The new crown leads a more active life. In addition to being carried through the streets of West Warwick each year, the crown rests with several local families. . . . At the end of the festa each year, there is the *sortes*, or drawing of lots among the members of the Holy Ghost Society. Six families are chosen. One is selected to keep the crown for the next 46 weeks. The five other *domingas* [designated crown keepers] each host the crown for one week.

Source

Pawtuxet Valley (Rhode Island) *Daily Times,* September 1, 1978, unsigned feature article that was part of the extensive newspaper coverage of the Festa of the Holy Ghost.

Childhood Memories of the Festa

These recollections were published in a newspaper interview with Mary Pacheco of West Warwick, Rhode Island. She was born Mary Mello, in West Warwick, of parents who came to America from the Azores in 1900. She is known locally as an authority on the festa.

I can remember the aroma of *Masa,* Portuguese sweetbread, that was escaping from almost every home in Roverpoint village on Thursday and Friday of that week. I can remember the chickens cackling before they became that holiday meal. And the never failing "Sweetrice with cinnamon" a sure treat.

Most of all I recall the shiny window panes framed in starched curtains and the young lassies with rag curls so they'd be real curly-tops for the big Sunday parade.

With a chuckle I can recollect how many slept on the wood or linoleum floors so that the master bedroom had a guest-like appearance. The snow-white dust ruffle and counterpane of heavy embossed cotton with matching pillow shams were kept perfect until the relatives came. We were poor but for this occasion it almost always meant a new dress. The village seamstress would purchase a pattern or make one up and come Sunday afternoon, after the big parade, 20 to 25 youngsters from our area would all have the same design but in different fabric patterns.

It was really a great time as we followed the Crown for the six weeks of transfer. Every night we would go to the host's house and sing the rosary. The lady who was our leader had a high loud voice and the din was something as the young boys and girls tried to out-do her. Actually many of us would try to hurry it along because it meant a thick slice of *masa* and some homemade rootbeer afterwards.

Portuguese Labor Day Festa

AMERICA   CELEBRATES

LABOR DAY

Source

Pawtuxet Valley (Rhode Island) *Daily Times,* August 29, 1975.

And that's not all:
Other Portuguese communities have similar festivals which originated in the Old World. The St. Paio celebration in Naugatuck, Connecticut, is forty years old. It honors the patron saint of Torreira, a Portuguese seacoast town. For residents of Naugatuck of Portuguese descent, it is the most important social event of the year. It occurs annually on or near Labor Day.

September
18-19

LAGUNA INDIAN SAN JOSÉ DAY

In the areas of early Spanish influence in the Southwestern part of the United States, fiestas featuring Catholic masses and processions, carnival atmosphere, markets, dancing, and entertainments honor various patron saints. These are village ceremonials and are not sponsored by commercial organizations. They are traditional, with histories going far back to the time of the Spanish conquest. The Laguna festival honoring St. Joseph is a fine example. The pueblo of Laguna, some 45 miles west of Albu-

querque, New Mexico, was established about 1697. A Catholic mission was built there soon after and the official name of the village became "San José de la Laguna." The fiesta, the origins of which are lost in the last two and one-half centuries, was originally celebrated on St. Joseph's Day, March 19. However, the date was eventually shifted to September 18-19 because of better weather conditions and because the plentiful late summer harvest encouraged the exchanges of food and goods.

The Laguna Fiesta

Evan Z. Vogt observed the fiesta on several occasions and recorded the following:

An observer's first impression of the fiesta is that thousands of people move rather aimlessly through a welter of activities during the two days of festivities. But after continued observation and systematic interviewing over three or four successive seasons, the initial impression gives way to an understanding of the fiesta situation as a highly structured series of events. The fiesta is at one and the same time: (*a*) a religious ceremonial which combines Catholic vespers, masses, and processions honoring St. Joseph, with a Laguna Harvest Dance in the plaza; (*b*) an enormous "native" market for the exchange of economic goods; and (*c*) a carnival with merry-go-rounds, tent dances, bingo and other games of chance, hot dog and hamburger stands, etc....

LAGUNA INDIAN SAN JOSÉ DAY

The main cultural groups represented, in order of numbers attending, are as follows: Navahos (predominantly from parts of the Eastern Navaho area); Lagunas; Acomas; Spanish-Americans; Anglos; Zunis; Eastern Pueblos. . . .

Most Laguna families move in from the farming villages in the week preceding San José's Day. As "hosts," they prepare for the fiesta by whitewashing the inside and plastering the outside of the church, cleaning the floor and repairing and plastering the walls of the plaza, and cleaning and plastering their houses. There is singing and dancing practice for the Harvest Dance, and food preparation which includes baking bread in great quantities, roasting corn, and butchering sheep and cattle.

Meanwhile, the "guests" are also making preparations. The Navahos butcher sheep, weave rugs, and make jewelry to trade at the fiesta. . . . [The] Navahos are cognizant of Pueblo ceremonial calendars and use this knowledge to full advantage in planning trading expeditions. Traditionally, Navahos also engaged in trading ritual consisting of prayers and songs; today they still think of the dangers of being bewitched and carry "gall medicine" as a protection against witchcraft at the fiesta. Some Navahos also visit a "curer" in Acomita for witchcraft cures at this time. The Zunis make jewelry to sell, and the more devout say prayers and sing sacred songs the night before they leave for Laguna. The Spanish-Americans from the Rio Grande Valley pick fruit to sell; a few from the nearby villages make plans for selling liquor to the Indians who attend the fiesta. Precautions against possible witchcraft are also taken by Spanish-Americans, who wear crosses and "rosarios" (containing the image of the Virgin Mary and Infant Jesus) to ward off witches. Families in the Eastern Pueblos prepare turquoise (especially in Santo Domingo), chile and melons (especially in Isleta), and other goods to sell or trade.

The Anglo and Spanish-American concessionaires who bring the merry-go-rounds, bingo games, etc., to Laguna operate on fixed annual schedules, moving from one fiesta to another throughout New Mexico, and they plan their arrival at Laguna for the afternoon of September 18.

For all cultural groups, travel to the fiesta is now almost entirely by automobile. On the way to the main pueblo of Laguna the incoming "guests" stop in the farming villages at the homes of their Laguna or Acoma "host-friends," leave gifts (Navahos leave mutton, rugs, or jewelry; Zunis leave jewelry; Spanish-Americans leave yard-goods, soap, or towels; and Isletas leave chile, melons, or other foods) and often spend the night of the 17th with them before proceeding on to the fiesta grounds. . . .

By late afternoon on the 18th, the market and carnival aspects of the fiesta have been set in motion. . . .

While the market and carnival continue almost without interruption for two days, the religious aspects of the fiesta are divided into a series of definitely spaced events. The first of these is the evening vesper service which begins with the ringing of the Catholic church bells at 7:30 P.M. on the 18th. . . . Special prayers are said for St. Joseph, and after the service the priest announces that it is time for confession. In each of these years (I did not attend the service in 1947 or 1949) only a few Lagunas went forward to confess.

During the evening, the market and carnival continue along much the same lines as in the afternoon, but there is a noticeable increase in the size of the crowd and a number of new emphases are apparent. Additional Spanish-American families arrive for the evening dance. The younger unmarried members dance in the meeting house while their parents (who inevitably accompany the girls as "chaperones") sit on benches outside and visit with one another and with passing Indian friends. . . .

After the carnival closes at midnight, a group of Navahos usually gathers either near the stands or out in the camp area to sing Enemy Way songs and hold what is traditionally called a "squaw dance.". . .

The activities of St. Joseph's Day are initiated by a sparsely attended mass at 7 A.M. At 9 A.M. there is Solemn High Mass in the church. . . The virtues of St. Joseph (respect, kindliness, and justice) are stressed, as well as the fact that St. Joseph is the universal patron of the church "and our own patron here at Laguna." After an offertory, the formal church service ends, and the priest asks the governor and his lieutenants to come forward and "talk to the people." The priests then leave while speeches are made in the Laguna language by the governor and by seven other members of the Tribal Council who also stress the fact that this is the fiesta for St. Joseph and ask the people to prepare to carry the wooden image of the saint in the procession out to the plaza. . . .

After the speeches, the priests return and sprinkle holy water on the wooden image of St. Joseph. The image is then lifted from its niche by the parish priest and handed to two Laguna women who take turns carrying it in the procession which, after leaving the church, passes south of the plaza and enters the plaza on the east. The governor and his staff lead the way, making symbolic "trails" with their staffs of office; next comes an acolyte bearing a gold cross, followed by the women carrying the wooden image; the choir, which sings hymns about St. Joseph; the main body of the procession;. . . and, finally, the priests. . . .

Upon arrival in the plaza, the image of St. Joseph is placed on a table at the north side in a bower constructed of poles, covered with cornstalks. The front of the bower is left open and on either side of the entrance is a poplar tree. After a prayer the priests leave, the crowd disperses, and Laguna officials are left sitting with the saint during the rest of the day. . . .

LAGUNA INDIAN SAN JOSÉ DAY

Dancing in the plaza begins shortly after the procession (about 11 A.M.) and continues until almost sundown. The Darawee—the so-called "corn dancers" or "harvest dancers"—alternate with a team of younger men who perform a more secular dance. The 20 Darawee dancers (10 men and 10 women) are accompanied by a chorus of 10-12 men with drums. The chorus comes in first, singing, gesturing with their hands, and beating time with their feet. The dancers follow in two long lines, two men abreast, followed by two women abreast....

The more secular dance was formerly a Comanche dance..., but is now either a Hoop Dance, an Eagle Dance, or is even omitted altogether...

During the dancing, gifts of food (principally corn, bread, and green chile) are brought into the plaza by Lagunas and Spanish-Americans and placed in front of Saint Joseph. Later in the afternoon this food is distributed to the crowd by the Laguna officials....

During the last period of dancing, the Darawee and the more secular dance team perform simultaneously in the plaza. Shortly before sundown the dancers leave, the priest reappears and St. Joseph is returned directly to the church by a very small procession consisting of the priest, the governor and his lieutenants, the women who carry the image, and about forty others—all Lagunas and Acomas. Inside the church, St. Joseph is returned to his niche, and the religious phase of the fiesta ends when the priest leads those present in the Lord's Prayer....

The market and carnival activities, which have continued throughout the day as an adjunct to the religious phases of the fiesta, are again stressed on the evening of the 19th, and there are no changes from the evening before. Many people leave the fiesta on the night of the 19th, but the main exodus takes place on the morning of the 20th. The visiting Navahos, Pueblos, and Spanish-Americans finish their trading activities and break camp. Final stops are made at the homes of Laguna or Acoma friends in the farming villages on the way out, and at this time the visitors are fed and given gifts (usually corn, melons, bread or other foods) in exchange for the gifts left at these houses at the beginning of the fiesta. Mutual expectations are expressed to the effect that "we'll see you again next year at the fiesta." This gift exchange pattern takes place within the framework of an institutionalized "friend" relationship.... The friendships are initiated in various ways. In some cases, especially those involving other Pueblos, members of the two families may have met years ago at an Indian Service boarding school. In the cases involving Navahos, the original contacts were often made two or three generations ago and the "friend" relationship is maintained by the younger generation through the years. No bargaining is involved in the exchange of gifts; no questions are raised as to amount or quality of the gifts. But controls are present in the pattern, especially in the case of visiting Pueblos, by the fact that the visits will be returned and goods exchanged again when the Lagunas go to fiestas in other pueblos. In the case of the Navaho-Laguna relationship, the Navahos may decide to go to a different house the following year at fiesta time if they do not receive gifts in return that compensate them adequately for the goods they brought. On the other hand, if the Navaho visitors are "stingy" with their gifts, the Laguna hosts will provide less in exchange. In brief, a continuing process of adjustive reciprocity makes the system workable.... For the Lagunas, the fiesta for St. Joseph is the high point in the annual calendar of events. The important religious meanings centered in both the Catholic church and the ancient Harvest Dance are combined with the economic meanings centered in the market place and the recreational values in the carnival. All phases are now important in the Laguna definition of a good fiesta. The Lagunas also feel strongly their responsibilities as hosts to hundreds of visitors. The Spanish-American and Eastern Pueblo visitors are regarded as having many of the same interests in the fiesta, especially since these groups are also Catholic and have similar celebrations in their own villages. There is likewise a strong feeling of solidarity with Zunis, whose customs are similar and whose visits will be returned at Shalako time when Laguna families go to Zuni. The Navahos, on the other hand, are regarded as peripheral participants. There is no expectation that they will attend the church services or that their visits will be reciprocated by Laguna attendance at Navaho ceremonials....

There is clearly no consensus among the seven cultural groups attending the fiesta as to the religious meaning of the celebration and no common set of sacred values. Rather, the fiesta is articulated as a multicultural system in terms of varying definitions and varying roles played by cultural groups in such a way that the critical functions of trade and of feeding and entertaining a large, diverse crowd are carried out. These mutual role-expectations for fiesta behavior have shown remarkable stability and continuity over a long time span....

Source

American Anthropologist, LVII (1955), 820-39. Edited from a scholarly article, fully referenced, by Evon Z. Vogt. His findings are based on visits to the Laguna Fiesta in 1947, 1949, 1951, and 1952. The study was part of the Comparative Study of Values in Five Cultures, a project of the Laboratory of Social Relations at Harvard University.

October

4

FEAST OF ST. FRANCIS OF ASSISI

Francis of Assisi (1182?-1226), one of the greatest of the Christian saints, was distinguished for his joyous piety, asceticism, and compassion. The son of a prosperous merchant, he offered extravagant generosity to the poor, which caused his father so much concern that the father had his son legally disinherited. Soon thereafter, Francis began to minister to lepers near Assisi and to frequent a ruined chapel known as *Porciúncola*, which he rebuilt and is said to have punningly called his "portion" or "little inheritance." It was here that he sensed his

vocation and though a layman began to preach and gather disciples. In 1209, he received papal permission that led to the establishment of the Franciscan order. The order expanded enormously, travelling throughout Italy, France, Spain, and the Holy Land spreading the tenets of humility, poverty, and devotion. St. Francis died on October 3, 1226. He is notable for his love of nature and his humility. One legend relates how he preached a sermon to sparrows at Alviano and another that he saved bees from freezing to death.

St. Francis of the Pets

[Today] is the Feast of St. Francis. At Holy Cross School in Springfield, Delaware County [Pennsylvania], students brought their pets—dogs, cats, rabbits, hamsters, even hermit crabs—to be blessed yesterday by the Rev. Frank Truger of the school. [Caption for newspaper photograph.]

Source

Philadelphia Inquirer, October 4, 1978.

Blessing the Animals in New York City

The blessing of the animals has become quite a spectacle in New York City and has featured a good bit of humor and whimsy in the last few years. In 1988, for instance, 10 billion algae in a flask, a

turtle rescued from a Chinese restaurant where it was to have been made into soup, and a 14-foot tall ginkho tree were blessed. This account comes from an article by Ari L. Goldman:

Animals are not normally part of the cityscape. There are "no dogs" signs in store windows and "no pet" clauses in city leases. Yesterday, however, animals were given center stage at the Cathedral of St. John the Divine, a church that often draws its inspiration from the Middle Ages.

For its annual celebration of the Feast of St. Francis, the cathedral opened its doors to an 8,000-pound elephant, a dromedary, a macaw with a 30-word vocabulary, other birds, dogs, cats and a skunk named Respect. One by one, the animals were blessed at the altar in the cathedral, which is the length of two football fields. . . .

The procession of animals came at the end of a joyous two-hour religious service of dance, communion, jazz, preaching—and occasional barking.

For some, it was just another side show at an Episcopal cathedral that celebrated its centennial with a performance by an aerialist and that one Easter displayed a sculpture of a female Christ named Christa.

But to the Rev. James Parks Morton, the innovative dean of St. John the Divine, the blessing of the animals was a serious, if not exactly solemn, occasion, and one particularly appropriate for New York. "Animals are like vest-pocket parks," he said.

"They help get the urban dweller rooted in reality. Life has to be more than a series of trips on the subway to the office and back again. Animals give us a fundamental link to creation." . . .

Among the 4,000 worshipers at the service were Blanca Guzman and her daughter, Felisa, who brought their dog, Luna, from their home in the Bronx for a blessing. "We want her to be with us for a long, long time," said the younger Ms. Guzman, tugging at the leash of their 4-year-old Siberian husky. "She's a good companion," said her mother, who stays home with Luna when her daughter is at work. "I only wish she would be a better guard dog. Luna looks tough, but she doesn't bark."

As Robert Gilmor of Huntington, L.I., took his cat, Tom, for a blessing, he said his wish was that the cat "would become a vegetarian."

"He brings home chipmunks, mice, squirrels and birds," said Mr. Gilmor, whose raincoat was covered with white hairs from Tom's coat. . . .

The festival took in not just animals but everything God created, as was evident from the service for the day, known as "Missa Gaia/Earth Mass." The piece was performed by the Paul Winter Consort, the Omega Liturgical Dancers and the cathedral's choristers, chorus and singers, with the added sounds of wolf, whale and loon. The mass was commissioned by the cathedral and first performed there in 1981.

FEAST OF ST. FRANCIS OF ASSISI

The work has the essentials of the mass—the Kyrie, Sanctus, Benedictus, Agnus Dei—as well as the text of the "Canticle of Brother Sun," a prayer written by St. Francis.

Still, as was appropriate, the animals had the final word. Pete Brandon of Manhattan took his macaw, Captain Casanova, to Dean Morton for a blessing. In the silence of the church, the dean put his hand over the beak of the red, green and blue bird and whispered a prayer. Captain Casanova, digging into his own vocabulary for a response, announced: "Come on! Let's go!"

Source

New York Times, October 5, 1987. Copyright © 1987 by The New York Times Company. Reprinted by permission.

October
9

LEIF ERICSON DAY

Born in Iceland sometime before 1000 A.D., Leifr Eirikson was the son of Norseman Eric the Red, who discovered and colonized Greenland (the largest island in the world). After spending his youth in Greenland, Leif visited Norway and was converted to Christianity. About the year 1000, King Olaf I commissioned him to convert the Vikings of Greenland. According to the "Saga of Eric the Red" in the *Hauksbok* collec-

tion of sagas, he was blown off course on his return voyage from Norway to Greenland and as a result reached the coast of North America, where he found grapes and self-sown wheat. After collecting specimens, he continued his voyage to Greenland, where he successfully introduced Christianity. In another version of the story, from the "Saga of Olaf Tryggvason," the Icelander sets out from Greenland and spends the winter at Vinland, a point somewhere between Virginia and Nova Scotia. Although this version is more complete, the account from the "Saga of Eric the Red" enjoys more general acceptance. Because the date and place of Erikson's "discovery" of America are uncertain, in 1964 the originators of this celebration arbitrarily selected October 9 to commemorate it. This seemed appropriate because of its proximity to Columbus Day and because the first organized body of Norwegian emigrants landed in America on October 9, 1825.

AMERICA CELEBRATES

LEIF ERICSON DAY

Leif Erikson, Norseperson

Proclamation 4524
Leif Erikson Day, 1977

By the President of the United States of America

A Proclamation

Once again it is appropriate for Americans to honor the intrepid Norse explorers who overcame hardship and adversity to reach our shores so long ago.

The United States is a young Nation, but our debt to that courageous Norseperson, Leif Erikson, predates 1776 and recalls a distant age when brave adventurers sailed forth into the unknown. As a people we continue to embody this spirit of bold discovery, and we take pride in his historical exploits.

As a mark of respect for Leif Erikson and the Norse explorers, the Congress of the United States, by joint resolution approved September 2, 1964 (78 Stat. 849, 36 U.S.C. 169c), authorized the President to proclaim October 9 in each year as Leif Erikson Day.

NOW THEREFORE, I, JIMMY CARTER, President of the United States of America, do hereby designate Sunday, October 9, 1977, as Leif Erikson Day and I direct the appropriate Government officials to display the flag of the United States on all Government buildings that day.

I also invite the people of the United States to honor the memory of Leif Erikson on that day by holding appropriate exercises and ceremonies in suitable places throughout our land.

IN WITNESS WHEREOF, I have hereunto set my hand this twenty-third day of September, in the year of our Lord nineteen hundred seventy-seven, and of the Independence of the United States of America the two hundred and second.

Jimmy Carter

From the *Congressional Record*

(Mr. MICHEL asked and was given permission to address the House for 1 minute and to revise and extend his remarks.)

Mr. MICHEL. Mr. Speaker,... How ... can you account for President Carter's proclamation, quoted in the Washington Post the other day, which decrees that Leif Ericson was not in fact a Norseman. The President has declared that Ericson and all his countrymen, excuse me, countrypersons, were Norsepersons.

If this is indeed a sign that history is being rewritten, I must express grave concerns. What is it going to cost to rewrite all those history books and reprogram those of us already educated in the old-fashioned way of doing things?

I think our President ought to explain this new application of his power. He is ultimately responsible. One of his first actions as President was to proudly display on his desk a reminder that "the buck stops here," a reminder first made famous by that great leader and great President, Harry S. Truperson.

Source

Federal Register, September 27, 1977, 38-39. The remarks of Robert H. Michel, Eighteenth District of Illinois, the House of Representatives, were first published in the *Congressional Record* of September 30, 1977.

Leif Ericson and Columbus

This discussion of the Norse holiday was prepared by Lee Linder, Associated Press staff writer. His informant, Ivar Christensen of Media, Pennsylvania, is of Norwegian birth and is president and founder of the Leif Ericson Society which promotes this celebration:

Here we go again. Who really discovered America?

Supporters of two main contenders celebrate their conflicting claims on the same day, Oct. 9.

Officially, though not legally, it's Leif Ericson Day.

Legally, though not officially, it's Columbus Day—pushed forward from the formal Oct. 12 by Congress to make a long weekend possible.

Ivar Christensen, president of the Leif Ericson Society, which claims the Viking hero landed in North America in 1004 (488 years before Columbus sailed into the New World), has scheduled a gala dinner-dance near his headquarters office in Media [Pennsylvania] "and we have invited various Italian organizations and also will have our Viking ship 'Raven' parked outside," he said.

"It's an inspiring ship and some of the non-Vikings might walk a big circle around it because those dragonheads mounted on it are intimidating," he said. "But we've encouraged the Sons of Italy to bring a replica of the Santa Maria (the Columbus flagship) to see which looks best."

The party will wind up a three-day Scandinavian Festival, sponsored jointly by the Danish, Finnish, Icelandic, Norwegian and Swedish societies to mark Ericson's historic voyage to America, not yet recognized in most history books.

"It's really a friendly thing because there is no dispute any longer over who discovered America—is there?" Christensen said.

Source

Philadelphia Inquirer, October 11, 1978.

October
12
COLUMBUS DAY

By sailing westward, Christopher Columbus reached the New World, landing on a small island in the Bahamas which he named San Salvador on October 12, 1492. The anniversary of his landing was formally celebrated for the first time by the Society of St. Tammany, also known as the Columbian Order, in New York City in 1792 and was made a legal holiday by presidential proclamation a century later at the opening of the Columbian Exposition in Chicago. Now by federal law it is celebrated on the first Monday in October.

Although Columbus to his dying day believed he had reached the East Indies, and although other sailors and explorers may have preceded him to America, and although America is named for a navigator, Amerigo Vespucci, who followed after him and extended his discoveries, Columbus Day serves as a tribute to the revelation of a New World. A native of Genoa, Italy, Columbus is the particular hero of Italian-Americans, and Columbus Day has become for them a patriotic occasion of importance.

Columbus Day Pageant

Charles Speroni prepared this account. His sources, in addition to personal observation, included John J. Mazza of San Francisco, "who since 1941 has been playing the role of Columbus in the pageant," and San Francisco newspaper files.

Although the celebration [of Columbus Day in San Francisco] takes place on a Sunday, the festivities actually begin on the preceding Saturday night when, at a Grand Ball, the young woman who is to play the role of Queen Isabella in the pageant is chosen by popular vote, and crowned. This past year [1947] October 12 fell on a Sunday. On the evening of October 11, the Columbus Day Ball and the Coronation of the Queen were held at the Aquatic Park Building. On Sunday the ceremonies began with Solemn High Mass, which was—and always is—celebrated in the Church of Saints. Peter and Paul, in the North Beach district, where most of San Francisco's

Italians reside. The civic festivities, however, did not begin until the afternoon, when, at one o'clock, a parade assembled at the Civic Center and then proceeded down Market Street to Kearny Street, Columbus Avenue, Stockton Street, Filbert Street, and Powell Street. No fewer than five thousand marchers passed before the reviewing stand opposite the Church of Saints. Peter and Paul. Thousands of people watched the impressive procession of more than eighty units.

This first float was the Queen Float, with the Queen, Rose Amodio, and her ladies-in-waiting. Then followed the official cars, the band of the 2d Infantry Division, the San Francisco Naval Base band and marching sailors, the Coast Guard band, and many other bands, hundreds of horses and riders in their dazzling trappings, the Irish Freedom League float, howling Red Men improvising war dances, the blue-clad Vallejo Rainbow Girls patrol, colorful drill teams of the Native Daughters of the Golden West, the Italian Catholic Federation's drum and bugle corps, the showy red-and-orange clad drum corps of the Chinese girls of Old St. Mary's Church, hundreds of marching young men from the Salesian Boys Club and the San Francisco Boys Club. The parade lasted more than two hours.

Even before the parade ended, throngs of people had gathered at Aquatic Park where, since half-past one, other festivities had been in progress: a symphony orchestra played several selections; the

San Francisco Fire Department gave an exhibition of water-front fire fighting, and so on. By the time the parade was over, a large percentage of the spectators had arrived at Aquatic Park. The bleachers set up for the occasion were filled to capacity, and the rest of the crowd moved about restlessly, trying to secure a place from which to get a glimpse of the beach where Columbus was soon to land.

While the spectators were waiting for the Queen and her retinue to arrive, one of the officials of the day gave the address of welcome. A soprano sang "God Bless America," the audience joined in the Pledge of Allegiance, and a group of dancers performed some Spanish dances. Meanwhile, on the beach, only a short distance from the blue waters of the bay, several tepees had been erected, and squatting and walking among them, in colorful Indian costume, were numerous members of the Improved Order of Red Men, and of the Degree of Pocahontas. A few of them participated in typical Indian dances.

Finally, with some delay, the Queen arrived on her float with her attendants. They alighted and went to take their places on a platform which had been set up not far from the Indian tepees. Everything was now ready for the "landing" of Columbus. Thus, a few minutes later, three boats, provided by the Italian fishermen of the city and rigged up to resemble the famous *Santa Maria, Pinta* and *Niña*, entered the cove and cast anchor a short distance from the shore. Columbus and a few of his men

AMERICA CELEBRATES

COLUMBUS DAY

descended into a rowboat, came ashore, and proceeded to the Indian village. The Admiral uttered a few words of thanks to God for having guided him to the Indies, and smoked the pipe of peace with the Indian chief. Then, accompanied by some of his men and a few Indians, he walked over to the platform representing Queen Isabella's court in Barcelona, and there was met by Cardinal Mendoza, beautifully clad in bright red. The Cardinal escorted Columbus into the presence of the Queen, who was surrounded by three ladies-in-waiting and three children, all dressed in appropriate costumes. She graciously listened to the great navigator's account of his voyage, while looking with interest at the gifts and the Indians he had brought back; and when he finished his report, she thanked him for all he had accomplished.

Thus ended the colorful pageant. Later in the afternoon, prizes were awarded to the winning organizations that had participated in the parade, and in the evening the entire celebration closed with the annual Columbus Day dinner, at which the principal speakers were General Mark Clark and Dr. Herbert C. Clish, Superintendent of Schools, City of San Francisco....

[By] 1892 the Italians of New York, San Francisco, and a few other American cities had been celebrating Columbus Day for several years. As far as I was able to ascertain, the Italian population of New York City began to celebrate the discovery of America on October 12, 1866. The honor of having begun these Columbian festivi-

ties goes to the *Compagnia del Tiro al Bersaglio di New York* ([Italian] Sharpshooters' Association of New York). Their example was soon followed by other Italian associations in other parts of our country, so that by 1869 very elaborate festivities—in New York, a parade, sharpshooting contests, dancing, a banquet, and Italian ships in the harbor gaily decorated with flags—were held not only in New York, but also in Philadelphia, St. Louis, Boston, Cincinnati, and New Orleans.

As far as can be learned, it was in 1869 that Columbus Day was first celebrated in San Francisco. This city, however, observed Discovery Day on Sunday, October 17. On that day flags were displayed from various armories of the city. At noon the procession formed and started from the corner of Post and Montgomery streets in this order: A. D. Grimwood, Grand Marshal, assisted by his aids; a band of music; the Swiss Guards; a triumphal carriage, drawn by four horses and decorated with a half hemisphere on which was the "eagle, bird of freedom," as if it had just alighted on the newly discovered continent to claim it as its own. In the center of the car was a statue of the great Discoverer, and in the rear of the platform was a raised dais on which were seated two young ladies, one dressed to represent Isabella of Spain, the other, America. The whole was decorated and surmounted by Italian, American, and Spanish flags. Then came the Lafayette Guard with a brass band; the California Jaeger corps; the Car of State with thirty-two young ladies dressed in white and bearing in their hands the colors of the United States and of the other republics of America. Then, in barouches, came the President of the Day, the Orator of the Day, the Italian and Spanish consuls; a band; the Garibaldi Guard; the *Santa Maria*, a large boat rigged in imitation of the caravel which bore Columbus to our shores. The boat carried Columbus with an escort of several sailors in red shirts and dark pantaloons. Then came the decorated wagon of the Italian gardeners, bearing a young lady surrounded by the implements of agriculture. Then another float with a pyramid of punch bottles (it advertised an Italian liquor store), decorated with flowers, ribbons, and so forth. The procession moved through the main streets, and on to the City Gardens, where an oration was delivered on the exploits of Columbus. The festivities ended with a dinner provided by the Garibaldi Guard (hence the red shirts and dark pantaloons of the sailors on the *Santa Maria*.)

Source

Western Folklore, VII (1948), 326-29. From "The Development of the Columbus Day Pageant of San Francisco."

Italian-American Columbus Day

John Alexander Williams emphasizes the "transformation of Italian-Americans from immigrants to ethnics" in his study and identifies Columbus "as an ethnic hero" and Columbus Day as an amalgam of a traditional Italian saint's day festival and an Anglo-American patriotic ceremony.

For much of the nineteenth century, the celebration of Columbus in literature,

the arts, and ritual remained in Yankee hands. But while the "Italianization" of Columbus began in eastern cities such as New York and Philadelphia, Italian-Americans in the West made significant contributions to this process....

One of the interesting questions about the Columbus Day complex is the extent to which it combined Italian and Anglo-American elements. The landing pageant and the costuming of Columbus impersonators, for example, may owe much to the John Vanderlyn painting, *The Landing of Columbus*, commissioned for the U.S. Capitol rotunda in 1839 and reproduced widely on U.S. postage stamps in 1869 and 1892. The Columbus Day parades (generally not a feature of the Anglo-American Columbus Day before 1892) may owe much to Italian religious processions, especially if we consider the importance of Columbus statues in the Columbus Day complex. The Italian-American community of Walla Walla, Washington, erected its Columbus statue in 1910 and, according to local historians, the annual Columbus Day festival dates from that year. Meanwhile, in 1907 Colorado became the first state to make Columbus Day a legal holiday, thanks to a drive led by local *prominenti* aided by the Italian consul in Denver. The holiday and its associated practices and artifacts remain an important cultural landmark for Italians. For example, when during the recent restoration of California's Gold Rush era capitol in Sacramento architects proposed eliminating an anachronistic Columbus statue that had been installed in

COLUMBUS DAY

the capitol rotunda under Anglo-American auspices in 1882, Italian-American politicians and organizations raised a storm of protest, forcing the reinstallation of the statue.

Source

Folklife Center News, XI (Summer 1989), 11-12. From "Italian Regionalism and Pan-Italian Traditions."

Columbus Day Turkey Shoot

Datelined Lackawaxen, Pennsylvania, this article by staff writer Mark Fineman notes that live turkey shoots were a colonial sport and that today most sportsmen shoot at paper targets in competitions for frozen turkeys, and the article quotes condemnation of the event by officials of humane societies.

Keith Geiges squinted down the barrel of his .22-caliber rifle yesterday [October 11, 1981] afternoon, trying desperately just to sight his target.

It wasn't much to shoot at—just a tiny white head with a minute speck of red blending into a dense autumn background of crimson and gold woods.

So tough was the shot that Geiges was about to make at 2:30 P.M. yesterday that 21 contestants before him, each paying $1 a shot for the same chance, had come up empty. But finally, on the 57th shot of the afternoon, Geiges, 22, of Newfoundland, Pennsylvania, got lucky.

And the crowd cheered when he finally blew the turkey's head off.

Welcome to the 30th Annual Turkey Shoot, an event that has become something

of a legend to the folks in this rural Pocono Mountains township in Pike County.

Every Columbus Day weekend since 1951, thousands have come from miles around to the little hamlet called Bohemia, about 150 miles north of Philadelphia near the New York border, to watch contestants take their best shots at the head of a caged turkey 75 yards away.

The event is the featured attraction in the Central Valley Fire Department's annual fund-raising event, which comes complete with food, plenty of beer and a room featuring bingo, wheels of fortune and other games of chance....

It was well after noon yesterday when fire company member Walter Frisbie drove his battered blue pickup truck into the wooded enclave. Ten live white turkey hens, worth a total of $105, were caged in the back of the truck.

Frisbie, who runs the booth at the live turkey shoot, drove 75 yards back into the woods to what folks around here call the "Turkey Bunker." It's a simple, 5-foot-high cinderblock wall with steel plating on its face.

Just behind the wall is a weathered and cracked orange plywood crate with a hinged door. On the top of the crate, just above the wall, are two hinged slats, each with a semicircle cut out. The crate holds the turkey in place; the slats hold its neck.

And at 2 P.M., just before the first contestant loaded his .22-caliber short-barreled rifle (long barrels are prohibited), the two "spotters" crouching behind the wall slipped the first turkey into the crate and went to work. One spotter is called the watcher. He looks for the first sign of blood on the turkey's head after each shot is fired. The other is called the gooser. He prods the caged turkey's rear end with a stick to make sure the turkey keeps its head above the wall.

"All set?" Frisbie shouted to the spotters when the turkey's head appeared above the wall. Then Frisbie turned to the large crowd that had gathered and called out: "OK, who's going to kill the first turkey?"...

"Oooh, oooh, oooh; yep, yep, yesi-ree, you've got 'em," Frisbie finally shouted when Keith Geiges' bullet hit the turkey between the eyes.

Seconds later, a big red flag flew up behind the turkey bunker. One of the two spotters immediately grabbed the wounded turkey from the crate, raised his hatchet and finished the job. ("It's more humane that way," Tussel had said earlier. "The turkey doesn't suffer one bit.")

Source

Philadelphia Inquirer, October 12, 1981.

October—November

Hindu New Year
DEWALI, HINDU FESTIVAL OF LIGHTS

Hinduism is considered one of the world's oldest living religions. Made up of many sects, it was not founded but rather evolved over a period of four thousand years on the Indian subcontinent. Beliefs include the doctrine of *karma*. According to this system, a person's actions produce future consequences in a series of lifetimes. Gods and goddesses have numerous aspects but are all considered to be forms of the

one Supreme Being. The word *dewali* means cluster of lights, and illumination by lamps, fireworks, and bonfires are an important feature of the week-long festivities that mark the beginning of the Hindu New Year. It is a particularly holy day for devotees of Vishnu, the Preserver. One story relates how Vishnu killed a filthy and obnoxious demon on this day, but the most widely held belief is that Dewali honors the coronation of Rama, a manifestation of Vishnu, following his conquest of the demon ruler of Sri Lanka, Ravana, who had stolen his beloved wife. During Dewali, effigies of Narakasura or of Ravana are burned, Hindu merchants settle their accounts, presents are given, fairs are held, and games of chance are played.

Dewali in New Jersey

Nearly 1,000 Hindu families in the Philadelphia area will gather tomorrow [November 15, 1981] for their annual Dewali celebration at the Osage School, opposite the Echelon Mall in Voorhees, New Jersey.

Dewali is the most important Hindu festival, similar to Christmas in the Western world.

The world's 500 million Hindus celebrate this day with festivities, worship, gift exchanges, good wishes, fireworks and the decoration of homes with lights.

On this day, Hindus believe, Shri Ram (God incarnate) returned to his kingdom after 14 years of self-imposed jungle residence and after having defeated the fierce 10-headed demon Ravana.

The day signifies victory of light (knowledge) over darkness (ignorance), truth over falsehood and spirituality over immorality.

The celebrations in New Jersey will include folk and classical dancing, devotional music, religious discourses, the *Arati* (ceremony of lights) and a dinner. The programs are free, sponsored by the India Temple Association, a nonprofit organization that serves the cultural and religious needs of Hindu families in the area.

Source

Philadelphia Inquirer, November 14, 1981. Unsigned news item for a regular Saturday column of religious news titled "In the Churches and Synagogues."

Food for Dewali

Food writer Marilynn Marter provided this culinary information:

[The] festive meals prepared during Dewali, the Indian Festival of Lights, which begins today [November 1, 1978] and peaks Tuesday night [November 7] with a family feast similar to Christmas dinner, are typically vegetarian.

The vegetarian meal is natural on this pure and auspicious day when families get together to say prayers and friends and relatives visit and exchange gifts of sweets, dried fruits and nuts.

As described by Amar Bhalla [of Philadelphia], owner of the Indian restaurant Siva's and an excellent cook himself, the holiday is celebrated not only with sweets but also with new clothes, firecrackers and family entertainment such as card games, which are most common in northern India. Homes are lit by earthen pots with wicks set in wax or oil. Natural materials prevail.

In earlier times the poor served dinner on cleaned banana leaves and in little "cups" made from the leaves. The modern meal, however, is presented in individual *thalis*, which are round serving trays, typically of stainless steel, though sometimes of silver or brass. Each *thali* holds four or five little cups, called *katoris*, for the separate foods being served.

Bhalla prepared a typical *thali* for us, including vegetable balls called *Sabji Kofta* and *Dahl* (cooked lentils), for which his recipes appear [below]. Also on the menu was *Began Bhurta*, eggplant roasted, mashed and cooked with tomatoes, herbs and spices. These were accompanied by a yogurt-cucumber-tomato mixture called *Raita*, a rice pilaf and *Samosa*, a pastry filled with peas, potatoes, raisins, herbs and spices. The traditional puffed bread, *puri*, and tortilla-like *papadum* were the bread selections.

DEWALI, HINDU FESTIVAL OF LIGHTS

Sabji Kofta
(Vegetable Balls)

1½ pounds mixed, diced vegetables of your choice, cleaned and peeled as needed
4   cloves garlic
¼   ounce fresh ginger root, grated
¾   teaspoon salt
¼   teaspoon *garam masala* (commercial or homemade spice mixture)
2   ounces dry bread crumbs

Gravy:
4   ounces butter
4   ounces chopped onion
4   ounces grated onions
½   teaspoon red (cayenne) pepper
½   ounce ginger
8   cloves garlic
1   rounded teaspoon ground coriander
1½   teaspoons salt
½   teaspoon *garam masala*
8   ounces sliced tomatoes
2   green chili peppers, optional
1   cup water
1   teaspoon chopped fresh coriander leaves

Steam-cook diced vegetables, adding garlic, ginger and salt. When tender, mash the mixture. Add *garam masala* and bread crumbs. Mix thoroughly and divide mixture into 10 to 12 equal parts, shaping into balls 1 ½ to two inches in diameter. In a skillet, fry the vegetable balls in oil until golden brown. Serve hot with gravy. Makes four to six servings.

To prepare the gravy, heat butter, add onions and fry until golden. Remove from heat; add red pepper and stir until the color of the pepper is infused into the butter. Add ginger, garlic, coriander, salt, *garam masala* and tomatoes; cook until *masala* (spice mixture) is fried and "ghee" (clarified butter) separates from it. Add green chilies and water; simmer until raw flavor of garlic disappears and sauce thickens. Serve hot over vegetable balls and sprinkle with fresh coriander leaves. . . .

Dahl
(Cooked Lentils)

Dahls or cooked lentils are the most popular of Indian foods. About 60 different varieties of lentils are used for thick, soup-like mixtures also called *dahls*. This *dahl* recipe from Bhalla also contains kidney beans, which, when cooked and mashed along with the lentils, result in tiny, chewy bits that resemble ground meat. Once again, the feeling or impression of meat is found in a purely vegetable recipe.

8   ounces whole black beans (*urad dahl*), available in Indian or Oriental groceries
2   ounces kidney beans
4   cups water
2   ounces fresh ginger root, grated, divided
2½   teaspoons salt
12   cloves garlic, finely chopped
5   tablespoons clarified butter, divided
3   green chilies, chopped fine
½   teaspoon *garam masala*

Wash beans several times, removing grit. Boil water; add beans. Cover and return to a boil, cooking about five minutes. Add one ounce ginger, salt, garlic and one tablespoon butter. Simmer three to four hours. (Alternatively, you may pressure cook the beans at 15 pounds pressure for 30 minutes, allowing the pressure to drop by itself. Uncover and cook the beans further in the same pot or another pan over low heat for 30 minutes more.) Stir and mash beans occasionally during cooking (except in pressure cooker) until reduced to a creamy thick consistency.

Heat remaining four tablespoons butter with remaining one ounce ginger. Add green chilies and *garam masala*. Mix with the cooked *dahl* and serve. Makes four or more servings.

Source

Philadelphia Inquirer, November 1, 1978.

October   November

31 ^{to} 2

HALLOWEEN, ALL SAINTS', ALL SOULS' DAYS

All Saints' or All-Hallows' Day is November 1, which according to pagan custom begins as the sun sets the evening before. A festival of the dead, it was made into a celebration of all the known and unknown saints and martyrs of the Catholic Church in the seventh century. Originally, it was celebrated on May 13, but was shifted to its present date in the eighth century. All Saints' Day is followed by All Souls'

Greenwich ghosts and goblins

Day, November 2, another Christian adaptation of pagan festivals for the dead. This is a day of intercession for dead souls that have not yet been sufficiently purified, in the belief that the prayers of the living will help. It originated as a memorial in the tenth century.

Unlike All Saints', All Souls' Day was abolished by the Church of England, although it is recognized informally by many Protestants. Thus the two days have become combined in modern secular tradition. Mumming, pranks, bonfires, decoration of graves, belief in the return of ghosts or dead souls, fortune-telling and ritualistic games are associated with the eves and days of both November 1 and 2 in America.

"Trick or treat," the Halloween threat of little children, is apparently a recent American phenomenon, as distinct from pranks and mischief long customary on this holiday. It seems to be related to the Gaelic practice of giving cakes to the poor at Samhuinn or "summer-end," a seasonal festival that coincides with All Souls' Day. They came to be called "soul-cakes," and in return recipients were obligated to pray for a good harvest. Somewhat closer is an English Plough Day custom. Ploughmen went about begging for gifts, and if they did not receive anything, threatened damage to the grounds with their ploughs.

Trick or Treat

The following was collected by Catherine Harris Ainsworth, who was interested in identifying vestiges of Celtic influence in recent American Halloween practices:

Hallowe'en, when I was a child in the 1920s in the state of North Carolina, was noticed and celebrated, but not always; and when it was, with a marked degree of caution and frugality. There was some candy but not big brown paper bags full of it as there was for my younger daughter in Michigan in the 1950s. I do not recall the custom or phrase of "trick or treat" in North Carolina or in Florida when my older daughter was in her childhood in the 1940s. In fact, I first heard the expression when I was in Holly, Michigan, in 1955. An acquaintance, born in 1911, who grew up in Philadelphia, Pennsylvania, said he did not hear the expression there. The young people, did, he recounts, indulge in "mischief night," when they did destructive, mischievous acts on the night before Hallowe'en....

> Trick or treat,
> Smell our feet.
> We want something
> Good to eat.

Source

New York Folklore Quarterly, XXIX (1973), 164, 176. The rhyme was obtained from Jonny Davis, who chanted it as a ten-year-old in Niagara Falls, New York, c. 1972.

And that's not all:
See "More on All Souls' Day," especially the rhyme of Indian children in which they threaten to break windows if they are not given presents.

Halloween Junkpile

The very small village of Danbury, New Hampshire. has long had an unusual way of celebrating Halloween. Junk (old cars, bathtubs, broken bicycles, lumber, barrels, and other trash) mysteriously appears in the center of the common during the night, and no one seems to have had a hand in it. Although such littering, even by supernatural beings, is illegal, the town constable doesn't bother to interfere. In fact, the one time a lawman did try to investigate and stop proceedings, he was burned in effigy. Most of the residents figure that no one gets hurt, property isn't damaged, and the stuff is cleared away the next day, so why not? But there are those who feel that the whole thing is childish and lowers the town's image. Whatever, the tradition seems as well established as "trick or treat" and will undoubtedly continue as long as spirits do mischief at All Hallows.

Source

Reported orally to T.P.C. by a graduate student at the University of Pennsylvania. Recalled upon seeing the custom written up by Dave Zilavy in the October, 1988, issue of *Yankee* magazine.

Halloween Egg-Throwing

Constance L. Hays reported on this Halloween custom:

It's Halloween. It's egg time.

It's time for young people to buy them by the dozen and for grown-ups to worry about the impact of eggs on their neighborhoods.

And these last few days, the grocery store managers of New York have been the actors in a small, annual morality play: Is it mischief or is it mayhem? To sell or not to sell?

To many, holiday egg-buying is simply a phase of growing up.

"I used to throw eggs myself when I was younger," said Mohammed Marini, the manager of a Key Food grocery store in South Brooklyn. Mr. Marini said he doubled his egg order last week, to 8,216 eggs, to satisfy both shoppers with legitimate egg needs as well as the seasonal surge in demand.

But Won Kyu Lee, manager of Frank's Big Apple Deli frowns on such antics.

"We don't sell eggs to kids," said Mr. Lee, who added that he was hit by an egg Saturday night. "This is not play," he said. "This is almost bad."

Still, what remains a seasonal mystery is why the egg—a self-contained food that sells for 6 to 9 cents each and is carefully decorated on other holidays—

makes such an attractive weapon. Is it the size? The hard shell? The ghoulish pleasure of seeing, post-collision, the slimy, yellowish mess that results when the yolk, the white and the shell shatter against someone's shirt, car or house?

"It's cheaper than tomatoes," said Robert Vallo, a 14-year-old from South Brooklyn. He and two of his friends, Joseph Hajaistron, 14, and Anthony Sanzone, 13, were riding their bicycles around their neighborhood yesterday afternoon, but, having purchased five dozen eggs, were prepared for a night of egg warfare.

They wore long pants with big pockets on the legs, and several sweaters and jackets, all with lots of pockets. And they wore the indispensable hooded sweatshirt—Anthony had his hood strings pulled tight, almost covering his face—that is necessary to protect the adolescent head from eggs filled with chemical hair remover.

"Last year, a couple of my friends came into school the next day with bald spots," Joseph said.

Why throw that kind of egg? "To be mean," he said, adding, somewhat sanctimoniously: "We're in it for the fun. We stay in open areas, where there are no houses." Homeowners, he discovered after an angry one punched him last year, do not appreciate having to remove dried egg.

Tricia Joyce, a social worker who works at a mental-health clinic in Flushing, Queens, said mothers in the area were worrying about the impact of eggs on their neighborhoods. In recent days, she said, "kids were throwing so many eggs that they couldn't really walk into their apartment buildings without slipping and sliding."

Eggs were selling briskly yesterday at the Key Food in South Brooklyn. "There's some kids buying eggs now," Mr. Marini said, sprinting to a checkout aisle to prove his point. Two small boys, both wearing hooded sweatshirts, were purchasing a dozen eggs. Grade A. Large.

"What are you buying the eggs for?" Mr. Marini asked them.

The boys blushed. "It's for my mother," one whispered.

Once outside the store, the boys fled down the street, in the direction of a local Chinese restaurant called Me and My Egg Roll, clutching their sack of eggs.

Kaz Zahrieh, the manager of another Key Food store, on Nostrand Avenue in the Bedford-Stuyvesant section, said egg sales soared over the weekend, coinciding with eggs meeting tragic fates on the exterior walls of his store.

"They come in with their masks on and everything," Mr. Zahrieh said. "It's a mission."

Source

New York Times, October 31, 1988. Copyright© 1988 by The New York Times Company. Reprinted by permission.

Halloween Apple Games

Catching or dipping for apples was a means of divination among the Druids and survives in the folklife of countries influenced by Celtic culture. Since the apple is also a common love charm, the practice seems to be associated with the selection of a lover. It is, as well, a Christmas game, originally a fertility rite, during a season when other fertility rites were regularly performed. There appears to be no reason to play this game on Halloween except that apples are plentiful at this time. This item was remembered from her childhood in North Carolina by Catherine Harris Andrew:

In Elkin, North Carolina, which is in the Piedmont area of Southern United States, bobbing for apples was standard fare at all private Hallowe'en parties and at public Hallowe'en festivals given at the school or at a church to raise money for the institution. At any fall carnival, as well as at Hallowe'en, bobbing for apples was considered great amusement and entirely appropriate. A dozen or more apples were put into a large galvanized tub of water and contestants, for a prize, attempted to capture an apple with their teeth without the assistance of their hands. I have experienced, also, a variation of the bobbing-for-apples in which an apple was suspended in a doorway by a string tied to its stem, and contestants were to snag it with their teeth, again without the help of their hands. It is interesting to note also, that when my cousins moved into my community from a more remote and mountainous one and gave a Hallowe'en party, they had bobbing for apples as one of the games at their party. Since they had hardly had time to become acquainted with our community customs, I believe that they, too, acquired

AMERICA CELEBRATES

HALLOWEEN, ALL SAINTS', ALL SOULS' DAYS

this custom from our common Scottish ancestors. Perhaps bobbing for apples is the modern expression of the role of the mystic apple in the old Celtic ceremonies and fairy tales.

Source

New York Folklore Quarterly, XXIX (1973), 167-68.

Halloween for Grown-Ups

Don Shirley filed this report on activities in the nation's capital:

Halloween isn't just for kiddies any more.

Hundreds of grown-ups, more or less, roamed the main drags of Georgetown [District of Columbia] Wednesday night, wearing a glittering variety of Halloween garb. Costumes dotted the landscape around 19th and M streets, too, and at a number of bars and private parties around town.

San Francisco may not have been impressed; Halloween is a longstanding tradition for adults there. But even there changes are taking place, says an observer of the Bay Area social scene. Its Halloween scene used to be dominated by gays; now straights are dressing up and indulging themselves, too.

The Washington Halloween scene Wednesday night was an event for people of many ages and races and sexual orientations.

Though many of the revelers were young adults, some were not so young. As a carload of older folks wearing masks inched through the traffic, they were asked if they were going to a party. An old woman lifted her mask and shouted out that no, she was going to the Miss America pageant.

It was that kind of night.

A trio of George Washington University students—dressed rather conservatively as a Roman, a witch and a pirate—confessed that they had actually been trick-or-treating among the posh homes of Georgetown. At their ages? "If you ate dorm food, you'd go trick-or-treating too," replied the pirate.

A group assembled for dinner at the Foundry included a duck, a "priest," a Great White Hunter, a bat and an assortment of other creatures. In real life they were workers on the Hill, at the Brookings Institution, the Pan American Union and at other formidably starchy institutions, but tonight they were expressing their "real, inner selves," they said.

Except for one woman: "I didn't have the breasts for Dolly Parton so I decided to come as a little old man instead," she explained.

At the corner of Wisconsin and P streets, the windows of Avant-Garde, a new boutique, seemed to be shaking. A closer look through the fog on the windowpane revealed the wiggling bodies inside, dancing the night away. Owner Alain

Chetrit had moved out all the clothes and installed a disco for Halloween, open without charge to anyone who was strolling by, and the place was packed with gyrating dancers wearing elegant and exotic costumes.

Outside the store was a campaign worker for Republican mayoral candidate Arthur Fletcher, passing out brochures to the disco crowd. She applauded Chetrit's opening of his doors to the public and said Fletcher would do the same thing if elected.

Down the street, at La Serre, was a group that might have disagreed. "Trick or treat with Marion Barry," said the invitations, and inside, the Democratic mayoral candidate was dispensing conversation and handshakes while surrounded by pumpkins and orange and black crepe paper. Discreet little masks were available at the door, but not many people were wearing them.

On the sidewalk outside La Serre practically everyone was wearing a mask of some sort, and few of them were discreet.

The Potatoheads were holding court at the corner of Wisconsin and M. These were little figures with enormous heads who liked to silently surround individual strollers. Rugged interrogation by the press finally exposed them as normal-sized pals from Cheverly who occasionally had to dart behind buildings to take off their heavy heads and give their bodies a break. Such are the burdens of Halloween.

The Potatoheads said they had been called everything from homosexuals "to Devos to cute little honeys."

Two young bottles of Tanqueray and Michelob, walking down Wisconsin en route to Sarsfield's, were asked why so many people were doing this sort of thing this year. One of them ventured the opinion that a whole new school of whacko comedy has become popular lately—what with the Coneheads, Steve Martin, "Animal House"—and everyone wants to join the fun.

Source

Washington Post, November 2, 1978.

The Greenwich Village Parade
A Modern Observance

Greenwich Village is situated in lower Manhattan, New York City. It was designated an historic district in 1969. It was once a separate village and has become noted as a literary and artistic district. Columnist Joel Opppenheimer reported this information:

Over the last couple of years the Halloween Parade through the West Village and the late-evening masquerade party at the Theatre for the New City have been enjoyed with ever-increasing attention by me and my family. The parade starts from Westbeth in the early evening, and I can stand at my living-room window while the crowds begin to gather and Ralph Lee's fantastic and beautiful creations take their places, and then, when things seem ready to start, the kids and I can run down the

HALLOWEEN, ALL SAINTS', ALL SOULS' DAYS

fire stairs and slip right in. The watching has to be integrated, of course, with steady runs to the door for the hordes of trick-or-treaters availing themselves of Westbeth's soft touches. This year I got dressed a bit myself (tailcoat, top hat, Swiss army all-leather motorcycle jodhpurs, Adidas, rubber glove in handkerchief pocket, wristwatch on bicycle chain draped across chest), to the amusement of my adult neighbors, the scorn of the teenagers, the bemusement of the four- to 10-year olds, and the complete disinterest of the younger-than-fours, all of whom just said "Hewwo Joel," as if I looked like that every day.

Ralph Lee's creations are of course masks and figures; this year we walked in company with a four-humped camel and a tall Medusa, while some sort of gigantic general strutted, chest covered with medals. Before, behind, and around us, a huge, sectioned snake, supported by bamboo poles in the hands of 15 or so volunteers, wove its way on a route that ended at Washington Square Park. We were led by a hay wagon for the very little ones and an honest-to-God marching band, which I never saw but kept hearing loud and clear. Along the way we were greeted by ghosts on a Bleecker Street fire escape, the traditional scarecrow riding up and down the flagpole at Seventh Avenue, pumpkin-headed goblins on a low roof on Twelfth Street, windowsful of Victorian grotesques in the brownstone on Charles where two years ago a lifesize Punch and Judy was acted out as we paraded by, and then,

predictably, a hail of eggs from one of those lovely high-rises that make the Village what it is today.

Traffic on Seventh Avenue was agreeably stalled; my neighbor said, "God, do they have to wait until the whole parade goes by?" and I answered "I hope so." Once a year it's nice to be able to cross Seventh Avenue in safety. I suppose it's corny, but the parade is the one time all year that the Village feels like we all keep saying it does year 'round: warm and pleasant and small-towny. People yelled hellos all along the route, joined in, dropped out, and generally were there for fun and not hassles. Of course, fame has begun to take its toll—I'd estimate that fully 42 per cent of the marchers this year were dressed as photographers or videotapers or filmmakers, but for once they seemed part of the thing, rather than interlopers and disrupters. They tended to converge on a marvelous Dracula, who brought along his own upright rolling coffin, and who later showed up at the Theatre for the New City's party selling the opportunity to be photographed with him as a benefit for this chronically under-funded artistic endeavor.

The Theatre for the New City is the work of Crystal Field and George Bartenieff, with lots of dedicated help, and it goes on, somehow, year to year. Its productions, to my taste, have been spotty—some great, some awful, and some in between; whatever else, it always provides its actors and playwrights and the whole theatre with enthusiasm and élan. I suspect that a million-dollar endowment would ruin it forever, but someone ought to be able to give it something less than that just to keep it with us. The Halloween Ball started a year or two ago as a fundraiser, and this year it was just splendid. There was a giant swing band and a reggae-band and a loud rock band and a quiet jazz trio, and there were singles acts, including that great lady of everything, Rosalyn Drexler, singing. There were jugglers, and small plays, and a graphologist, and a sign for a phrenologist, although I never saw one in action. And there was a parade of costumes with prizes of a year's pass to the theatre and a lottery ticket. I had the honor to be one of the judges, for which I received no remuneration, no bribes, and a great deal of calumny because I picked a woman with terrific breasts as the Most Poetical. Why not?

All in all, the evening seemed a suitable way to say good-bye to the streets for the next six months, and when we hit them again, it'll be in the individual outbursts of spring. This was a huge and good and happy gathering of all of us, grown-ups and children, men and women, straights and gays, blacks and whites, all the dualities out there, holding off the darkness and the ghosts, and saying Good-bye, Sun, see you next year.

Source

Village Voice, November 14, 1977. From the column "Mix and Mask."

A Policeman's Lot

The New Yorker carried this report:

Time was when the Greenwich Village Halloween Parade was a small-town affair, a procession of kids and attendant parents straggling down streets where half the houses still had boot scrapers on the front steps. That time is no more. With floats on flatbed trucks, and with steel-drum, Dixieland, and conga bands, and crowds of revellers, the marchers barely distinguishable from the gawkers, the parade has gone big time. It requires major arteries on which to disport itself. It also requires police, to keep the revellers moving and happy. We know a sergeant of the Auxiliary Police Force in the Sixth Precinct, and when we learned that he was going to be on duty at the parade we decided to spend the evening in his company.

On the way to the precinct house, the sergeant told us about crowds. The passersby in the early darkness still seemed normal enough, with the exception of the odd demon. Sixth Avenue, up which the parade would flow, was lined with blue sawhorses. "Sixth Avenue will be the worst," the sergeant said. "It's where all the people will go as soon as they get off the subways at Sheridan Square or West Fourth Street. When the parade used to end in Washington Square, that was bad for crowd control, because it was harder to leave. Union Square, where the parade ends now, is better—people can take the subway right there. One problem with the Halloween parade is that it's at night.

The Greenwich Village Parade

AMERICA CELEBRATES

HALLOWEEN, ALL SAINTS', ALL SOULS' DAYS

Halloween isn't like Thanksgiving or St. Patrick's Day, when you can see what's happening. The other problem is that people think, It's the Village, I'm gonna have a good time."

The Auxiliaries of the Sixth Precinct—there were seven of them that night—rendezvoused in a room on the second floor of the precinct house on West Tenth Street. The commanding officer, a trim, white-haired man, who had supplied himself with a bullhorn for the evening, gave them their posting—a pedestrian passage across Sixth Avenue, at Fourth Street. This represented an innovation. The year before, Sixth Avenue had been a sealed column—you couldn't cross. This year, there would be a human sluice. "Remember, folks," the C.O. said. "Be firm but gentle."

Back on the streets, the crowds had become thicker, and distinctly odder. We passed a flamenco dancer, a headless woman, a bearded Aunt Jemima. Geishas were out in force. We took up a position between a hot-dog cart and a sawhorse just west of the crossing place. The crossing had two lanes, and it was the job of the Auxiliaries, and also of some regular officers, to keep people, or whatever, moving in the right direction. There were ninja, wizards, pharaohs, droogs, cows, lobsters, sandwiches, mice, a dinosaur squiring a belle. A young man in normal clothes came along shouting, "I'm a full marching band! You didn't notice the disguise, right?" The spectators included lots of out-of-towners. Two men

in bow ties and with earnest faces stopped near us, and one asked, speaking precisely, with European vowels, "Could you explain where we go to see something?" Others—from closer to home, apparently—spoke of catching the eleven-thirty train to Hoboken. Every tenth person, it seemed, wanted to take a shortcut through the crossing's sawhorses; these jaywalkers were firmly but gently rebuffed. "My favorites are the people who say they *live* here," the sergeant told us. "Like, they don't know what October 31st is?"

At about seven-thirty, the real parade appeared, heading north on Sixth Avenue, and caused a surge along the already dense sidewalks. From where we stood,the individual marchers were invisible, and even the more elaborate displays—the plant from "Little Shop of Horrors," the Brooklyn Bridge, bagpipers—reached us in fragments: bars of music, glimpses of superstructure. We did get a good view of a green-and-white paper snake about twenty feet long. The only sign we saw of a politician was a placard that said "Al Gore."

The Auxiliaries waved three men off a windowsill; a fourth man grabbed the bottom rung of a fire escape but gave up trying to climb it before he had to be restrained. At one point, Death, carrying a scythe, decided to cross Sixth Avenue, and slipped under a sawhorse. The sergeant waved him back. "How do I get in the parade?" a bat-winged lizard carrying a sceptre crowned with a skull wanted to know. The sergeant told her (for the lizard was a woman) to go down Cornelia Street and left on Bleecker. "Ah, come on," she said, in unghoulish disappointment. We bought two hot dogs for a corpse who couldn't reach the pushcart.

After about an hour and a half—when the cold was beginning to spread from fingers and toes into the thighs—a sanitation truck came up the avenue. It was so bright and shining that we took it for a prop, but it was followed immediately by five sanitation trucks that were unmistakably real, and by a squad car with its cherry flashing. The commanding officer called through his bullhorn "Dismissed!" In no time, the streets filled with people. We lost our sergeant.

Source

New Yorker, November 11, 1988, 32-3. From "The Talk of the Town."

The Halloween Sadist

This item comes from a feature by Richard Moran:

Although Halloween itself dates back over several centuries, the myth of the Halloween sadist is a relatively new invention. It was created during the early 1970s when some of the nation's most prestigious periodicals began reporting the discovery of the Halloween sadist as a dangerous new type of killer. [The idea that the Halloween sadist was "created during the early 1970s" is certainly not correct. One of the editors of the present volume recalls being warned against such persons in the 1930s.]

Newsweek magazine, for example, warned that "several children have died and hundreds have narrowly escaped injury" from dangerous objects concealed inside Halloween goodies. And the *New York Times* cautioned that the plump red apple that junior gets from the kindly old woman down the block "... may have a razor blade hidden inside."

Legislators in California and New Jersey responded to the alleged threat by passing tough new laws. A few communities even tried to ban trick-or-treating altogether. Schools started training children to inspect their goodies for tampering.

Soon everyone from Dear Abby to the local police chief began giving advice on how to protect children from Halloween sadists. But those of us who study crime for a living have long been skeptical about the actual existence of Halloween sadists. For it seems implausible that a homicidal maniac would limit his attacks to one night a year. And it sounds too much like the Halloween legend itself.

At long last, the record has been set straight. In 1985 two California State University professors, Joe Best and Gerald Horiuchi, published a study which concluded that the Halloween sadist was essentially a myth. After an exhaustive examination of the nation's newspapers, covering a 15-year period (1959-1984), they managed to locate only 76 cases of tampering with Halloween candy.

HALLOWEEN, ALL SAINTS', ALL SOULS' DAYS

Most reports turned out to be either mistaken or fraudulent: Only 20 cases resulted in injuries, and all of them were minor. There were two deaths, but one involved a child who ate heroin hidden in candy he found at his uncle's house; the other child was poisoned by his father, who put cyanide in his candy to make it look like he was killed by Halloween sadist. . . .

The truth is that unless you're a nutrition buff, you really don't have to worry about your child's Halloween candy. What you need to worry about is flammable costumes, masks that obscure a child's vision, and your kid getting hit by a car in the dark. Take some precautions here, but forget about the candy. Let your child be a child, at least one night a year.

Source

Philadelphia Inquirer, October 29, 1987.

To See Your Future Husband on Halloween

Divination is commonly associated with Halloween in Britain because at the time, according to old beliefs, the veil between the living and the dead is partially lifted, and clairvoyants, witches, diviners, and ghosts are about. A child born on Halloween is supposed to have second sight, and if a young woman wishes to catch a glimpse of her future husband, her chances are good provided she performs certain rites and is lucky. The following items were collected by Annie W. Whitney and Caroline C. Bullock:

Maryland

If you are born on Hallowe'en, you can see and read things in dreams.

On Hallowe'en melt some lead and pour it from an iron spoon into cold water. The form that it assumes will be prophetic of your future life. One girl who tried it saw the lead take the shape of a coffin, and her husband took up the trade of an undertaker after her marriage.

On Hallowe'en, run around the square with your mouth full of pins and needles. Come home and look in the glass, and you will see your future husband, if you are to be married; but if not, you will see a coffin.

If you drop two needles into a bowl of water, you can tell by the way they move in the water whether you and your lover will come together.

On Hallowe'en, put some apples in a tub of water, and name them with a label. Let a girl kneel over the tub, shut her eyes, put her hands behind her, and try to catch an apple with her teeth. The one she succeeds in catching will be her future husband.

Suspend some apples, labeled with names over a doorway, blind-fold a girl with her hands behind her, and let her try to bite an apple. The one she bites, will be her future husband.

Walk around your house three times or around the town, with a mouthful of water in your mouth, and you will marry the first man you meet.

Walk into a room backward at twelve o'clock at night on Hallowe'en, looking over your left shoulder, and you will see your future husband.

Put three chestnuts on a hot stove. Name one for yourself and the others for two men. If one jumps and bursts, that lover will be unfaithful; if one blazes or burns, that one has some regard for the one making the test. If the girl's nut burns with one of the lovers, they will marry before the next Hallowe'en.

On Hallowe'en go chestnutting with a party. The one finding the first burr will be the first to marry. If the burr opens easily, the love will not last long, if it is hard to open the love will last.

Bake small cakes, and put in one a piece of money, in another a ring, in a third a rag, and in a fourth a thimble. You can tell who will be rich, who will be married, who will be poor, and who will earn her own living.

Take three dishes, and in one put clear water, in another milky water, and have the third one empty. Blindfold a girl, and if she touches the clear water, she will marry a bachelor; the milk water, a widower; the empty one, she will not marry at all. This must be tried three times.

If you eat a salt cake and go to bed backwards without speaking, you will dream that your future husband will bring you a drink of water. If the cup be of silver or gold, you will be wealthy; if of glass moderately rich, and if of tin, you will be poor. If you help yourself to a drink, you will never be married, and if the vessel out of which you drink is a gourd, you will be a pauper.

A salt cake was eaten by a girl in Emmittsburg [Maryland] on Hallowe'en. She went to bed without speaking, and dreamed that she was sitting in a certain house looking out of a window and longing for someone to bring her a drink of water, and getting weary of waiting, she went into the kitchen and helped herself from a tin bucket with a tin cup. Returning to the window, she was just in time to see a dark-haired man ride away. She was never married, and is terribly poor.

Source

Memoirs of the American Folklore Society, XVIII (1925), 123-35. "Folk-Lore from Maryland."

North Carolina

Joseph D. Clark supplied these items:

If you stand in front of a mirror at twelve o'clock on Halloween, the man you are to marry will look over your left shoulder.

If on Halloween you take a mirror and walk down the stairs backward, you will see in the mirror the person you will marry.

On Halloween night, if one holds up a candle and looks in a mirror, the face of one's future husband or wife will be seen.

Look into a spring with a lightwood torch at midnight on Halloween and see the face of your future husband (or wife).

To See Your Future Husband on Halloween

HALLOWEEN, ALL SAINTS', ALL SOULS' DAYS

Look into the well at eleven o'clock on Halloween Day and your future will be disclosed.

On Hallow Eve, if an egg placed in front of the fire by a young woman in love is seen to sweat blood, it is a sign that she will succeed in getting the man she loves.

On Halloween, children used to put corn meal by the side of their beds, and then ghosts would write with it the name of the man each was to marry.

Source

North Carolina Folklore Journal, XX (1972), 135. As cited in a general article in on Halloween.

To See Your Future Hus-band on Halloween

Tennessee

Neal Frazier collected this lore in middle Tennessee:

On Hallowe'en night, peel an apple and toss the peeling over the left shoulder. The letter formed is the initial of the girl's future husband.

Source

Tennessee Folklore Society Bulletin, II (October 1936), 10.

And that's not all:
For other days and ways of divining a future mate, see "New Year's Beliefs"; "Seeing the Future on Midsummer Eve"; and "May Day Predictions."

Halloween Bonfires

Halloween bonfires are a survival of the Druid practice of building hilltop fires to celebrate important festivals. November 1 was the Druid New Year and marked the return of winter. The Scottish custom of fire-jumping is another Druid survival. It took place on May Day or Beltane and was believed to bring good luck.

Michigan

The following was reported by Catherine Harris Ainsworth in a study of Celtic influences on American Halloween practices:

In Bloomfield Township, Michigan, in the Upper Long Lake's Estate subdivision from 1955 to 1961, I attended yearly with my younger daughter a huge bonfire built on the shore of the lake for the celebration of Hallowe'en. All of the children of the subdivision came to the bonfire for apple cider and doughnuts and stood around in their various costumes.

Source

New York Folklore Quarterly, XXIX (1973), 169.

Maryland

This lore was collected by Annie W. Whitney and Caroline C. Bullock:

In East Market, on the Eastern Shore [of Maryland before 1935], on Hallowe'en night boys jump over bonfires or ride over them, as was done in Scotland.

Source

Memoirs of the American Folklore Society, XVIII (1925), 6. "Folk-Lore from Maryland."

And that's not all:
See "A Beltane Fire" and "No Rooz."

Devil's Night Fires

Bill McGraw filed this report:

The eve of Halloween has been called Devil's Night for decades in Detroit, but for years it was a time for soaping windows, ringing doorbells and other harmless pranks.

False fire alarms and broken windows were generally the worst Devil's Night problems until the early 1980s, when fires began breaking out after dark on and around Devil's Night. Mass arson erupted in 1983, when 650 fires were reported on Devil's Night alone.

There was a similar outbreak the next year.

By 1985, reports of Detroit's bizarre ritual had spread around the globe. News crews from Europe and Japan roamed city streets capturing the blazes, while fire buffs—people fascinated with fire-fighting lore and technology—gathered in the city each year for what the nationally circulated trade journal Firehouse called "the Super Bowl of fire fighting."

According to city officials, fires have declined each year since 1984, when there were 810 fires on Oct. 29-31.

Source

Detroit Free Press, October 31, 1989.

Washing the Tombs on All Saints' Day

This item was collected by Marvy Evelyn Hill, a student of folklore at Wayne State University, in 1961. Her source was Mrs. Hazel Heine, age 55, of New Orleans, Louisiana.

Cemeteries in New Orleans are all made of vaults above the ground. This is necessary because of the swampy condition of the land.

On All Saints' Day the vaults or tombs are washed, whitewashed and profusely decorated with flowers and wreaths. The favorite flower for this occasion is the chrysanthemum.

In New Orleans the downtown cemeteries are particularly festive. The women weep and gossip, men discuss local politics, and children run in and out of the criss-crossing aisles. The street vendors do a lively business selling gumbo, snowballs, pralines, peanuts, balloons, mechanical birds and toy skeletons.

The outlying districts have a custom not practiced in New Orleans. At night on All Saints' Day candles are lighted in the cemeteries giving an eerie aspect to the surroundings.

Schools and some business establishments are closed in New Orleans on this day.

Source

Wayne State University Folklore Archive, 1961.

The Day of the Dead and All Souls' Day in Pueblo Cultures

The original date of this ceremony was reckoned by the moon and fell in October. Here Elsie Clews Parsons describes the Day of the Dead among the Pueblo natives of Zuñi, Acoma, and Laguna, New Mexico.

HALLOWEEN, ALL SAINTS', ALL SOULS' DAYS

Towards the end of October the Zuñi celebrate *ahoppa awan tewa* ("the dead their day"). It is announced four days in advance from the house-top by *santu weachona'we*, the saint's crier. He also calls out that it is time to bring in wood. A portion of whatever is cooked on *ahoppa awan tewa* is thrown on the house-fire by the women, or carried by the men to the "wide ditch" on the river-side, where possessions of the dead are habitually buried.

At nightfall boys go about town in groups, calling out, "*Tsale'mo, tsale'mo!*" and paying domiciliary visits. At the threshold they make the sign of the cross, saying the "Mexican" prayer, *polasenya*; and the inmates give the boys presents of food—bread or meat. In spite of the "Mexican" features of *ahoppa awan tewa*, the Zuñi assert that the day has always been observed by the people, and that it is in no wise a Catholic ceremonial.

In Catholic Acoma the Catholic character of the day is of course recognized. It is known as a church celebration to fall on a calendar day, November 1 or 2, guessed my informant. At Acoma, too, parties of boys, as many as ten perhaps, will go around town, calling "*Tsale'mo, tsale'mo!*" They also ring a bell. Their "Mexican" prayer is, "Padre spirito santo amen." They are given food. Food is also taken to the cemetery and placed around the foot of the wooden cross which stands there in the centre. The war-chiefs stand on guard. By morning, however, the food has disappeared. What becomes of it my informant did not know.

At Laguna, food is also taken to the cemetery. The day is called *shuma sashti* ("skeleton day"); and to give to the dead on *shuma sashti*, the fattest sheep and the best pumpkins and melons are saved. A story goes that once a young man was told by his mother to bring in for the occasion the fattest two lambs of their flock. The young man objected. Soon thereafter he fell sick, and he lay in a trance for two or three days, until the medicine-man restored him. On coming to, he reported he had been with the dead. The church was full of them. Happy were they who had been well-provided for by their families. The unprovided were befriended by the provided.

On *shuma sashti*, candles are set out on the graves. A little ball of food made up of a bit of everything served to eat is also put on the fire. The boys who go about getting food call out, "*Sare'mo, sare'mo!*" Their "Mexican" prayer is called *porasinia*.

Source

Journal of American Folklore, XXX (1917), 495-96.

All Souls' Day in Pueblo Cultures

Aurelio M. Espinosa emphasizes linguistic evidence to support his view of the importance of Spanish and Roman Catholic influences in the celebration of this holiday:

[Concerning All Souls' Day at Zuñi, Acoma, and Laguna . . .] I beg to make here a few additional suggestions and some corrections to the notes of Mrs. Parsons. . . .Even where the church exists and the Catholic curate is present, as is the case in pueblos like San Juan and Isleta, I have reasons for believing that the Catholicity of the Indians is not genuine. In spite of this, however, it is too much to assume that the religion of the Spaniards has not left its influence among them; and, in fact, many of their old ceremonials and festivals seem to have been more definitely established through the introduction of the new Catholic doctrines and ceremonies.

The All-Souls-Day festival of Zuñi, Acoma, and Laguna, is certainly a continuation of the Catholic festival. The Zuñi festival, which comes late in October, comes sufficiently close to the date of the church calendar to prove this. Furthermore, the whole ceremonial seems to be a direct continuation of the Catholic church feast, the assertions of the Zuñi Indians notwithstanding.

The leaving of food for the dead is not alone an Indian custom. Ethnologists and folk-lorists are familiar with this institution, which is found among many peoples, even in modern times.

The words which accompany the ceremony of the making of the sign of the cross are all Spanish. They are all perfectly clear. This shows how Catholic and how Spanish the ceremony still remains. There is no such thing as a Mexican prayer, *polasenya* (Zuñi) or *porasinia* (Laguna). These Indian vocables are regular phonetic developments of the first three words of the Catholic ceremony in question: *Por la señal*, [By the sign]. In New-Mexican Spanish,

and also in Andalusian Spanish, the current familiar pronunciation of these three words is *po la señal* or *po la señá*. This is exactly the Zuñi *polasenyá*. Mrs. Parsons does not write it with *a* final accented, but I presume that is the correct accentuation. The Laguna form, *porasiniá*, is also a perfectly normal Spanish dialectal development....

Mrs. Parsons finds it difficult to explain the Indian words *Tsalemo* (Acoma and Zuñi), *Saremo* (Laguna), which the Indian children repeat from house to house as they go forth begging for food on All-Souls Day. This also is a purely Spanish custom.... The complete version of the New-Mexican Spanish invocation is,

> *Oremos, oremos,*
> *angelitos semos,*
> *del cielo venemos.*
> *Si no nos dan*
> *puertas y ventanas*
> *quebraremos.*

> Let's pray, let's pray,
> We are little angels,
> From heaven we come.
> If you don't give to us
> Your doors and windows
> We will break.

The Zuñi and Acoma form *Tsalemo*, and the Laguna form *Salemo*, are Indian developments of the first word of the invocation. Curiously enough, these Pueblo Indians have preserved only the first word of the Catholic invocation, evidently taught to them by the old *padres*. In the current familiar Spanish pronunciation the first two

AMERICA CELEBRATES

HALLOWEEN, ALL SAINTS', ALL SOULS' DAYS

words of the invocation are thus divided into syllables:

Oremo, soremo.

The initial verse is frequently repeated before passing to the second; and hence,

Oremo, soremo,
soremo, soremo.

Soremo is the Spanish word that is now pronounced *Tsalemo* and *Saremo* by the Zuñi, Acoma, and Laguna Indians.

Source

Journal of American Folklore, XXX (1917), 495-96 and XXXI (1918), 550-52.

And that's not all:
See the "trick or treat" Halloween custom.

November

Thursday after Election Day
RETURN DAY IN DELAWARE

For some one hundred fifty years, it has been the custom at Georgetown, the seat of Sussex County, Delaware, to announce formally and festively the returns of the presidential election (which since 1845 falls on the first Tuesday following the first Monday in November) two days after the voting is over. This ritual came about as a result of an election reform in 1828 that allowed Delaware residents to vote in the "hundreds," as political subdivisions of the county were called. The tabulations would then be rushed by couriers to the county seat. Two days later, the tally sheets would be officially inspected and the totals posted. In more recent years the official announcement of two-day-old election returns isn't particularly exciting, but the colorful parades, picnics, military displays, songfests, and politicking that grew up around the announcement of the returns continue to attract festive crowds. Governors and members of the state congressional delegation, current and past, usually are present, along with a hoard of lesser politicos. Office seekers recently in contention shake hands in a display of unity, ride in the parade together, and begin preparing for the next political contest with a ceremonial "Burial of the Tomahawk." Since 1965, Return Day has been legally a "half-holiday" in Sussex County.

Early Return Days

W. Emerson Wilson supplied the following background:

In January, 1791, the General Assembly [of Delaware] directed that a commission choose a central site for a new county seat. This was done by May and the new town, named Georgetown after George Mitchell, one of the commissioners, was ready for the election of 1792.

Was the first "Return Day" held that year? One may assume that it was, but if

RETURN DAY IN DELAWARE

that is true it was much different than the "Return Days" of the present era. Voters had to drive into Georgetown to cast their ballots and it is unlikely that they would return two days later for the results. Undoubtedly the results of the election were known that night or the next day and the voters would stay over to learn the results.

As early as 1803 complaints about having to go to Georgetown over rough roads in bad weather, leaving their families at home unprotected, were made by large groups of men in the outer districts.

It took a long time in those days for the people to change customs, especially in Sussex County, so it was not until 1828 that the General Assembly adopted new election laws providing that the Presidential electors should be chosen by the people rather than by the Legislature and that the polling places should be in the hundreds [political subdivisions] rather than at the county seat. This meant that the election officers had to bring the results from each of the hundreds into Georgetown where they were turned over to the sheriff and tabulated and the results announced from the courthouse at noon on Thursday.

Thus the voters did not have to go very far from home to vote, but since there were no county newspapers in those days there was no way of knowing who had won the election. So many of the farmers decided to take a day off, load their whole families into wagons and go to Georgetown on Thursday to get the results.

It would seem that "Return Day" as we now know it probably started with the election of 1830 or the Presidential election of 1832. Certainly by the 1840s the custom was well established.

Several thousand persons would pour into Georgetown that morning coming on foot, in wagons drawn by mules, horses, or oxen, in carriages of all types and on horseback.

While waiting for the results the crowd listened to band concerts, wagered on cockfights, and engaged in other pastimes. Soon merchants saw an opportunity for gain and stalls and booths selling all kinds of food, clothing, and other articles were set up.

The results were read from the door of the courthouse at noon and were printed on a white sheet hoisted over the courthouse door. The winning candidates were placed on to the shoulders of their adherents and paraded around the Green. A large pole was erected in the Green and the emblem of the winning party was run up it. Generally an ox roast was provided by the winners.

However, the spirit of good feeling and reconciliation which marks the "Return Day" of the present was not always there in the old days. The losers quite often did not take their defeat with good grace and in one fight in 1844 a Dagsboro man was killed. . . .

One of the best descriptions of "Return Day" was that published in the *Wilm-*

ington Every Evening which sent a city slicker down to Georgetown to cover the event in 1872.... Excerpts from his story follow:

"Strolling from the Brick Hotel kept by a New Castle man, J. H. Wood, I found in front of the courthouse and on either side of the main street leading to the jail work benches, tables, and temporary stands, numbering 30 or 40 and called stalls and many were the boxes of confections on them.

"By 10 o'clock people of both sexes and all colors dressed in every manner and style, in wagons drawn by one, two and four horses with mule teams as well poured in from all directions. The ladies especially were gotten up well and I doubt not *Harper's* would have sent one of the best artists of the fashion world had they known of the day.

"By noon at least 2,000 persons had been added to the town's population for every avenue, lane, alley and street were lined with wagons in which old fashioned settees and chairs, some going back to Revolutionary times, had been installed as seats.

"Many dined at the hotels, others fared sumptuously in their wagons and carriages while others enjoyed roast beef, turkey, chicken, fish, coon, rabbits and possum at will, all of which could be had among the stalls cooked to order. Many ladies who had not visited the "Capitol" since the last "Return Day" could be seen

in the crowd buying nicknacks for 'the little ones.'

"A part of the programme of the day is to see that young girls are treated. A pretty young lady, whether acquainted or not, is licensed to receive a box of candy and be it said for the young gentlemen of Sussex that no pretty damsel goes away empty."

Source

Return Day Program Sussex County, Georgetown, Delaware, for November 9, 1972, 2, 5-6; from "History of Sussex County Return Day."

Politicking and Parading

William J. Wade added these remarks:

Return Day, of course, is much more than the announcing of the election results. The celebration that has grown up around the occasion has elements to please everyone. The main aspect of the celebration is still political, and in this regard Return Day offers those who come to Georgetown an opportunity to meet the candidates. The politicos themselves also made use of the occasion to mend fences and to garner support. As one member of the 1974 Return Day Committee noted, "More politicking goes on on Return Day than any other day of the year.... I guess they figure it's as good a time as any to get started for the next election."

Today the "politicking" generally gets started at a luncheon held for the candidates, where winners and losers circulate amidst supporters, accepting congratu-

AMERICA CELEBRATES

RETURN DAY IN DELAWARE

lations or condolences as the case may be. In earlier days, however, candidates, townspeople and all others assembled in Georgetown shared a repast in the streets of the town. In the town's public square, booths, stalls and stands were erected, complete with cooking stoves. From these booths "all kinds of edibles were for sale, such as Delaware biscuit, hot corn pone, with black molasses to pour over it, sweet potato biscuit, opossum, rabbit roasted upon a spit, white and sweet potatoes baked in hot ashes, fish, oysters, maninose (clams), fried chicken and hominy made in mortars chopped from a sturdy gum. . . . Always a large steer would be roasted in the open air and eaten. Hogsheads of beer, fresh cider, and vast quantities of Sussex County apple jack were consumed."

This tradition has also endured, only today, the street vendors offer a slightly different menu. Roast oxen is the principle food for modern revelers. The oxen, cooked on a spit in a lot just off the Georgetown Circle, is put to the fire on the day before Return Day so that it may be slowly turned and roasted, ready to be served to the waiting crowd at the next day's festivities. . . .

The well fed crowds are also treated to various forms of entertainment. The highlight of the day is the parade down Market Street. This tradition probably began at one of the early Return Days, growing out of the practice of some celebrants who would arrive at Georgetown "in carts drawn by oxen, or in wagons drawn

by six and eight horses gaily decorated with flags, ribbons and sleigh bells." No doubt these revelers would have used their decorated wagons to parade the winning candidates through the streets of Georgetown to receive the congratulations of the crowd.

Perhaps the most colorful of the Return Day parades took place in 1882, when Charles Stockley was elected Governor of Delaware. The Wilmington *Sunday Star* of November 12, 1882, described the parade as follows: "A procession moved through the town while the people cheered and guns boomed. A boat in bright new paint was mounted on wheels, rigged like a ship, and labeled the 'Old Constitution.' The craft was profusely decorated with a blue hen draped in ribbon and a dried coon skin was suspended from the mast. Six men on horseback moved in front and one hundred and twenty mounted men in the rear, all decorated and giving back to the crowd cheer for cheer. Standing on the quarter deck of the mimic ship, bowing to the multitude who enthusiastically applauded and saluted him, was the Governor Elect Charles Stockley. When the ship was drawn into the Square the people flocked from all sides to shake hands with the new Governor and at length he was lifted on brawny shoulders and carried into the Court House above the heads of the crowd, which cheered louder and louder."
. . .

Georgetown's own Senator Willard Saulsbury ably demonstrated that politics and liquor can be mixed and the spirit of

Return Day celebrations was often enlivened by this potent brew. Partisan political feelings, when mixed with alcohol, would occasionally lead to brawls when members of one party would rejoice too much over their defeated and crestfallen opponents. In general the high spirits of Return Day were not conducive to good order in the earlier days and, as William P. Frank noted in the 1970 Return Day Program, "The newspapers of the past century always commented on whether there was any trouble. For example, the *Morning News* in 1884 noted: 'Everything considered, the crowd was remarkably orderly and seemed jubilant over the county victory and the prospect for the inauguration of a Democratic president on the 4th of March next.'"...

While the parade has been the highlight of Return Day, the celebrants have often added gaiety and entertainment to the fete by attiring themselves in ludicrous costumes and riding or roaming through the streets of town. In the evening, by torch or by moonlight, there would be folk dancing on the green, where "fiddlers scraped the Virginia Reel and the Schottische and joy ran unconfined."

Source

Return Day Program, Sussex County, Georgetown, Delaware, for November 6, 1980, 5-6; from "Return Day."

And that's not all:
See "Shad Planking" and "Labor Day Politicking."

November

Fourth Thursday
THANKSGIVING

American Thanksgiving Day began in Plymouth Colony in 1621, when the Pilgrims who had migrated to Massachusetts gave thanks that the new land had been good to them and that they had been able to harvest a good crop their first year. The first officially designated day of thanksgiving was in 1631 in Massachusetts. Abraham Lincoln was the president to proclaim the day a national celebration, and he set the date as the last Thursday in November. This moveable date was changed by Franklin D. Roosevelt in 1939 to the fourth Thursday in November, although some states have been reluctant to shift. In Canada, the second Monday in October is celebrated as Thanksgiving.

Actually, days of thanksgiving with their prayers and feasting

are far older than Pilgrim times. The American celebration is an adaptation of Lammas (Loaf Mass) Day, August 1, which was celebrated in Britain if there was an abundant crop of wheat but not otherwise. On Lammas Day the farmers brought loaves of bread made from the successful crop to mass (thus Loaf Mass Day) as a token of thanksgiving. Moreover, thanksgivings for successful crops are common enough to all agricultural peoples, as the selections that follow testify, though usually the dates are later than August 1 when the yield of crops in addition to wheat is known. Harvest Home observances mark the end of seasonal tasks involving the work community and at the same time express gratitude for the bounty of nature.

Origins of Thanksgiving

Jay Allen Anderson prepared the following overview:

Our modern Thanksgiving is a combination of two very different and very old holidays: 1) the harvest home feast celebrated when the main crops were harvested and 2) the formal day of thanksgiving proclaimed by a community's authorities to focus on a particular event, such as a military victory, or the need for rain....

For almost ... two hundred and fifty years, these two kinds of "thanksgiving" remained quite distinct. Very few formal "days of thanksgiving" coincided with harvest. They were proclaimed at various times in all regions of the English colonies and were popular. No special foods became associated with them. During the same period (1620-1870) harvest home feasts also flourished. The menus of these feasts differed along regional and ethnic lines. The harvest supper of the Germans in Pennsylvania, the Dutch in New York, the Scotch-Irish in Appalachia, the African Americans in the South, and the English in New England: all were unique. Because these regional ethnic cultures remained isolated and autonomous, their harvest home and thanksgiving day feasts continued to be local and provincial in character.

During and after the Revolutionary War (1775-83), a desire for national rather than local holidays developed and an attempt was made to combine harvest home with the formal day of thanksgiving. George Washington noted in his orderly book on October 31, 1777, "Tomorrow being the day set apart by the honorable Congress for Public Thanksgiving and praise, and duty calling us devoutly to express our grateful acknowledgements to God for the manifold blessings he has granted us...." Later in 1789 as President, he appointed the last Thursday in November as a national thanksgiving day. Regional feeling was, however, still too strong for the feast to be accepted nationally. But regionalism began to crumble in the nineteenth century as mass communications and transportation evolved. Hard surfaced highways, canals, and railways helped a national market develop. An industrial revolution began, cities expanded, and tens of millions of immigrants flooded in from Europe. A nationalistic spirit developed and pressure was put on both regional and immigrant ethnic cultures to adopt the new national, popular culture. Compulsory education in public schools insured a measure of common enculturation. The story of the Pilgrims became an ideal medium for fostering "Americanism." Regionalism's last attempt to thwart this nationalism came in 1861 when the southern slave owning states seceded, setting off Civil War. During the worst of the fighting, President Lincoln—in an attempt to bolster unionist spirit—appointed the last Thursday in November as an annual national Thanksgiving holiday. Soon afterwards, the northern

THANKSGIVING

regions won the war and the union was preserved. As regionalism quickly faded, the tradition of a combined harvest home and thanksgiving day feast celebrated nationally was accepted. The "new" holiday featured all the characteristics common today: a church service in the morning, followed by an afternoon's feast and a weekend of sports. The menu centered around roast turkey, stuffing, cranberry sauce, numerous vegetables, and pumpkin pie—the main dishes of the New England harvest home feast. Many of these foods had gained popularity because of their supposed connection to the Pilgrims. Thanksgiving as a national cultural event is now just about a century old and still relatively unchanged. In a nation of continual and rapid change, it remains surprisingly vital.

Source

Kansatieteellinen Arkisto 26, Suomen Muinaismuisto-yhdistys, 1975, 10-11. From a paper by Jay Allan Anderson presented at a conference on ethnological food research and published in the *Journal of the Finnish Society of Antiquities* of Helsinki. The first part "describes the feast as it is commonly celebrated today and traces its history."

And that's not all:
For support of Anderson's emphasis on officially proclaimed days of thanksgiving and the Pilgrim Fathers tradition, see "First Thanksgiving in Illinois."

Harvest Customs

Annie W. Whitney and Caroline C. Bullock collected these items:

Harvesters were in some places [in Maryland before 1925] liberally supplied

with a drink of cold water, ginger and molasses, and they always had an extra dinner given them. In other places ginger bread and egg-nog was the standard treat, and sometimes beer was substituted, this being in most cases home made, and made from hops.

The last day of the harvest was celebrated as a "Harvest Home," and the evening was given over to merriment, the neighbors coming from miles around to take part.

There were also husking parties; and a feature of this in some places was a chicken potpie baked in a Dutch oven, sweet potatoes and preserves being its necessary accessories. The favorite games at these husking parties were "sock-a-bout," "foul and fair," and "watch the candle."

It was customary during corn husking for the finder of the "red ear" to throw it to the prettiest girl, and then chase her until he had caught and kissed her. Then they danced together.

Source

Memoirs of the American Folklore Society, XVIII (1925), 122. "Folk-Lore from Maryland"; data on informants incomplete.

Papago Harvest Festival Songs

The Papago were an agricultural people who once occupied most of southern Arizona and northern Sonora, Mexico. They raised corn, beans, and cotton and their harvest songs invoked the rains, which brought a bountiful corn crop. Eight new songs were composed by each of the five participating villages whenever a harvest celebration was held, and the heart of the ritual consisted of the village groups, in sequence, masked and carrying rattles, performing their songs. J. Alden Mason obtained a full description of a Vigita, *or harvest festival, in 1919 from José Juan, "one of the singers at the festival of 1913." At the time Mason was studying the Papago language, and his texts and translation conclude his account.*

The [*Vigita,* or harvest] festival is held the last of November, supposedly every four years [by the Papago Indians]. But it depends largely upon the success of the harvest of the crops and it has now (1919) been six years since it was held. It may be held this year or may never be celebrated again, as the establishment of a government school, public power plant, and trader's store at Santa Rosa will naturally result in a speedy loss of conservatism.

The celebration of the *Vigita* is vested in the five principal villages of the Santa Rosa valley, though celebrants attend from all villages of the Indian Oasis and ally themselves with one or other of the five.... The festival is always held at Achi, which is considered the foremost Papago village....

The following eight songs were taken down as typical *Vigita* songs. They were sung by Achi at the last celebration.

1. geℵhu ŋe tcevaŋi cahkali wucanyi
   Over there the   clouds   in a row   come out.

   gaᴍhuŋ itoinaŋe dam ane muvitci
   Over there   our field   above,   there with corners

   ane wucanyi tuahi djuhku
   there   come out.   Thunders,   rains.

2. atci itoinaŋ mehk osekaitaŋ iuŋidjeh
   Achi   our field   far off   is heard   to shake.

   dama itonenami tcevahaŋi wucanyeh
   Above   shining   clouds   come out.

   ioh toinaŋ djuhku hunyi wucaℵYE
   Here   our field   rains,   corn   springs up.

3. vavahki eḍa vadjuhku'
   Big house   within   it rains.

   daᴍhana tcevahaŋi wucanyeh
   Up above   clouds   come out.

   sapowekaki namenoahi djuhku'
   Well hear   that thundering,   rains.

4. winyim itoinaŋe winyim itoinaŋe
   Winyim   our fields.   Winyim   our fields.

   damaiŋe huℵya pewuwahkime
   on them   corn   springs up.

   yatci toinaŋe yatci toinaŋe
   Achi   our fields.   Achi   our fields.

   tamaiŋe hunya pewuahkime
   on them   corn   comes out.

   ak'tcin it.oinaŋe ak'tcin it.oinaŋe
   Akchin   our fields.   Akchin   our fields.

   yanegam it.oinaŋe anegam oinaŋe
   Anekam   our fields.   Anekam   fields.

5. yahtci t.oinaŋe damain cudaˑki merikuhte mamasemel
   Achi   our fields   on   water   ran   ran.

   iakonyehite iotam vahcaℵ nawitcu huhunyi
   Here look   people!   Yonder   clown   ears of corn

   behkeme behkeme
   bears away.   bears away.

6. wewesi u'si wehtceh wewesi u'si wehtceh
   All   sticks   are there.   All   sticks   are there.

   we's ametcutca kakai pevaupanyime
   All   we stand up   lay across.

   wes amatcutca vaupah
   All   we stand up   lay across.

7. muhkisi tcewana kahtce
   Dying   world   here lay.

   muhkisi tcewana kahtce
   Dying   world   here lay.

   daᴍhanai hunyi wuca
   Above it   corn   comes out.

   mudatatci kiohta
   Bend   stalks.

   damhana wuca djuhku
   Above   comes out.   Rains.

8. yalisi tcetcetoˑki litol vavu'ca
   Little   green   Montezuma is coming out.

   yalisi dodo haiyu hunyi vuca
   Little   white   corn   is coming out.

mumui	tcewaŋ	akenyapenyukena
Many	clouds	rain on me.
mumui	tcewaŋ	akenyapenyukena
Many	clouds	rain on me.
tcewaŋ	iwucanye	kenyapenyukua
Clouds	come out.	rain on me.

Source

American Anthropologist, XXII (1920), 14, 24-25.

Chinese Harvest Moon Festival

Moon Cakes

According to Chinese belief, the moon influences crops and therefore is an object of happy veneration at harvest time when it becomes full. Originally an agricultural festival, this holiday is celebrated on the fifteenth day of the eighth moon, said to be the time when the moon is brightest. Bakeries and candy shops display moon-shaped confections. William Hoy observed festivals in "sizable Chinese colonies," mainly of Cantonese origin, in San Francisco, Oakland, Los Angeles, Sacramento, Marysville, Bakersfield, Fresno, San Diego, Visalia, and other cities. He prepared this account:

Chief symbol of [the Chinese Harvest Moon] festival is the "moon cake," a small cake made in the shape of the moon, about one inch thick, stuffed with sweetened and pulverized soya beans of several varieties, mixed with shelled melon seeds and whole egg yolks, and baked to a golden brown.

Accompanying the moon cakes is the *pomelo*, a fruit similar to our grapefruit except that it is twice as large and the meat is sweet. However, the *pomelos* grown in California are usually fairly sour, as the climate is not very favorable for the growth of this tropical fruit. As substitutes, apples, oranges, and other California citrus fruits are used.

Also part of the Moon Festival are little figures of rabbits and other animals made from candied sugar, and cookies shaped into miniature pigs enclosed in Chinese-style reed cages. The use of rabbits has special significance: Chinese mythology has it that there is a rabbit in the moon who is forever busy pounding out the elixir of life.

No traditional ceremonies are connected with this festival other than taking the day off from toil and gathering family members together for a good dinner and the enjoyment of moon cakes afterward. In former days, however, some California Chinese families performed the ceremony of honoring the moon by placing moon cakes, fruits, and lighted incense sticks on a table up on the roof or on a balcony. Then, at the stroke of midnight, when the moon becomes full, the ceremony of "capturing the moon" is observed. This is done simply by catching the moon's reflection in a basin full of water. This ceremony, however, is more or less forgotten today [in 1948].

Source

Western Folklore, VII (1948), 248. From a description of "Native Festivals of the California Chinese."

Day of the Moon Cake

Fred Ferreti filed this report:

Today is the Day of the Moon Cake.

Actually, it is the Autumn Moon observance, celebrated by the Chinese on the 15th day of the eighth month of the Chinese lunar calendar, which this year [1980] falls on Sept. 23. It is not only the day of the full moon, but the time each year when the full moon is most intense. In Chinese mythology the moon is a traditional female element, and because of that the *yin*, the feast of the autumn moon, is, according to Chinese belief, essentially gentle and quiet.

Unlike most Chinese festivals, which are preceded by days of preparation and often followed by days of recovery, the Autumn Moon observance lasts but one day, and on this day families eat a good deal of fruit, particularly fruit with many seeds, to symbolize fertility. And they eat lots of moon cakes, since this is the one day in the year that the cakes, because of their composition, become symbolic as well as enjoyable.

Moon cakes are simple affairs. At their heart is a thickened paste of lotus seeds, to which nuts might be added. The paste is rolled into balls and these are covered with dough. The paste-filled balls are then pressed into carved wooden molds of various shapes and out come round or squarish cakes with calligraphic designs celebrating the holiday. These are brushed with egg yolk for glaze before baking.

Though moon cakes are available throughout the year in [New York] Chinatown bakeries, it is on Autumn Moon Day that they become special, as well as symbolic. Preserved duck egg yolks, representing the moon, are often placed in the middle of the lotus seed centers. The cakes are marked with one, two, three or four red dots to indicate the number of duck eggs inside.

For a couple of weeks the Chinatown bakeries have been trying feverishly to keep up with the demand for moon cakes, as people have been buying them and storing them, waiting for today.

One day last week, almost a hundred people were lined up in front of the Lung Fong Bakery, waiting to buy moon cakes.

Choon Wah Lee, the owner, showed a visitor a rear storehouse packed to the ceiling with cartons of preserved duck egg yolks from Taiwan. Two huge Hobart mixers were working the dough. In the bakery's basement, other mixers were combining lotus seeds, sugar, oil and water into the paste.

"It's really not all lotus seeds," Mr. Lee confided, "because they are too expensive. We add some crushed lima beans to make the paste thick." All around were pails of paste waiting to be taken upstairs to the production line.

Does anyone mind that there are lima beans in the lotus seed paste, Mr. Lee was asked. "No," he said. "They cannot be tasted. The cakes are still very, very good."

Source

New York Times, September 23, 1980.

AMERICA CELEBRATES

THANKSGIVING

Lithuanian Harvest Dances

It is widely believed that Lithuanian harvest dances originated in pagan ceremonies designed to propitiate the forces of nature. For instance, Blezdingėlė has been explained as a fertility dance suggesting death as the swallows fly southward in the winter and regeneration as they return in the spring; and the Malūnas and Rugučiai, with movements imitating the harvesting and grinding of grain, are magical rites to express thanks for a plentiful crop. This discussion of the dancesss and Chicago's festival was prepared by Vytautas Beliajus, a native of the Lithuanian agricultural village of Pakumprys who emigrated in 1923 to the United States, where he taught Lithuanian dances and founded the folklore magazine, Viltis. The dance festivals are international. They are held every five years in Chicago.

By their very nature, the Lithuanian folk dances are of the agricultural-ceremonial type. The social dances were for everyone's participation, but the folk dances were demonstrations in which only those versed in the dances participated. The dances described chores in the fields and other related subjects.... *Kubilas*, the Tub, was a fast-moving dance that demonstrated the joy at a bountiful harvest. Choice vegetables were placed in a tub while the dancers spun round it. *Rugučiai* demonstrates the harvesting, gleaning, scythe honing, and so forth. There is a multitude of figures for *Malūnas*, the dance of the Mill which produces the flour for the daily bread. *Blezdingėlė* originally was danced in the fields—as the swallows left the countryside in the autumn to return next spring; so did the field workers bid their farewell. This dance, by the way, won great acclaim from about 120,000 spectators at a *Tribune* sponsored Festival [in Chicago] in 1944,

when the everchanging "V" formation of the dance was interpreted as being "V" for Victory sign during those war years.

Source

Sixth Lithuanian Folk Dance Festival, July 6, 1980, 75. From an article on "The Changing Scene of the Lithuanian Folk Dance in the U.S." from the program of the dance festival.

Seneca Green Corn Dance

The Green Corn Festival or Busk was part of the elaborate harvest ceremony of the southwestern and northeastern Indians. After the corn ripened, it was not to be eaten until the Great Spirit was properly thanked. Often a sacred arbor was built and a large fire lighted under it, and dances and other rites were performed about this fire. Among the Iroquois, of whom the Senecas were part, the thanksgiving observance, with which the ritual began, took place in the council house. The entire celebration, with its prayers, dances, feasting, and games, sometimes lasted for a week or more. In fact, in his description of Onondaga festivals, Joshua Clark states that "when the green corn becomes fit to use ... the first ears are broken off to be roasted or boiled" at "the most joyous and merry-making festival in the Indian calendar," and a second or extension of the corn festival takes place "after the corn harvest; usually about the first of November." Differences in growing season affected the timing of this widespread ritual. This account was written by Mrs. Harriet Maxwell Converse, by adoption a member of the Snipe Clan of the Seneca nation. The festival took place in the Cattaraugus Reservation, Newtown, New York. It was attended by "between 500 and 600 Indians... and during the three days there was no irreverence, vulgarity, nor any unseemly conduct."

Among the festivals of the Iroquois Indians, one of the most important is the *Ah-dake-wa-o*, or Green Corn Festival, commonly called the Green Corn Dance. This dance continues for three days, and, though varied in proceedings, the ceremonies of each day terminate with a feast. Like all the religious ceremonies of the red man, "thanksgivings" predominate in this, the *Ah-dake-wa-o*. The "Great Feather Dance," included in this festival, is also religious, and, that guests from each nation may unite in the universal thanksgivings, and join in this dance, these festivals are never "called" the same day of the month on the separate reservations.

In the distribution of the various offices and duties pertaining to the ceremonies, the matrons, as well as the men, take share. They are denominated *Ho-non-de-ont*, or "Keepers of the Faith," and to their care is entrusted the "preparations" for the feast. As the festival-time draws near, these matrons are also appointed to visit the cornfields at sunrise every day, and bring to the council-house several ears of corn, there to be examined by one of the "head men," who decides, when it is in fit condition for eating, the date when the feast shall be called.

This year [1890] the "summons," or invitations, from the chiefs at the Cattaraugus Reservation were sent to those who were to be the active participants and guests from Tonawanda and Allegany reservations that, on September 10th, at sunrise, the introductory ceremony of the *Ah-dake-wa-o* would begin at the council-house on the Cattaraugus Reserve. This council-house, located one mile from Lawton Station on the Erie Railroad, and standing on a prominent elevation in the centre of an open space of eight acres of undulating grassy ground, was erected on the spot where the Seneca Indians, withdrawing from the Buffalo Reservation, felled the trees of the dense forest, and made the settlement they called "The New Town." This little Indian village, retaining its old name through having lost its significant "The," is now known as Newtown. The council-house, a one-storied wooden structure about eighty feet long and fifty feet wide, constructed in accordance with the cardinal points of the compass—north, south, east, and west—has two entrances, one at the northeastern end of the building, designed for the women, and the other at the opposite southwest end for the men only; and although the council-house has no inner division, the women always sit apart from the men during a council or a dance. At the east end of the building, within a brick chimney that juts out about four feet from the wall, yawns a huge fireplace, in which still remained the ashes of the last feast (in the old times these ashes were not removed save at the New Year festival); the long crane that hung within its smoke-begrimed depths suggested the swinging of the great kettles of the corn soup and succotash of the winter-time feasts. On the three sides of the chimney above the fire-place are projecting shelves, on which were deposited the various donations to the feast which had been presented by the "foreign" guests and friends. At the west end of the building stands an old-fashioned iron stove, rusty and fireless during the summer time, but in which great

THANKSGIVING

logs can be thrust to the comfort of the participants in the winter festivals. On the south and west sides of the council-house, and extending lengthwise, are three rows of undivided seats, not unlike the pews in very old churches, arranged step-like, one above the other; and for further accommodation ordinary wooden benches are provided in the east end of the house, that all may be seated during the ceremonies. In the centre of the room two benches were apportioned to the singers and musicians. One of these benches was well worn in deep ridges, the result of the vigorous strokes of the turtle-shell rattles in the hands of the musicians.

It is the custom for the *Ho-non-di-ont*, or men keepers of the faith, to build at sunrise, on the morning of the feast, the "first fire," and to place upon it tobacco and some ears of corn as a special offering to the Great Spirit, and, while the offering was burning, to ask his blessing, after which the fire is extinguished and a new one built in its place by the women who have charge of the public feast. Although the "summons" called for a convening of the people at sunrise, yet at eight o'clock the councillors had not assembled, which delay, however, was afterwards explained. The great variety of vehicles that had brought the guests to the festival were ranged around the outer edges of the grounds; groups of young men playing ball; young women and girls sauntering about, evidently intent in the "chat of pleasant conversation;" old men with tottering steps, elderly women with pathetic gaiety slowly

making their way to the council-house; matrons hurriedly busy preparing the soup and succotash boiling vigorously in large iron kettles suspended over the great logs that burned with a glow suggestive of comfort and warmth in the chill mist that veiled the far-away hills,—all added to the picturesqueness of a scene that was striking in its effectiveness.

It was not long before a general movement in the assemblage gave notice that the ceremonies were about to begin. The women slowly entered the building by the northeast door, the men passing in at the southwest entrance and arranging themselves with order in the seats; the musicians, with their turtle-shell rattles, had already taken their places on the benches appropriated for them; and when quiet prevailed—and there is no congregation of people who remain so perfectly quiet as an assemblage of Indians at a religious "gathering"—the "head speaker" began the feast ceremonies with an invocation to the Great Spirit. The men, with uncovered heads, bent in reverent attention (Indians never kneel), and the women looked solemn and earnestly serious as the speaker, in low voice, rendered his prayer. After a pause, lifting his voice, he proceeded with the following address (I give the *literal* translation):

"My friends, we are here to worship the Great Spirit. As by our old custom we give the Great Spirit his dance, the Great Feather Dance. We must have it before noon. The Great Spirit sees to everything in the morning; afterwards he rests. He gives us land and things to live on, so we must thank Him for his ground and for the things it brought forth. He gave us the thunder to wet the land, so we must thank the thunder. We must thank Ga-ne-o-di-o [Handsome Lake, the prophet of the "new religion"] that we know he is in the happy land. It is the wish of the Great Spirit that we express our thanks in dances as well as prayer. The cousin clans are here from Tonawanda; we are thankful to the Great Spirit to have them here, and to greet them with the rattles and singing. We have appointed one of them to lead the dances."

During this speech the men remained with their heads uncovered. At its conclusion, and following a slight pause, a shout from outside the council-house gave notice that the "Great Feather" dancers were approaching.

The "Great Feather Dance," one of the most imposing dances of the Iroquois, is consecrated to the worship of the Great Spirit, and is performed by a carefully selected band of costumed dancers, every member of which being distinguished for his remarkable powers of endurance, suppleness, and gracefulness of carriage. As they drew near to the council-house the swaying crowd gave way, permitting the leader and his followers to pass through the west door, where, taking their places at the head of the room, they remained stationary a moment as the speaker introduced the leader to the people and proceeded, in a voice keyed to a high pitch, to offer the ceremonial "thanks," the dancers, meanwhile, walking around the room, keeping step to the slow beating of the rattles. Each "thanks" was followed by a moderately quick dance once around the room, and terminating at the halt into a slow walk, which was continued during the recital of each "thanks" until all were rendered.

THE THANKSGIVINGS

We who are here present thank the Great Spirit that we are here to praise Him.

We thank Him that He has created men and women, and ordered that these beings shall always be living to multiply the earth.

We thank Him for making the earth and giving these beings its products to live on.

We thank Him for the water that comes out of the earth and runs for our lands.

We thank Him for all the animals on the earth.

We thank Him for certain timbers that grow and have fluids coming from them [referring to the maple] for us all.

We thank Him for the branches of the trees that grow shadows for our shelter.

We thank Him for the beings that come from the west, the thunder and lightning that water the earth.

THANKSGIVING

We thank him for the light which we call our oldest brother, the sun that works for our good.

We thank Him for all the fruits that grow on the trees and vines.

We thank Him for his goodness in making the forests, and thank all its trees.

We thank Him for the darkness that gives us rest, and for the kind Being of the darkness that gives us light, the moon.

We thank Him for the bright spots in the skies that give us signs, the stars.

We give Him thanks for our supporters, who have charge of our harvests. [In the mythology of the Iroquois Indians there is a most beautiful conception of these "Our Supporters." They are three sisters of great beauty, who delight to dwell in the companionship of each other as the spiritual guardians of the corn, the beans, and the squash. These vegetables, the staple food of the red man, are supposed to be in the special care of the Great Spirit, who, in the growing season, sends these "supporters" to abide in the fields and protect them from the ravages of blight or frost. These guardians are clothed in the leaves of their respective plants, and, though invisible, are faithful and vigilant.]

We give thanks that the voice of the Great Spirit can still be heard through the words of Ga-ne-o-di-o (by his religion).

We thank the Great Spirit that we have the privilege of this pleasant occasion. [Vigorous dancing followed this, all shouting in gladness, in which the speaker joined.]

We give thanks for the persons who can sing the Great Spirit's music, and hope they will be privileged to continue in his faith.

We thank the Great Spirit for all the persons who perform the ceremonies on this occasion.

With this the thanksgiving ended. There is an Iroquois harvest festival in which is included thanksgivings for all the harvest, when each grain and fruit-producing tree, vine, or bush is separately recognized.

The speaker then ordered the dance to begin, and the dancers, who in single file had walked slowly around the room during the recital, save at the interludes of the "thanks," began a movement of a more animated character.

In all its features and characteristics the Feather Dance is quite unlike the War Dance. In its performance the dancer remains erect, not assuming those warlike attitudes of rage or vengeance which so plainly distinguish the two dances. All the movements of the Feather Dance are of a graceful character, its undulating and gentle motions designed to be expressive of pleasure, gladness, and mildness. Each foot is alternately raised from two to eight inches from the floor, and the heel brought down with great force in rhythm to the beat of the rattles. At times there was an indescribable syncopated movement of wondrous quickness, one heel being brought down three times before it alternated with the other, the musicians beating the rattles three times in a second, every muscle of the dancer strung to its highest tension, the concussion of the foot-stroke on the floor shaking the legging bells; the lithesome, sinuous twistings and bendings of the body momentarily accelerated by the dancers' shouts of rivalry mingled with the plaudits and encouraging cries of the excited spectators, as they filed swiftly round and round the council-house, were thrilling to a degree of intenseness! The dancers accompanied themselves by joining the singers in a weird syllabic chant consisting of but two notes—a minor third—which was strongly accented as they sang the *Ha-ho—Ha-ho—Ha-ho*; then with quicker time all joined in the refrain, *Way-ha-ah, Way-ha-ha, Way-ha-ah*, and terminating in the strong guttural shout, *Ha-i, ha-i*, as the dancers bowed their heads in accent.

In this dance there were fifty men in costume, for whom, at the "rest" intervals, a refreshing drink, made from the juce of the wild blackberry, added to sweetened water, was provided. In the slower movements many of the women, at the exhortation of the speaker urging all to unite in the Great Spirit's dance, joined the dancers at the foot of the column, finally forming an inside circle.

At noon the costumed dancers went to their homes, returning again in ordinary citizen's dress. During their absence an opportunity was offered to any person who might desire to have children named, or names changed. A child three months old was "presented" for a name, the babe having been the realization of a dream. Before its birth its "grandfather" had dreamed that a boy would be born who would be a great hunter, and as the older Indians have strong faith in dreams, this child was particularly mentioned as a proof of the infallibility of the dreamer. The name given was "The Swift Runner."

The speaker of the day then made a short address, inviting all to partake of the feast. This was the signal for the young men, who then came in, bearing two great kettles, of the capacity of eight gallons each, and containing, one the beef soup, and the other the succotash. One of the *Honon-di-ont*, in a prolonged exclamation, said grace, in which he was joined by a swelling chorus from the multitude in acknowledgement of their gratitude to the Great Giver of the feast. As the red men do not sit down together at a common repast, except at religious councils of unusual interest, the succotash and soup were distributed in vessels brought by the women for the purpose, and all the guests carried equal portions to their respective homes, there to be enjoyed at their own fireside.

It was near sunset when the feast was over, and the people slowly dispersed, making way to their homes, a few, however, remaining for the social dances not included in the religious feast. Previous to their departure a faith-keeper announced that, according to the ancient ways, the

THANKSGIVING

feast games between the rival clans would be played on the next day. He also cautioned them that they "must not be dejected if they lost, as they had heard by the Great Spirit that what they lost on earth would be returned to them in heaven. If they won they must not boast, nor hurt the feelings of their opponents, but assume their victory with dignified silence."

The second day opened with the *Gus-ka-eh*, the peachstone or Indian dice game. This was played in a dish a foot in diameter, and four articles were contributed as a donation to a "pool." A good deal of excitement prevailed during the betting, which was a privilege extended to any of the members of the contending clans. The Wolf, the Bear, Beaver, and Turtle clans played against the Deer, Snipe, Heron, and Hawk. The game was won by the latter clans. There were no other events of particular interest that day. It was expected that the game would continue all day (the festival cannot go on until this game is finished, and it sometimes lasts two or three days), but on this occasion it proved of short duration. At the end of the contest a feast was offered, as on the previous day, and there were more social dances in the evening to "entertain the visiting guests from Tonawanda and Allegany."

The third day was "Women's Day"—the women opening the ceremonies with a dance, for which there were special singers, and songs accompanied by a small drum and rattles made of horns, about four inches in length, and not unmusical in

effect. The women dance entirely unlike the men. They move sideways, raising themselves alternately upon each foot, from heel to toe, and then bringing down the heel upon the floor at each beat of the rattle and drum, and keeping pace with the slowly increasing column that moved around the council-house with a quiet and not ungraceful movement. After some urging by the faith-keeper, two thirds of the women present joined in the circle, also many young girls, and children from four years upwards.

There was no pairing or taking of partners in any of the dances, as each individual danced alone. Following this "women's" dance came another, in which both men and women joined, called the "Thank Dance for the Crops." After that another women's dance, the "Shuffling Dance," followed by the men's dance, "Shaking of the Rattle." For each of these dances there were different steps and songs. Next came the "Snake Dance," beginning with four men clasping hands, the leader shaking a rattle and singing; others, including the women and children, gradually joining the dance line until there was not room enough in the council-house for the circle within circle of dancers. This dance, which includes in its movements the "hunting" for the snake, and represents the action of its body in swift gliding and in the convulsions of death, lasted about three quarters of an hour.

There had been a misty rainfall all the day, but as the dancers were exulting in enthusiasm the sun separated the clouds, and, as an Indian expressed it, "looked in" upon them through the west window, filling the room with its cheery glowing. The nodding plumes, the tinkling bells, the noisy rattles, the beats of the high-strung drums, the shuffling feet and weird cries of the dancers, and the approving shouts of the spectators, all added to the spell of a strangeness that seemed to invest the quaint old council-house with the supernaturalness of a dream!

As the sun neared its setting the dancers stopped in a quiet order, and the "speaker of the day" bade farewell to the clans, "active officers," and guests, wishing them a safe journey homeward under the guidance of the Great Spirit; and admonishing them all to lead good lives for another year, and hoping they might be privileged to meet again to thank the Great Spirit for his goodness, he dismissed the "gathering," and, after invoking the blessing of the Great Spirit, declared the Green Corn Festival of 1890 ended.

A final and bountiful feast was then served, after which the people peacefully separated, and in an orderly way departed for their homes.

Source

Journal of American Folklore, IV (1891), 72-77. Reprinted from the *Buffalo Express* of October 12, 1890.

And that's not all:
See "Florida Seminole Green Corn Dance" and "Games at the White Dog Feast."

Bread and Apple-butter Thanksgiving

Andrew S. Berky describes the traditional thanksgiving service of the Schwenkfelder, a persecuted Protestant sect. He quotes extensively from Phebe Earle Gibbons's Pennsylvania Dutch and Other Essays. Gibbons was a Quaker journalist. How the traditional fare originated is not certain, but Berky points to contemporary records of the Schwenkfelder colonists giving thanks for fresh water, bread, and apples obtained immediately after landing in America in 1734.

Bread, butter and apple-butter play an unusual role in Schwenkfelder culture. For the past 226 years, the Schwenkfelders have observed, on September 24, a thanksgiving service (*Gedaechtnisz Tag*) which is unique in several aspects. The only fare provided at the traditional meal consists of water, bread, butter and apple-butter. This service of thanksgiving was instituted on September 24, 1734, by the Schwenkfelder immigrants, two days after their arrival in Pennsylvania. It has been observed annually thereafter in remembrance of the safe voyage and the rescue from intolerance; as a measure of gratitude for the blessing of freedom; as a reminder of the responsibility for the preservation and extension of freedom to others; and as an expression of gratitude to God for his grace and guidance. . . .

The Schwenkfelders did not construct meeting-houses until the 1790s, so the annual services were held in individual homes. The difficulties attendant to serving one or two hundred people a full course meal from the "kitchen" of a log or plank house are evident. In all probability, the

THANKSGIVING

traditional meal was served on long plank tables set up near the house, crocks of apple-butter were brought up from the cellar or spring-house, and loaves of bread were gingerly removed from the warm bake oven.

With the construction of meeting-houses, the scene for the annual *Gedaecht-nisz Tag* services shifted, and so did the method of serving. Phebe Earle Gibbons has provided us with a vivid description of one of these "yearly meetings."...

> [The Rev. C. Z. Weiser] tells us, that whoever is not providentially prevented is bound to attend their yearly reunion. Nor has it been found necessary thus far to enter an urging statute to secure the presence of the fraternity. The "seeding" is done, the corn stands in shocks, and the farmwork of September is timely put aside, in order that all may participate in the memorial ceremonies of the 24th with a light, gay, and thankful heart. It is on the day and day before that you may feast your eyes on many a well-laden carriage, the horses all in good condition, moving on towards one of the Schwenkfelder meeting-houses, selected in rotation, and one whole year in advance. The aged and infirm of both sexes stay not behind. The young men and women are similarly enough clad to be considered uniformed. So too are the mothers arrayed in a manner very like to one another, with snow-white caps and bonnets that never vary. The sons and daughters do

indeed not love the habits of their elders any the less, yet only the wicked world's a little more.

The morning service opens at nine o'clock, and is filled out with singing, praying, and recitals of portions of their ancestral history. All is gone through with in the Pennsylvania German dialect, but withal reverentially, solemnly, and earnestly, just as though it were newly and for the first time done.

At twelve o'clock, the noonday feast is set. This is the feature of the day. It consists of light and newly-baked rye bread, sweet and handsomely printed butter, and the choicest apple-butter. Wheat bread is now used. (At a Schwenkfelder house I ate apple-butter, sweet, because made from sweet apples, and seasoned with fennel, of which the taste resembles anise.) Nothing beyond these is set, but these are of the first water. The bare benches, but lately occupied by devout worshippers, serve as tables, along which the guests are lined out. Not in silence, nor in sullenness, do they eat their simple meal, but spicing it with cheerful talk, they dine with hearts full of joy. Still, you need fear no profane utterance or silly jest. They are mindful of the spirit of the occasion, of the place in which they congregate, and of the feast itself, which the singing of some familiar hymn has consecrated. If any one thirst, let him drink cold water.

And now think not that they feign simply to eat and drink—that the meal from first to last is but a poor pretense. A full and hearty dinner is "made out" there. It is a bona fide eating and drinking that is done in the meeting-house of the Schwenkfelders on their *Gedächtniss Tag* (anniversary). They are all hard-working men and women—farmers and farmers' wives and farmers' children. They are sunburnt, healthy, and hungry besides. And why should they not relish the sweet bread, with their sweet butter and apple-butter, then? Even strangers who attend and are hospitably entertained by the society show that one can make a full hand, even at such a table.

At two o'clock the tables become pews again, and the afternoon exercises are conducted according to the programme of the morning. These concluded, a general invitation is again extended to partake of the baskets of fragments gathered up and stored away in the rear of the meetinghouse. A fraternal handshaking closes the anniversary for the year. The reflection that many part now who may never meet again on earth causes tears to trickle down some furrowed cheek, which generally proves more or less contagious, as is always the case in a company of hearts, when those tears flow in sincere channels. Hence, though all were happy all day long, they now feel sad.

To appreciate the meaning and spirit of this apparently homely scene, it is necessary to know that it is a memorial service all through. It was on this very 24th of September, 1734, that some seventy (forty) families of Schwenkfelders, who had landed on the 22d, and declared their allegiance on the 23d, held their thanksgiving service, in gratitude to God for a safe deliverance to the colony of Pennsylvania. They had arrived in the ship St. Andrew, at Philadelphia, as fugitives from Silesia.

Poor, but feeling rich in view of their long-sought liberty, they blessed God in an open assembly. We may judge their store and fare to have been scant and lean indeed; and to perpetuate the original service of their fore-fathers from generation to generation, they statedly celebrate their *Gedächtniss Tag*.

The poor fare before them is finely designed to impress the sore fact of their ancestors' poverty indelibly upon their minds, memories, and hearts. They eat and drink in remembrance of former days—the days of small things. They join thereto at the same time a gladsome worship, in thankfulness for the asylum opened up for them from their former house of bondage, and which proved so fair a heritage to their people ever since.

This description by Phebe Earle Gibbons presents a fairly accurate picture of the *Gedächtnisz Tag* scene throughout the

THANKSGIVING

19th Century. The setting for "bread and apple-butter day" changed to its present form in the early years of the present century when the Schwenkfelders closed the old meeting-houses and moved into larger church structures, equipped with kitchens.

The traditional meal is now served on tables in church social rooms, the plain garb of the 19th Century has been replaced by modern dress, the sermons and hymns are rendered in English in lieu of German, but the fare—bread and apple-butter—remains the same, as it has for the past two and a quarter centuries.

Source

Pennsylvania Folklife, XII (Fall 1961), 42-43.

First Thanksgiving in Illinois

The sources of Isabel Jamison's historical sketch are newspapers and local informants, listed in her text:

As we all know the first-comers into the Sangamo Country [Illinois] were for the most part, Kentucky pioneers, and, since the south and south-central portions of the state were about all that could be considered "settled" at that time, it naturally followed that the customs and traditions of the South predominated. The population turned out to celebrate New Year's, the 8th of January [Battle of New Orleans], Washington's birthday, the Fourth of July and Christmas, with much enthusiasm and in most cases, explosion of gunpowder and ringing of bells. The three purely patriotic holidays were further distinguished in the

late [18]30's by the firing of a *"feu de joie"* at sunrise. Thanksgiving was merely a tradition of the "Yankees," whom the Kentuckians lumped carelessly as shrewd itinerants addicted, according to popular report, to the tinkering of clocks and the vending of wooden nutmegs in their natural habitat, and who, being transplanted to western soil, could "dicker" in such a masterly and efficient manner that the party of the second part was considered fortunate if he escaped with his eye teeth intact....

In the late [18]30's there was a small settlement of "Yankees" a few miles west of Springfield, who, according to an old settler with whom I talked, "were left pretty much to themselves and were not much thought of." It is quite possible that these derelicts of the prairie sea may have celebrated a quiet Thanksgiving of their own if they felt that they had any occasion for it, but if so, nobody seems to have noticed, or, at least, commented upon it. But when Simeon Francis, editor of the *Sangamo Journal* from 1831 to 1855, came to Springfield, he, being a native son of Connecticut in good and regular standing, openly deplored the absence of any regular observance of the Yankee holiday in his adopted western home. It was quite to be expected, therefore, when the *Chicago Democrat*, in the autumn of 1838, published what purported to be a Thanksgiving Proclamation issued by Governor Joseph Duncan, that the *Sangamo Journal* promptly copied it, while the editorial columns of the paper reflected the pleasure its editor felt on account of the adoption by Illinois of the Yankee holiday; nor did he fail to remind his readers that a pumpkin was indispensable to a correct observance of the day—and would some subscriber have the kindness to send him one?

Certainly the Proclamation had all the ear-marks of the genuine article, being couched in sounding phrases, and duly signed and sealed.

In the *Sangamo Journal* of December 1st, 1838, the editor made the following statement to the public:

"We are constrained to believe that the Proclamation purporting to have been issued by Governor Duncan for a "Day of Public Thanksgiving, Prayer and Praise," published in last week's paper, is a forgery. We have come to this conclusion with much regret, because, in the first place, a proclamation for the observance of a day for public thanksgiving, prayer and praise we would consider proper and appropriate; and, in the second place, we were loth to believe that any man having access to the columns of a newspaper, would deliberately perpetrate such a forgery. The spurious Proclamation first appeared in that vehicle of loco focoism, the *Chicago Democrat*."

As wild turkeys and pumpkins were plentiful, to say nothing of other ingredients necessary to a proper culinary observance of the day, it is very probable that the Proclamation was productive of some orthodox Thanksgiving dinners, forgery or no forgery.

Of one of these, at least, we are certain—a "stag party" which took place at the American House in Springfield, a pretentious building just completed by Elijah Iles, to reinforce the hotel accommodations of the new State Capital. It was the most ambitious structure that had, as yet, been provided for public entertainment in Springfield, and while most of the hotel proprietors in the town were Kentuckians or Virginians, the American House opened triumphantly November 24th, 1838, under the auspices of a real, live Bostonian. Thus it happened that, when this adventurous pilgrim from the city of beans entered the arena of public hospitality in Springfield, a few kindred spirits, hungry and thirsty for real Thanksgiving cheer, quietly planned among themselves to hold a rousing little celebration that would, so to speak, "knock the spots" off anything the Battle of New Orleans or Washington's Birthday had ever shown Sangamon county in the line of good cheer.

Mine host, Clifton, was only too pleased to demonstrate, so early in the game, what Boston enterprise could do in the way of banquets, and accordingly on Thanksgiving—at the hour of midnight—a little band of self-convicted Yankees (the late Mr. Edward R. Thayer, who related the story to me, being one of the number) sat down in the dining room of the American House, to such a Thanksgiving dinner as we read about—and the participants probably dream about, afterwards.

AMERICA CELEBRATES

THANKSGIVING

As the solid viands disappeared, and the liquid refreshments began to stir the blood of young New England to greater enthusiasm, its expression became more vociferous. Songs and toasts went around the board, and the fun was at its height when the door at the end of the banquet hall swung open and the small, determined figure of the hostess of the American House stood upon the threshold. There was a glint in her eye that boded no good to the hilarious guests. Her voice rang through the suddenly silent room with a finality that was convincing:

"Men"—she said—"I cannot call you *gentlemen,* since you are behaving like anything else—I will not allow this uproar! Do you not know that this house is full of guests who are unable to sleep on account of this disgraceful carousal?"

Like an assemblage of naughty boys detected by the schoolmistress in the act of affixing a bent pin to her chair, the descendants of the Pilgrim Fathers sat in abashed silence. Finally, mine host, Clifton, who had probably had previous experience in dealing with emergencies of a similar character, rallied to the rescue. "Come along, boys," he exclaimed, "let's go down to the wash-room where we can make all the noise we want to." He led the way; each man grasped such portion of the good cheer of the occasion as was nearest to him and followed....

No regular Thanksgiving celebration was held during the following two or three years.... However, by 1841, the northern part of the state had begun to feel the influence of a population that was drifting in from the East and which had, generally speaking, been brought up on Thanksgiving dinners; and the Presbyterian State Synod, at its fall meeting that year, adopted a resolution recommending to the churches under its care, the observance of Thursday, November 25th, as a day of Thanksgiving for the blessings of the past year. [In 1842 Governor Thomas Carlin officially proclaimed] the last Thursday of November next as a Day of Thanksgiving....

Mr. Francis, of the *Sangamo Journal* ... delicately hinted that "since a goodly portion of the community was not thoroughly broken to Thanksgiving observances and might not possess the knowledge of what was required by immemorial usage," he would offer a few suggestions, not as to the spiritual preparations which would be attended to by the "dominies," but on strictly material lines. We trust that his suggestions, which follow, were accepted in the helpful spirit in which they were given:

"A large supply of the good things of life are required, such as turkies, chickens, geese, partridges, and such like. Families give out their invitations to the dinner a week ahead, so that all can go like clockwork. All the eatables, including a large lot of pumpkin pies, are prepared for the oven the night beforehand.

"At 11 o'clock on Thanksgiving Day, all the supernumeraries of the family (leaving only those at home necessary to perform the duties of cooking) proceed to church where the service is of great length, rendered so by the singing of one or two extra hymns. This is done to impress the inner man with due solemnity of the importance of the Day—and also has the effect of sharpening the appetite of the outer man for the things that are about to be set before him. There is no hesitancy that we have ever discovered under such circumstances, in hastening from the church to fulfill their respective engagements. The tables are soon filled and the important business of eating is performed with all due deliberation. The old then retire to talk over the occurrences of younger days, the children romp, and the young men and girls prepare for the interesting duties of the evening—what those are, all can judge. At such times the young ladies are generally at home, and the young men are generally more courageous than usual.

"The remaining part of the week, (Thanksgiving should always be set on Thursday, as Governor Carlin has very properly done in this case), should be spent in visiting, social parties and such, and when Saturday night comes, in reckoning up matters it is usually found that, in neighborhoods, old grudges are healed, new courtships are under progress, and the people are generally better satisfied with their condition and happier by far than before the Thanksgiving holiday. And we trust that Governor Carlin's Thanksgiving will be productive of these good fruits."

In closing his suggestions, Mr. Francis urged everybody to remember the poor, as Thanksgiving is a most fitting time to remember the widow, the orphan and the distressed; also not to forget to "send the 'dominie' a couple of turkies," which would indicate that the pastor's quiver was well-filled, unless, indeed, the "turkies" of that day were inclined to be skinny.

Source

Journal of Illinois State Historical Society, XI (1918-1919), 370-77.

Pumpkin Pie

Margaret Louise Arnott provided this information:

. . . While no mention has been made of the pumpkin being a part of the first Thanksgiving dinner, the Northeastern Indians did raise some, which in all probability they gave to the Pilgrims, and certainly the "pompion" was known to and eaten by the later colonists. Pumpkins, native to the Western Hemisphere, came through the normal trade routes from Central and South America, and were experimented with by the North American Indians centuries before Columbus reached the West Indies. They were boiled, baked in ashes, used in making bread, and dried. In the beginning the Pilgrims stewed "pompion" and mixed it with Indian cornmeal to make bread, but they also filled the pumpkin shell with milk, sugar and spice and baked it in the fireplace. The Indians themselves baked the pumpkin with honey. Today Pumpkin Pie is a part of most traditional

AMERICA CELEBRATES

THANKSGIVING

Thanksgiving dinners. Recipes for this dish are endless, and methods of serving provide an equal variety. Comparison can be made between a simple New England Pumpkin Pie which can be found in almost any good cookbook, and a recipe found in a hand written cookbook of Martha Washington. The New England pie calls for 1½ cups cooked pumpkin, ⅔ cups brown sugar, 1 teaspoon cinnamon, ¼ teaspoon each of ginger and nutmeg, ½ teaspoon salt, 2 eggs slightly beaten, 1½ cups milk and ½ cup cream. The recipe of Martha Washington is copied here in its entirety: "Pare and cut into pieces a good pumpkin. Put it into a granite or porcelain kettle with not more than a teacup of water; cover the kettle and steam the pumpkin until tender. While it is hot, add a tablespoonful of butter to each quart. Press the whole through a colander, rejecting every particle of water. Also sprinkle over, while the pumpkin is hot, after it goes through the colander, a tablespoonful of flour to each quart. Now take a quart of this strained pumpkin, add to it six well-beaten eggs, a cup of sugar, a quarter of a teaspoonful of mace, a tablespoonful of ginger, a quarter of a nutmeg, and one gill of brandy. Have the dishes lined with good, rich paste, pour in the mixture, put strips of twisted paste across and bake three-quarters of an hour in a quick oven."

Source

Kansatieteellinen Arkisto 26, Suomen Muinaismuisto-yhdistys, 1975, 22-23. From a paper titled "Thanksgiving Dinner: A Study in Cultural Heritage."

Thanksgiving Turkey with Ethnic Dressing

Margaret Louise Arnott also provided the following:

. . . Today in the United States [Thanksgiving] is celebrated by many Americans whose roots do not stem from Britain and therefore whose taste varies. Generally, it has been found roast turkey remains central to the meal but that the accompanying dishes are those of another cuisine. The Puerto Rican will serve turkey, rice and beans, with *Arroz con Dulce,* a pudding made of rice, sugar, coconut milk, and milk, spiced with cinnamon and ginger in place of pumpkin pie. Among the Armenians, the old country people serve the traditional Armenian foods but do use turkey because it is similar to chicken and will feed a large number of people. Those born in the United States vary in custom but most have turkey with pilaf and the Armenian bread, *Cheorig,* while all the food is seasoned with oriental spices. Pumpkin pie is not generally served by the old country people but the new generation does use it, though there is no hard and fast rule. On the other hand, the Greek community tends to serve the traditional American menu, even in those families which adhere regularly to the Greek cuisine. However, the salad and condiments, namely feta cheese, are Greek, and sweet sauces or candied yams are avoided. Families from India usually depend upon being invited by an American family, but when they are not, since most of them are vegetarians, they tend to keep to their own cuisine. The

Italians mix the menu, serving soup, roast turkey, ravioli, macaroni, pumpkin pie, wine and coffee. They cannot tolerate the sweet potato. The Poles use turkey with various vegetables, but serve apple pie and lots of beer and whiskey.

Source

Kansatieteellinen Arkisto 26, Suomen Muinaismuisto-yhdistys, 1975, 20-21. From a paper titled "Thanksgiving Dinner: A Study in Cultural Heritage."

Thanksgiving Parades

This news release is from a publicity file prepared by Jean McFaddin, Director of Special Productions for Macy's, New York:

Macy's, New York

The [1979] Parade starts off at 77th Street and Central Park West, promptly at 9:00 A.M. All units proceed south on Central Park West to Columbus Circle, then around to Broadway; down to Times Square and then to 35th Street. The Streets of New York are Macy's stage for this annual event. Between 35th and 34th Streets the Parade elements stop for performances, and then again on 34th Street between Broadway and 7th Avenue. The Finale of the Parade is signaled by the arrival of Santa Claus, a huge Mass Band Finale, and Macy's own choir, plus elves, toy soldiers and more! This choreographed finale truly reaffirms that the Holiday season has officially begun and Macy's continues to be the Miracle on 34th Street.

The Macy's Parade was originated and is completely directed and operated by Macy's employees. As the lead banner proclaims, the event is presented as a "Holiday Treat for Children Everywhere." The first Parade was held in 1924, entertaining an estimated audience of over 10,000. At that time, we started at 145th Street and Convent Avenue and included elephants, camels, and monkeys in the line-up. Today, the Parade delights two million spectators along the line of march. Of course, that figure varies according to weather conditions. However, rain or shine, the show always goes on, and it captivates well over 80 million television viewers on the NBC and CBS television networks.

Macy's huge balloons, a unique trademark for the store, made their first appearance in 1927. They were designed by master puppeteer, Tony Sarg (who also created the Christmas Fantasy windows at the store). Construction is carefully executed by the Goodyear Aerospace Corporation, in Akron, Ohio.

Parade preparations are year round, handled by Special Productions Department Staff and design artists. Operations are at their highest pitch on Thanksgiving Eve. When the balloons arrive by truck at 77th Street and Central Park West, they are removed from their shipping crates and anchored by sandbags and giant nets which secure them during inflation.

Between 6:00 A.M. and 7:30 A.M. on Thanksgiving Day, over 2000 Macy's employees who will march in the Parade, arrive at Herald Square for professional costuming and makeup. These enthusiastic

AMERICA CELEBRATES

THANKSGIVING

Thanksgiving Parades

employees come from all over the tri-state area; some as far away as Albany, New York, 150 miles north! When each group is ready, they are bussed to the Starting Line. While these in-store preparations take place, the Goodyear technicians check the weather bureau for barometric pressure, a key element in determining the mix of helium and air that goes into each balloon. Hundreds of employees who have been assigned to their favorite balloon are standing by. Parade divisional marshalls test walkie-talkies so that they can maintain the correct order of elements and keep in contact with the Herald Square staging area.

The Parade floats built and assembled in New Jersey, will be brought through the Lincoln Tunnel and are unfolded to their individual shapes. Twenty-nine Chevrolet Caprices will pull Macy's Parade floats from their home in New Jersey to New York and through the two and a half mile Parade route.... These cars have been specially selected to complement the color scheme of each float, according to the Float's motif and music selections.

The marching bands, selected from all over the country, have arrived and are placed on Central Park West. The celebrities who appear in the Parade cause additional excitement as they are escorted to their respective floats.

The countdown begins 10 seconds of 9:00 A.M. Promptly at 9:00 A.M., the grand marshalls and lead banner, cross the inter-

section. The show is on. The Holiday has finally arrived!

Source

Macy's 53rd Annual Thanksgiving Day Parade, 1979.

Gimbel's, Philadelphia

This press publicity was prepared by Christian Mattie, Jr., of Gimbel's, Philadelphia:

Step right up ladies and gentlemen, boys and girls, and feast your eyes on beauty, color, thrills and excitement as Gimbel's presents "The Circus" and our 60th Annual Thanksgiving Day [November 22, 1979] Parade.

It all started on Thanksgiving Day in 1920 when Ellis Gimbel gathered fifteen cars and fifty people and a fireman dressed as Santa Claus and called it a parade. Little did Mr. Gimbel know that he would create such a prestigious tradition. Now the Gimbel's parade has the distinctive honor of being nationally acclaimed as the oldest and largest parade of its kind in America. The parade has grown in size from fifty to over 3,000 participants. Last year it was estimated that close to one million people lined the streets of Philadelphia to watch this fantastic parade while many more viewed it on television....

This year amid a myriad of color, animation and excitement, the Benjamin Franklin Parkway will act as a Midway for "The Circus." Twenty-four floats, each averaging over fifty feet in length, will glide along the parade route on Thanksgiving morning introducing "Two-Two the

Clown," ferocious lions, dancing ladies, performing horses, penguins playing merry tunes on horns and balancing nimbly on a colorful ball, "Two-Foot Teddy," talented canines, and a Tom Thumb wedding. Don't be surprised if you see a huge purple elephant—it's only "Eleanor the Elephant." And there is music provided by, what else, but a carousel, holding colorful figures and revolving gayly while the ticket taker looks on. And what circus would be complete without clowns! We'll have clowns that bob, slide and tumble, and laughing and crying clowns. All floats are animated, like the high wire act, or the lions jumping through rings of fire.

And there's more! In a clash of color and excitement, we'll find approximately 2,000 bandsmen from California to New York, and Maine to Florida, forming on the broad steps of the Art Museum. They're mostly high school youngsters, filled with anticipation and proud to strut their stuff for the city and national television....

This year, the real "star of the parade," Santa Claus, will make his appearance on an exciting fifty-five foot float towed by his regal reindeer and surrounded by Santa's six beautiful snow maidens. The festivities reach a climax at the official welcoming of Santa Claus in front of the Gimbel store when he is greeted by the Queen of the Thanksgiving Day Parade. Our queen is picked from thousands of six to twelve year old girls and it is her duty, along with her Court of Honor consisting of four girls, to present the key of the city to Santa.

Let's not forget—in keeping with the spirit of Thanksgiving, each year over 5,000 underprivileged and orphaned children of Greater Philadelphia are invited to be special guests of Gimbel's and sit in reserved reviewing stands at City Hall.

Source

News from Gimbel's, 1979.

Hudson's, Detroit

Thanksgiving Parades

The following comes from a press kit prepared by Diane Girard Brown and Kathy Pitton of the J. L. Hudson Company of Detroit, Michigan:

Santa's Thanksgiving Day Parade officially marks the beginning of the Christmas season for many Detroiters.

The first parade was staged in 1924. There were interruptions in 1941 and 1942 because of a shortage of materials at the start of World War II.

This year [1979], more than 2,500 people will march in the parade. Another 300 work behind the scenes on repair and preparation of floats and other chores.

Employees begin setting up the parade at Hudson's Fort Street Events Studio at 3:30 A.M. on Thanksgiving Day. At 4 A.M., a Detroit Police escort arrives to take the floats down to the parade starting point at Woodward Avenue and Putnam.

Marchers arrive later in the morning to be costumed, made-up and receive last-minute directions. There is no dress re-

THANKSGIVING

hearsal. The parade itself is the first and only run through.

The first parade consisted of horse-drawn lumber and milk wagons, covered with papier-mâché and other decorative materials. About 150 employees participated in the event, which boasted 10 to 12 floats.

Because of a runaway horse team during one of the early parades, manpower was used for many years, with some 24 persons pulling a single float. Cold weather caused another problem when metal-rimmed wheels froze to the street surface. This led to the use of mechanical floats. This year's floats are pulled by tractors obtained from the Ford Motor Company.

Source

Hudson's News Bureau Release, November 5, 1979; from "Parade History."

Thanksgiving Prayer

Ella E. Clark supplied this account:

A religious thanksgiving ceremony of [an American Indian] tribe, the Umpqua, in southwestern Oregon, was observed many years ago by a pioneer, Samuel B. Flowers. Invited to attend a religious council on the bank of the Umpqua River, he cautioned his men to approach in a reverent manner. He had always been friendly with his Indian neighbors, and he knew that he was being honored with the invitation.

As he and his company entered the village, everything was quiet. All the men,

both old and young, were sitting on the grass in a great circle around a tall pine tree, their heads bowed low. After they had remained in that position for some time, the head man of the village arose and began to walk slowly around the council pine. Then he looked up at the sky and began his prayer of thanksgiving:

> "Oh, bright sun, Oh, noble sun, father of all living!" he said. Then he praised the sun for rising each morning to drive away the darkness and fill the world with light. He eulogized the power of the sun to melt the snow off the mountains, and to send the warm rains. He thanked the sun for making the fruits bloom, the leaves grow and the green grass cover the earth. He lauded the power of the sun over the sea and the river. He thanked the sun for sending the red salmon up the streams so that the Indians might have fish for food.

> Then the chief addressed the earth: "Oh, earth, mother of all living!" He poured out praises to the earth for feeding grass to make the elk and the deer, that the Indian might have meat for food to make them strong and brave. He thanked the earth for the wild fruits and berries which gave the Indians health and gladness. Then the chief paused. Looking about him he called loudly upon the wild streams to praise the sun and the earth. He commanded the rocks and the trees to praise them. He eloquently commanded his people to honor the sun and the

earth as father and mother of all living. He begged the sun and the earth to send good to the Indians and to guard them from harm.

When the chief had ended his prayer, he drew an arrow from the quiver hanging on his back and slashed his bare chest with the sharp point. The blood flowing over his heart was his oath of sincerity, of loyal devotion to the sun and the earth.

Source

Oregon Historical Quarterly, LXI (December 1960), 348-49. From an article on "Indian Thanksgiving in the Pacific Northwest." Clark's source was a collection of Indian legends compiled by the U.S. Federal Writers Project, "Oregon Oddities," No. 28, December 15, 1939. Specific date and place not given. Similar thanksgiving ceremonies among tribes in Washington, Idaho, and Montana c. 1900 are described by James A. Teit, *45th Annual Report, 1927-28,* Bureau of American Ethnology.

November

Day after Thanksgiving
BLACK FRIDAY

Black Friday is a term that has historically designated various Fridays on which a tragic or devastating event took place. Since World War II, the Friday after Thanksgiving, festive and frantic, has become the traditional date for the beginning of the Christmas commercial season. Merchants hope to see their accounts ledgered "in the black," that is, showing a profit, thus bringing a positive connotation to the term Black Friday. Because many businesses look to the Christmas purchasing season to maintain economic health, Black Friday

has come to be seen by many as a consumer bellweather that accurately forecasts the economy's climate as a whole. Though it evolved from a consumer-oriented society and has been nurtured by the advertising industry, Black Friday has something in common with the seasonal fairs held since the Norman Conquest in England and earlier on the Continent. In fact, trade fairs grew up at such religious festivals as the Olympic games of the Greeks and have continued to be associated with religious holidays.

Shopping Boom and Wall Street Crash

Barbara Demick filed this report:

Forget about the stock market crash. Forget about debts and deficits. No, this wasn't a day to worry. This was a day to do what American consumers do best, to shop.

"We lost money in the stock market. But what are you going to do? Sit home and cry about it? Christmas only comes once a year," said an enthusiastic Mary Irelan of Vineland, N.J., plunking down a credit card at the jewelry counter of Strawbridge & Clothier.

Her mother, Margaret Quinn, agreed wholeheartedly. "Sure, I lost a little bit in the market. But what the heck!"

Yesterday was "Black Friday," the traditional day-after-Thanksgiving kickoff of the Christmas shopping season.

This year, retailers and economists alike have anticipated the event with more than the usual anxiety. With the Oct. 19 [1987] stock market crash fresh behind us, many forecasters fear a slowdown of consumer spending that could drive the U.S. economy into recession.

But shoppers yesterday appeared to be blind to the woes of Wall Street. Right on cue, they were out there doing what they do every year.

Shopping malls and department stores around the Philadelphia area reported heavy traffic.

Brian Ford, a retailing consultant at the accounting firm of Arthur Young & Co. in Philadelphia, conducts an exploratory shopping trip through the New Jersey and Philadelphia malls on the day after Thanksgiving every year. Yesterday, he was bullish on Christmas.

"It was a fabulous shopping day. Just great. . . . I don't think I ever remember seeing it so crowded in the last three to four years," Ford said.

Retailers were braced for the day. Malls were decked with Christmas glitz. Some stores opened at 8 A.M. Some planned to stay open until 11 P.M.

There were extra sales clerks, extra security guards and even extra Santas. At the Center City John Wanamaker store, there were three Santas on duty, each in a separate chamber so that "each child thinks he or she has seen the *real* Santa Claus," said store publicist Joyce Mantyla.

Still, by 2 P.M., the Santa wait had reached three hours at Wanamakers. There were lines for the escalator, lines for the cafeteria, lines for gift-wrapping. Baby strollers were grid-locked in the aisles of the toy department as parents picked through bins of teddy bears, discounted 40 percent for a clearance sale. . . .

The weeks between Thanksgiving and Christmas are a critical season for many U.S. retailers, who, some say, coined the name "Black Friday" to refer to the day that the red ink on the income statement turns black.

Actually, "Black Friday" is not the biggest shopping day of the year. The heaviest spending usually comes in the week before Christmas.

But the early days are critical because they set the tone. If shoppers do not respond well, retailers are forced to do what they hate most during Christmas: to put merchandise on sale. That is an especially pressing fear this year because last month's stock market crash came too late for retailers to make big changes in their inventory levels.

Source

Philadelphia Inquirer, November 28, 1987.

November—December

25th Day of Kislev
HANUKKAH

Hanukkah (or Chanukkah) is an eight-day Jewish festival. It begins on the twenty-fifth day of Kislev, third month of the lunar year, which usually falls in December, near the time of the winter solstice. The story of Hanukkah is told in the first book of the Maccabees, in the *Apocrypha*. The Syrian king Antiochus Epiphanes (Antiochus IV) in 162 B.C. ordered that an altar to the Greek god Zeus be placed in the Temple at Jerusalem, profaning the Temple by attempting to force the Jews to make sacrifices to heathen gods. This provoked a successful rebellion led by Judah Maccabee, and the Temple of Jerusalem was cleansed and a new altar was dedicated in

165 B.C. According to a Talmudic legend, only a limited amount of consecrated oil was available for relighting the perpetual lamp, but miraculously it lasted for eight days. Thus Hanukkah was associated with the miraculous cruse of oil, and came to be known as the Feast of Lights and the Feast of Dedication. A *menorah* or candelabra, is lighted, one candle on the first evening, and the number of lit candles increases by one each night of the festival. The eight-branched candlestick has become a symbol of Hanukkah. It is a joyous holiday, celebrated with games, plays, gifts, and meals that feature *latkes* or potato pancakes.

Hanukkah Riddles and Problems

These items were collected by Ruth Rubin:

The Holiday of Chanukkah is an important week of joy and thanksgiving. During the days of the week, work continues as usual, but in the evenings songs are sung around the table, and puzzles, riddles, arithmetical problems and enigmas are provided for entertainment. Games of cards and "*Dreydl*" (teetotum or trendel) are played.

The following problems in arithmetic and riddles are among those which my mother used to ask [in Yiddish] during the Chanukkah holiday.

Riddles

1. It clothes the entire world, but walks naked. What is it? (*a needle*)

2. It stands in the middle of the square. When you shake its hand, it weeps. What is it? (*the town pump*)

3. It has four legs, but is not an animal? What is it? (*a bed*)

4. It has feathers, but is not a bird. What is it? (*a feather bed*)

5. Seventy fellows in a wooden hut and each and all are bald. What is that? (*a box of matches*)

6. All day it moves about the house and in the evening it stands in a corner. What is it? (*a broom*)

7. A thousand fellows who wear one belt. What's that? (*a bundle of straw*)

8. Two rhymed variants of a riddle about snow:

> Flies without wings,
> Builds without bricks,
> Sits without an arse,
> Departs without feet.

> Flies in without wings,
> Builds without bricks,
> Lies down like a lord,
> Rises like a fool.

This refers to the fact that when snow first falls, it is gentle and clean; when it melts and disappears, it is soiled and slushy. (This, of course, was the explanation given me by my mother.)

9. Dressed in seven petticoats and whoever undresses it must weep. What is it? (*an onion*)

10. Your father's son and no brother of thine? Who is it? (*you*)

11. Patch on patch and not a single stitch. What's that? (*a cabbage head*)

12. Looks like a horse, eats like a horse and his tail can see as well as his eyes. What is that? (*a blind horse*)

13. Why does a hare run to the woods during both summer and winter? (*because the woods won't come to him*)

14. When it rains what kind of tree does a hare sit under? (*a wet tree*)

15. A little barrel fell off the roof and there wasn't a barrel-mender in the world who could mend it. What was that? (*an egg*)

16. He climbs up and pokes about and takes it out and shakes it off and climbs down. What is that? (*a chimney sweep*)

Arithmetic Problems

1. A city slicker, walking up a country road, met a herd of geese. "Good morning, ye hundred geese," he greeted them, doffing his hat gallantly. "Ah," said the leading goose at the head of the herd, "but we are not a hundred. Now if you will

HANUKKAH

but double our number, and add to it half of our number, then a quarter of our number and then one of us, only then will we be a hundred!" How many geese were they?

(*Answer: 36*)

2. A farmer, who had been selling eggs at the market, was left with 35 eggs at the end of the day. When his three sons, who had been helping him all day, were gathering up the baskets for their return home, the farmer turned to them with the following problem: He asked his eldest to take *half* of the number of eggs; his middle son to take a *quarter*, and the youngest to take *two-ninths*. The sons started to divide the eggs in the manner their father had indicated, but they simply got nowhere. What should they have done?

(*Answer: Pretend that you have 36 eggs, one more than the actual number left over, and now PROCEED AS THE FARMER HAD INSTRUCTED HIS SONS TO DO. Lo and behold, it works! As to why it works—why does it work this way? Well, that's too deep for me, and Mother didn't have the answer for that one.*)

3. A man had to cross a lake in a rowboat. He had to take with him a lamb, a wolf and a head of cabbage. However, he was permitted to transport only *two* of these at one crossing. Now, if he left the wolf and lamb alone, the wolf would eat the lamb. If he left the lamb and cabbage alone, the lamb would eat the cabbage. The problem is to transport all three in a

minimum of crossings. How many crossings did he make and how did he manage the transportation of his three charges?

(*The answer to this problem can be resolved by many in different ways. I have been able to do it in seven trips:*

The man first crosses over with the lamb.

Then he returns and takes the cabbage across.

Then he returns with the lamb, leaves the lamb there and returns with the wolf.)

Source

New York Folklore Quarterly, XII (1956), 257-59.

Hanukkah and Christmas

David Harris filed the following item:

Billy Apple painted a holiday picture two years ago without any of the traditional signs of the season.

Conspicuously absent from his colorful poster were the decorated trees, falling snowflakes, galloping reindeer and likenesses of old St. Nick present in the artwork of his classmates.

Billy is Jewish, and to him the holiday season meant Hanukkah; therefore, it was only natural for him to draw a *menorah*.

"I just drew the Hanukkah *menorah* because that's what we have at home," Billy, a fifth-grade student at the Burnside Elementary School in Jeffersonville [Pennsylvania] said yesterday [December 12, 1980].

Little did he suspect that his artwork would be reproduced 50 million to 60 million times and distributed to homes across the nation. But it has—his painting was one of the 50 selected to be used on the traditional Christmas seals produced by the American Lung Association. The seals are used as a fundraising tool by the organization in its battle against tuberculosis and other lung diseases.

"This is the first time a Jewish holiday picture has been used on a Christmas seal in the 73-year history of the Christmas seal program," said Chalmers Stroup, executive director of the American Lung Association of Philadelphia....

Billy, who is 11 years old, drew the picture when he was 9. According to Barbara Forman, his art teacher, Billy had no idea that it would be entered in the lung association's seal contest. Billy's picture competed against the works of 700 other elementary school children in a statewide competition. The association selected one picture from each state for its seals.

Source

Philadelphia Inquirer, December 12, 1980.

Food for Hanukkah

This recipe comes from an article by Ethel G. Hofman on "dishes of Hanukkah."

Potato Latkes

4   large potatoes, peeled and grated

¼   onion, chopped
2   eggs
¼   cup flour
1   teaspoon salt
¼   teaspoon pepper
¼   teaspoon baking powder
    oil for frying

In a large bowl, place grated potatoes, onions and eggs. Stir to mix. Add flour, salt, pepper and baking powder, and mix well. Heat about one-half cup oil in the skillet. Drop mixture by spoonfuls into hot oil, flattening with a spoon. Cook until browned, about three minutes on each side. Drain on paper towels. Makes about 24 small *latkes* . Serve with Crisp Fresh Applesauce.

To make applesauce, pour one-half cup orange juice in the jar of a blender or the work bowl of a food processor. Add four unpeeled red apples, cored and quartered. Chop coarsely. Turn into small bowl and add sugar or honey to taste. Makes about 1 ¼ cups.

Source

Philadelphia Inquirer, November 27, 1983.

Hanukkah and Civil Liberties

Sally Johnson filed this report:

In an unusual variation on the debate over religious symbols on public property, city officials in Vermont's largest city [Burlington] have allowed a Jewish group to erect a menorah in City Hall Park.

AMERICA CELEBRATES

HANUKKAH

Early this week Sidney Baker, the city's superintendent of parks and recreation, said the Vermont Organization for Jewish Education could display a menorah from December 15 through December 23, the duration of the Jewish festival of Hanukkah. The organization is part of the Lubavitcher movement, a Hasidic sect that seeks to reawaken interest among Jews in Orthodox Judaism.

The decision by city officials came just one week after a Federal magistrate recommended that a cross be ordered removed from the front lawn of a courthouse in nearby Hyde Park because its presence violated the constitutional separation of church and state. That case was brought to court by the American Civil Liberties Union.

Scott Skinner, executive director of the Vermont chapter of the civil liberties organization, said he believed the Burlington menorah posed the same fundamental problem.

"Such religious symbols should not be displayed in front of public buildings because they give the impression of government endorsement of religion," Mr. Skinner said. He said his office had received complaints about the menorah.

The Jewish organization has been raising the menorah in the park for four years, but it attracted little attention the first two years because it was up for only one day, said Rabbi Yitzchok Raskin, who emigrated to Vermont from Brooklyn four

years ago. Last year, he said, it was on display for the full eight days of Hanukkah.

But the menorah has become a subject of real controversy only this year, said Joseph McNeil, the Burlington City Attorney, who said "there is a heightened awareness" of religious symbolism because of the dispute over the Hyde Park cross.

Rabbi Raskin insisted the message of the menorah transcended Judaism. He said the nine-pronged candlestick symbolizes "a universal message of freedom of the human spirit, freedom from oppression and the victory of good over evil."

"These principles are shared by a majority of the American people," he said. "The menorah represents this message to the entire world."

He added that the Lubavitcher movement was advocating the display of menorahs all over the country.

Mr. McNeil said at a news conference today that they had a constitutional obligation to allow the menorah to be displayed.

"City Hall Park is a public-forum location where the expression of political and religious viewpoints is not only tolerated but encouraged," Mr. McNeil said. "We are proud of that fact. We have had everything from peace demonstrations to carol singing."

"This has been a true New England town square in the best sense of that tradition," added his colleague, Assistant City Attorney John Franco.

The lawyers noted that in 1984, the Federal Court of Appeals for the second circuit, which includes Vermont, allowed a crèche to be displayed on public property in Scarsdale, N.Y., ruling that it was in a place that had often been a public forum....

Source

New York Sunday Times, December 20, 1987. Copyright © 1987 by The New York Times Company. Reprinted by permission.

And that's not all:
See "Supreme Court Ruling on a Creche Display."

December
24-25

CHRISTMAS EVE AND CHRISTMAS DAY

For more than three centuries Christ Mass was a moveable feast, and in many places it was celebrated on Epiphany, January 6, the day, according to the biblical account, when Jesus manifested himself to the Magi. Even after the Western church, using a solar calendar, settled on December 25, the Eastern church for almost a century continued to fix Christmas by the moon. The western date of Christmas was

made to coincide with the Roman midwinter festival of the Kalends. Kalends was preceded by seven days of tribute to the god of agriculture, Saturn. For devotees of Mithra, Kalends was preceded by the Birthday of the Unconquered Sun. Many of the pre-Christian rites are still celebrated as part of Christmas: the evergreen decorations, the exchange of gifts or *strenae*, the indulgence in food and drink, the license in kissing and sexually related activities, the mumming.

By 567 the twelve days between December 25 and January 6 (Old Christmas Day) had become days of revelry following the penitence and fasting in Advent. Many of the Christmas customs were common to various thanksgiving days and to New Year rites. Some are extremely old: ivy worship going back to the Dionysian revels of ancient Greece; mistletoe being the golden bough sacred to the Druids. But Christmas has also generated new customs. The Christmas card began in England in the nineteenth century; Santa Claus' reindeer date from about the same time in America. The Christmas tree was introduced in English-speaking lands by Prince Albert of Saxony as late as 1844. It is an adaptation of the *Paradeisbaum* (the decorated tree of life) so popular in German medieval drama and of the pagan *Tannenbaum*.

Christmas Eve Bonfires

Mary Ann Sternberg, an authority on Louisiana life, compiled this report:

As dusk falls on Christmas Eve, Nolan Oubre gives the signal to light the string of wooden pyres that seems to stretch to infinity along the spine of the Mississippi River levee. Over his car's PA system, he speaks the long-anticipated words: "It is now 7 P.M.; you may light your bonfires." It is ironic that the leathery, walrus-mustached Oubre would be among those charged with the setting of fires, causing a hundred curtains of purple and orange flame to rise into the black velvet night, crackling and popping and sparking showers of gold along the green flank of the man-made ridge. Ordinarily—as chief of the volunteer fire department in Gramercy, Louisiana (pop. maybe 3,500)—he is in charge of putting them out.

But the fire chief's role reversal is symptomatic of the fever that pervades rural St. James Parish each December. Between Halloween and Christmas, a host of locals devote thousands of hours to the construction of intricate log masterpieces. Most are 25-foot-high, tightly wrought pyramids. Some, like those of industrial maintenance worker Ronald St. Pierre, are detailed reproductions of familiar local subjects, such as a log cabin, an oil rig with derrick, a two-story plantation house with double-curved stairway, or a turn-of-the-century locomotive complete with cowcatcher and smokestack. A few whimsical constructions—PeeWee's Playhouse or the roughly cut digits of a graduation year—round out the field. But at the fire chief's signal, all of the structures—regardless of artistry or size—are uniformly torched.

Christmas Eve is the only time of year when River Road, once the only highway between New Orleans and Baton Rouge, becomes a curvy, two-lane gridlock from the Mt. Airy town line west to Convent. Nightfall brings thousands of pedestrians, who swarm back and forth among the cars inching along to get a close-up view of the blazing sentinels. The light radiating from within the geometric skeletons makes them look eerily akin to the chemical plants and refineries that dominate the flat landscape.

From the river waft the rollicking soprano notes of calliopes on paddle wheelers up from New Orleans, the hoarse bass of freighter horns and the insistent buzzing of small craft. The bounce of swamp pop and *chank-a-chank* Cajun music mixes with the blare of jam boxes, car horns and firecrackers, while smells of kerosene, sweet smoke, burned powder, beer and gumbo permeate the air.

Lighting bonfires on Christmas Eve in St. James Parish has been a holiday ritual since the 1880s, though its origin is still debated. The most popular explanation is that the bonfires were started to light the way for Papa Noël, the Cajun version of Santa Claus, as he paddled his pirogue to deliver gifts to good Cajun children—but traditionally Papa arrives on New Year's Eve.

CHRISTMAS EVE AND CHRISTMAS DAY

Others say the fires were functional, begun as navigational signals to help guide steamboats through the dense December fog; or religious, to light the way to midnight mass. Or the fires may have celebrated Epiphany, the Twelfth Night, when Christmas trees were taken down and burned, and chestnuts and potatoes roasted over the blaze. Most likely, the bonfires were introduced into the area by French Marist priests who, in 1864, took over Jefferson College (now Manresa House of Retreats) in nearby Convent. The Brothers built their fires on the batture next to the river and entertained their students. The practice caught on, but why it was moved from the traditional New Year's Eve to Christmas Eve remains a mystery.

Whatever its origins, the German-Acadian Coast Historical and Genealogical Society attributes the first Christmas Eve levee bonfire to merchant George Bourgeois in the town of Mt. Airy in 1884. He is said to have collected boxes and packing material in which merchandise for his New Camelia Plantation store arrived, massing them into a flaming heap on the levee across from his business. The flames were so large and salutatory that riverboats pulled right up to his landing to join the Christmas Eve celebration. Bourgeois had also built a game room behind his store where local men played poker and ate gumbo. Sometimes, when they arrived with their sons in tow, the entrepreneur gave the boys fireworks and sent them off to the levee to entertain themselves around a bonfire.

By the turn of the century, says Leonce Haydel, the area's acknowledged unofficial historian, scattered, private bonfires were built on Christmas Eve. Trash wood, scrap lumber, old boxes, cardboard, tires and anything else that fathers and sons could scavenge made a good bonfire in those early days.

Whether social pressure eventually demanded a grander style than that of a trash heap, or whether safety demanded more careful construction, the configuration of levee bonfires evolved from amorphous piles into a conical tepee shape. After World War II the bonfire tradition began to strengthen; and the individual bonfires began to reach higher with the introduction of the pyramid shape: the neat, articulated superstructure imposed over a tepee.

Gathering the wood (willow, which is abundant and fast-growing, is the material of choice) is still largely a father-and-son affair. Today a boy's rite of passage is likely to be the first time he uses a chain saw or the day he's allowed to drive the pickup truck, swaying with a bed of ragtag willow poles, back to the levee.

There, on December weekends, the entire community congregates, either to build bonfires or to offer moral support to those who do. The big night itself has evolved into a typical southern Louisiana festival, with souvenir hunters in search of logoed sweatshirts, and long lines of people waiting for a fresh batch of cracklings. But at its heart, Bonfires on the Levee is still a family-style celebration.

Source

Smithsonian, December, 1989, 146-50.

Christmas Cooking, Italian Style

Pauline N. Barrese supplied these traditional Christmas recipes:

In old southern Italy, it was habitual to retire and rise early during the year. Nevertheless, a few evenings before Christmas meant going to bed late, at least, for the young and older women, who helped one another prepare and bake their traditional *porcellate* [fruit cookies] and *biscotti* [biscuits] which required many hands. There was much rubbing of tired, sleepy eyes, but the pleasure of sharing the festive spirit was immense as goodies were placed one by one on oblong metal trays, then into brick ovens, cleaned of their ashes from burning wood that helped make them white-hot. After inserting the *balata* (a small, iron door) and securing it with wet rags around its edges, to prevent air escaping into those ovens, they chattered about the important day and waited for golden brown delicacies to come from the oven. . . .

The traditions of southern Italian holiday cooking are continued by many in the United States, and the recipes are offerings for rich and delicious holiday eating.

Biscotti Italiani

6 eggs
1 cup sugar
4½ cups flour
4 tsp. baking powder
8 oz. jar of maraschino cherries (chopped)
½ tsp. salt
¼ lb. butter (creamed)
3 oz. finely chopped almonds

Beat eggs with salt. Add sugar and beat thoroughly. Sift flour and baking powder. Add to eggs and sugar mixture. Add cherries, cherry liquid, butter and almonds. Mix well until dough is smooth. Cut dough into 4 even sections. On greased cookie sheets, spoon and shape dough into 4 oblong loaves, 5 inches wide and ¾ inch thick. Bake in 375 degree oven for 25 minutes. Remove from oven and cut into 1 inch slices. Let bake for another 10 minutes.

Porcellate Siciliani

¾ cup of shortening
½ cup of sugar
2 eggs
3½ cups flour
3 tsp. baking powder
⅓ tsp. salt
½ cup lukewarm water
2 tsp. vanilla extract
confectioner's sugar

Filling:
1 cup chopped, roasted almonds
3 cups ground dry figs
1½ cups ground raisins
4 tsp. grated orange rind
1¼ cups water

AMERICA CELEBRATES

CHRISTMAS EVE AND CHRISTMAS DAY

½ cup sugar
1 tsp. cinnamon

Place figs and raisins in casserole with water over low heat. Cook for 5 minutes stirring constantly. Remove from heat. Add almonds, orange rind, sugar and cinnamon. Let cool.

Combine all dry ingredients. Add eggs. Blend in shortening with hands until fine. Then add water and vanilla. Knead until smooth. Divide dough. Roll ⅛ inch thick into 3½ inch squares. Fill with fruit. Fold and pinch edges. Make horseshoe shapes. Place on cookie sheets. Bake for 25 minutes in 375 degree oven. Remove from oven. Cool. Sprinkle with confectioner's sugar. Makes 3½ dozen.

Source

New York Folklore Quarterly, XXI (1965), 189, 191-92; from an article on "Southern Italian Folklore in New York City."

A Christmas Wheat Sheaf for the Birds

The following is from an article on holiday celebrations by Bertha L. Heilbron who quotes from the travel account of Hugo Nisbeth, published in Stockholm in 1874:

Hugo Nisbeth, a Swedish traveler who visited Minnesota in 1872, commented: "It is not only the Scandinavians who celebrate Christmas here in America in a true ancient northern fashion, but even the Americans themselves have in late years begun to give more and more attention to this festival of the children and have as

nearly as possible taken our method of celebration as a pattern." He drove out onto the prairie near Litchfield, where he spent the Christmas holiday with one of his countrymen who was living in a sod house, built half above and half under ground.

Upon his return to Sweden, Nisbeth published a book about his travels in which he tells about the frontier festivities. The day before Christmas was spent in preparing for the celebration; among other things a "small sheaf of unthreshed wheat was set out for the few birds that at times circled around the house, in accordance with the lovely old Swedish custom." As in the fatherland, the principal celebration took place on Christmas Eve. "There was no Christmas tree, for fir trees are not yet planted in this part of Minnesota," he records, "but two candles stood on the white covered table and round these were placed a multitude of Christmas cakes in various shapes made by the housewife and such small presents as these pioneers were able to afford, to which I added those I had brought." Nisbeth was disappointed because the traditional Swedish Christmas dishes, *lutfisk* [codfish preserved in wood ashes] and rice porridge, were not served, but he observes that the "ham which took the place of honor in their stead banished all doubt that the settler's labor and sacrifice had not received its reward." After the meal the children were given their presents.

Source

Minnesota History, XVI (1935), 388-90.

Supreme Court Ruling on a Crèche Display

The following is excerpted from the March 5, 1984, Supreme Court decision on the action brought by Pawtucket, Rhode Island residents, individual members of the Rhode Island affiliate of the American Civil Liberties Union, and the Union itself challenging the city's right to include a crèche in its annual Christmas display. The action eventually came before the United States District Court for Rhode Island, which found that the city had "tried to endorse and promulgate religious beliefs" by the inclusion of the crèche in its display. The action was then referred to the Supreme Court. The "Opinion" in the 5-4 ruling that overturned the District Court finding was written by Chief Justice Warren E. Burger, the "Dissent" was written by Justice William J. Brennan.

From the "Opinion"

We granted certiorari to decide whether the Establishment Clause of the First Amendment prohibits a municipality from including a crèche, or Nativity scene, in its annual Christmas display.

Each year, in cooperation with the downtown retail merchants' association, the City of Pawtucket, R.I., erects a Christmas display. The display is situated in a park owned by a nonprofit organization and located in the heart of the shopping district.

The display is essentially like those to be found in hundreds of towns or cities across the nation, often on public grounds, during the Christmas season. The Pawtucket display comprises many of the figures and decorations traditionally associated with Christmas, including, among other things, a Santa Claus house, reindeer pulling Santa's sleigh, candy-striped poles, a Christmas tree, carolers, cut-out figures representing such characters as a clown, an elephant, and a teddy bear, hundreds of colored lights, a large banner that reads "Seasons Greetings," and the crèche at issue here. All components of this display are owned by the city.

The crèche, which has been included in the display for 40 or more years, consists of the traditional figures, including the Infant Jesus, Mary and Joseph, angels, shepherds, kings and animals, all ranging in height from five inches to five feet....

There is an unbroken history of official acknowledgment by all three branches of government of the role of religion in American life from at least 1789.

Our history is replete with official references to the value and invocation of divine guidance in deliberations and pronouncements of the Founding Fathers and contemporary leaders. Beginning in the early colonial period long before Independence, a day of Thanksgiving was celebrated as a religious holiday to give thanks for the bounties of nature as gifts from God. President Washington and his successors proclaimed Thanksgiving, with all its religious overtones, a day of national celebration and Congress made it a national holiday more than a century ago.

Executive orders and other official announcements of Presidents and of the Congress have proclaimed both Christmas

AMERICA   CELEBRATES

CHRISTMAS EVE AND CHRISTMAS DAY

and Thanksgiving national holidays in religious terms. And, by acts of Congress, it has long been the practice that Federal employees are released from duties on these national holidays, while being paid from the same public revenues that provide the compensation of the Chaplains of the Senate and the House and the military services.

Art galleries supported by public revenues display religious paintings of the 15th and 16th centuries predominantly inspired by one religious faith. . . .

Justice Brennan describes the crèche as a "re-creation of an event that lies at the heart of Christian faith." The crèche, like a painting, is passive: admittedly it is a reminder of the origins of Christmas. Even the traditional, purely secular displays extant at Christmas, with or without a crèche, would inevitably recall the religious nature of the holiday. The display engenders a friendly community spirit of good will in keeping with the season. . . .

To forbid the use of this one passive symbol, the crèche, at the very time people are taking note of the season with Christmas hymns and carols in public schools and other public places, and while the Congress and legislatures open sessions with prayers by paid chaplains would be a stilted over-reaction contrary to our history and to our holdings.

The Court has acknowledged that the "fears and political problems" that gave rise to the Religion Clauses of the 18th

century are of far less concern today. We are unable to perceive the Archbishop of Canterbury, the Vicar of Rome, or other powerful religious leaders behind every public acknowledgement of the religious heritage long officially recognized by the three constitutional branches of government. Any notion that these symbols pose a real danger of establishment of a state church is far-fetched indeed.

We hold that, notwithstanding the religious significance of the crèche, the City of Pawtucket has not violated the Establishment Clause of the First Amendment. Accordingly, the judgment of the Court of Appeals is reversed.

It is so ordered.

From the "Dissent"

. . . First, all of Pawtucket's "valid secular objectives can be readily accomplished by other means." Plainly, the city's interest in celebrating the holiday and in promoting both retail sales and good will are fully served by the elaborate display of Santa Claus, reindeer and wishing wells that are already a part of Pawtucket's annual Christmas display. More importantly, the Nativity scene, unlike every other element of the Hodgson Park display, reflects a sectarian exclusivity that the avowed purposes of celebrating the holiday season and promoting retail commerce simply do not encompass. To be found constitutional, Pawtucket's seasonal celebration must at least be nondenominational and not serve to promote religion. The inclusion of a distinctively religious element like the crèche, however, demonstrates that a narrower sectarian purpose lay behind the decision to include a Nativity scene.

The "primary effect" of including a Nativity scene in the city's display is, as the district court found, to place the government's imprimatur of approval on the particular religious beliefs exemplified by the crèche. Those who believe in the message of the Nativity receive the unique and exclusive benefit of public recognition and approval of their views. The effect on minority religious groups, as well as on those who may reject all religion, is to convey the message that their views are not similarly worthy of public recognition nor entitled to public support. It was precisely this sort of religious chauvinism that the Establishment Clause was intended forever to prohibit.

Finally, and most importantly, even in the context of Pawtucket's seasonal celebration, the crèche retains a specifically Christian religious meaning. I refuse to accept the notion implicit in today's decision that non-Christians would find that the religious content of the crèche is eliminated by the fact that it appears as part of the city's otherwise secular celebration of the Christmas holiday.

The Court also attempts to justify the crèche by entertaining a beguilingly simple, yet faulty syllogism. The Court begins by noting that government may recognize Christmas Day as a public holiday; the Court then asserts that the crèche is nothing more than a traditional element of Christmas celebrations; and it concludes that the inclusion of a crèche as part of a government's annual Christmas celebration is constitutionally permissible. The Court apparently believe that once it finds that the designation of Christmas as a public holiday is constitutionally acceptable, it is then free to conclude that virtually every form of governmental association with the celebration of the holiday is also constitutional.

The vice of this dangerously superficial argument is that it overlooks the fact that the Christmas holiday in our national culture contains both secular and sectarian elements. To say that government may recognize the holiday's traditional, secular elements of gift-giving, public festivities and community spirit, does not mean that government may indiscriminately embrace the distinctively sectarian aspects of the holiday.

Contrary to the Court's suggestion, the crèche is far from a mere representation of a "particular historic religious event." It is, instead, best understood as a mystical re-creation of an event that lies at the heart of Christian faith. To suggest, as the Court does, that such a symbol is merely "traditional" and therefore no different from Santa's house or reindeer is not only offensive to those for whom the crèche has profound significance, but insulting to those who insist for religious or personal reasons that the story of Christ is in no

AMERICA CELEBRATES

CHRISTMAS EVE AND CHRISTMAS DAY

sense a part of "history" nor an unavoidable element of our national "heritage."

Source

The United States Law Week: "Supreme Court Opinions," LII, #34 (March 6, 1984), Bureau of National Affairs, Washington, D.C.

And that's not all:
See also "Hanukkah and Civil Liberties."

Christmas Riddles

Mac E. Barrick collected and commented on the following riddles:

The joking question "What's black and white and red all over?" with the answer "A newspaper" is perhaps the most common example of a folk riddle collected in the United States in the twentieth century.... A number of riddles and riddle jokes, running throughout almost all types of riddles, at least in American collections, have several possible answers. These multiple-answer riddles are found in the repartee of minstrel shows ("What has four legs and flies?" "—A dead horse." "Wrong, two pairs of pants."), in folk conundrums of the early twentieth-century ("What goes around a button [a-buttin']?" "—A buttonhole." "No, a billy-goat."), and in the semisophisticated elephant jokes of the 1960's. Unlike ancient riddles of impossibility ("How many fish in the sea?"; "What am I thinking?"), whose purpose was to show the cleverness of the person answering the riddle as in the tale of the King and the Abbot, the purpose of these modern riddle jokes seems to be to make the person answering look ridiculous because he is

unable to guess which answer the riddler has in mind. Of course, no matter which answer is given, the riddler insists that the other is the correct one. Thus with the [multiple answer riddle] new answers continue to proliferate, such as the following collected in Shippensburg, Pa., in October, 1973: "What is black and white and red all over?" "—Santa Claus coming down the chimney on Christmas Eve." Although here more logically the progression of colors should be "red and white and black all over," the order of the original ... is preserved to mislead the victim into thinking that the answer is the same.

Source

Journal of American Folklore, LXXXVII (1974), 253, 257.

Christmas Office Parties

Linda S. Wallace filed the following report:

Quietly, without fanfare, a great corporate tradition is dying. The office Christmas party, which dates back more than 50 years, has grown up to become a big business risk.

As a result, the institution that simultaneously provided the ambitious with a proving ground and the lonely with fertile ground for romance, may be headed the way of the dinosaur, business consultants say.

Traditional holiday office parties, where people primarily came at night to socialize and drink, are on the way out, often replaced by brunches, alcohol-free breakfasts and year-end afternoon meetings to recap corporate goals.

The changing times, which reflect public concern about drinking and the widening scope of legal liabilities for alcohol-related behavior, have encouraged many employers to put the traditional party on the shelf, said Andrew Sherwood, chairman of The Goodrich & Sherwood Co. in New York, a management-consulting firm that deals with how people relate to one another. . . .

Sherwood said yesterday, "I think there is greater liability in terms of the employee who goes to the office party and kills a bunch of people on the way home or falls under a train . . . A number of things could happen that the company could be liable for."

Then, too, office parties do not serve the purpose they once did, Sherwood said.

"They started right after the Depression when there was a lot of bad news going on. People didn't have money, so I think companies got together and said, 'Why don't we put on a Christmas party for people who are struggling?'"

Another purpose was to boost employee morale and productivity.

"Today, there is very little productively to be gained [by] the traditional office party," Sherwood said. "What companies are doing is having year-end parties . . . they recap the year . . . maybe hand out

some service awards, and then people go home or go shopping."

Source

Philadelphia Inquirer, December 24, 1987.

Christmas and Non-Christians

Brenda Lane Richardson filed the following report:

In the Cobble Hill section of Brooklyn, a Christmas tree may help light Santa's way to the house of Kaid and Fatima Almontaser. The Almontasers are Moslems.

In Mount Vernon, New York, St. Nick may admire the origami on the tree prepared by Satomi Higashi, with a little help from her husband, Nobuyoshi. The Higashis are Buddhists.

In Los Angeles, Santa Claus is expected at the home of Alan Rachins and his wife, Joanna Frank, who play Douglas and Sheila Brackman on "L.A. Law," the NBC-TV series. Mr. Rachins and Ms. Frank are Jewish.

None of these parents celebrate Christmas as a religious holiday, yet all want their children to enjoy the romance of the season and to feel in step with much of the rest of the country.

Not everyone agrees with their approach, however. In Tacoma, Washington, for example, Rabbi Richard Rosenthal tells his 300-member Reform congregation that "Christmas is not for Jews." In Brooklyn, a Jehovah's Witness from Crown Heights teaches her sons to accept being different,

even at Christmas, which is just another day for Witnesses.

Such varied strategies highlight this generation of parents' conflicting attitudes about coping with Christmas. In many neighborhoods, the holiday takes center stage for a month and is almost unavoidable. It also poses a particular dilemma for parents who remember the pain of being different when they were children but take comfort in their own adult religious beliefs.

Mr. Rachins, 45 years old, recalled feeling isolated from his friends at Christmas. Today, although his 5-year-old son, Robbie Rachins, is still too young to feel such discomfort, he and his parents will greet the holiday with a ceiling-high tree and a gathering of friends. Carols will be sung, and Mr. Rachins and Ms. Frank may read "A Visit From St. Nicholas" to their son.

As in the Rachins-Frank household, Mrs. Higashi, 33, a homemaker, and her husband, 50, a martial-arts instructor, celebrate Christmas as much for themselves as for their children, Shintaro, 3, and Mie, 2. The family attends a Buddhist temple on Sundays, and there the children learn about their culture and meet other Japanese youngsters. But Mrs. Higashi said that they were also Americans and that Christmas was more than a religious holiday. "It's a custom of the United States," she said, adding that she did not want her children to feel "left out at such a fun time."

That attitude is criticized by the Jehovah's Witness, a 31-year-old hair stylist who, to protect her family's privacy, asked that her name not be used. She said her children must live without Christmas, in keeping with her church's beliefs. "We don't try to hide the fact that we're different," she explained. "We are trying to be different, and we have to be up front about that."

In the hair stylist's case, her 11-year-old son is forbidden to participate in Christmas-related activities, including parties at school. When these occur, he sits apart from his classmates. The isolation, he said, did not upset him, since God would reward his steadfastness with a life after death. "I keep it up, and I won't die," he said.

Mr. Almontaser, 47, came to the United States from Yemen in 1965. A co-owner of the Near East Restaurant in Cobble Hill, he said that despite the traditional Moslem aspects of their lives, the five of his six children who live in the United seemed comfortable with themselves and with American society.

Still, Mrs. Almontaser, 43, wears a robe and veil, and Mr. Almontaser and his brother Abdullah pray daily at the nearby Islamic Mission of America mosque. The Almontaser children, who range in age from 5 to 17, study the Koran, attend mosque weekly and visit Yemen each summer. But they also exchange gifts among themselves and with Christian friends, and Ali, 13, recently decorated his own two-foot vinyl tree. "As an American, I have feelings for Christmas," he said....

Mensah Wali, 45, of Brooklyn observes Kwanza, an African-American holiday that extends from Dec. 26 to Jan. 1 and honors blacks of African-American ancestry. The name, Kwanza, is Swahili for "the first fruits of the harvest."

Mr. Wali has been teaching his children about Kwanza. "It reflects important principles, such as unity among blacks, self-determination, sharing workloads and responsibilities and creativity," he said.

Many blacks, he said, have replaced Christmas with Kwanza: "It has become an alternative for black parents who don't know what to say to their kids."

A transportation coordinator for the New York City Board of Education, Mr. Wali is the father of JaJa, 10, and Namyamka, 9. He said that if his children insist on celebrating Christmas, "it won't be a problem—when they say they want to be more like other kids, they'll be paying their own rent."

Paula McNabb, 42, a psychotherapist who is the mother of Michael, 7, and Katie, 3, said that while it can be comforting for a child to understand who he is, a sense of being different and separate can cause dangerous feelings. "They can last into adulthood and cause low self-esteem," she said.

Ms. McNabb, and her 43-year-old husband, Dennis, also a psychotherapist, are Catholics who live and work in a predominantly Jewish neighborhood in Great Neck, L.I. Two years ago, Mrs. McNabb said, Michael wanted to celebrate Hanukkah. She encouraged him to learn about the holiday and to participate in some Hanukkah customs, such as making the toy tops called dreidles.

Source

New York Times, December 16, 1987. Copyright © 1987 by The New York Times Company. Reprinted by permission.

Numerology in the "Twelve Days" Carol

The following calculation is that of William H. Riker, Lawrence College, Appleton, Wisconsin:

The recently popular carol, "The Twelve Days of Christmas," which is presumably of medieval origin, contains a charming example of medieval numerological wit. In our day numerological fancies are so out of style that it is perhaps necessary to point out in wholly prosaic terms the exact nature of the witticism.

It is to be noted that on the first day the true love gave one gift (a partridge in a pear tree), on the second day he gave three gifts (two turtle doves and a partridge in a pear tree), etc., so that on the twelfth day he gave seventy-eight fanciful gifts. Since on each xth day, he gave the sum of the first x natural numbers, a convenient formula for the sum of these superficially senseless gifts is:

AMERICA CELEBRATES

CHRISTMAS EVE AND CHRISTMAS DAY

$$S = \sum_{i=1}^{n} \left(\frac{x_i(x_i+1)}{2} \right)$$

where "S" denotes the sum of the gifts, where the large sigma denotes the operation of summation over 1, 2,..., n cases, where "x+7i" denotes the number of the day and where "n" denotes the total number of days.

When this formula is applied to the case of n equals 12, as in the carol, it turns out that the giving is far from senseless for the lady has received exactly 364 gifts— enough to last until next Christmas. A modern might ask, "What about the 365th day?"; but I am sure that to the medieval mind there was no need for a gift from a mortal giver on Christmas Day itself.

Source

Journal of American Folklore, LXXII (1959), 348.

December 26-January 1

24-25

KWANZA

Meaning "first fruits" in Swahili, Kwanza, or Kwanzaa, is a traditional African celebration which offers an alternative to Christmas celebrations and has been adopted by many Black Americans since 1966. In characteristic thanksgiving fashion, many Africans celebrate the first harvest of their crops with singing, dancing, and feasting. African-Americans find in Kwanza not only the opportunity to re-establish community ties and celebrate the unity of the family, but also the chance to

re-establish their links to an African past. Kwanza is celebrated for seven consecutive days. A candle is lit each day and the traditional symbols are displayed on the mat or Mkek. Discussions of the meanings behind

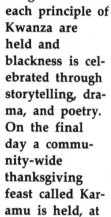

each principle of Kwanza are held and blackness is celebrated through storytelling, drama, and poetry. On the final day a community-wide thanksgiving feast called Karamu is held, at which children receive gifts and elders are honored.

A Celebration of Blackness

TRADITIONAL SYMBOLS OF KWANZA

MKEKE = straw mat to represent a foundation

MAHINDE = corn plant to symbolize growth

KINARA = candleholder with seven candles

(one for each Kwanza principle)

MATUNDA = first fruits of the harvest

KIKOMBE = unity cup used to toast and praise the ancestors

ZAWADI = gifts of love for the children (watoto)

AMERICA CELEBRATES

KWANZA

COLORS OF KWANZA

RED
... represents the struggle of the black people.

BLACK
... represents the beauty of the black people.

GREEN
... represents growth, the symbol for new life.

PRINCIPLES OF KWANZA
(expressed with African proverbs)

UMOJA (oo-MOH-jah) = unity

(When spider webs join together, they can tie up a lion)
—*Ethiopian proverb*

KUJICHAGULIA (koo-gee-CHAH-goo-lee-ah) = self determination

(No matter how full the river, it still wants to grow)
—*Zairean proverb*

UJIMA (OO-GEE-mah) = to work together

(When two elephants fight, only the grass will suffer)
—*Nigerian proverb*

UJAMAA (oo-jah-MAH-ah) = to share with others

(A brother is like one's shoulder)
—*Somalian proverb*

NIA (NEE-ah) = purpose

(He who learns, teaches)
—*Ethiopian proverb*

KUUMBA (koo-OOM-bah) = creating beauty

(A tall tree is the pride of the forest)
—*Nigerian proverb*

IMANI (ee-MAH-nee) = faith in yourself and in the beauty of blackness

(He who cannot dance says the drum is all bad)
—*Ashanti proverb*

Source

Information provided by Cora Burns Forcell, Librarian-in-Charge, Black Resource Center, Los Angeles. Letter dated August 24, 1988, and leaflet published by the Afro-American Resource Center in Compton, California.

Kwanzaa in Detroit

Denise Crittendon filed this report:

Lee Thomas lit a green candle, then turned to face his family.

"The principle of today is *nia*," he said. "*Nia* is purpose. The purpose of my life is to do the best I can for my fellow man."

Nia, he explained, is from the East African language of KiSwahilia. It also represents one of the seven principles of the African-American holiday known as Kwanzaa (first fruits).

Kwanzaa, which started about 20 years ago in Los Angeles, is beginning to spread throughout Metro Detroit, Thomas said.

This year the seven-day Kwanzaa tradition began Dec. 26 and will end tonight [January 1]. Each day focused on a principle or basic value. In addition to *nia*, Kwanzaa celebrates *umoja*, unity; *kujichagulia*, self-determination; *ujima*, collective work and responsibility; *ujaama*, cooperative economics; *kuumba*, creativity; and *imani*, faith.

During the weekend, the Thomases—Lee, his wife, Sheryl, and their daughters Khalia, 12, and Shaura, 9—dressed in flowing African garments and gathered around the dining room table in their Detroit home. One by one, they recited their intentions for the new year and lit several of the seven candles.

The seventh candle will be lit tonight, signifying the end of Kwanzaa. Also, a special ceremony is planned that often includes storytelling, poetry recitals and gift exchanges.

"It is not an African holiday. It's American, but it is based on African tradition," Sheryl Thomas said. "It's a relatively new holiday that has become more socially accepted in the last 10 years.

"We started observing it because we like the principles. In Kwanzaa, you are perpetuating a positive self-image and our children need that."

One of the first principles is unity, *umoja*. "When you think about our race, we need unity. We've never had a tradition that is both historical and contemporary, something we can pass on to our children," she said.

But, for most, Kwanzaa hasn't replaced Christmas.

"We sent Kwanzaa cards and we sent Christmas cards" she said. "We're Christian so we celebrate both."

Source

Detroit News, January 1, 1990. Reprinted with the permission of the *Detroit News*, a Gannett newspaper, copyright 1990.

ABBREVIATIONS

The following abbreviations are used in the Source sections for publications that are cited frequently:

Baughman

Baughman, Ernest W. *A Type and Motif-Index of the Folktales of England and North America.* Indiana University Folklore Series, 20. The Hauge: Mouton & Co., 1966.

Folklore in America

Coffin, Tristram Potter, and Hennig Cohen. *Folklore in America.* Garden City, N.Y.: Doubleday Anchor, 1966.

Folklore from the Working

Coffin, Tristram Potter, and Henning Cohen. *Folklore from the Working Folk of America.* Garden City, N.Y.: Doubleday Anchor, 1973.

Motif

Thompson, Stith. *Motif-Index of Folk Literature.* 6 vols. Bloomington, Ind.: Indiana University Press, 1955.

The Parade of Heroes

Coffin, Tristram Potter, and Hennig Cohen. *The Parade of Heroes.* Garden City, N.Y.: Doubleday Anchor, 1978.

Tale Type

Aarne, Antti, and Stith Thompson. *The Types of the Folktale.* 2d. ed. Folklore Fellows Communications No. 184. Helsinki: Academia Scientiarum Fennica, 1961.

TEXT CREDITS

New York Folklore Quarterly, v. VII, 1951; v. VIII, 1952; v. X, 1954; v. XI, 1955; v. XII, 1956; v. XVI, 1960; v. XXII, 1963; v. XXI, 1965; v. XXIV, 1968; v. XXVIII, 1972; v. XXIX, 1973. All reprinted by permission of the New York Folklore Society.

New York Times, October 2, 1978; May 4, 1980; October 5, 1987; December 16, 1987; December 20, 1987; March 28, 1988; September 6, 1988; October 17, 1988; October 31, 1988; April 29, 1989; July 14, 1989. Copyright © 1978, 1980, 1987, 1988, 1989 by The New York Times Company. All reprinted by permission.

The *New Yorker* Magazine, November 11, 1988. © 1988 The New Yorker Magazine, Inc. Reprinted by permission of the publisher.

Pennsylvania Folklife, v. IX, Fall, 1958. Reprinted by permission of the publisher.

Philadelphia Inquirer, February 1, 1978; December 12, 1980; July 12, 1982; November 27, 1983; March 7, 1984. All reprinted by permission of the publisher.

Prospects: An Annual of American Cultural Studies, v. IV, 1979 for "Emancipation Day, Sacred and Profane" by William H. Wiggins, Jr. Reprinted by permission of the author and *Village Voice.*

Providence Sunday Journal, April 15, 1990 (reprinted from *The Baltimore Sun*). © 1990, The Baltimore Sun Co. Reprinted by permission of *The Baltimore Sun.*

Southern Folklore Quarterly, v. IX, 1945; v. XXIV, 1960. Both reprinted by permission of the publisher.

Southwestern Journal of Anthropology, v. II, 1946. Reprinted by permission of the publisher.

The Swarthmorean (Swarthmore, Pennsylvania), June 30, 1989. Reprinted by permission of the publisher.

Village Voice, November 14, 1977.

The *Washington Post,* November 2, 1978; April 17, 1980. © 1991, The *Washington Post.* Both reprinted with permission.

Western Folklore, v. VII, 1948. Reprinted by permission of the publisher.

PHOTO CREDITS

Photographs appearing in *America Celebrates!* were received from the following sources:
Photograph by Herb Moscovitz; reproduced by permission of Mummers Museum: p. 1; © Charles Hornbrook Photo Co.: p. 28; AP/Wide World Photos: pp. 41, 56, 67, 111, 123, 138, 167, 244, 252, 282; Photo © Gary Vasquez: p. 77; Courtesy of Sweetwater Jaycees: p. 101; Photograph by Jean Dupuis: p. 108; Photograph by Robert McCrory: p. 156; Photograph by Jim N. Barker, Jr., Wakefield Ruritan Club: p. 160; © Richard Bram/NQF: p. 174; Reproduced by permission of the Indianapolis Motor Speedway Corp.: p. 191; Courtesy of Cheyenne Frontier Days: p. 229.